THE OFFICIAL

NICK HOLT

With a foreword by LAUREN LAVERNE

BOOKS

1 3 5 7 9 10 8 6 4 2

BBC Books, an imprint of Ebury Publishing
20 Vauxhall Bridge Road,
London SW1V 2SA

BBC Books is part of the Penguin Random House group
of companies whose addresses can be found at
global.penguinrandomhouse.com

Penguin
Random House
UK

This book is published to accompany BBC Radio 6 Music.

BBC Books would like to thank Lorna Clarke, Paul Rodgers, Anna Manley,
Lauren Laverne and all the 6 Music presenters and teams.

First published by BBC Books in 2016

www.penguin.co.uk

A CIP catalogue record for this book is available from the British Library

ISBN 9781785941757

Typeset in India by Thomson Digital Pvt Ltd, Noida, Delhi
Printed and bound in Great Britain by Clays Ltd, St Ives PLC

Penguin Random House is committed to a sustainable future
for our business, our readers and our planet. This book is made from
Forest Stewardship Council® certified paper.

For everyone I have driven barmy with
my quizzes over the years

Contents

FOREWORD
By Lauren Laverne

I've been working at 6 Music for almost a decade. My time at the station has taught me some amazing things. David Byrne talked me through his all-time *Desert Island Disco* floor-fillers (he relies on Frankie Smith's 'Double Dutch Bus' to get the party started, FYI). Bootsy Collins told me what he learned from James Brown (in a 4/4 funk song, the beat should be 'on the 1'). Laurie Anderson shared the three rules for life that she drew up with her partner, Lou Reed:

1   Don't be afraid of anyone

2   Get a really good bullshit detector

3   Be really, really tender

In our time on air, Sir Paul McCartney, Stevie Nicks, Smokey Robinson and Iggy Pop have all popped in to tell us the stories behind their songs. It is a privilege to have been able to winkle information out of so many of my music heroes, but on balance – statistically speaking – they aren't the ones who've taught me the most. Not even close.

I can thank the 6 Music listeners for that. They are the smartest, funniest, most informed and forthright people I have never met. It's a pleasure to share my mornings with them.

Daily conversation with the 6 Music family has taught me everything, from how to keep going when you're rowing solo across the Atlantic (one listener, Tara, needed a seriously motivational soundtrack that she could

11

stand to listen to for 70 days – plenty of Prodigy!) to what it feels like to hear music for the first time (Jo Milne, who had cochlear implant surgery just hours before the broadcast, experienced that live on air with us, and wrote about it in her book, *Breaking the Silence*). We've learned about the healing power of music from a father and daughter who repaired their relationship by trying to reassemble his lost record collection, and another listener who had to relearn everything about the music she loved when brain cancer robbed her of her memory.

As well as sharing their personal passions, our listeners are also a repository for fascinating information about every genre and era of music. They are knowledgeable and opinionated about the records they love and the cultural context around them, too. Film, art, books, fashion... they know it all.

Whether it's floating a controversial-but-compelling theory surrounding the subject matter they claim unites the B52s 'Roam' and Toni Basil's 'Hey Mickey', debating which precise lineup of the Muscle Shoals Swampers best represents the FAME studios sound, or telling you which brand of sunglasses Prince used to wear (his own, marked with his Symbol – our listener knew because she caught them when he threw them into the crowd) every day is a school day and a fantastic club night rolled into one.

My team draws on this knowledge daily. Each programme has a feature that invites our listeners to show off what they know on air. Over the years we've picked their brains to create 'Peoples Playlists' on topics as diverse as the Roland 808 drum machine, birdsong, archaeology, the solar system, insects, dystopia, utopia and the collaborations of David Bowie. They are interested in everything from club bangers to music theory. So whether you're discussing Frankie Knuckles or Theodore Adorno they will be happy to contribute.

All of this makes working at 6 Music endlessly surprising, fascinating and wonderful, and is why we've produced this book, with 99 brain-palpating quizzes. The subject matter is as wide-ranging as our playlist, ranging from the classic to the current and touching on every genre the 'alternative' universe encompasses, from old-school rock 'n' roll to disco, punk, funk, hip-hop, electronic and (way) beyond. We hope you'll enjoy it and polish up your musical knowledge in the process. Perhaps you'll get to share it with your friends and family, too. Like music itself, that's what makes it even more fun.

Good luck, and thanks for listening!

Lauren x

INTRODUCTION

A word about music.

It is a passion, not a hobby, for many, and I suspect those are the kind of listeners that veer towards 6 Music, where the journey is one of discovery as well as heritage. Passion for music leads to strange habits: the frequenting of dingy second-hand vinyl stores in damp basements; the drive of more than 100 miles to see the final show by some soon-to-be-defunct cult band for the last time in a room above a pub in Scunthorpe; the scarcely uncontrollable urge to send virulent hate-mail to the producers of TV talent shows. If, like me, you suffer from all these traits, then you will probably enjoy the book. If you are thinking, 'Oh, TV talent shows aren't so bad!', maybe gently replace the book on the shelf and save your hard-earned cash.

'(We play) music which records history, because without the knowledge of history, you cannot determine your destiny. Music about the present; because if you're not conscious of the present, you're like a cabbage in the society.'

So goes the introduction to Misty in Roots' brilliant 1979 live album, *Live at the Counter Eurovision 79* (a favourite of John Peel). I have tried to balance the two, past and present, but the past intrudes so clearly and purposefully on the present in music, that there is an inevitable bias towards history. The 21st century music scene is vibrant and colourful and multi-faceted, but this is the legacy of the founding fathers of rock and roll, the stars of the fifties, sixties and seventies who built the foundations on which stands today's palace of musical pleasure.

A word on quiz books.

What makes a decent quiz book? If I had to answer in one word, it would be: Variety.

Variety of subject matter is important, even within the confines of a music quiz book. So we have tried to include questions across the whole spectrum of musical genres, albeit with a heavy nod to the 6 Music playlist..

Variety of format helps too. We have tried to set different challenges throughout the book: some timed quizzes, some chains and connections; all that jazz (except without the jazz).

Finally, variety of difficulty. Within each quiz there are a couple of questions to which the occasional radio listener will know the answer, and one or two which will tax even those with specialist knowledge.

One last note: there is a lot of reference in the book to chart positions and hits in the UK and the US. Until the digital era the chart was a genuine measure of success, and the weekly run-down was a must-listen event. They mattered.

Enjoy the book.

Nick

QUIZ 1

6 MUSIC RECOMMENDS

Because that's much of what 6 Music sets out to do; they put records in front of their audience for them to decide whether or not they appreciate the music. There are no visuals, no marketing fluff, no advertising – just the music. 6 Music Recommends is a theme that runs throughout the shows. On the weekend that I write this, the channel showcased a whole 15 hours of brand new music. That is some commitment to musical endeavour as opposed to commercial opportunism.

In a quiz book I can't just ask questions on brand new music – they're all about memory and knowledge of a whole pantheon of (in this case) popular music. But equally I couldn't ignore the thread that is 6 Music Recommends. So here is a personal take on that thread – 30 questions on bands that I first heard while listening to 6 Music over the years.

Answers: page 459

1   *La Di Da Di* was the third album (2015) by which art-rock band? Who is their singer and keyboard player noted for his distinctive and experimental guitar style?

2   John Bramwell is the lead singer in which Manchester band, who are a hit on the live circuit if not in terns of record sales? What was their only UK Top 40 single, taken off their third album, *Gods and Monsters*?

3   Who crashed through the fame barrier with a live performance of their single 'Seasons (Waiting on You)' on US talk show *Letterman* that became a YouTube phenomenon? What is the name of their singer?

4   The Black Keys comprises two chaps, a guitarist/singer and a drummer: who are they?

5   What were Foals exhorting us to forget in their song 'Spanish Sahara'? From which 2010 Mercury Prize-nominated album was it taken?

6   What was the 2007 release by Rilo Kiley that became their first album to seriously chart? What was the side-project band formed by one of the band's main songwriters, Blake Sennett, releasing their first album, *Me First*, in 2004?

7   What kind of sex gave The Vaccines their first UK Top 40 hit? And what was the street-art-related title of their third album?

8   If *Youth Novels* (2008) was first and *I Never Learn* (2014) was third, who is the artist, and what was second in 2011?

9   In 2003, Sufjan Stevens released an album named after a US state, claiming it was the first of a series of 50 such albums he intended to make: what was the state? What was Stevens' 2015 release, his first to make the Top 10 of the UK album chart?

10 *Give You the Ghost* was the 2012 debut album by which cult electronic band? Who is their lyricist, singer and keyboard player?

11 What are the names of the Söderberg sisters from Swedish folk-pop band First Aid Kit?

12 What was the 2014 album from War On Drugs that gradually crept up the charts after good reviews and word-of-mouth approval? According to the title of the album's epic fourth track, what is 'in between the waves'?

13 *Instant Coffee Baby* (2008), *Susan Rode the Cyclone* (2010) and *A Season In Hull* (2016) are all albums by which witty pop rockers? Which cult musician and artist collaborated with the band on their 2015 album, *Great Big Flamingo Burning Moon*?

14 Which band survived the departure of main songwriter and singer Tim Smith in 2012? What was the album they released the following year after ditching all of Smith's material and starting afresh?

15 Who played drums on the Queens of the Stone Age album, *Songs for the Deaf* (2002)? And who provided guest vocals on both this and the band's previous album, *Rated R*?

BONUS TRACKS

16 Which south London shock-rockers released their second album of boundary-pushing tracks, *Songs for Our Mothers*, in 2016? Which post-punk singer and influence did they reference in a 2014 single?

17 Peter Liddle was the singer and lyricist in which English folk rock band, who released their first album in 2012, another in 2014, and then split? How did he love you, in the band's 2011 single, 'No Rest'?

18 Which city gave Editors their first UK Top 10 hit? And in their second, what were the saddest things the band ever saw?

19 Paul Janeway is a soul singer who gives his name to which Alabama six-piece collective? What was their semi-urban debut album from 2014?

20 Whose eponymous 2012 debut album included the singles 'WOR' and 'Default'? According to the title of their 2015 follow up, where were they born?

21 Who released the *By Default* album in 2016? What induced death on the second track form their 2009 debut album, *Baby Darling Doll Face Honey*?

22 Héloïse Letissier is a French singer with which band? What was her 2014 release, a massive mainstream hit in France that picked up airplay and sales on its release in a UK version in 2016?

23 With which band was Kurt Vile recording before embarking on his solo career? What is the name of Kurt's backing band?

24 The Hutchison brothers, Scott and Grant, from Selkirk in Scotland, were founder members of which contemporary band? What was their 2016 album, produced by Aaron Dessner of The National?

25 Who dropped 'We Are…' from their band name in August 2013? What was the title of their intense 2011 debut album?

26 The 2013 hit *Take Me to Church* was a global hit for which Irish singer-songwriter? Which other Irish singer recorded a song with the same title on her 2014 album, *I'm Not Bossy, I'm the Boss*?

27 *Thank Your Lucky Stars* was a very swift follow-up (released two months later) to which 2015 album by Beach House? What connects the band to the TV show *The Wire*?

28 If Brittany Howard is playing guitar and singing, which band are you watching? What was the band's much-praised 2012 debut album?

29 Which indie guitar icon worked with Modest Mouse on their 2007 album *We Were Dead Before the Ship Even Sank*? Who is Modest Mouse's primary singer and lyricist?

30 Sante Fe musician Zach Condon is the lynchpin of which band? What is his primary instrument when they play live?

QUIZ 2

THE BEATLES

Most polls to decide the best band in the history of rock and roll come up with one answer, and they are probably right. We all have our favourites, but most followers of rock music would concur that without the Beatles, much of what followed would have been very different. They were a rock and roll band who became a sophisticated songwriting team who became a challenging psychedelic outfit who became successful solo artists: what a CV! You will occasionally come across people who will tell you that the Beatles were crap – please tell them to shut up. Here, we have mixed questions about the Beatles with ones about the four individual members of the group.

Answers: page 460

1   In 2009, the remastered versions of the Beatles' albums hit the charts. Which of them went highest (to No5)? And which 92-year-old topped the album chart in the same week with a greatest hits album to coincide with the seventieth anniversary of the start of the Second World War?

2   What connects W.C. Fields, occultist Aleister Crowley, Robert Peel, Dylan Thomas, Karl Marx and Marlon Brando? Where do pop artists Jann Haworth and Peter Blake fit in?

3   Which Paul McCartney Beatles lyric did novelist A.S. Byatt say had the 'minimalist perfection of a Beckett short story'? Which McCartney composition from the same album, *Revolver*, was on the reverse of the double-A-side number one single?

4   In 'Lucy in the Sky with Diamonds', of what were the yellow and green flowers made, and what were the rocking-horse people eating?

5   What connects the Beatles' songs 'If I Needed Someone', 'Taxman', 'While My Guitar Gently Weeps' and 'Here Comes the Sun'? Which track from *Sgt Pepper's Lonely Hearts Club Band* belongs in this group?

6   How many holes did the Beatles find in Blackburn, Lancashire? Where did they tell us?

7   Who played the drums on 'Back In The USSR' on the *White Album*? And to which American song was 'Back in the USSR' a tongue-in-cheek response?

8   To where do the Beatles travel to help out in the animated film *The Yellow Submarine*? Which bad creatures have taken control there?

9   Who produced all of the Beatles' albums except *Let It Be*? Which instrument did this classically-trained musician play on some Beatles tracks?

10 'Across the Universe', 'The Long and Winding Road' and 'Get Back' are on which Beatles album? Where were they filmed playing live for a documentary of the making of the album?

11 Who directed the 1965 film *Help!* in which the Beatles did battle with an evil cult? What was the film that the same director made with the band in the previous year as a fictional documentary of their lives?

12 Ringo had a UK Top 10 hit and a number one in the US with which lyrically dubious rock-and roll-cover in 1973? Which US rockabilly guitarist and singer had the original hit with this Sherman Brothers song in 1961?

13 'I Saw Her Standing There'; 'It Won't Be Long'; 'A Hard Day's Night'; 'No Reply'; 'Help!'; 'Drive My Car'; 'Taxman'; 'Sgt Pepper's Lonely Hearts Club Band'; 'Back in the USSR'; 'Yellow Submarine'; 'Come Together'. What is the significance of this list of Beatles' songs, and what completes the set of twelve?

14 What was Ringo's first major hit as a solo artist in 1971? On which multi-artist live album released later that year did he play it?

15 Which song off *Sgt Pepper* was a reworking of a tune Paul McCartney wrote when he was 15? Who were the grandchildren?

BONUS TRACKS

16 What was the most commercially successful single, written by George Harrison, by his post-Beatles supergroup the Travelling Wilburys? What fictitious name did he adopt for this project?

17 'Roll Over Beethoven', 'Money (That's What I Want)' and 'All My Loving are on which Beatles album? And who wrote 'Roll Over Beethoven'?

18 The success of the single 'My Sweet Lord' made which George Harrison album the best-selling album by a solo Beatle? The opening track, 'I'd Have You Anytime', was co-written with Bob Dylan; which other Dylan song does he cover on the album?

19 The Beatles covered a Smokey Robinson track on *With the Beatles*: what was it? And which Larry Williams song off *Help!* was their last cover version with an attributable songwriter?

20 What was the name of the record label set up by George Harrison in the mid-seventies, sharing its name with a poorly-received album from 1974? Which single, taken from 1987 album *Clouds*, got him back into the UK Top 10 for the first time in 14 years?

21 From 1963 to 1969, every Beatles single went to number one – apart from one. What was the exception, written at the same time as the songs for *Sgt Pepper's Lonely Hearts Club Band*? What was the last of these number one singles (it was the story of a marriage)?

22 Which two John Lennon solo albums hit number one in the UK (the second largely because it coincided with the singer's murder)?

23 What instrument did George Harrison use for the first time on 'Norwegian Wood' on *Rubber Soul*? He would later take lessons on the instrument from which maestro?

24 Which John Lennon song was re-released and topped the UK charts in January 1981, a month after his death? Which Lennon song off the same album

did Roxy Music cover and take to number one in his memory two months later?

25 'And Your Bird Can Sing', 'Got to Get You Into My Life' and 'Eleanor Rigby' are on which Beatles album? In which year was it released?

26 When Rocky Raccoon fell back in his room on the *White Album,* what did he find? Which other animal is celebrated in a particularly silly George Harrison song on the same LP?

27 The Beatles' last live tour was in 1966: what controversy during this visit to the US set them against playing live?

28 What were the two duets Paul McCartney recorded with Stevie Wonder on the album *Tug of War?*

29 What is the significance of skiffle group the Quarrymen to the history of The Beatles? How about Rory Storm and the Hurricanes?

30 Paul McCartney has released eight solo pop albums since 1990. Can you name the two missing from this list: *Off the Ground* (1993); _____ (1997); *Run Devil Run* (1999); *Driving Rain* (2001); *Chaos and Creation in the Backyard* (2003); *Memory Almost Full* (2007); *Kisses on the Bottom* (2009); _____ (2013)?

QUIZ 3

MONEY MONEY MONEY

It makes the world go round, don't you know? Or does it? Maybe, in fact, it is the canker that eats at our social fabric and ruins the lives of millions? Whatever your views, it is a subject that has attracted the attention of songwriters since the dawn of time – and all of these songs have some link to the demon Mammon. It's only the third quiz, we're still warming you up, so just straight questions here: nothing cryptic, two sections of fifteen. This is a cross-genre quiz, so there are rappers and rockers, punks and poseurs – something for everyone.

Answers: page 461

1   What band did Glen Matlock form after leaving the Sex Pistols? Which bandmate went on to enjoy great success with Ultravox?

2   Who mused, on a song off their debut album, *Gordon* (1988), what they might do with $1,000,000? What was this Canadian band's most successful single, which appropriately spent a week at the top of the US chart?

3   The Greedies, who had a minor hit with rocking Christmas song 'A Merry Jingle' in 1979, were an occasional amalgam of friends, mainly from which two hard rock and punk bands?

4   'Easy Money' was a popular Billy Joel song off which 1983 album? Which 2012 Bruce Springsteen album had a song with the same title?

5   What was Donna Summer's bestselling eighties album, with a title track about a single woman trying to make ends meet that went top three in the US? Which British reggae act collaborated with her on the next single from the album, 'Unconditional Love'?

6   Which song, written with Lenny Kaye, closed side one of the vinyl release of Patti Smith's *Horses*? Which Durham punk band did a fabulous cover of the song on their debut album, *Moving Targets*?

7   'Money Trees' was a track on which Kendrick Lamar album from 2012? Which other rapper shared vocal duties on the song?

8   Travie McCoy's 2010 single 'Billionaire' featured vocals from which other American singer? In the song, McCoy envisages himself standing alongside Oprah Winfrey and which other world figure?

9   Who played guitar and co-wrote the songs with Adam Ant in his most successful period? What was the bitchy song the pair wrote and aimed at Ant's departed wife on his first solo album, *Friend or Foe*?

10 Where did the hero of the Pet Shop Boys song 'Opportunities' study? What phrase in brackets completed the song title?

11 Which US rock band signed a binding contract never to tour again after their 2015 farewell tour, to allay suspicions of a 'cash-in'? By contrast, which band unashamedly entitled a 1996 reunion the 'Filthy Lucre' tour?

12 'Money' was the first track, side two of the vinyl release of which classic Pink Floyd album? Who sang lead vocals?

13 What did Steve Miller advise Billy Joe and Bobby Sue to do in 1976? How and where did they do it, as revealed in the lyric of the song?

14 In the Beatles' song 'Can't Buy Me Love', what does the singer offer to buy the unnamed girl? What was lacking on 'Can't Buy Me Love' that was present on all the previous Beatles' singles?

15 Who co-wrote Dire Straits' most successful single, 'Money for Nothing', as well as providing distinctive backing vocals? On which album did it first appear?

BONUS TRACKS

16 What was the second single (after the title track) from Madonna's *Like a Virgin* album in 1984? To which Hollywood star did the singer pay homage in the video to accompany the song?

17 Which British rapper had a song called 'Money, Money' on his 2009 album *Tongue n' Cheek*? Which other song, a single from the same album, warned against spending money you don't have?

18 Whose 360° tour, lasting from 2009-11 and incorporating 110 shows, is the highest grossing tour of all time? Which band, famous for their voracious appetite for cash, have played four of the top 20 highest-grossing tours?

19 What does money do, according to the opening track of Cyndi Lauper's debut album, *She's So Unusual*? Tom Gray originally wrote the song for which American cult new wave band?

20 Which Barrett Strong hit did the Beatles cover on *With the Beatles*? On which label was Strong's original released?

21 Apart from current members of the Rolling Stones or former Beatles, which two pop acts appeared in the *Sunday Times* Rich List 2016?

22 In the last song she recorded before her death, Janis Joplin asked the Lord for which type of car? What was the consumer item she requested in the second verse?

23 Which well-known song begins with a demand for rent from a landlord and continues with a plea to a girlfriend for financial help, rejection, and the conclusion that women are only after men for one thing? It was a US No1 in 1953 for Clyde McPhatter and which newly formed backing band?

24 Who were the *Billion Dollar Babies* in 1973? Which No1 single off the band's previous album fuelled the sales of this follow-up?

25 The song 'Who Wants to be a Millionaire' was written for the 1956 film *High Society*. Who wrote it, and who sang it as a duet with Celeste Holm?

26 'Mo Money Mo Problems' was a posthumous US number one single for which rapper? On whose Bad Boy label was this single and the accompanying album *Life After Death* released?

27 Who teamed up to reach number one in the US with 'Rich Girl' in 1977?

28 Who is Curtis Jackson III, and what was his 2003 debut album called?

29 What was Simply Red's first chart single? With which previous band did singer Mick Hucknall first record the 1986 hit 'Holding Back the Years'?

30 What was the main attraction of the ATV music catalogue owned by Australian entrepreneur Robert Holmes à Court, and who bought it from him in 1985?

QUIZ 4

CLASSIC ALBUMS #1: THE SIXTIES

This is a really straightforward section. We give you three tracks from an album and the year of release. You give the artist and album title. Fair exchange? Then no robbery has occurred.

Option: if you are reading the quizzes out loud, try giving the quizzers two tracks — if they can identify the album from these, they get both points. If they need the third track, which is usually the charm (the big single or stand-out track), then they just get one.

Answers: page 462

1   'Death of a Clown'; 'David Watts'; 'Waterloo Sunset' (1967)

2   'I am a Rock'; 'Kathy's Song'; 'Richard Cory' (1966)

3   'A Boy Named Sue'; 'I Walk the Line'; 'Folsom Prison Blues' (1969)

4   'Black Angel's Death Song'; 'Sunday Morning'; 'Venus in Furs' (1967)

5   'Wouldn't It Be Nice'; 'Sloop John B'; 'God Only Knows' (1966)

6   'Bright Lights Big City'; 'Mystic Eyes'; 'Gloria' (1965)

7   'The Night Time is the Right Time'; 'Tombstone Shadow'; 'Bad Moon Rising' (1969)

8   'Slim Slow Slider'; 'Cyprus Avenue'; 'The Way Young Lovers Do' (1968)

9   'You Shook Me'; 'Communication Breakdown'; 'Dazed and Confused' (1969)

10 'Bummer in the Summer'; 'Alone Again Or'; 'A House is Not a Motel' (1967)

11 'One Woman'; 'Walk On By'; 'By the Time I Get to Phoenix' (1969)

12 'She Has Funny Cars'; '3/5 of a Mile in 10 Seconds'; 'White Rabbit' (1967)

13 'Crazy Man Michael'; 'The Deserter'; 'Matty Grove' (1969)

14 'Brief Candles'; 'Care of Cell 44'; 'Time of the Season' (1968)

15 'Death Cab for Cutie'; 'I'm Bored'; 'The Intro and the Outro' (1967)

BONUS TRACKS

16 'All Along the Watchtower'; 'Gypsy Eyes'; 'Voodoo Chile' (1968)

17 'Frosty the Snowman'; 'Winter Wonderland'; 'I Saw Mommy Kissing Santa Claus' (1963)

18 'Motor City is Burning'; 'Starship'; 'Ramblin' Rose' (1969)

19 'Spanish Harlem'; 'I Call Your Name'; 'California Dreamin'' (1966)

20 'Do You Want to Know a Secret?'; 'Misery'; 'Love Me Do' (1963)

21 'Stray Cat Blues'; 'Street Fighting Man'; 'Sympathy for the Devil' (1968)

22 'Mary, Mary'; '(I'm Not Your) Steppin' Stone'; 'I'm a Believer' (1967)

23 'Captain Soul'; 'Wild Mountain Thyme'; 'Eight Miles High' (1966)

24 'Afterglow of Your Love'; 'Happiness Stan'; 'Lazy Sunday' (1968)

25 '(You Make Me Feel Like A) Natural Woman'; 'Come Back Baby'; 'Chain of Fools' (1968)

26 'Sitting on Top of the World'; 'I'm So Glad'; 'Badge' (1969)

27 'Smash the Mirror'; 'The Acid Queen'; 'Pinball Wizard' (1969)

28 'Satisfaction'; 'I've Been Loving You Too Long'; 'A Change Gonna Come' (1965)

29 'The Partisan'; 'Lady Midnight'; 'Bird on a Wire' (1969)

30 '24 Hours from Tulsa'; 'Mama Said'; 'Anyone Who Had a Heart' (1964)

QUIZ 5

ROCK AND ROLL

Time to get on the blower to Grandad: it's Teddy Boy time! It's all about the early days of rock and roll, when bequiffed boys and girls in ra-ra skirts shocked elders with their filthy gyrations. Here are two quizzes. The first is on a variety of the music makers and snaky hip-shakers of the late fifties and early sixties.The second has an Elvis theme, with questions about the King and artists influenced by his legendary status.

Answers: page 463

1   Who had the biggest selling single of the fifties with 'Rock Around the Clock'?

2   Which singer, who died in 2002, was dubbed the 'King of Skiffle'? With which major recording artist did he and fellow skiffle star Chris Barber appear on live album *The Skiffle Sessions* in Belfast in 1998?

3   Who had a UK number one with 'Shakin' All Over' (1960)? Which technically gifted guitarist joined the band a year or so later and was to reform them ten years after the lead singer's death?

4   Which singer was known as The Big O? He wrote a song about his wife and sold it to the Everly Brothers when he was hard up early in his career: what was the song (and his wife's name)?

5   Who was lead guitarist in Cliff Richard's backing band on his early hits? What was the title of his first UK number one with his own band, the Shadows?

6   What was the stage name of Ellas McDaniel, a blues guitarist whose unique sound pioneered some of the early rock and roll guitar greats? What was his song that was later covered by Quicksilver Messenger Service and George Thorogood?

7   Charles Weedon Westover had a number one in both the UK and the US in 1961 with 'Runaway'. Under what name did he record, and which supergroup recorded the song in tribute in 1990 after Westover committed suicide?

8   Who had a one-off 1958 hit with 'To Know Him is to Love Him'? Who formed the group and wrote the song before embarking on his successful production career?

9   'Don't want your love anymore...' begins which US and UK 1960 number one single by the Everly Brothers? What were the names of the two brothers?

10 Which 1961 John Leyton song was the first UK number one single produced by Joe Meek in his tiny London studio? And what was Meek's next hit, the following year, which saw a British band top the US charts for the first time?

11 Who wasn't in sight when Little Richard woke up this morning in 1957? And which blues legend named all his guitars after her?

12 Which pretty pretty lady was a Top 10 hit on both sides of the Atlantic for Buddy Holly in 1957? What did she do in 1959?

13 Johnny Paris, a saxophone player, was the primary member of which instrumental rock and roll band? What was the band's biggest selling single, a UK number three in 1959?

14 'Such a Night', 'Just Walkin' in the Rain' and 'Yes Tonight Josephine' were all UK number one singles for which pre-Presley heartthrob? Which 1982 Dexy's Midnight Runners single references him in the lyric and features him in the accompanying video?

15 Which tale of teenage lust gave Chuck Berry his first UK Top 20 hit (and a number two in the US)? Which song, to his mortification, gave him his only number one in both territories?

BONUS TRACKS

16 In 1993, a commemorative Elvis stamp was issued. What phenomenon did the US mail service report over the next few weeks?

17 'Dixie', 'All My Trials' and 'The Battle Hymn of the Republic' are the three parts that make up which of Elvis' favourite live songs? The first and last parts reference which event in US history?

18 In 2005 Elvis' catalogue was rereleased in the UK and three singles topped the charts. Which was the first (becoming the first song to go straight to number one twice)? Next was 'One Night' — why was its success notable in chart-history terms?

19 What was Elvis' first UK number one in 1957, after 'Heartbreak Hotel', 'Don't Be Cruel' and 'Hound Dog' all stalled at number two? Which Leiber & Stoller song gave him a follow-up the same year?

20 Which record label acquired the rights to Elvis' output in 1956? Who was the singer's manager who negotiated the deal, at huge personal benefit to himself?

21 A remix of which Elvis song by Dutch DJ Junkie XL topped the charts in 2002? Which hit 2001 Steven Soderberg crime film utilised the song and prompted the remix?

22 Which film, a Western that shares its titles with one of Elvis' softer ballads, saw the singer make his screen debut? Where, in 1973, did Elvis play the first live gig to be screened across the world via satellite?

23 A rendition by Elvis of which Frank Sinatra standard hit the UK Top 10 in 1977, a few weeks after Presley's death? Who wrote the famous words to this song?

24 Which two soundtrack albums from movies in which he starred in 1960 and 1961 became US and UK number one hits for Elvis?

25 What was the single released just before Elvis' death in 1977 that then topped the UK chart? It was his first number for seven years – what was the previous one?

26 'Calling Elvis' was a song about an Elvis fan who believed the King was still alive. Who released it as a single, and on which 1991 album, the band's last, did it appear?

27 Both Frank Zappa and country star Jerry Reed have recorded songs using which oft-cited phrase concerning Elvis? And where did Tiny Tim claim to have seen Elvis, in a parody of his own 1968 hit?

28 Who had his only major commercial success with the song 'Walking in Memphis' (1991)? Which female singer took the song back into the charts in 1995?

29 Where did Kirsty McColl's 1981 single place a man who claimed to be Elvis? Which Billy Bragg song gave Kirsty her only UK Top 10 solo hit, three years later?

30 Who released a download-only single from his 2005 album, *Patience*, called 'John and Elvis are Dead'? Who was the John referred to in the title?

QUIZ 6

PEOPLE'S PLAYLIST: ALL AROUND THE WORLD

The People's Playlist is an opportunity on the 6 Music website for you folks to submit cool (or otherwise) themed playlists. This book is our opportunity to do the same – and to test your knowledge with some quickfire quizzes in the process.

Here's the first such quiz, and the theme here is All Around the World: all the questions or answers feature a location in the title or the name of the act. There are 40 questions – if you fancy an extra challenge, set yourself a time limit to complete it. Five or six minutes should do the trick.

Answers: page 464

1   Gary Daly and Eddie Lundon are the main men in which Liverpudlian band, who had their greatest successes in the eighties?

2   Which Scottish band released an album in 1997 called *Songs from Northern Britain*?

3   Who took a 'Spanish Stroll' in 1977?

4   Which city was the subject of a 20-minute suite by 10cc on their 1975 album *Original Soundtrack*?

5   What was the Smashing Pumpkins' second album, their commercial breakthrough?

6   Which city lent its name to an instrumental track on David Bowie's *Low*?

7   Where in Africa did Dylan wander on *Desire*?

8   What made 'a hard man humble', according to Murray Head on his hit from the musical *Chess*?

9   Which American band had only one UK Top 10 hit, 'Africa', in 1982?

10 Which Caribbean island was a big hit for the Gibson Brothers?

11 Which one-hit-wonder German band were 'Big in Japan' in 1984?

12 Who were 'California Dreamin'' on their version of a song first released by Barry McGuire in 1965?

13 Where did Odyssey state they were from in 1977?

14 And how, four years later, did they state they were returning there?

15 Which area of New York, sometimes known as 'El Barrio', is the subject of a Leiber and Stoller song that became a hit for Ben E King in 1960?

16 Where should you be sure to wear some flowers in your hair?

17 Which city 'Got Blurry' for Parquet Courts in 2016?

18 Who were the Passions in love with in 1981?

19 How long did it take Prince to go 'Around the World' in 1985?

20 According to a song from their first album, where did the Dead Kennedys take their holiday?

21 Which place was the subject of the Human League's first single from *Hysteria*, their follow-up to *Dare*?

22 Who were '(Drawing) Rings Around the World' in 2001?

23 Which classic eighties track was kept off the UK number-one spot by Joe Dolce's novelty song 'Shaddap You Face'?

24 What was the Jam's first UK Top 20 single, released between their first and second albums?

25 Where did the lights all go out in the 1967 Bee Gees song?

26 Whose 2005 album *Road to Rouen* spoofed the title of *Road to Ruin*, an earlier Ramones album?

27 Which city took George Ezra into the UK Top 10 for the first time?

28 Who took a *Rocket to Russia*?

29 Which organisation went from 'Miami 2 Ibiza' in 2010, with Tinie Tempah along for the ride?

30 Who had a 'China Girl' in 1983?

31 Which principality lent its name to a 2007 album by Caribou?

32 Which country did Manic Street Preachers take into the British Top 10?

33 In which US state did the National find a 'Bloodbuzz' in 2010?

34 Who sang about Toulouse on their first album, Dagenham on their second, Sweden on their third and Los Angeles on their fourth?

35 Whose debut album, released in 1998, was *Music Has the Right to Children*?

36 'I once had a girl, or should I say, she once had me.' So begins which Beatles song?

37 The title of which Beastie Boys album nodded to New York in 2004?

38 What sort of mambo did Rosemary Clooney enjoy in 1955?

39 Which Oasis album saw them go 'All Around the World'?

40 'New York, London...' Where else was everyone talking about 'Pop Muzik' in 1979?

QUIZ 7

NAME THE BAND #1

Another absurdly simple task. Here are the line-ups of 60 bands of varying vintages and varying levels of fame. All you need do for your point is to identify the band. If the band is still active, the line-up may not necessarily reflect the current line-up and is more likely to be taken from a classic phase in the band's career. For example, if we gave you the Who, the answer would be Daltrey, Townshend, Entwhistle and Moon.

Answers: page 465

1   Steve Askew, Nick Beggs, Limahl, Stuart Neale, Jez Strode

2   Brian Aubert, Chris Guanlao, Joe Lester, Nikki Moninger

3   Robert Bell, Paul Buchanan

4   Jeffrey Daniel, Howard Hewett, Jody Watley

5   Karl Astbury, Sam Forrest, James Galley, David Jones

6   Chris Edwards, Ian Matthews, Tom Meighan, Serge Pizzorno.

7   Les Chadwick, Les Maguire, Freddie Marsden, Gerry Marsden

8   Thom Green, Cameron Knight, Joe Newman, Gus Unger-Hamilton

9   Jonathan Higgs, Jeremy Pritchard, Alex Robertshaw, Michael Spearman

10   Craig Adams, Mick Brown, Simon Hinkler, Wayne Hussey

11   Bethany Cosentino, Bobb Bruno

12   Jules de Martino, Katie White.

13   Eric Bloom, Albert Bouchard, Joe Bouchard, Allen Lanier, Donald Roeser

14   Tom English, Duncan Lloyd, Paul Smith, Archis Tiku, Lukas Wooller

15   Mike Kerr, Ben Thatcher

16   Francis Buchholz, Matthias Jabs, Klaus Meine, Herman Rarebell, Rudolf Schenker

17   Brian Briggs, Jonathan Ouin, Oli Steadman, Rob Steadman

18   Obie Benson, Duke Fakir, Lawrence Payton, Levi Stubbs.

19   Eddie Chin, Peet Coombes, Annie Lennox, Dave Stewart, Jim Toomey

20   Ben McKee, Daniel Platzman, Dan Reynolds, Wayne Sermon

21   Robbie Bennett, Adam Granduciel, Charlie Hall, David Hartley, Anthony LaMarca

22 Jello Biafra, East Bay Ray, Klaus Flouride, Ted

23 Brain Bell, Rivers Cuomo, Mikey Welsh, Patrick Wilson

24 Tunde Baiyewu, Paul Tucker

25 Selwyn Brown, Basil Gabbidon, David Hinds, Alphonso Martin, Ronald McQueen, Steve Nisbett, Mykaell Riley

26 Bilinda Butcher, Colm Ó Cíosóig, Debbie Googe, Kevin Shields

27 Donald Johnson, Jez Kerr, Martin Moscrop, Peter Terrell, Simon Topping

28 Bob Benberg, Rick Davies, John Helliwell, Roger Hodgson, Dougie Thomson

29 Jon Coghill, John Collins, Bernard Fanning, Ian Haug, Darren Middleton

30 Saul Adamczewski, Severin Black, Adam J Harmer, Ciaran Hartnett, Lias Kaci Saoudi, Nathan Saoudi

BONUS TRACKS

31 Lilian Lopez, Louise Lopez, Tony Reynolds

32 Rob B, The Head, Owen If

33 Lux Interior, Poison Ivy Rorschach, Nick Knox

34 Mike Hugg, Paul Jones, Tom McGuinness, Mike Vickers

35 Davy Carton, John Donnelly, Leo Moran, Derek Murray, Anthony Thistlethwaite

36 Jerry Allison, Joe Mauldin, Niki Sullivan

37 Pete Birrell, Ray Crewdson, Bernie Dwyer, Freddie Garrity, Derek Guinn

38 Dean DeLeo, Robert DeLeo, Eric Kretz, Scott Weiland

39 James Edward Bagshaw, Adam Smith, Samuel Toms, Thomas Walmsley

40 Rod Argent, Paul Atkinson, Hugh Grundy, Chris White

41 Andy Bell, Gareth Farmer, Alex Lowe, Will Pepper

42 Joey Burns, John Convertino, Paul Niehaus, Jacob Valenzuela, Martin Wenk, Volker Zander

43 Mark Chadwick, Jeremy Cunningham, Simon Friend, Charlie Heather, Jonathan Sevink

44 Nicky Byrne, Kian Egan, Mark Feehily, Shane Filan, Brian McFadden

45 Jack Bessant, Dominic Greensmith, Kenwyn House, Gary Stringer

46 Bernie Clark, Roddy Frame, Campbell Owens, Dave Ruffy

47 Sarah Cracknell, Bob Stanley, Pete Wiggs

48 James Allan, Rab Allan, Paul Donoghue, Jonna Lofgren

49 Jeremiah Fraites, Byron Isaacs, Neyla Pekarek, Stelth Ulvang, Wesley Schultz

50 Patrick Fitzgerald, Dan Goodwin, Julian Swales

51 Mike Cooley, Patterson Hood, Brad Morgan, John Neff, Spooner Oldham, Shona Tucker

52 Jimi Goodwin, Andy Williams, Jez Williams

53 Peter Cox, Richard Drummie

54 Dot Major, Hannah Reid, Dan Rothman

55 Tom Fleming, Ben Little, Chris Talbot, Hayden Thorpe

56 Elliott Easton, Gre Hawkes, Ric Ocasek, Benjamin Orr, David Robinson

57 Jonathon Aherne, Toby Dundas, Joseph Greer, Dougy Mandagi, Lorenzo Sillitto

58 Paul Foad, Peter Hammond, Jane Munro, Lesley Woods

59 Kirk Brandon, Mickey Donnelly, Neil Pyzer, Alan St Clair, Stan Stammers, Dolphin Taylor

60 Christian Hardy, Nick Hemming

QUIZ 8

DJs & RADIO

In the decades since pop music became a fixture on the airwaves, an unexpected cult has grown up around the men and women whose job title implies that they're there simply to cue up the records. Some disc jockeys do their thing unobtrusively: picking and playing the music, telling us a little about what we're hearing, letting us make our own judgements. Other DJs take a very different tack: as they fill the airwaves with banter and chat, daft games and dafter jingles, music sometimes feels like an afterthought. On BBC 6 Music, all our DJs enjoy theselves on air, but we're really all about the tunes. Here are 30 questions on some of the best-known radio DJs of the last 50 years.

Answers: page 466

1   Which DJ's mid-morning programme on BBC Radio 1 included a sentimental feature called 'Our Tune'? For which station did this DJ work after leaving the BBC, presenting occasionally from 1997 and regularly from 2002 until 2011?

2   *Come Find Yourself* is the 1996 debut album by which New York band, who favoured a cartoon gangster image? Which current BBC 6 Music presenter fronts the band?

3   Which radio station boasted the most powerful transmitter in Europe from the thirties to the sixties? On which famous medium wave frequency did the station broadcast?

4   Which track by Ocean Colour Scene was used as the main theme for Chris Evans' show *TFI Friday*? What was the name of the earlier programme, also hosted by Evans on Channel 4, that helped to set the light entertainment blueprint for the show?

5   Who was the first female DJ to present the Breakfast Show on BBC Radio 1? Which TV show does she currently present, having previously been a contestant on its parent programme?

6   What was the full name of the Australian-born DJ known affectionately by his colleagues as 'Fluff'? What's the name of the chart programme he presented on BBC radio from 1961 to 1972?

7   In 2015, which independent rock station was rebranded as Radio X? Who left talkSPORT to host both Radio X's drive-time show and a Saturday football-based programme called *Kickabout*?

8   'When Britain was an Empire, we were ruled by an emperor. When we became a kingdom, we were ruled by a king. And now we're a country, we're ruled by Margaret Thatcher.' Who was censured for telling this joke on BBC Radio 2 in the early eighties? What was the name of the sci-fi hero alter ego he used in both his radio and TV shows?

9   In which city was the inaugural 6 Music Festival launched in 2014, and who played the festival's first headline set?

10 Now a presenter on BBC Radio 2, 'Whispering' Bob Harris presented which influential TV rock programme in the seventies? In recent years, with which style of music has he been most associated?

11 Who took over the BBC Radio 2 breakfast show from Brian Hayes in 1993 and turned it into a national institution? Who was the show's traffic presenter from Splott in Wales, light-heartedly referred to as the 'Totty from Splotty'?

12 Between 1976 and 1982, which children's programme gave DJ Noel Edmonds his big break on TV? Why did Edmonds quit *The Late Late Breakfast Show* in November 1986?

13 In January 2004, who did Chris Moyles replace as presenter of BBC Radio 1's Breakfast Show? Who was Moyles's chief sidekick on many of his radio shows?

14 Who presents The Music News on 6 Music? With which band did he have UK top 20 singles (including 'Daydreamer', 'Stardust' and 'Being Brave') in the 1990s before starting a new career in journalism?

15 Who took over the Breakfast Show on BBC Radio 1 from Chris Moyles in 2012? On which BBC One magazine show does he now frequently work as a guest presenter alongside Alex Jones?

BONUS TRACKS

16 David Hamilton, Tony Blackburn and Kenny Everett all featured on which London-based oldies station, which launched in 1988? Which enthusiastic sports commentator, now a familiar TV voice, worked on the station's live football coverage?

17 Who was the first DJ to broadcast on BBC Radio 1 in 1967? Which reality show did he win in 2002?

18 Which Radio London DJ was the first to play Graham Parker and Dire Straits on the radio, and was hugely instrumental in launching the success of Ian Dury? What was the title of his 1970 book, one of the first and most influential histories of rock and roll?

19 Who was BBC Radio 1's first female DJ? Which music TV show did she co-present from 1978 to 1982, playing an important part in making the programme more relevant to a younger audience?

20 Which 6 Music DJ was behind the classic Sunday acid jazz sessions at Dingwalls in Camden Town from 1986 to 1991? What was the name of the show he ran on BBC Radio 1 for thirteen years before moving to 6 Music?

21 Simply Red's 'Something Got Me Started' launched which independent radio station in September 1994? Which spicy presenter joined the station in 2013 as co-host of the breakfast show alongside Jamie Theakston?

22 In radio history, what is the significance of *MV Fredericia*, a Danish passenger ferry? After whom was it renamed following its refurbishment?

23 Which DJ's name is most readily associated with the words 'in the afternoon'? Where did Mr Angry, a spoof caller to his show, hail from?

24 Which BBC 6 Music presenter was formerly known as 'Lard'? With which band did he play bass between 1978 and 1983?

25 Who presented *God's Jukebox* on BBC Radio 2 from 2006 to 2010, and kept the name of the show for a late-night slot he has curated at the Latitude festival? Which popular TV music quiz did he host for 17 series?

26 Which DJ was the subject of David Cavanagh's 2015 book, *Good Night and Good Riddance*? And which DJ of similar vintage released an autobiography in the same year called *Still Whispering After All These Years*?

27 Which DJ was the original co-presenter of *The Evening Session* on BBC Radio 1 with Steve Lamacq? She moved to a mid-morning slot after which of her colleagues left to join BBC Radio 5 Live?

28 In the nineties, which two comedians invented the DJ characters Smashie (Mike Smash) and Nicey (Dave Nice)?

29 'Flirt Divert', 'Innuendo Bingo' and 'Your Call' have all been features on which DJ's BBC Radio 1 afternoon show? Which BBC Radio 5 Live and *Match of the Day 2* presenter once co-hosted the show?

30 Which erudite American BBC Radio DJ co-founded Classic FM and contributed regularly to BBC Radio 4's long-running arts programme, *Kaleidoscope*? What is the name of the programme he started in 1988, showcasing the best of the American music scene?

QUIZ 9

LOU REED

From the release of the Velvet Underground's debut in 1967 until his death in 2013, Lou Reed stood out as one of rock music's most individual and uncompromising figures. Like David Bowie, a sometime collaborator, Reed stood for progression and experimentation. His albums weren't always commercially successful, and his music was rarely the sort of thing with which to give yourself a lift after a bad day at the office. But he was always distinctly, uniquely Lou. The first section of this quiz covers Reed himself, while the second covers three other artists who score low on the chuckle-ometer: Leonard Cohen, Neil Young, and one latter-day acolyte, Nick Cave. Enjoy. Or, if not, wallow.

Answers: page 467

1 Reed's 2003 opus *The Raven* is a series of recitals and musical pieces based around the work of which American author and poet? Which New York painter and friend of Reed's from the Factory days provided the art for the cover?

2 Where did the Velvet Underground play a nine-week residency in 1970, gigs made famous by the official 1972 release of bootleg tapes recorded on the final night (Reed's last performance with the band)? Which pounding track opens the set?

3 Reed contributed vocals to the 1988 album *Boom Boom Chi Boom Boom* by which New York band? On which of his own compositions did he sing?

4 On 'Good Evening Mr Waldheim' from the 1989 album *New York*, which African-American politician and which religious leader came in for some stick alongside the Austrian head of state named in the title?

5 On what occasion did the *New York Times* publish a poem by Reed called 'Laurie Sadly Listening'? Who's the 'Laurie' referred to in the title?

6 Who was Reed's tutor at Syracuse University, an American poet to whom he dedicated the Velvet Underground song 'European Son'? To which artist is Reed and John Cale's 1990 album *Songs for Drella* dedicated?

7 The *Children in Need* version of Reed's 'Perfect Day' was released in 1997 by popular demand after appearing on TV in what capacity? Which film had already increased the song's profile earlier in the decade?

8 Which Velvet Underground song did Canadian band Cowboy Junkies include on their classic album *The Trinity Session* in 1988? And who had previously covered the song on their 1972 album *All the Young Dudes*?

9 What's the title of Reed's 1975 notorious double album, a squall of feedback and noise lasting nearly two hours? And what's the live album he made in 2008 in an attempt to bring some of this material into a live context?

10 Which fiercely distorted and dissonant Velvet Underground track lasts for 17 minutes in its original studio version? On which album, the band's second, did it appear?

11 What was the title of Reed's greatest hits released in 2004, acknowledging his place in the artistic life of his hometown? Which song from *Transformer* was reworked and rereleased around the same time, taking the singer back into the UK Top 10?

12 Who replaced Angus MacLise as the drummer in the Velvet Underground before they had even set foot in a studio? What was the most notable feature of this drummer's 1991 solo album, *I Spent a Week There the Other Night*?

13 What was the final album Reed released as a solo artist without any credited collaborators? Which long-term associate of Reed's played bass on the album, as he did frequently on Reed's records from the 1980s to the 2000s?

14 'Waltzing Matilda' is the first part of a three-part song cycle that makes up the title track of which 1978 Reed album? Whose voice is heard in the spoken section of the third part, 'Slipaway'?

15 Which two titles from the following list are not the names of studio albums released by Reed: *The Blue Mask, Coney Island Baby, Heroin, New Sensations, Sally Can't Dance, Sex with Your Parents, Legendary Hearts*?

BONUS TRACKS

16 If 'Like a drunk in a midnight choir' is the second line, what's the first? And on which Leonard Cohen album is this the opening track?

17 What was Nick Cave's third solo album, a collection of covers with a Biblical quote for a title? Which Reed-penned song did Cave include on the album?

18 Which musician has played on every Nick Cave & the Bad Seeds album so far except *Push the Sky Away*, released in 2013? And which original Bad Seed returned for the album, his first record with Cave since 1986?

19 What's the title of the 1972 album that put Neil Young firmly up front as a solo artist? What, loosely speaking, did the album acquire 20 years later?

20 When Young went to Hollywood and Redwood and crossed the ocean, for what was he searching? Which of the song's lyrics seems much more apt when Young sings it today?

21 What was Leonard Cohen's outerwear of choice on *Songs of Love and Hate*? Which historical figure is recognised in the title of the last track on the album?

22 Which 2012 album saw Neil Young & Crazy Horse rip up a number of traditional folk songs in their own inimitable style? Which British anthem ended the album?

23 What are the titles of the two discs on the 2004 double-album release by Nick Cave & the Bad Seeds?

24 Which Leonard Cohen song gave the singer his only UK singles chart entry in 2007 when it was rereleased amid a surge of interest in his work? On which 1984 album did the song initially appear?

25 What's the name of the violent Australian western, directed by John Hillcoat, for which Nick Cave wrote the screenplay, as well as composing the soundtrack with Warrn Ellis? And what's the title of the stylised 2014 documentary about Cave, directed by Iain Forsyth and Jane Pollard?

26 Which Oliver Stone film from 1994 featured three tracks from Leonard Cohen's 1992 album *The Future*? In the title track from that album, what does the singer want to see the return of, alongside Stalin and St Paul?

27 Fed up with younger artists failing to speak out against the Bush administration, Neil Young released a politically charged album in 2006. What was it called? Which controversial track on it called for dramatic anti-government action and included excerpts from George W Bush's speeches?

28 Which 2012 Leonard Cohen album became his highest charting album in the US when it reached No3, 45 years after his first album came out? What's the title of the 2014 follow-up, released a few months before the singer turned 80?

29 Under what name did the band that became the Birthday Party release their first album, *Door, Door* in 1979? And what's the name of the Nick Cave project that made two noisy albums in 2007 and 2010?

30 *Weld*, *Year of the Horse* and *Road Rock* are all examples of what? And what was the album of feedback and noise that accompanied the initial release of *Weld*?

QUIZ 10

NOW PLAYING @6

I love Tom Robinson's show on Saturday evenings. That is to say, I love the show that Tom broadcasts on Saturday evenings — I rarely actually listen to it on Saturday evening, but that is the joy of modern radio: we can listen to stuff when we like. The benefits of the internet are the subject of much debate, but 'Play Again' would be most people's idea of a good thing. Tom likes a theme and, as this is a quiz book, themes are the order of the day. All the songs and artists in this section involve questions in some way; either they have an overt question in the title, or the lyrics are written in a heavily interrogative style. As usual, they are all two-part questions.

Answers: page 468

1   What was the title of Hazel O'Connor's debut album, the soundtrack to a film of the same name? Which interrogative single from the album was a last-dance-at-the-disco classic in the eighties?

2   What was the all-important question asked by Department S in 1980? Where did the band get their name?

3   In 1970, who asked 'Who'll Stop the Rain?' And who was the group's leader and songwriter, still recording and playing today?

4   What was the title of the EP released by the Arctic Monkeys a few months after the release of their debut album in 2006? What was its lead track?

5   Which are the only two David Bowie singles to contain a question mark in the title?

6   'Is It Wicked Not to Care?' appeared as the third track on which classic Belle and Sebastian album? Which Scottish singer provided the vocals, as she did on numerous occasions before embarking on a solo career?

7   What was the best-selling album of the nineties? It never topped the bestseller lists for one single year. Robson and Jerome sold more in 1995; which album by a Canadian singer outsold it in 1996?

8   Who sang the first line of Band Aid's 'Do They Know It's Christmas?' in 1984? Who sang it at Live Aid in 1995?

9   Who thought getting to the top of the UK album chart in 1970 was merely *A Question of Balance*? Who wrote and sang lead vocals on the opening track, 'Question'?

10 What geographical question did a famous Bacharach and David song ask in 1968? And who took it into the Top 10 on both sides of the Atlantic?

11 The Who are a band whose name inevitably led to punning titles. Which two Who albums are grammatically interrogative, even though the question mark wasn't used on either?

12 On his debut album, *Doggystyle*, Snoop Dogg asked two fundamental questions in one song title. Which one?.

13 'Who Killed Bambi?' appears on the Sex Pistols' *Great Rock 'n' Roll Swindle* album. Who sings it? And who did kill Bambi?

14 'What Becomes of the Brokenhearted' was a UK Top 10 hit twice for which singer? The 1974 re-release was even more successful than the original, which gave the singer his first big hit in which year?

15 '(What's So Funny 'Bout) Peace, Love and Understanding' is a song best known for the version by which new wave singer and his band? His producer, Nick Lowe, wrote the song and recorded it first with which earlier band?

BONUS TRACKS

16 What was Buzzcocks' first UK Top 40 single, in 1978? Which durable Northern Irish band (with a question mark in their name) have covered it?

17 Who had a massive hit with 'Why Do Fools Fall In Love' in 1956, aged 14? What was the second line of the song?

18 Who reached number three on the UK chart with 'Who's That Girl?' in 1983? Who released a single with the same title in 1986 (from a movie of the same name) and hit number one in the UK and US?

19 Originally a B-side, which 1986 song by the Smiths seemed to query the linear nature of time? A later version by US band Love Spit Love was the theme for which TV sci-fi series from 1998 to 2006?

20 What did Duran Duran want you to please, please tell them now? Surprisingly, given how big they were, they only ever had two UK number one singles — what was the other?

21 'Who Cares What the Question Is?' was the opening track on *Octopus*, the third album by which British indie band? From where do they hail (it's the same place as Level 42)?

22 What question took girl group the Shirelles to the top of the US chart in 1960? Carole King, who co-wrote the song, released her own version a decade later on which classic album?

23 'What Can I Do?' was a track from the second (and Mercury Prize-winning) album by Antony and the Johnsons. What was the album, and who provided additional vocals on the track?

24 Which Tamla Motown song was segued with 'Tainted Love' to give Soft Cell their first major hit? Who was the other half of the band alongside Marc Almond?

25 What self-pitying question did Pet Shop Boys ask on their second single off their second album? Which British sixties pop great joined them on the track?

26 What rhetorical question did Bat For Lashes ask on her first album, *Fur and Gold*? What is the real name of the artist who records as Bat for Lashes?

27 Who collaborated with Rihanna on her 2010 single 'What's My Name?' What is Rihanna's full name?

28 The opening track on Bob Dylan's second album is a series of questions. Where was the answer, and what was the album?

29 Who took the bitter break-up song 'Who's Sorry Now?' to the top of the UK charts in 1957? In which Marx Brothers film did the song appear in 1946?

30 Which crucial culinary question, combining mastication and slumber, was a novelty hit for skiffle legend Lonnie Donegan in 1959? What song about his father's employment was his third and final UK number one in 1960?

QUIZ 11

THIS IS REGGAE MUSIC

No apologies here for including a lot of questions on Bob Marley and the Wailers. Reggae snobs may moan 'There's more to reggae than Bob Marley, you know ...' but Marley is by some distance the most successful and far-reaching reggae artist ever.

Yet there are also questions here on other pace-setters and pioneers as well as a few on the modern scene - although Jamaican music is now failing to penetrate the market in the way it did in the classic roots era.

Answers: page 469

1 he 1976 album *CB200* was by which reggae star, born Lester Bullocks, but naming himself after an American gangster? Where did the album title come from?

2 By what name were Marcia Griffiths, Rita Marley and Judy Mowatt collectively known? What was their primary employment?

3 What sweet chorus did the 'Three Little Birds' sing on *Exodus*?

4 Which Tina Turner B-side provided a surprise UK number one for Aswad in 1988? Where did they get their name?

5 'Fighting Against Conviction' was one of many heavily political songs on whose brilliant 1976 first solo album, *Blackheart Man*? His 1990 album *Time Will Tell* was affectively a tribute to which other artist?

6 Which two brothers supplied the rhythm for the Wailers in their seventies heyday? With which Lee Perry house band were they previously employed?

7 *Marcus Garvey* was a classic Island Records album released in 1975: who made it? And who was Marcus Garvey?

8 What were the two UK Top 20 singles recorded by Bob Andy and Marcia Griffths (as Bob and Marcia) in 1970 and 1971?

9 Who performed live on US TV singing 'Bush Doctor', a song about the legalisation of cannabis? Who duetted with him on the lead single from the *Bush Doctor* album, '(You Gotta Walk) Don't Look Back'?

10 In which London auditorium was Bob Marley and the Wailers' famous 1975 live album recorded? What was the title of the other live album released in Marley's lifetime, in 1978?

11 Pato Banton had a number one hit in the UK with a 1994 version of 'Baby Come Back', performed with two members of which prominent band? Who wrote the song and also had a number one with it in 1968 with his multiracial band the Equals?

12 Which 1984 compilation went in to become the best-selling reggae album of all time? Which is the only album to have spent more weeks on the US chart?

13 Who released the 1995 dancehall album *Til Shiloh*, reflecting his new Rastafarian beliefs? Why has he not released any more albums since 2010's *Before the Dawn*?

14 Which two members of the original Wailers left the band in 1974 to pursue their own careers?

15 Shaggy had the first reggae-based number one in the UK for some years with his 1993 smash 'Oh Carolina'. Who recorded the original song in 1960? What was Shaggy's next number one, two years later?

BONUS TRACKS

16 In which city did the late seventies ska revival begin with the formation of The Special AKA? What was the name of the record label they formed?

17 What was the UK Top 10 album for dancehall pin-up Sean Paul? Which Jamaican DJ collaborated with him on the hit single 'I'm Still in Love with You'?

18 Which 1973 Wailers album featured the original version of 'I Shot the Sheriff'? What was the name of the sheriff?

19 Which ragga duo had the 700th official number one in the UK in January 1994 with a cover of a Chubby Checker classic? What was their debut single from the previous year that reached number three?

20 Which reggae cover was the longest track on the first album by the Clash? Who recorded the original version a year previously?

21 Who blended roots reggae with softer lovers rock on albums like *Night Nurse* and *Private Beach Party*? What was the nickname accorded the star?

22 Bob Marley's 'No Woman, No Cry' is an account of growing up in which deprived area of Kingston? To which country did Marley relocate from Jamaica in 1976?

23 Dawn Penn had been around on the Jamaican music scene for some while before hitting paydirt with a 1994 revival of which song? Which major recording artist covered it on her 2005 debut album, *Music in the Sun*?

24 Cecil Campbell helped to give birth to ska and reggae music: what is his stage name? What was the name of his famous backing band?

25 *Skylarking* (1972) was the debut album of which roots reggae singer? With which British hip hop band did he become associated in the nineties, singing on all of their studio releases?

26 What was the last Bob Marley and the Wailers album released while Marley was still alive? What was the compilation of previously unreleased material released in 1983?

27 Whose 1997 debut album *Maverick A Strike* saw him hailed as a saviour of British reggae? In which city was he born into a family of jazz musicians?

28 Which record label, famous for its series of reggae box sets, was originally set up as a sister company to Island records before being sold to Saga in 1975? Which youth movement identified itself with the label before being hijacked by racists in the seventies and eighties?

29 'The Tide is High' was originally released by which rocksteady band? Who was the song's composer who later had a successful solo career, including a UK Top 10 hit with a cover of 'Help Me Make it Through the Night'?

30 Which Bob Marley hit the UK Top 10 when it was remixed by DJ Funkstar Deluxe in 1999? On which 1971 album did it initially appear?

QUIZ 12

GIRLS & BOYS

A simple theme: this section is all about girls' and boys' names that feature in the titles or lyrics of hit songs from the last 60 years. There are two sections, both straightforward: the first 20 questions spotlight the girls, while the rest are all about the boys.

Answers: page 470

QUIZ 12 GIRLS & BOYS – THE GIRLS

1   What's the name of the girl in the title of Blondie's soaring 1999 comeback single, which reached number one in the UK? In the same year, who released a darker song about a girl with the same name, killed in a sweatshop while working illegally in the US, on their album *The Battle of Los Angeles*?

2   'Rosalita (Come Out Tonight)' is a longtime live favourite by which major rock act? Which band included a thunderous version of Bob Seger's 'Rosalie' on their memorable 1978 live album *Live and Dangerous*?

3   Which girl lent her name to the title of the debut single by the Fratellis? And which 'Mistress' was the first single from *Here We Stand*, the group's second album?

4   Which girl's name gave Steve Winwood the title of one of his two UK Top 20 singles? Who persuaded Amy Winehouse to join him in a cover of the Zutons' song about a girl with the same name?

5   What was the name of the Welsh witch that Fleetwood Mac, led by Stevie Nicks, sang about on their self-titled 1975 album? And who was namechecked, again by Nicks, on the group's epic album *Tusk* (1979)?

6   Which salacious schoolgirl gave the Boomtown Rats a UK Top 20 hit in 1977? And which real woman did the band profess never to have loved on their second album, *A Tonic for the Troops*?

7   Who was a friend of the Killers on their first album, *Hot Fuss*? On the same record, how did the band suggest we should smile?

8   How did Judy present herself on John Fred & His Playboy Band's 1968 top five hit, its title inspired by The Beatles' 'Lucy in the Sky with Diamonds'? And what was Judy on the Ramones' self-titled debut album?

9   Who lent their name to two very different songs by Tom Jones (in 1968) and Queen (on *Innuendo*, from 1991)? Who covered Tom's song on *The Penthouse Tapes* (1976)?

10 Which two women are referenced by name in titles on *Songs of Leonard Cohen*, the Canadian singer's 1967 debut?

11 How often was Charlotte, according to the Cure in their 1981 single inspired by a book by Penelope Farmer? And a year earlier, what was Iron Maiden's Charlotte?

12 What (or who) was the breakthrough 2008 single for Scottish indie band Glasvegas? Who (or what) was invited by the band to take their hand in 2011?

13 'Mandy' was an American number one hit for which singer in 1974? Which boy band took the song to the top of the British charts in 2003?

14 Which two male singers have recently sung about a girl called Candy, one on *Sunny Side Up* (2009) and the other on *Take the Crown* (2012)?

15 Which band took 'Emma', a song about an actress who commits suicide, into the US and UK Top 10 in 1974? Which real actress inspired a number one hit for Mika in 2007?

16 U2 have featured female names in the titles of two tracks, one on their 1981 album *October* and the other from the more recently released *Songs of Innocence*. What are they?

17 Which girl's name made the UK Top 10 in hits by Neil Diamond in 1971 and Status Quo two years later? Which other female name had previously given Diamond his first UK hit single in 1970?

18 Which soul classic, a hit for Wilson Pickett, features the line 'ride, Sally, ride', which took on new resonance after American astronaut Sally Ride became the first American woman in space in 1983? What did Eric Clapton want his Sally to do in 1977?

19 Which band asked Alice what the matter was in 1994? And who, in 1976, were living next door to Alice?

20 Who picked a fine time to leave Kenny Rogers? And what did she leave behind?

THE BOYS

21 Which two punk bands sung separately about Harry in 1978 and 1979?

22 Which Leiber and Stoller song, which shares its name with a cartoon character, was a hit for the Coasters in 1959? Which Coldplay album features a song with the same title?

23 Daniel was leaving tonight on a plane in a 1973 hit for which British singer? And in 2009, which singer knew when she saw him that Daniel had a flame in his heart?

24 Which couple were a hit for John Cougar in 1982? Under what name does Cougar record today?

25 Who wrote and recorded Johnny B Goode in 1958? Which band included a track called 'Johnny Bagga Donuts' on *180*, their debut album from 2013?

26 Which Shel Silverstein song became Johnny Cash's biggest US hit single in 1969? Where was Cash's version recorded?

27 Who took 'Fernando' and 'Angelo' to the top of the UK charts in 1976 and 1977 respectively?

28 Whose 'Jimmy' was so good they named him twice in 1979? Who sang about 'St Jimmy' on their classic album from 2004?

29 Who did Sinéad O'Connor sing about in 1987, a song covered by Placebo in 2003? And which namesake soul singer starred in a song by Van Morrison that was later a hit for Dexys Midnight Runners?

30 'Johnny and Mary' was a standout track on the 1980 album *Clues* by which British singer? Who sang on DJ Todd Terje's 2014 cover of the song?

QUIZ 13

STADIUM ROCK

You know the bands we mean: the ones who play venues so big that all you can see is a tiny speck half a mile away, even though you paid £65 for a ticket. Their popularity is one reason why festivals have become so popular: it's sometimes better to stand in a field with 20,000 like-minded folk than sit in row Z at Wembley Stadium or Old Trafford, staring enviously at the empty seats in the corporate enclosure. Anyway, these two sections contain five questions each about six of the world's biggest bands, past and present: Fleetwood Mac, Queen, Muse, the Who, U2 and Led Zeppelin.

Answers: page 471

1   Fleetwood Mac started as a straight-up blues band under whose leadership? Who replaced him as guitarist and songwriter between 1971 and 1974, a relatively fruitless period in the group's history?

2   Who stepped into Freddie Mercury's shoes when Queen reformed in 2004? What's the title of the only album he recorded with the band?

3   What's the name of the three-part symphony that concludes Muse's *Resistance* album? Which call to arms begins the record, and became the first Muse track to break into the American Top 40?

4   The Who were one of the first bands to play a concert at a football ground. At which London stadium did the group play to 80,000 fans in 1974 and 1976? What was notable about the second show?

5   U2's *Rattle and Hum* was both a documentary film and an album, featuring new tracks, live tracks and covers. A live version of which Beatles song opens the album? And which track from the record became the band's first British number one?

6   Who sued Led Zeppelin and was later given a co-writing credit for 'Whole Lotta Love', released on the band's second album? Which other song by the same blues musician closes the album?

7   Taken from their debut album *My Generation*, what was the Who's first UK Top 10 hit? The band never had a number one single but did twice reach number two, with 'My Generation' – and which song about a young lad who was dressed as a girl by his mother?

8   The title of Muse's album *Black Holes and Revelations* comes from a line in the second track 'Starlight', but what kind of black hole lends its title to track three? And which six-minute epic closes the album?

9   Which two artists are credited alongside Queen on the *Five Live* EP, a British number one recorded at a tribute concert to Freddie Mercury in 1992?

10 Which 1987 album signalled U2's step up from adored live band to global rock superstars, putting the band at the top of the US albums chart for the first time? Which photographer (and, later, film director) worked with U2

throughout the first half of their career and shot the album's memorable cover in the California desert?

11 Which eight-minute song on Led Zeppelin's *Physical Graffiti* is told by 'a traveller of both time and space'? And which ten-minute opener to the band's album *Presence* is not about the Trojan War, as the title might suggest, but was inspired by the poetry of William Blake and a range of hills in Morocco?

12 Which Queen song reached number one in the UK singles chart twice, in 1975 and 1991? Why was it reissued?

13 What's the title of the US chart-topping live album recorded during their 1997 tour by the classic mid-seventies line-up of Fleetwood Mac? And what's the name of the successful 2003 studio follow-up, recorded without Christine McVie?

14 'Drowning Man', 'Two Hearts Beat as One' and 'New Year's Day' are all tracks on which 1983 U2 album, their first to top the UK charts? What's the opening track, a tough observation on the damage caused by the Irish troubles?

15 Which of Led Zeppelin's albums has sold the most copies? What's distinctive about its cover?

BONUS TRACKS

16 On the album *Quadrophenia*, each member of the Who has a 'theme' song. What are the songs designated as 'Pete's Theme' (for Pete Townshend) and 'Keith's Theme' (for Keith Moon)?

17 What was the first film soundtrack album to be released by Queen? And the songs for which film formed the basis for the group's number one album *A Kind of Magic*?

18 Released in 1981, *Bella Donna* and *Law and Order* are the debut solo albums by which two members of Fleetwood Mac?

19 What's the name of the post-traumatic disorder, through which victims of kidnapping develop a bond with their captors, that gave Muse the title of the lead single from their 2003 album *Absolution*? And what 'scared the hell' out of Matt Bellamy on the same album?

20 What are the two UK number one singles taken from U2's 2004 album *How to Dismantle an Atomic Bomb*?

21 Which track from Led Zeppelin's 1973 album *Houses of the Holy* gave its name to a live album and film, released three years later? And which Zeppelin album features a track called 'Houses of the Holy', originally recorded for the album of the same name but not featured on it?

22 The name and the heartbeat of Fleetwood Mac comes from the rhythm section, consisting of which two musicians?

23 Which 16th-century composer's work did Muse adapt into the title track of their 2015 album *Drones*? Which song, most famously recorded by Nina Simone, did the band cover on their earlier album *Origin of Symmetry*?

24 What's the title of the studio album Queen released after Freddie Mercury's death, using existing songs and vocal tracks the late singer had written and recorded? Where is the statue of Freddie Mercury that features on the cover?

25 The successful use of the Who's 'Who Are You' as the theme tune to the American forensic procedural drama *CSI: Crime Scene Investigation* led to two more Who tracks, both from the album *Who's Next*, being used for the spin-off series, *CSI: Miami* and *CSI: NY*. What are they?

26 Under what name did U2 and Brian Eno join forces to release their 1995 album *Original Soundtracks 1*, a series of songs for mostly imaginary films? Recorded for a documentary produced by Bono, which song from the album features an operatic segment sung by Luciano Pavarotti?

27 Through which door did Led Zeppelin arrive on their 1979 album, the band's last before John Bonham's death? What was the title of the aptly named album released three years later, two years after the group had disbanded?

28 What was the contrast between love and lies that gave Fleetwood Mac two hit singles from their 1987 album *Tango in the Night*?

29 What's the title of Muse's 1999 debut album? On which Australian label was the album distributed in the UK?

30 Who replaced Keith Moon as the drummer in the Who? And which son of a famous drummer stepped in when the band started playing live again in 1999?

QUIZ 14

DAVID BOWIE

The difference in quality between David Bowie's best music and his worst is spectacularly extreme. Bowie could be magnificent, a colossus showing the way forward with each shift of musical style, as he was in the seventies. He could be cheeky and challenging and innovative, experimenting with new sounds and techniques. He could be a pop diva, as he was in the eighties when he produced a string of pop hits that audiences lapped up. Or he could be a bit rubbish, as he was for most of the nineties. Yet he was never dull.

Answers: page 472

1   'V-2 Schneider' was a David Bowie track dedicated to Florian Schneider, a big influence on Bowie's work in the late seventies: who was Schneider? And on which Bowie album was 'V-2 Schneider' the opening track on the second side of vinyl?

2   In which 1986 fantasy movie did Bowie play Jareth the Goblin King? What part did he play in the 1988 Martin Scorsese film *The Last Tempation of Christ*?

3   Who took Bowie's song 'The Man Who Sold the World' into the UK Top 10 in 1974? Who produced the version as well as playing guitar and singing backing vocals?

4   Why did Bowie change his stage name from David Jones, his birth name? And where did 'Bowie' come from?

5   'In Drive-In Saturday' what did 'Buddy' do? What was his female friend's non-verbal response?

6   In which city was Bowie living at the time of his death in 2016? Which US city did he once say should be burned to the ground after he had a hard time while living there?

7   Bowie wrote the track 'Fame' based on a guitar riff from his collaborator, Carlos Alomar, and ideas from which musical legend, with whom he had been jamming in the studio? Which soul crooner co-wrote 'Fascination' from the same album?

8   By what name was David and Angie Bowie's son Duncan known in his early years? What was his first, highly successful, feature film as a director, released in 2009?

9   The Buzz, Doppelganger, the King Bees, Lower Third, Riot Squad, Skeleton Men. Which two of these were NOT bands in which Bowie played as a youngster?

10 Which female star sang 'Under Pressure' with Bowie at the 1992 memorial concert for Freddie Mercury? Who formed a more lasting partnership with Bowie when she married him four days later?

11 Which Bowie song was the result of an infatuation between Iggy Pop and a Vietnamese woman, Kuelan Ngoyen? On which album did Bowie's version of the song (co-written with Iggy) appear?

12 In 1993 Bowie released a hastily written and produced soundtrack album to which TV series? Who wrote the source novel on which the series was based?

13 What was Bowie's final album, released days before his death in early 2016? Which album pushed it off the number one slot in the UK album chart?

14 Which Bowie subject thought he'd blow our minds? And which one had a police bike and a turned-up nose?

15 *Lodger* was the final album in David Bowie's late seventies Berlin trilogy. What were the first two?

BONUS TRACKS

16 Which collaborator did David Bowie once describe as a 'little old orange on a stool'? What was the single, a number three hit at Christmas 1982?

17 Who was the Puerto Rican guitarist who worked with Bowie for nearly 30 years from *Young Americans* in 1975? And who provided the searing lead guitar on 'Heroes' and 'Teenage Wildlife'?

18 Which modern TV cop show starring John Simm and Philip Glenister took its title from a David Bowie song? And what nickname did Glenister's unreconstructed seventies cop give himself?

19 Which disco maestro produced the album *Let's Dance* alongside Bowie? Which Texas blues guitarist took time out from his own band Double Trouble to play guitar?

20 What persona did Bowie adopt for his *Station to Station* period? Which song, originally sung by Johnny Mathis in a 1957 film of the same name, elicited an extraordinary, albeit occasionally out of tune, vocal performance from an allegedly coked-up Bowie?

21 David Bowie played on two albums in 1989 and 1991 as part of which hard rock band? Which John Lennon song did they cover?

22 The storyline of 'Ashes to Ashes' referenced which earlier Bowie hit? What costume did Bowie wear in the promotional video?

23 *Pin-Ups* (1973) was an album of cover versions. Which songs by the Who and Pink Floyd did Bowie cover?

24 Which Beach Boys song did Bowie cover on *Tonight* (1984)? And who duetted with him on the album's title track?

25 'Jump They Say' (1993) was Bowie's last UK Top 10 single for 20 years. From which album was it taken? Which song from 2013 album *The Next Day* ended the hit drought?

26 What was the massive tour undertaken by Bowie in 1983 to support the release of *Let's Dance*? What was his very poorly received following tour, in 1987?

27 Some of the music for Bowie's album, *Low*, came from rejected material from the soundtrack to which 1976 film, in which Bowie starred? Who was the director?

28 Which 1999 Bowie album was the first full LP made available to download over the internet, prior to the release of the physical album? Why did the lead single off the album have far to go?

29 Which 1986 rock musical directed by Julien Temple starred Bowie and gave him a hit single with its title song? Which young model and star and (later) serial rock spouse had the film's major role?

30 Which former member of Nirvana played guitar on 'I've Been Waiting for You' from Bowie's 2003 album *Heathen*? On which song from the same album did Pete Townshend play guitar?

QUIZ 15

ACCEPTABLE IN THE 80S

It's fair to say that the eighties' reputation precedes it. Readers of a certain age who grew up during this most maligned of decades may remember parts of it rather fondly. For almost everyone else, it was a heinous time for music – and, for that matter, fashion. Leg warmers and bouffant hair wasn't a good look even then, and it certainly isn't today. There are two sections to this quiz, some questions in the usual format and then three quickfire memory rounds.

Answers: page 473

1   Clare Grogan was the singer with which pop-punk band in the 1980s? The band's main composer, Johnny McElhone, went on to have a string of UK Top 10 hits with which other Scottish band?

2   Who had a massive Christmas hit in 2003 with 'Mad World'? Who sang the original eighties hit?

3   Stedman, Lorraine, Denise, Doris and Delroy Pearson were the five siblings in which British pop-soul band? What was the title of their chart-topping second album?

4   Kid Creole & the Coconuts' 1982 album *Tropical Gangsters* was a hit on the back of two hit singles: one about a police informer and one a protestation of non-parenthood. What are their titles?

5   Which 1987 Christmas single by the Pogues re-entered the UK Top 20 every year from 2005 to 2015? Who sang lead vocals on it alongside Shane MacGowan?

6   What was Abba's final UK No 1 single from 1980? And what was their last album, from Novembet the following year?

7   Foreigner were massive in their native US but were never as big in the UK. What was the principal exception, a worldwide number one hit in 1984? The band's English co-founder, Mick Jones (not that one), had previously been a member of which scary-sounding prog rock band?

8   Featuring session singer Carol Kenyon sharing vocal duties, 'Temptation' became the first UK Top 10 hit for which band in 1983? From which album was it taken?

9   Songwriter, singer and guitarist Paddy McAloon was the prime mover, and remains the solitary member, of which pop band who emerged during the 1980s? Containing their only Top 10 single, 'The King of Rock 'n' Roll', what's the title of their most successful album?

10 What's the name of the hit collaboration between David Bowie and Queen in 1981? Which 1982 Queen album did it appear on?

11 What was the first Police album with an English-language title? Written about the troubles in Northern Ireland, what was the first single from the album?

12 What's the full name of the band usually referred to as OMD? (To get the full two points, you have to spell it correctly.

13 What's the name of the vocalist with the Style Council who was also Paul Weller's wife? With which eighties pop band had she previously cut her teeth as a backing singer?

14 *Elvis and Me*, Priscilla Presley's memoir of her late husband, inspired which classic Depeche Mode song? Which country legend later covered the song as part of his *American Recordings* series?

15 What were the two British number ones from Adam & the Ants' third studio album in 1981?

BONUS TRACK 1

Name the artists behind these hit songs:

1 'China in Your Hand' (1987). 2 'Reap the Wild Wind' (1992). 3 'Sign Your Name' (1987). 4 'Wouldn't It Be Good' (1984). 5 'Every Time You Go Away' (1985). 6 'You Take Me Up' (1984). 7 'Oblivious' (1983). 8 'If She Knew What She Wants' (1986). 9 'Torch' (1982). 10 'Smalltown Boy' (1984).

BONUS TRACK 2

And these, all of them number one singles.

1 'Japanese Boy' (1981). 2 'A Good Heart' (1985). 3 'I Owe You Nothing' (1988). 4 'Oh Julie' (1982). 5 'Rock Me Amadeus' (1986). 6 'Fame' (1982). 7 'I Should Have Known Better' (1984). 8 'Move Closer' (1985). 9 'Hand on Your Heart' (1988). 10 'Down Under' (1983).

BONUS TRACK 3

Finally, match the album to the band or artist that recorded it.

1 *Some People* (1985). 2 *Globe of Frogs* (1988). 3 *Before Hollywood* (1983). 4 *EVOL* (1986). 5 *English Settlement* (1982). 6 *Pretty Hate Machine* (1989). 7 *Like Gangbusters* (1983). 8 *A Date with Elvis* (1986). 9 *In the Flat Field* (1981). 10 *Turn Back the Clock* (1988)

Artists: Bauhaus, Belouis Some, the Cramps, the Go-Betweens, JoBoxers, Nine Inch Nails, Robyn Hitchcock & the Egyptians, Johnny Hates Jazz, Sonic Youth, XTC.

QUIZ 16

PEOPLE'S PLAYLIST: WEATHER WITH YOU

The theme of the second People's Playlist quickfire quiz is the weather – and it's remarkable how many more songs have been written about summer and sunshine than about gloom and rain. Even the collection of depressives and miserabilists that make up the rock music community can't get worked up about fog or mizzle, with the honourable and obvious exception of Lindisfarne. The format is the same as before: 40 quick questions, and maybe get that egg-timer out again if you fancy an extra challenge.

Answers: page 474

1   Where does the title to this playlist come from?

2   Who wanted to know 'Why Does It Always Rain on Me' in 1999?

3   Who had a hit with a disco version of the sixties classic 'Macarthur Park' in 1978?

4   Who topped the album chart in 2010 with *Messy Little Raindrops*?

5   One side of Electric Light Orchestra's 1977 album *Out of the Blue* consisted of four tracks called 'Concerto for a Rainy Day'. What was the fourth track from the suite, which reached number six in the UK singles chart?

6   What was George Ezra's interrogative first single?

7   Which U2 song was used as the theme tune to *The Premiership*, ITV's Premier League highlights programme?

8   *Sounds Good Feels Good* was a chart-topping album for which Aussie power pop band?

9   Which 1984 single gave Don Henley his only UK Top 20 hit?

10   Who were lazing on a 'Sunny Afternoon' in 1966?

11   What was a UK number two hit for the Weather Girls in 1982?

12   Which Spice Girl went one better and took the same song to number one in 2001?

13   Where did the Sex Pistols like to holiday?

14   'Something in the Air' was taken to number one in 1969 by which stormy band?

15   Where was it raining for Buddy Holly?

16   When did Mungo Jerry have their biggest hit?

17   'Here Comes the Rain Again': whose observation in 1984?

18   Where did the sun always shine for A-Ha?

19 Who were the 'Riders on the Storm'?

20 Robert van Winkle had his big hit 'Ice Ice Baby' under which cooler name?

21 Joe Zawinul played keyboards in which jazz fusion band of the seventies and eighties?

22 Who tried to think up *50 Words for Snow* in 2011?

23 Which blues guitarist wrote the much-covered classic 'Stormy Monday' – or, to give it its full title, 'Call It Stormy Monday (But Tuesday Is Just as Bad)'?

24 Who was 'Frozen' at the top of the UK singles chart in 1998?

25 The musical *Jersey Boys* tells the story of which vocal group?

26 What meteorological downer got to the Walker Brothers in 1966?

27 With which band was Cozy Powell the drummer between 1975 and 1980?

28 Which British R&B band, named after a Sonny Boy Williamson II song, had some success in the early eighties with their albums *Don't Point the Finger* and *Third Degree*?

29 Who couldn't live without the 'Rain' in 1976?

30 Before their success at Eurovision, what was Katrina & the Waves' biggest hit?

31 Who had us thinking of 'Little Fluffy Clouds' in 1990?

32 Who advised us to *Dodge and Burn* in 2015?

33 'Oh, where have you been, my blue-eyed son?' So begins which Dylan classic?

34 Where did the Lovin' Spoonful spend their summer in 1966?

35 Whose first album brought a *Howlin' Wind* in 1976?

36 'Here Comes the Summer' was whose second single in 1979?

37 Who were concerned about 'Fifteen Feet of Pure White Snow' in 2001?

38 What was Snow's big 1993 hit, reaching number one in the US and number two in the UK?

39 What, in 1987, was the first UK Top 10 single for the Jesus and Mary Chain?

40 Who wanted to *Push the Sky Away* in 2013?

QUIZ 17

GUITAR GIRLS

The only artist to win the Mercury Music Prize on two occasions, PJ Harvey has long been one of the most exciting and provocative voices in British rock, and is the subject of part one of this quiz. Part two focuses on a pair of similarly pioneering female musicians, Chrissie Hynde and Patti Smith, before we end with a short mix-and-match quiz.

Answers: page 474

1   What does the 'PJ' in PJ Harvey stand for? And in which English country was she born? (2)

2   With which longtime bandmate did Harvey make the 1996 album *Dance Hall at Louse Point*? What's the title of their second co-credited album, released in 2009? And what was the name of the band in which the pair previously played together? (3)

3   *Murder Ballads* (1996) and *Angels with Dirty Faces* (1998) featured Harvey duetting with which two artists? (2)

4   Which two albums by Harvey have won the Mercury Music Prize? (2)

5   What's the only cover version on Harvey's second album, *Rid of Me*? (1)

6   What is Rob Ellis's contribution to most of Harvey's albums? (1)

7   Who provides backing vocals on a number of tracks on *Stories from the City, Stories from the Sea*, especially 'This Mess We're In'? And which Bad Seed worked extensively on the album? (2)

8   Whose life did Harvey chronicle in the opening track of *Uh Huh Her*? Where, on the same album, was the cat? And whose darker days were the subject of the closing track? (3)

9   Producer and engineer Flood contributed to Harvey's 2016 album *The Hope Six Community Project*. Under what name is he credited? And which veteran dub poet added guest vocals to 'The Ministry of Defence'? (2)

10 What refrain does Harvey repeat at the end of 'The Words that Maketh Murder' on *Let England Shake*? From which rock and roll classic are they borrowed? (2)

BONUS TRACKS

11 Which song gave the Pretenders their only number one hit in 1979? Written by Ray Davies and produced by Nick Lowe, what had previously served as their debut single?

12 Through her relationship with keyboard player Allen Lanier, Patti Smith sang vocals on a few recordings by which American rock band? What was the first single she released under her own name, a cover of a traditional song made most famous by Jimi Hendrix?

13 What was the last album Smith released in 1979 before taking a break to spend time with her family? Which Swedish band played a version of 'Dancing Barefoot', taken from this album, when Smith was awarded Sweden's prestigious Polar Music Prize?

14 What's the name of the Rockpile guitarist who played on a number of Pretenders tracks in the 1980s, when the band's line-up was constantly in flux? And which frequent Talk Talk collaborator was the band's *de facto* guitarist between 1984 and 1986, playing on almost every track on *Learning to Crawl* and *Get Close*?

15 Patti Smith was honoured by the French Ministry of Culture in 2005, partly in recognition of her love and knowledge of the work of which major French poet? Where did Smith play a three-and-a-half hour gig the following year, the last ever show at this legendary punk venue?

16 Which song from *Last of the Independents* gave the Pretenders their most recent UK Top 10 hit? Which girl band took a weak charity version of the song to number one?

17 What's the title of the Pretenders' 1995 live acoustic album? What was the role of the Duke Quartet on the album?

18 Which veteran guitarist from the New York scene played in Patti Smith's band at Meltdown on London's South Bank in 2005, when Smith was the curator of the festival? At the show, which album did the band play in its entirety?

19 What's the title of Chrissie Hynde's first solo album, released in 2014? Which former tennis megastar played guitar on the album?

20 Smith's album *Twelve* featured a selection of covers by artists she admires. Which Paul Simon song from *Graceland* features on the album? And which REM song from *Automatic for the People* is the album's bonus track?

Match the singer(s) to the band.

21 Helen Marnie. 22 Kiana Alarid and Neely Jenkins. 23 Ellie Russell. 24 Emily Kokal and Theresa Wayman. 25 Amy Lee. 26 Courtney Love. 27 Kathleen Hanna. 28 Corin Tucker. 29 Kat Bjelland. 30 Nina Gordon and Louise Post.

Bands: Babes in Toyland, Bikini Kill, Evanescence, Hole, Ladytron, Sleater-Kinney, Tilly & the Wall, Veruca Salt, Warpaint, Wolf Alice.

QUIZ 18

THE SMITHS

Marr and Morrissey were a sublime match, a hard-working and deeply gifted musician paired with a flamboyant and provocative frontman. The two joined forces to produce some of the finest music made in Britain during the eighties, a period when creativity and originality in the music industry seemed to be at a low ebb. The pair have had their ups and downs since they split – and there will be no reunion. But with the Smiths, as with all truly great bands, 'There Is a Light that Never Goes Out'.

The first section of this quiz is on the Smiths and Morrissey, and is followed by a few questions on other indie bands from the pre-Britpop era.

Answers: page 475

1 What are the Smiths' four studio albums? (4)

2 And what's the name of the 1984 compilation of singles, B-sides and radio sessions that's sometimes mistaken for their fifth? (1)

3 Who were the drummer and bassist in the Smiths? (2)

4 After working with various other groups as a session musician and a full-time band member, Johnny Marr finally released two solo albums in 2013 and 2014. What are they called? (2)

5 Why wouldn't the singer of 'This Charming Man' go out tonight? (1)

6 Who was invited to 'boot the grime of this world in the crotch'? (1)

7 Which Smiths song castigates us for kicking a person when they're down? And what, apparently, did Antony say to Cleopatra while opening a crate of ale? (2)

8 What are Morrissey's two forenames? (2)

9 Whose is the first voice we hear on *The Queen is Dead*, singing 'Take Me Back to Dear Old Blighty' before the title track kicks in? (1)

10 Which art-house film director made a video that featured 'The Queen is Dead', 'There is a Light that Never Goes Out' and 'Panic'? (2)

11 Which Smiths song is sung by two families at a barbecue in the third series of *Gavin and Stacey*? And which Irvine Welsh novel includes a chapter named after the song? (2)

12 Fill the gaps in this list of Morrissey's solo studio albums: *Viva Hate*; *Kill Uncle*; *Your Arsenal*; _____; *Southpaw Grammar*; *Maladjusted*; *You Are the Quarry*; _____; *Years of Refusal*; *World Peace is None of Your Business*. (2)

13 'Sweetness, I was only joking when I said...' ...what? And which Smiths song is under discussion? (2)

14 What was the title of the Smiths' 1983 debut single on Rough Trade? Who took a version of the song, recorded with members of the Smiths, into the UK Top 30 the following year? (2)

15 According to Morrissey's singles catalogue, what is he the last of (1989), what did November spawn (1990), who was the one for him (1992) and what brought him closer (1994)? (4)

BONUS TRACKS

16 *Swagger* (1990) is the finest moment by which Bristol band, still fronted by poet-vocalist Gerard Langley? What is Wojtek Dmochowski's role in the band?

17 The jarring, funky 'Rip It Up' was a 1982 hit for which Scottish post-punk band? What's the name of their lead singer and guitarist, who has gone on to enjoy a fine solo career?

18 Canadian Claire Boucher records under which name? What's the name of her third album, made in three weeks using Apple's GarageBand software and featuring the single 'Genesis'?

19 What important indie institution was launched in 1980? Which Spizzenergi single was the first to benefit?

20 Sonya Aurora Madan was the Indian-born lead singer in which nineties band, a favourite of Morrissey? What ambiguous declaration did they make in the title of their debut album?

21 Who played drums on *Psychocandy*, the hard-edged debut by the Jesus & Mary Chain? Which successful band has he fronted for more than 30 years?

22 What's the title of the jangly, infectious first album by Scottish band Aztec Camera? And what was the band's most successful single, reaching number three in 1988?

23 Tracey Thorn and Ben Watt released ten albums between 1984 and 1999 under which name? Which 1994 song of theirs shot back up the charts in 1995 after it was remixed by Todd Terry?

24 Martyn Ware and Ian Craig Marsh left the Human League in 1980 to form which electronic band? Which other band did they start around the same time, featuring singer Glenn Gregory?

25 The title of which Welsh-born singer's debut album, *World Shut Your Mouth*, was also the title of his most successful single, taken from his third album?

Before starting a solo career that has embraced poetry and scholarly mysticism as well as music, with which band was he the singer?

26 The Cure's debut single 'Killing an Arab' is based on a novel by which French author? Which album, released ten years later, remains their bestselling effort, and was the first album of theirs to enter the American Top 20?

27 'The Pictures on My Wall' was the 1979 debut from which Liverpool band? Who is their charismatic lead singer, who told anyone who would listen (and still will) that they were the best band on the planet?

28 Which Irish band, contemporaries of U2, audaciously kicked off their career in 1981 with a double album, *A New Form of Beauty Parts 1–4*? Who was their singer, who left in 1986 to pursue a solo career that has included both acting and soundtrack work?

29 What are the first two tracks on the Stone Roses' eponymous debut album (1989), which blew away any suggestion that the band had been over-hyped?

30 Released in 1993, *New Wave* is the Mercury Music Prize-nominated album by which band? What was the lead single from their second album, *Now I'm a Cowboy*?

QUIZ 19

CRAIG CHARLES FUNK & SOUL

Every Saturday evening, Craig Charles plays his pick from the world of funk and soul. Mixing contemporary acts with a healthy dollop of classic soul and disco-funk epics, Craig gives us an enthusiastic insight into his musical universe, a universe inhabited by tear-jerkin' dons and divas, bass lines made of mahogany and sharp-dressed bands.

Part 1 of this quiz roughly follows a feature of Craig's show, The Funk Family Tree: each questions refers back to the previous one in some way, as is the way with music. The connections can help – knowing question 3 can give you an insight into 2 and/or 4 – but you need to get into the chain. Part 2 features artists represented on the 3CD set curated by Craig, from classic cuts to underground gems.

Answers: page 476

1   Which former jazz producer moved over into pop and film, composing scores for films like *In Cold Blood*, *In the Heat of the Night* and *The Italian Job*? With which major pop artist did he produce three massive-selling albums from 1979 to 1987?

2   Which soulful jazz guitarist's 1980 album *Give Me the Night*, produced by (1), reached number three in the US chart? What was his 1976 hit album that won a hatful of Grammies?

3   *Share My World* (1997), featuring (2) on guitar, was the third album by which American R&B singer? She had a UK Top 10 hit with the song 'As' (1999); it was a lead release off a *Best of ...* album by which artist, who duetted on the track?

4   'As' was written by Stevie Wonder. On which classic 1976 album did it appear? 'Sir Duke', the biggest single off that album, was a tribute to which jazz legend?

5   Stevie's 1981 hit, 'Happy Birthday', was also an homage. Whose birthday was he celebrating? What was the name of the song that referenced the same person that was a hit for Dion in the US and for Marvin Gaye in the UK?

6   What was Marvin Gaye's first single after he left Motown, which was a Top 10 hit on both sides of the Atlantic in 1982? Which other Motown legend was in the middle of a six-week run at number one in the UK with 'Hello' when Gaye was shot dead by his father in 1984?

7   From which multi platinum-selling album was 'Hello' taken? And with which Motown band did Lionel Richie sing before going solo?

8   Which 1985 hit single by (7b) post-(6b) was a tribute to both Marvin Gaye and Jackie Wilson, who died the previous year? And who wrote and recorded the 1972 tribute 'Jackie Wilson Said (I'm in Heaven When You Smile)'?

9   Which British band took the song in (8b) to number five in the UK singles chart in 1982? And which tribute to another soul legend had given them a number one two years earlier?

10 What term is often ascribed to work by white artists that has the feel and sound of black music? Which proponents of this genre had a US number one single with 'Holding Back the Years' in 1985?

11 A cover of which Harold Melvin and the Blue Notes song gave (10b) a second US number one? Who was the Blue Notes' lead singer from 1972-75 before pursuing a solo career?

12 (11b)'s signature tune, 'Love TKO', was co-written by Cecil Womack, who together with his wife, Linda, made up Womack & Womack. Who was Linda's famous soul singer father? Which of his songs had its biggest success when it featured in a Levi 501's ad in 1986, reaching number two in the UK chart?

13 (12b) also featured in the cult 1978 John Landis film, *Animal House*. Which other famous soul stomp, written by Richard Berry, was sung by John Belushi and others at a frat-house toga party? Who recorded it on his 1964 debut album *Pain In My Heart*?

14 (13b)'s biggest UK hit was a song written with Steve Cropper and released just after the singer's tragic demise in a plane crash: what was the song? What was the name of the band, often used as the Stax house band, which regularly backed him and in which Cropper played guitar?

15 The band in (14b) backed Bill Withers on his first album, *Just As I Am*. What was the single off the album that gave him his first Top 10 hit in the US? Who took the song to number one in the UK with a version off his own debut solo album, *Got to Be There*?

BONUS TRACKS

16 'Spotlight on Lou Rawls ...' runs the song 'Sweet Soul Music'. Otis Redding and James Brown also come under the spotlight (Otis co-wrote the song), along with which other two acts?

17 *The Headphone Masterpiece* was the 2002 debut album from which soul/rock/blues singer? With which prolific hip hop duo did he have some minor success with his song, 'Seed'?

18 In the early seventies, who needed a little more time? Who was their fabulously named singer?

19 Which soul singer's only big hit was her 1970 song 'Band of Gold'? What was the subject matter of her single the following year, 'Bring the Boys Back'?

20 Harry Wayne Casey was the leader of a pop/funk/soul band. By which two initials was he known? What was their only UK number one?

21 Brass players Cynthia Robinson and Jerry Martini, drummer Gregg Errico and bassist Larry Graham were all honorary members of which multi-racial soul family? Which 1968 hit single that demonstrated their near-psychedelic sound?

22 The singles 'That Lady' and 'Summer Breeze' were taken from *3+3*, a brilliant 1973 album by which soul band? What was the significance of the LP title?

23 The 1967 album *I Never Loved a Man the Way I Love You* was the eleventh album and commercial breakthrough for which prolific soul singer? What was her first US number one single?

24 'Ladies' Night' (1979) was the breakthrough single for which soul/disco act? Which girl band joined them on a 2003 re-issue?

25 Which soul singer, born Paul Williams, had a hit in 1972 with a song about an extra-marital affair, 'Me and Mrs Jones'? Which sportswear company did he sue in 2000 after they used the song in an ad without permission?

26 Mabon 'Teenie' Hodges and his brothers, Leroy and Charles, were an integral part of the backing band for which American soul singer? Which single gave him his only US number one?

27 *Coming Home* was the 2015 debut album of which US soul/gospel prodigy? What product was the title track used to advertise that year?

28 Who had a hit in 1984 with the soul/funk classic 'Somebody Else's Guy'? Better known as a session singer, on whose 1991 hit, 'Don't Talk Just Kiss', did she sing?

29 What was the biggest selling single in both the US and the UK for the funk band Heatwave? Who directed a 1997 movie of the same name?

30 Which 1970 single took Edwin Starr to the top of the US chart for three weeks? What is it good for?

QUIZ 20

PROG ROCK

Prog has made a comeback in recent years, so once again the music scene sees bands of great musical proficiency offering lengthy instrumental compositions with neo-classical learnings and labyrinthine narratives. Time to indulge yourself.

The first section here is straight questions. The second section deals with the long epic pieces of which prog rock bands were so fond (and still are: there are a couple of contemporary bands in there with the old geezers). In this section, you have to match the track to the artist, and also take a punt on the length of that particular epic. You don't have to be spot on: we have given you parameters to fall between.

Answers: page 477

1   What was Genesis's 1974 double-album rock opera called? What is the name of the character whose journey through life it charts?

2   *Warrior on the Edge of Time* (1975) was the highest charting album by which prog band, who are still recording and playing today? On whose science fantasy epic novels was the work based?

3   Ray Manzarek and Bobby Krieger reunited in the 21st century to play the songs of which sixties band, of which they were both members? Who replaced the band's charismatic, long dead singer?

4   Take an element from The Nice, one from King Crimson, and one from Atomic Rooster – what have you got? (Exact details for both points).

5   John Lees and Les Holroyd both still record and tour as different incarnations of which seventies prog rock band? What was the band's signature tune, off 1971 album *Once Again*?

6   Which member of Pink Floyd left in 1979 but rejoined for the 1987 album *A Momentary Lapse of Reason*? Which other key member, the band's lyricist, left in 1985 but played with the band at Live 8 in 2008?

7   Which two musicians have been the mainstay of the jazz-tinged progressive band Steely Dan, both in the seventies and since they reformed n 1993?

8   Which 1973 Yes album consisted of four sides of vinyl with one track each, the first of which was entitled 'The Revealing Science of God (Dance of the Dawn)'? Who was their singer, with a distinctive falsetto?

9   Who wrote and produced the rock opera *The War of the Worlds*? And which dramatic luminary narrated the album version?

10 *Demons and Wizards* (1972) was the breakthrough album for which London heavy prog band? From which Charles Dickens novel did they get their name?

11 Genesis released ... *And Then There Were Three* ... in 1978: which two members of the original band had left by then?

12 Greek prog rock band Aphrodite's Child's third album 666 was an expansive 1972 Biblical epic. Who was the band's musical guiding light and who provided the falsetto vocals, which he put to good use in a subsequent solo career?

13 The 1981 album *My Life in the Bush of Ghosts* was a collaboration between David Byrne and which other avant-garde music figure? What was this artist's previous contribution to David Byrne's career?

14 Which singer made a good decision in not performing under his birth name, Derek Dick? With which band did he enjoy commercial success in the eighties?

15 Which band were named after an English agriculturalist? What was their 1972 album that consisted of one 40-minute track?

BONUS TRACKS

Match the epic pieces of self-indulgence to the bands. And guess how long the track was.

1. 'Tarkus', 1971; 2. 'Supper's Ready', 1972; 3. 'Fugazi', 1984; 4. 'The End', 1967; 5. 'In-a-Gadda-da-Vida', 1968; 6. 'Time Was', 1972; 7. 'The Great Nothing', 2000; 8. 'The Gates of Delirium', 1974; 9. 'Moonchild', 1969; 10. 'Shine On You Crazy Diamond', 1975; 11. 'The Fountain of Lamneth', 1975; 12. 'Nine Feet Underground', 1971; 13. 'Hellbound Train', 1972; 14. 'The Truth Will Set You Free', 2002; 15. 'Heavy Horses', 1978

The bands, in alphabetical order: Caravan; The Doors; Emerson, Lake & Palmer; The Flower Kings; Genesis; Iron Butterfly; Jethro Tull; King Crimson; Marillion; Pink Floyd; Rush; Savoy Brown; Spock's Beard; Wishbone Ash; Yes.

QUIZ 21

WORLD MUSIC

We have ample opportunity to broaden our listening and get beyond the output of the US and Britain but many people seldom do. This is changing slowly, especially as Western artists such as Damon Albarn promote these musicians hard and absorb their sounds and techniques into their own compositions.

Here are two sections on world music. The first section is straight questions; the second simply asks you to match 15 artists to their geographical roots.

Answers: page 477

1 Which British magazine, founded in 1999, champions world music and sponsors awards for artists in that field? From which culture is the magazine's name taken?

2 Which musician co-founded the WOMAD festival in 1982? What was the name of the world music label he established in 1989?

3 *Dimanche à Bamako* was a 2005 breakthrough success for which Malian duo? What disadvantage have the couple overcome?

4 Which Congolese band consists of four paraplegic instrumentalists and a percussion section of street children? Which side project of the band released their debut album, *From Kinshasa*, in 2015?

5 Argentinian musician Astor Piazzolla was perhaps the most famous performer of which style of traditional dance music? Which Paris-based multi-national band blended this music with dance beats and samples on their 2006 album *Lunático*?

6 'Hips Don't Lie' was a worldwide number one single for Shakira with contributions from Wyclef Jean. In which two countries were these two stars born?

7 Ibrahim Ag Alhabib is the founder and main composer of which African guitar band? Which African culture do they represent?

9 What was the Ry Cooder-produced 1997 album that gave a number of talented Cuban musicians a wider audience? Who was the German director of the 1999 documentary of the same name?

10 Which flamenco guitar band found popularity in the UK with their 1989 album, *Mosaique*? Where are the band from?

11 Which multi-lingual artist released his debut album *Clandestino* in 1988? For years he was a busker on the streets of which city?

12 Who, in 2005, organised a benefit concert against world poverty in Cornwall, featuring exclusively African artists, in response to criticism of the mainly

white line-ups at the global concerts organised by Bob Geldof's organisation? Which Senegalese star headed and hosted the event?

13 Which classic 1970 Santana album contains the tracks 'Oye Como Va', 'Se a Cabo' and 'Samba Pa Ti?' What was the brilliant Nicaraguan musician Jose Areas' contribution to the album?

14 *Music in Exile* was the 2015 debut of which African guitar band? They got their break when a group of European musicians went on a talent-spotting mission to which country?

15 What was the name of the South African vocal group who rose to fame through their work on Paul Simon's 1986 album, *Graceland*? Who produced their successful 1987 follow up, *Shaka Zulu*?

BONUS TRACKS

Match the artist to his/her geographical roots:

16 Pioneering Nigerian musician and composer;

17 New York gypsy-punk blues act;

18 Aboriginal rockers and protesters;

19 Brazilian goth metal band;

20 Acclaimed diva of Portuguese fado singing;

21 Percussion-heavy Zimbabwean band beloved of the late John Peel;

22 Albino pop star from Mali;

23 Mexican Flamenco guitarists;

24 Jamaican guitarist and pioneer of the ska guitar sound;

25 Senegalese singer and percussionist;

26 Iran's best-known master of traditional Persian music;

27 Trinidadian pop-reggae star;

28 Indian fusion musician and film composer;

29 Alternative rock duo from Leamington Spa;

30 Bermudan singer-songwriter.

Choose from these artists: Bhundu Boys; Gogol Bordello; Raghu Dixit; Salif Keita, Fela Kuti; Cheikh Lo; Mariza; Nizlopi; Heather Nova; Billy Ocean; Ernest Ranglin; Rodrigo y Gabriela; Sepultura; Shajarian; Yothu Yindi.

QUIZ 22

MICHAEL JACKSON

The Prince of Pop, as Michael Jackson was hailed, was one of the bestselling artists of the eighties and nineties. While he was surrounded by rumour in the later years of his life, the fact remains that he was one of the finest purveyors of a pop tune that the music industry has ever seen.

Here are 30 questions about Michael and the rest of the Jackson clan, both as solo artists and as the iconic family group.

Answers: page 478

1   Michael Jackson had 13 US number one hits while he was still alive. How many did he have in that time in the UK: was it seven, twelve or fifteen? How old was he when he died in 2009?

2   Who was the oldest brother in the original Jackson 5 line-up? Who was replaced by Randy in 1975?

3   Which songwriter, previously in disco band, Heatwave, wrote the title track and two other songs on *Thriller*? He was a keyboard player from Cleethorpes: in which English county is it?

4   In the mid-seventies, Michael Jackson released two solo albums that bombed: what were they called?

5   Who was the mystery girl who sang on the track 'In the Closet' off the *Dangerous* album? She had a massive French hit with 'Ouragan' (1986): what was the UK version of the song, a minor hit?

6   What was the full title of the 1995 Michael Jackson record usually referred to as *HIStory*? Which Lennon/McCartney song was covered on the album?

7   The single 'Son of a Gun', from Janet Jackson's album *All for You*, referenced which 1972 song in brackets in the title, and was largely a rehash of that song? Who performed a spoken-word segment?

8   Which Paul McCartney song did Michael Jackson cover on *Off the Wall*? And which track on *Thriller* featured a Macca vocal?

9   Who directed the 18-minute video for the title track off *Bad*? Which classic 1961 musical film does it heavily reference?

10 Which rapper co-wrote and appears on the track 'This Time Around' on *HIStory*? Which single off the album saw Jackson accused of anti-Semitic lyrics?

11 Which label launched the career of the Jackson 5? Which of the label's stars 'presented' their debut album?

12 Which Rod Stewart song did Janet Jackson cover on *Velvet Rope* (1997)? And which Joni Mitchell song was sampled on 'Got 'Til It's Gone' from the same album?

13 How old was Michael Jackson when he released *Thriller*? What was the time lag before his next album, *Bad*?

14 Who is the unfortunate victim of an attack in 'Smooth Criminal' from *Bad*? Which other girl is mentioned by name in the title of the album's preceding track?

15 What was the title of the 1997 Michael Jackson album that was a remix of songs from *HIStory* with a handful of new songs? Which disco dude played the funky guitar on the title track?

BONUS TRACKS

16 Which Michael Jackson song reached number one in the UK when it was re-released off a compilation album after the success of *Off the Wall*? On which earlier (1975) album did it appear?

17 What are Janet Jackson's middle names, as cited in the title of her 2004 album? Who was Janet's first husband, a soul singer whom she married while still a teenager and divorced a year later?

18 What was the Jackson 5's debut single for Motown? What was the name of the four-man songwriting team created by Motown purely to write hits for the family?

19 Which song from *Bad* was the theme tune to Michael Jackson's 1988 portmanteau film, *Moonwwalker*? Which band went higher than Jackson in the UK charts with a cover of the song in 2001?

20 In which year did Michael Jackson die, and what was the name of the personal doctor found responsible in court for his death?

21 Which movie director shot the *Thriller* video? Which horror-movie star provided the speaking voice and maniacal laughter?

22 Which of the Jackson brothers had a twin, Brandon, who died shortly after being born? Which Jackson sibling was born after Jermaine but before Marlon?

23 Which 1977 single gave the Jacksons en masse their only UK number one? Which record company released it, having signed the band when they left Motown?

24 Which Michaael Jackson album became the first album by any artist to spawn five US number one singles? Which female artist emulated this with her 2010 album, *Teenage Dream*?

25 Whose daughter did Michael Jackson marry in 1994 and divorce in 1996? Who became his second wife later that year?

26 Who duetted with Michael Jackson on 'Scream', the first track on the new-material section of *HIStory*? And who wrote the UK number one single, 'You are Not Alone', off the album?

27 Which 1980 song, co-written by Stevie Wonder, was the first UK Top 10 single for Jermaine Jackson? His only other UK Top 10 hit, 'Do What You Do', featured which model in the promotional video before she married a high-profile English rock star?

28 What was the title of Michael Jackson's first solo album, and also the lead single off the album? Which other hit single from the same album was a cover of a 1958 Bobby Day hit?

29 What was the only single from *Dangerous* (1991) to reach number one in the UK? Which child actor featured in the video?

30 What was the last studio album released by Michael Jackson during his lifetime? And what was the posthumous 2014 album of 'new material that went to number one in the UK?

QUIZ 23

THE NUMBERS GAME #1

Here is another simple quiz. Question one requires one answer, question two requires two, right up to question ten, which requires ten. (I've thrown in a question 5a to bring the total number of answers to 60, like the other chapters). Only give the required number of answers per question. Extra ones will be ignored.

Answers: page 479

1 What was the only Elvis UK number one with the word 'love' in its title?

2 What were the Specials' two UK number ones?

3 Three compilations, from Queen, Abba and Bob Marley, have spent the most weeks on the UK chart. Which three original studio albums come next in the list, with 629, 519 and 474 weeks respectively?

4 Name the four films to feature Prince and his music.

5 Name the five studio albums released by Queens of the Stone Age since their 1998 eponymous debut.

5a 'Maggie May' was Rod Stewart's first UK number one: what are the other five?

6 Which six artists have enjoyed more than ten UK number one singles? (Not including the Shadows, as more than half of their entries were as Cliff's backing band).

7 The Top 10 chart of best-selling albums by girl groups contains seven different groups. Who are they?

8 What were the Human League's eight Top 10 singles?

9 The Beatles wrote nine songs with girls' names in the title: how many can you name? (cover versions are not allowed, and nor are 'Lady Madonna', as Madonna is a generic reference in the song, or 'Penny Lane', as this is a street name).

10 Can you name New Order's ten albums?

QUIZ 24

FESTIVALS

As live music becomes an ever-more important source of income for artists faced with declining record sales, so festivals have become an ever-more important part of the music calendar. Yes, they've been hijacked by commerce to an extent, but they still offer plenty of value if you can survive for three days without a shower. (Don't mention the mud.) This quiz starts with 15 straightforward questions, then continues with a quickfire test of your knowledge of festivals both national and international.

Answers: page 480

1   Where did Led Zeppelin play two massive outdoor shows in 1979, shows that would prove to be their last UK appearances for more than 20 years? When the band reunited to play at London's O2 in 2007, who replaced the now-deceased John Bonham on drums?

2   Which multi-arts festival started in 2009 at Henham Park in Suffolk? Which Northern Irish band were the first act to headline the main Obelisk Stage?

3   What's the name of the festival held every August Bank Holiday weekend that takes its name from a famous Liverpool club? The festival takes place in Daresbury – in which English county?

4   Which annual festival originated in Strathclyde but moved to Balado Airfield in Kinross between 1997 and 2014? Which Perthshire venue hosted the event in 2015 and 2016?

5   Which festival takes place in Great Tew in Oxfordshire, having vacated the site from which it originally took its name? Confusingly, another festival now takes place on the original site: what's it called?

6   In which US state is Woodstock, site of arguably the most famous festival of them all in 1969? And who directed the 2009 film *Taking Woodstock*, about the birth and organisation of the event?

7   Which festival provided Matthews Southern Comfort with a number one hit without them even being there? Band leader Iain Matthews was previously the singer with which English folk rock band?

8   Which Danish festival was started by two high school students in 1971? What's the bizarre 'sporting' event that takes place on the Saturday of the festival?

9   Of the following bands, which two did not play at Woodstock in 1969: Santana, the Band, Derek & the Dominos, Arthur Lee & Love, the Grateful Dead, Creedence Clearwater Revival, Sly & the Family Stone?

10 At which 1969 festival in the US did the Hell's Angels, who were providing unofficial security, get involved in a fracas that led to the death of Meredith Hunter? Which band were on stage when the fighting broke out?

11 Drawing nearly 90,000 visitors each year, what is the biggest music festival in Belgium? What's the name of the one-day event held a week later that showcases older, longer-established acts?

12 Who, in 2008, became the first hip hop artist to headline Glastonbury? Which rapper filled the same Saturday-night slot in 2015?

13 What's the name of the annual food and music festival that Alex James hosts on his Oxfordshire farm? Which famous chef is his collaborator on the project?

14 Which festival takes place at the Petrovaradin Fortress in Novi Sad, Serbia every year? And what's the name of the coastal spin-off that started in 2014?

15 What has been the official capacity of the Glastonbury Festival from 2007 to 2016? What is the name of the closest village to the site?

16 Since 2000, who are the only two solo female acts to have headlined Glastonbury's Pyramid Stage?

17 Where has the Governors Ball taken place on the first week of June since 2011? What happened on the Sunday in 2016 when Kanye West was due to headline?

18 T Rex played to 1,500 people in Somerset in 1970: what did they start in doing so? Who stepped in at the same venue the following year when Pink Floyd cancelled their show?

19 Which festival takes place on the weekend after the August Bank Holiday in a Dorset pleasure garden? Which record label curated a day at the festival in 2012?

20 Conceived by Perry Farrell of Jane's Addiction as a one-off event, which festival has taken place annually in Chicago's Grant Park since 2005? Which South American city was the first outside the US to use the same brand for its music festival (there are now four in South America and one in Berlin)?

BONUS TRACK 1

Match the British festival to the venue.

21 Lulworth Castle, Dorset. 22 Steventon, Oxfordshire. 23 Charlton Park, Wiltshire. 24 Victoria Park, London. 25 Donington Park, Leicestershire. 26 Escot Park, Devon. 27 Robin Hill, Isle of Wight. 28 Southbank Centre, London. 29 Brecon Beacons, Wales. 30 Brighton.

Festivals: Beautiful Days, Bestival, Camp Bestival, Download, the Great Escape, Green Man, Lovebox, Meltdown, Truck, WOMAD.

BONUS TRACK 2

Now, do the same thing in reverse for these international festivals.

31 Primavera Sound. 32 Splendour in the Grass. 33 Secret Solstice. 34 Coachella. 35 Bonnaroo. 36 Magnetic Fields. 37 Edge of the Lake. 38 South by Southwest. 39 Bahidorá. 40 Burning Man.

Venues: Austin, Barcelona, Byron Bay, California, Iceland, Manchester (Tennessee), Mexico, the Nevada desert, Rajasthan, Switzerland.

QUIZ 25

EARWORMS

Earworm (n:) A catchy song or tune that runs continually through the mind

The 6 Music morning-show presenter, Shaun Keaveny, likes listeners to text or tweet with their earworms. The result is a barrage of requests for songs you end up humming to yourself in an annoying manner for the rest of the day. Happily, Shaun doesn't play all of them.

The songs that get under your skin – and stick in your brain – tend to be cheesy pop hits rather than cool album tracks. How often have you found yourself humming along to a popular hit you heard in a shop that day? 'NO' you declare, this must not be – but it's too late, you are stuck with Justin Bieber or Taylor Swift rattling around in your head. This author accepts no responsibility for any earworms you pick up attempting this chapter...

Answers: page 481

1   A recent online poll determined that which Spice Girls song was the most prevalent earworm? What year was it released?

2   What was the song from *Rocky III* that was a huge hit in the US for American rock band Survivor? Which follow-up, from the *Rocky IV* soundtrack three years later, also went Top 10?

3   From which Abba song was the hook from Madonna's' Hung Up' sampled? Which other Abba song, with its irritating 'a-hah' chorus, came out just before it as a double-A side with 'Angel Eyes'?

4   Monica, Erica, Rita, Tina, Sandra, Mary: what are we talking about and who finished the sequence?

5   What was the mini-album released by Lady Gaga 15 months after her debut effort, *The Fame*? What was the lead single?

6   'Dum dum dum dooby doo wah' went the hummable intro to Roy Orbison's first UK number one in 1960: what was the song? Which classic track off Bruce Springsteen's *Born To Run* name-checks it?

7   Which track, with an unmistakeable rock riff, kicked off the second side of Michael Jackson's *Thriller*? Which eighties rocker played the guitar solo in the middle of the song?

8   'Don't You Want Me' was a massive Christmas number one in the UK for the Human League in 1981. Who provided the female vocals in duet with Phil Oakey? And where did her character work at the song's outset?

9   'What's that coming over the hill...?' What was it, in 2006? And who were asking?

10 'YMCA' by the Village People was a gay sing-a-long pop classic. In the video were a cop, a Native American, a GI, a leather-clad biker and which other two costumed dudes?

11 The Proclaimers' 'I'm Gonna Be (500 Miles)' came from their successful 1988 album, the title of which reflected their roots. What was the album and which football club play the title track before their home games?

12 Which Culture Club song was 1983's best-selling single in the UK? Which three colours are mentioned in the chorus?

13 What, in June 2014, was the debut single by Meghan Trainor that rocketed her to international stardom? What was the title of her debut album (there's a clue in the question)?

14 Which animated character hit number one with a mobile ringtone of a famous tune in 2005? What was the tune, which had also reached number one 20 years earlier when it was the theme to the movie *Beverley Hills Cop*?

15 Which song was released as a single off Deep Purple's *Machine Head* album and became one of the most recognisable rock riffs ever? Which rock festival is cited in its first line?

BONUS TRACKS

16 Which 2001 UK number one hit saw a revived Kylie cause a national epidemic of earworms with its chanted intro? The song was written by Cathy Dennis and Rob Davis; the latter formerly played guitar in which seventies pop band?

17 'Who Let the Dogs Out?' – well, who did, in 2000? And which Nickelodeon movie gave the song a big leg-up?

18 Which profoundly dumb but hummable single by Carly Rae Jepsen was the best selling single across the globe in 2011? In which country's version of *Pop Idol* did Jepsen first gain exposure?

19 Which hip hop band had a huge 2005 hit with a song that was essentially a 'celebration' of boobs and bums? What was the follow-up, with a guitar run from Dick Dale and the Deltones' 'Misirlou'?

20 'Oh Mickey, you're so fine...' Who sang this in 1981? What was the original title of the song when it was recorded by British bubblegum pop band Racey in 1979?

21 'Rivers of Babylon' was originally recorded by the Melodians in 1970: who turned it into a UK number one in 1978? What was the B-side, which gained almost equal airplay and was equally invasive on the ears?

22 Which former *American Idol* winner released the eardrum-plaguing single 'Since U Been Gone' in 2004? According to her in 2012 (and to Friedrich Nietzsche), what makes you stronger?

23 Which 1986 earworm was the only UK Top 10 hit for Swedish band Europe? What was the stage name, evocative of a fifties rock and roller, of their singer, Rolf Larsson?

24 You might hope that 'Barbie Girl' in 1997 was Danish band Aqua's only hit, but no – their next two singles also hit number one. What were they?

25 'I get knocked down, but I get up again!' we all chanted in 1997. Who were the band, and what was the song's title?

26 Which two punk-era singles did One Direction merge into a pop earworm that topped the UK charts in 2013?

27 Who won Eurovision for the United Kingdom in 1981 with 'Making Your Minds Up?' What risque stage routine did they perform while singing it?

28 With its classic rumbling intro, which White Stripes song gave the band their first UK Top 10 hit single in 2003? On what was that now-familiar intro played?

29 Which 1978 UK and US number one, a female emancipation anthem written by Freddie Perren and Dino Fekaris, is believed to be the most sung song in karaoke bars across the western world? Who had the original hit with the song?

30 Which song, originally released in 2012 by Jamaican singer OMI, was a massive global hit in 2015 after a remix by Felix Jaehn late the previous year? Who promoted the song in the UK and was even seen on a viral promo video singing the tune himself?

QUIZ 26

CLASSIC ALBUMS #2:
THE SEVENTIES

This is another really straightforward section (as per Quiz 4). Here are three tracks from an album and the year of release. You give the artist and album title.

Option: if you are reading the quizzes out loud, try giving the quizzers two tracks – if they can identify the album from these, they get both points. If they need the third track, which is usually the charm (the big single or stand-out track), then they just get one.

Answers: page 482

1   'Graveyard'; 'Memories'; 'Poptones' (1979)

2   'Chemistry Class'; 'Green Shirt'; 'Oliver's Army' (1978)

3   'Little Green'; 'The Last Time I Saw Richard'; 'This Flight Tonight' (1971)

4   'Bed and Breakfast Man'; 'My Girl'; 'Night Boat to Cairo' (1979)

5   'Another Star'; 'Knocks Me Off My Feet'; 'Isn't She Lovely' (1976)

6   'Any Major Dude Will Tell You'; 'Monkey in Your Soul'; 'Rikki Don't Lose that Number' (1974)

7   'Even the Losers'; 'Don't Do Me Like That'; 'Refugee' (1979)

8   'Disorder'; 'Shadowplay'; 'She's Lost Control' (1979)

9   'Eddie You Should Know Better'; 'Pusherman'; 'Freddie's Dead' (1972)

10 'Kinky Reggae'; 'Concrete Jungle'; 'Stir It Up' (1973)

11 'Have a Good Time'; 'My Little Town'; '50 Ways to Leave Your Lover' (1975)

12 'Savage Circle'; 'Something That I Said'; 'Babylon's Burning' (1979)

13 'Scissor Man'; 'Ten Feet Tall'; 'Making Plans for Nigel' (1979)

14 'Space Monkey'; 'Privilege (Set Me Free)'; 'Because the Night' (1978)

15 'Dagenham Dave'; 'Burning Up Time'; 'Something Better Change' (1977)

BONUS TRACKS

16 'The Needle and the Damage Done'; 'Old Man'; 'Heart of Gold' (1972)

17 'Electric Guitar'; 'I Zimbra'; 'Life During Wartime' (1979)

18 'Take the Long Way Home'; 'Goodbye Stranger'; 'The Logical Song' (1979)

19 'Midnight Moses'; 'Hammer Song'; 'Isobel Goudie' (1972)

20 'Mamunia'; 'Mrs Vanderbilt'; 'Jet' (1973)

21 'One Way or Another'; 'Sunday Girl'; 'Heart of Glass' (1978)

22 'The Wanton Song'; 'Ten Years Gone'; 'Kashmir' (1975)

23 'Fire in Cairo'; 'Grinding Halt'; '10:15 Saturday Night' (1979)

24 'I'd Rather Be the Devil'; 'Dreams By the Sea'; 'May You Never' (1973)

25 'She's So Modern'; 'Like Clockwork'; 'Rat Trap' (1978)

26 'TVC-15'; 'Word on a Wing'; 'Golden Years' (1976)

27 'Adam Raised a Cain'; 'Badlands'; 'Prove It All Night' (1978)

28 'Grey Lagoons'; 'In Every Dream Home a Heartache'; 'Do the Strand' (1973)

29 'Men of Good Fortune'; "Caroline Says I'; 'Caroline Says II' (1973)

30 'Sweet Talkin' Woman'; 'Wild West Hero'; 'Turn to Stone' (1977)

QUIZ 27

PAUL WELLER

From his beginnings as the angry young man riding the crest of the punk wave to his current status as one of the grand old stagers of the British rock scene, Paul Weller has packed a punch for nigh on 40 years. He's still trying new things, too: witness the experimental sounds on *Saturns Pattern*, his 12th solo album from 2015. The first section of this quiz is dedicated to Weller in all his incarnations, while part two covers a number of modern acts who arguably share something of his fiercely adventurous spirit.

Answers: page 483

1   What's the title of Paul Weller's 2004 covers album? Whose song 'The Bottle', a hard-hitting exploration of alcoholism, did he choose to include on it? (2)

2   The Jam covered a Wilson Pickett song on their second album and a Tamla Motown classic on their fourth: which two songs? (2)

3   What do the Jam songs 'Smithers-Jones', 'London Traffic', 'Circus' and 'Don't Tell Them You're Sane' have in common? (1)

4   On *Setting Sons*, what was Weller doing up on the hill? With whom did he have an extremist scrape? And who got fired? (3)

5   'They smelt of pubs and...' What else? And on which Jam song? (2)

6   Ripped-up concrete, an electric train, damp on the walls and smelling stale perfume are all what? (1)

7   Which four Jam singles reached number one in the UK? (Two were double-A sides; either side is acceptable.) (4)

8   What was the only Jam single written by Bruce Foxton? And in which single, written by Weller and Foxton, did they watch the flames grow higher? (2)

9   Which title is shared by a collection of Jam covers by artists including Garbage, Noel Gallagher and the Beastie Boys, and a box set of Jam live performances released in 2015? Where does the title come from? (2)

10 Which Weller album is the best-selling record of his solo career? Where does the title come from? And what's the name of the ballad from the record, now a live favourite, that reached the British Top 10? (3)

11 What was the only Style Council album to top the UK charts? Which comedian and TV presenter provided the vocals for 'The Stand Up Comic's Instructions'? (2)

12 Which favourite book of Weller's, which he picked when he was on *Desert Island Discs*, was also the title of a late Jam single? (1)

For the next five questions, simply name the Weller solo album from which the following tracks are taken.

13 'Mermaids', 'Friday Street' and 'Brushed'. (1)

14 'Song for Alice', 'Sea Spray' and 'Echoes Round the Sun'. (1)

15 'With Time and Temperance', 'Back in the Fire' and 'Sweet Pea, My Sweet Pea'. (1)

16 'Has My Fire Really Gone Out?', 'Moon on Your Pyjamas' and 'Sunflower'. (1)

17 'Sleep of the Serene', 'Paperchase' and 'That Dangerous Age'. (1)

BONUS TRACKS

18 'Three Dollar Hat', a song on the Dead Weather's third album *Dodge and Burn*, is a duet between which two band members?

19 *Cockahoop* (2003) is the solo debut by which singer and future BBC 6 Music DJ? What's the title of her 2012 collection of Christmas songs, taken from a duet she made with Tom Jones on his *Reload* album?

20 2D, Russel Hobbs and Murdoc Niccals: who or what are they? And who or what is missing?

21 Which Northern Irish singer and songwriter wrote the theme tunes for *Father Ted* and *The IT Crowd*? What's the name of the band that occupies the majority of his time?

22 Which band's commercial peak was the 1997 album *Tellin' Stories*? What was the tragedy that befell the band halfway through recording it?

23 Which film-maker's dialogue was sampled by Fun Lovin' Criminals on 'Scooby Snacks'? Where were they swashbucklin' on their third album, *Loco*?

24 Who went to the top of the UK albums chart in 2005 with their second album, *Tourist*? What was the anthemic single that helped bring about their success?

25 Who was Aimee Mann with in 1995, according to the title of her second album? For which 1999 Paul Thomas Anderson movie did she provide the bulk of the soundtrack?

26 Steve Cradock is the guitarist in which Birmingham Britpop band? With which other major artist has he been a regular collaborator and touring musician for the last 20-odd years?

27 *Speech Therapy* (2009) and *Dead* (2014) were both Mercury Music Prize-winning albums released on the Big Dada label – but by which artists?

28 Which established Scottish band had a UK number one album with *White on Blonde* in 1997? Who is their singer and lyricist, who released a couple of solo albums before resuming her career with the band?

29 What did the weak become, according to the Streets in 2002? And what didn't come for free for the group two years later?

30 Which 1990 number one by the Beautiful South featured a duet between Dave Hemingway and Briana Corrigan? In the group, Hemingway also shared vocal duties with which male singer?

31 Before his solo career as Fatboy Slim, Norman Cook had number one hits with 'Caravan of Love' (an Isley Brothers cover) and 'Dub Be Good to Me' – with which acts?

32 *Alone with Everybody* (2000) was the first solo album from which singer and songwriter? Which band did he front before going solo?

QUIZ 28

PEOPLE'S PLAYLIST: DRINK & DRUGS

Here are 40 questions that broach the topics of drink and drugs: some with humour, some with regret, some with self-regard and braggadocio. Kids – don't try this at home. The same format as before: 40 questions, single answers, and it's more fun if you give yourself a time limit. Get your mum and dad to help – it may amuse you to find out how much they know about these particular topics...

Answers: page 484

1   What did John Lee Hooker have along with his 'One Bourbon'?

2   Which hallucinogenic paradise, accessed via the 'bridge of sighs... under dreaming spires', was 'all too beautiful'?

3   Who released albums called *Drunk Enough to Dance* and *A Hangover You Don't Deserve* in 2002 and 2004?

4   Who chronicled his battle against drugs in 'A Junkie's Lament', which appears on his 1976 album *In the Pocket*?

5   Who admitted to a penchant for 'Cigarettes and Alcohol'?

6   Which self-confessed heavy cannabis user sang about a 'Bake Sale' on his 2016 eponymous album?

7   'However Much I Booze' is a confessional track on which Who album from 1975?

8   Who wrote 'Cocaine', the song Eric Clapton popularised on his *Slowhand* album?

9   Which Irish singer made famous the bleak song 'Whiskey Didn't Kill the Pain'?

10 'Nicotine, Valium, Vicodin, marijuana, ecstasy and alcohol.... C-c-c-c-cocaine!' goes the refrain on 'Feel Good Hit of the Summer' by which band?

11 What did Dr Feelgood take with their alcohol?

12 'One pill makes you larger, and one pill makes you small...' What do the ones that mother gives you do?

13 Apart from whisky and lager, which other two drinks are drunk in the verse to Chumbawumba's 'Tubthumping'?

14 Which number one hit by the Shamen received substantial airplay in 1992 despite clearly being an endorsement of recreational drugs?

15 Which cocktail was the subject of a Beastie Boys single in 1997?

16 The Byrds' 1966 album *Fifth Dimension* includes which classic drug-trip track (denied at the time), one of the first great psychedelic rock songs?

17 What did Snoop Doggy Dogg like with his juice?

18 Hip hop bands are often happy to make overt drug references. In 2003, who took some 'Hits from the Bong'?

19 A minor US hit for both Ray Stevens and Johnny Cash, 'Sunday Mornin' Comin' Down' is a day-after reflection that was written and recorded by which singer-songwriter?

20 Who released a track called 'Ten Crack Commandments' shortly after his death in 1997?

21 In 1998, Stereophonics sang about 'The Bartender and...' Who else?

22 What was the sugar on the pill that eighties Leicester band Gaye Bykers added to their name?

23 Who topped the indie chart in 1980 singing about 'Beer Drinkers and Hell Raisers', a cover of a song by ZZ Top?

24 What was Roxy Music's fix in 1975, 'face to face' and 'toe to toe'?

25 Mark Lanegan's second solo album advocated whiskey for which supernatural being?

26 Who 'Traded in My Cigarettes' on his 2010 debut album?

27 Which band enjoyed a 'Marguerita Time' in the UK Top 10 in 1983?

28 Who made 'Rehab' profitable in 2006?

29 Nina Simone, Elkie Brooks and Jeff Buckley all expressed a preference for which drink?

30 Which West Coast band sang about 'Amphetamine Annie' in 1968?

31 Who reached number two in 1976 with a 'A Glass of Champagne'?

32 Who had an album called *One Way Ticket to Hell and Back* in 2005?

33 What were Cliff's two key elements for a fine Christmas in 1988?

34 Who were 'Sorted for E's and Whizz' in 1995?

35 Who had the 'Liquor Store Blues' on his 2010 debut album *Doo-Wops and Hooligans*?

36 'Mama (Loves a Crackhead)' was a single from which British rapper's first album, released before he hit paydirt with his second?

37 What were naughty boys Calvin Harris and Tinie Tempah doing in the British top 10 in early 2013?

38 Who sang about 'Sweet Leaf' (marijuana) in 1971 and 'Snowblind' (coke) in 1972?

39 Who had a 'Liquid Lunch' on her 'Shocking' 2013 album?

40 Which band sang about 'Special K' on their 2000 album *Black Market Music*?

QUIZ 29

THE SEVENTIES

Long hair and loons don't tell the whole story of the seventies, a decade during which social unrest was followed by a spell of retrenchment and conservatism that carried over into much of the eighties. It may have been an era of three-day weeks and power cuts, but it was also a period defined by great leaps forward in human rights and freedom of expression. Here are 30 questions about it. If you get stuck, call your dad.

Answers: page 484

1   What was the title of War's 1975 US Top 10 single about cruising around in a 1948 Chevy? Which American comic duo featured the song in their 1978 stoner comedy *Up in Smoke*?

2   Which song became Golden Earring's biggest hit in 1973 and an enduring school disco favourite for the next 20 years? In which country did the band enjoy most success?

3   Who came *Alive!* in 1976 on one of the biggest-selling live albums ever released? Featuring a wah-wah guitar intro, what was the album's lead single that gave the singer his only UK Top 10 hit?

4   Whose mum gave Dr Hook their first UK Top 10 single in 1972? Later that year, which magazine held a dream for them?

5   How did 'Pigs', 'Sheep' and 'Dogs' have an impact on the albums chart in 1977? Which famous London landmark featured on the cover of the record?

6   Who replaced Bernie Leadon as the guitarist in the Eagles between 1975 and 1976? What was his only UK Top 20 single as a solo artist, taken from the album *But Seriously, Folks...*?

7   *City to City* was a big-selling album by Scottish songwriter Gerry Rafferty largely due to the success of which single, featuring a famous saxophone solo? With which band had Rafferty previously been the singer?

8   Which band's finest moment was 'More than a Feeling', the opening track to their first, eponymous album in 1976? Which US city were the band from?

9   Queen's anthems 'We Will Rock You' and 'We Are the Champions' are the opening two tracks on which album from 1977? What's the name of the next track on it, which seems to belong on their earlier 1974 album?

10 Who connects pop band Slik with Band Aid? With which hard rock band did he play guitar from 1979 to 1980 as an emergency replacement for Gary Moore?

11 Which seventies prog rock band featured Sonja Kristina on vocals and the classically trained violinist Darryl Way? What was their only hit single?

12 *Manifesto*, Roxy Music's 1979 'comeback' album (they had only been away for four years), spawned two UK Top 10 singles. What were they?

13 Which Geordie folk rock band released an album called *Fog on the Tyne* in the summer of 1971? Who duetted with the band on a new version of the title track in 1990, taking the song back to number two?

14 'Yodelling has no place in popular music,' begins a chapter of Stuart Maconie's book *Cider with Roadies*. To which 1973 hit was he referring? And what was the title of the band's even more successful follow-up single?

15 By what name were Mick Ronson, Trevor Bolder and Mick Woodmansey better known in 1972? With which prog band did Bolder have a long career from 1976?

BONUS TRACKS

16 Which member of the *Dad's Army* cast had a UK number one with 'Grandad' in 1970? Which T Rex single, their first significant UK hit, was kept at number two by it?

17 Michael Parkinson, Christopher Lee, John Conteh and Clement Freud are among the celebrities who posed as escaped convicts for the cover of which classic seventies album? Which track was the first single to be taken from it?

18 Which rock and roll revival band from Leicester enjoyed ten UK Top 10 singles between 1974 and 1978? What was their only number one?

19 According to Boney M, who 'brought up her sons to handle a gun'? And who was 'a cat who really was gone' and 'big and strong, in his eyes a flaming glow'?

20 'Save the Children', 'Wholy Holy', 'Mercy Mercy Me (The Ecology)' are all tracks from which 1971 Marvin Gaye album? Who produced it?

21 Which seventies TV series lauched the career of Julie Covington? Which member of Roxy Music co-wrote the show's songs with Howard Schuman?

22 On his 1973 album *Billion Dollar Babies*, what did Alice Cooper tell us he didn't want to be any more? But what, on the same album, did he want to be?

23 Which track from Fleetwood Mac's *Rumours* became the theme tune for the TV coverage of Formula 1? Which Stevie Nicks song, originally the B-side of 'Go Your Own Way', was added to later reissues of the album?

24 Which movie soundtrack stayed at number one on the albums chart for 18 weeks in 1978? Which classic soundtrack from 1965 has spent the most total weeks on the UK chart?

25 Which band started as an offshoot of the Move, when Roy Wood and Jeff Lynne wanted a side project to develop some different ideas? And which band did Wood go on to form in 1972?

26 'I won't laugh at you, if you boo hoo hoo...' What's next in the lyrics to Slade's first UK number one? And what was their sixth and final chart-topper, released late in 1973?

27 In 1971, what became Diana Ross's first solo UK number one hit in 1971? Which then-BBC Radio 1 DJ is credited with having persuaded her label to release the song as a single?

28 Which 1974 single gave Status Quo their only UK number one? And with which 1977 hit did the group open Live Aid at Wembley Stadium?

29 Mott the Hoople acquired a loyal following during the early seventies. What was their preferred form of 'Boogie'? And from where did they travel all the way to the UK top 10 in 1973?

30 Who were the brothers at the heart of seventies glam pop band Sparks? What's the title of their brilliant 1974 album, which spawned the singles 'This Town Ain't Big Enough for Both of Us' and 'Amateur Hour'?

QUIZ 30

GIRL POWER

This quiz spotlights female artists of all eras, from Dusty to Duffy and Lulu to Lily. As in life, so in rock and roll – women are hideously under-represented. After 15 straightforward questions, there are two mix-and-match quizzes, one on girl groups of the nineties and one on singers in edgier outfits (the bands, not the clothes...).

Answers: page 485

1   Who encouraged us to 'Smile' as she went to the top of the UK charts with her debut single in 2006? She topped the albums chart with her second album – what's it called?

2   In 1998, which 52-year-old singer became the oldest female solo artist to reach number one in the UK singles chart? Eight years earlier, a cover of which minor hit for Betty Everett had given this artist her first UK number one for 25 years?

3   Cherie Currie was the provocative lead singer of which prototype all-girl punk band? Who portrayed Currie in a 2010 biopic of the group?

4   Shakespears Sister took their name from a song by which eighties indie band? Who joined founding member Siobhan Fahey when she decided to make her solo project a duo?

5   Whose first album was titled *Alf* after the nickname by which she was known? Which old Billie Holiday standard gave the singer her highest-charting single in 1985?

6   In 1981, who became the first all-female band to reach the top of the US charts with a self-penned album? Co-written by guitarist Jane Wiedlin and Terry Hall, what was their debut single?

7   It was 1980 before a sole female artist had a number-one album in the UK. Who broke the duck? And with which album?

8   Which female singer had a UK Top 10 hit in every decade from the sixties to the noughties? With which group did she collaborate on her nineties chart-topper 'Relight My Fire'?

9   Which TLC album from 1994 remains the biggest-selling album by an all-girl group in the US? Which single from it gave the band their first American number one, also reaching the Top 10 in the UK?

10 Natasha Khan is better known by which name? What's the name of her side project with the band TOY?

11 Who was a *Diva* in 1992, a Gorgon in 1995 and naked in 2002? Which song, taken from the soundtrack of Francis Ford Coppola's *Dracula*, gave her a number three hit in 1993?

12 Who was *The It Girl* at the height of Britpop? What does she do now?

13 The Spice Girls released ten singles between 1996 and 2000. Which was the first? And what was the significance, commercially, of 'Stop'?

14 Who were *Equally Cursed and Blessed* in 1999? Two years later, which playground game prompted the title of their next and final record?

15 Who wanted us to 'Push It' in 1987, then suggested 'Let's Talk about Sex' in 1991? Alongside the members in the group's name, what's the name of the DJ who completes the trio?

16 Which 15-year-old from Swindon hit the top of the UK charts with her debut single, 'Because We Want To', in 1998? Which DJ, 16 years older than the singer, became her first husband?

17 Which band consists of sisters Este, Danielle and Alana plus drummer Dash Hutton? What's the title of their 2013 debut album, which topped the UK charts?

18 Which guitarist co-produced Duffy's bestselling 2009 album *Rockferry*? What was Duffy's less successful follow-up?

19 Which four-member girl band were the main rivals to the Spice Girls in the late nineties? What was their first UK number one, which outsold all the Spice Girls' records except 'Wannabe'?

20 Which leather-clad rocker topped the UK charts with 'Can the Can' in 1973? Released a year later, what was her other British number one?

BONUS TRACK 1

Match the song to the girl group who recorded it.

21 'All Fired Up'. 22 'Hole in the Head'. 23 'Stickwitu'. 24 'Blame It on the Weatherman'. 25 'I Quit'. 26 'Never Ever'. 27 'All the Things She Said'. 28 'I'll Stand by You'. 29 '2 Become 1'. 30 'Whole Again'.

Groups: All Saints, Atomic Kitten, B*Witched, Girls Aloud, Hepburn, Pussycat Dolls, the Saturdays, Spice Girls, Sugababes, tATu.

BONUS TRACK 2

Finally, match the band to their lead singer.

31 Big Brother & the Holding Company. 32 Ex Hex. 33 The Breeders. 34 The Go-Go's. 35 T'Pau. 36 Eurythmics. 37 Halestorm. 38 The Slits. 39 The Heartless Bastards. 40 Cowboy Junkies

Singers: Belinda Carlisle, Kim Deal, Carol Dekker, Lzzy Hale, Janis Joplin, Annie Lennox, Margo Timmins, Mary Timony, Ari Up, Erika Wennerstrom.

QUIZ 31

PUNK I

There's a lot of punk in this book. BBC 6 Music is a bulwark of independent-spirited sounds – and without punk, so much of the best music of the last 35 years wouldn't have been made, much less had the commercial success that it continues to enjoy. Everything from indie rock to grime and hip hop have been influenced by this fleeting musical moment, as influential now as it's ever been. Here are 15 questions on the bands that ushered in the first flowering of punk rock, followed by a quickfire round to whet your appetite for the next one...

Answers: page 486

1   Who boasted that he belonged to the 'Blank Generation'? Of which innovative new wave band had he previously been a member?

2   'Do Anything You Wanna Do' was the first and only UK Top 10 single from which rousing pub rock band? Which guitarist joined the band after *Teenage Depression*, their first album?

3   'Shake Some Action' is the title of a 1976 single and album by which band, considered a major influence on the US punk scene? Which British guitar player took time off from Rockpile to co-produce the album?

4   Whose 1975 album *Go Girl Crazy!* was one of the first American punk rock albums to hit the record stores? Which 1961 surf song did the band cover on the album, a song also later covered by the Ramones on *Leave Home*?

5   'Personality Crisis' is the opening track on which 1973 album, a key release in the pre-history of punk and new wave? Who was the band's glam lead singer, who has since released four albums under the moniker Buster Poindexter?

6   Which two movers and shakers of the new wave era were the singers in the 101ers and Kilburn & the High Roads?

7   Ricky Gardiner wrote the distinctive riff for which classic Iggy Pop song? Which band covered it on their 1987 covers album *Through the Looking Glass*?

8   Who managed the seventies all-female rock band the Runaways? Their debut single was co-written by Joan Jett – what was it called?

9   Which band did Johnny Thunders form, along with Jerry Nolan, when they left the New York Dolls? Who was the third original member of the band?

10 Which pub rocker had a minor hit with a cover of the Trammps' hit 'Hold Back the Night' in 1976? What was their third album, released a year later and their first to hit the UK Top 20?

11 *Down by the Jetty* is the 1975 debut album by which Canvey Island R&B band? Who was their singer and harmonica player?

12 It starts with clapping from the audience, then a rant from the MC: 'I wanna see a sea of hands out there… Five seconds of decision… It's time to move – time to get down with it, brother. It's time to testify – are you ready to testify? Are you ready?' Which band are about to play 'Ramblin' Rose'? And on which 1968 album, a punk progenitor?

13 If 'Sheena is a punk rocker', what are Judy and Suzy?

14 Whose 1976 live album *Stupidity* briefly topped the UK album chart? Which Chuck Berry cover closed the album?

15 *Raw Power* was a prototype punk album by which American band? What was its opening track, which later gave its name to a hugely influential American punk magazine?

BONUS TRACKS

Punk was all about the fast blast, so here are 15 questions for which the answer is simply a song or album title plus the name of the band. You have two minutes and 28 seconds, the length of the Undertones' 'Teenage Kicks'…

16 A convicted brothel keeper was the subject of the opening song on which band's first album?

17 'I'm lying in the hospital, I'm pinned against the bed.' Which macabre punk song begins with these lines?

18 'Alarmed by the seduction, I wish that it would stop.' What's going on?

19 'Everybody's doing just what they're told to, because nobody want to go to jail.' So what's the answer?

20 'When I done them things, I done them just for you. And now I'm getting out, I'm coming back for you.' What statement comes next?

21 'Up on the roof, out in the street, down in the playground, the hot concrete.' But where can you hitch a ride to and escape?

22 Leon Trotsky, Lenny Bruce, Shakespeare and Sancho Panza are all referenced in which Top 10 hit?

23 'They just want money, we can take it or leave it, what we need….' Was what?

24 'Don't ask us to attend 'cos we're not all there.' What were we?

25 'I am Governor Jerry Brown, my aura smiles and never frowns, soon I will be President…' Who made this scathing attack on the Governor of California?

26 'I'm in distress, I need a caress… I'm not on the make, I just need a break…' And?

27 Who waited for her mum to put out the light before putting on her make-up and her skin-tight jeans and heading to the Pillar Bar?

28 Which classic punk single begins with the spoken words 'Is she really going out with him?'

29 'Oh, you know her, won't you look at that hair? Yeah, you know her, check out those shoes.' Which early single by which New York band?

30 'He always beat me at Subbuteo, 'cos he flicked to kick and I didn't know.' A genius couplet from which 1980 pop-punk single?

QUIZ 32

TEATIME THEME

Every teatime, Stuart Maconie asks you to name three connected tracks to listen to with a cuppa and a Jammie Dodger. This quiz works on the same principle (but don't you dare get crumbs on this book!). There are two points available here. If you can add a bit of detail, such as identifying two of the songs or artists, take two points. If you just guess the theme, it is only one.

The second part of the quiz is rather more literal: the theme is teatime, and goodies that may be consumed then. An example: the first question is about Cream, who were a band but can also be enjoyed with a bowl of strawberries at teatime...

Answers: page 487

1 Ian McCulloch; Martha and the Muffins; the most commercially successful Pink Floyd compilation album

2 Bob was asking for admittance; Bruno was excluded; Zep were buying a means of entry

3 Lily and Matchstick Men at An Exhibition

4 What connects *In The Future* and *Heretic Pride*, two albums released in 2008? What connects Fleet Foxes to them in the same year?

5 The Beatles and the Jam did it Larry Williams' way, Foreigner couldn't do it on their 2009 comeback album, and Oasis begged God not to do it to them: what?

6 The Killers sang about one, the Byrds gave theirs an honorific, and Blur thought they were one on their 2015 comeback album. What?

7 If Billy Joel didn't do it at all, Adele did it to the rain and Snow Patrol did it to the Third Bar. What??

8 Blur's was a rural retreat, Madness's was a bit of a laugh and Ed's was made of plastic bricks. What?

9 The Beastie Boys deemed it worth fighting for, Pink wanted to get it started, and Courtney Barnett didn't even think it worth the bother. What?

10 Lynn was unapologetic regarding one, the Beatles dreamed about one under the ocean and Siouxsie's was a long way away. What?

11 The Prodigy did it on *Fat of the Land*, Taylor Swift did it on *Fearless* and Pink Floyd did it on the *The Dark Side of the Moon*. What is it, it and where did Laura Marling do it?

12 For MGMT it preceded Feel, for Lana Del Ray it followed Body, and for Jonelle Monae it was a lady; what was it? What was it for Duran Duran in 1997?

13 If Beethoven composed the sonata, and Glenn Miller the serenade, what is it and how did it work for Toploader and Thin Lizzy?

14 It was bad for Bastille, Kanye's was in the leaves and Norah's was only young. What is it and what type do Mike Kerr and Ben Thtacher have?

15 Van Halen did it, House of Pain did it all over the place, and Metallica suggested you did it in the fire. What is it, and who did it on his 2009 album *R.O.O.T.S.* (with help from Nelly Furtado)?

BONUS TRACKS

16　Who was the drummer in the late sixties band Cream that included Eric Clapton on guitar? What band did he and Clapton form with Ric Grech and Steve Winwood after Cream broke up?

17　Who were the bass player and drummer in the Jam alongside Paul Weller?

18　What snack was Kacey Musgraves' lead-off single from her second album, *Pageant Material*? What was the title of her first?

19　Who sang 'Joy Division Oven Gloves' and from which LP, with a title spoofing a famous U2 album, was it taken?

20　Steve Mason, formerly of the Beta Band, released an album called *Black Gold* in 20106 under which name? What was the 2016 album he released under his own name?

21　What did Marilyn Manson couple with cake on his first album? What is Manson's birth name?

22　Errol Bown was the singer in which multi-racial pop group in the seventies and eighties? What was their only UK number one (1977)?

23　What kind of tea did Nirvana sing about on their *MTV Unplugged* album? To what is the song a reference?

24　What type of pie did the Beatles sing about on the *White Album*? Who sang about the same treat on his 1999 album, *Play*?

25　What were All Saints drinking at the top of the UK singles chart in 2000? And where did Squeeze drink theirs?

26　What does Snoop Dogg offer for dessert on his 2015 album *Bush*? Which former Gap Band singer helps him out on the track?

27　In the 1963 Searchers song, if his sweet got sweets, what did his honey get? What was coupled with this to give them another hit later that year?

28 The Beatles' 'Strawberry Fields Forever' was released as a double-A side single with 'Penny Lane'. For which album was it originally intended? How, in 2013, did Justin Timberlake want to ingest his strawberries?

29 Who had a UK Top 10 hit with 'Milk' off their debut album in 1995? Who declared 'Ernie' to be 'the fastest milkman in the West' in 1971?

30 David Gates was the singer in which Californian band of the late sixties and early seventies? What was their biggest UK hit, in 1970?

QUIZ 33

IN THE YEAR 2525

Fancy a date? They are the essence of this quiz. Each question has a birth and a death (usually), a UK chart topper, and a world event. Identify the year. Two points if you are spot on. One point if you are a year out.

Answers: page 488

1   Kelly Clarkson is born and Alex Harvey dies; Adam Ant has 'Goody Two Shoes' at number one; Pope John Paul II is the first Pontiff to visit Britain.

2   Jack White is born and Tim Buckley dies; 'January' is number one for Pilot; *Monty Python and the Holy Grail* is released in cinemas.

3   Ed Sheeran is born and Serge Gainsbourg dies; 'Do the Bartman' from *The Simpsons* hits number one; John McCarthy is released after being held hostage in the Lebanon for five years.

4   Sinéad O›Connor is born and Johnny Kidd dies; 'Strangers in the Night' takes Frank Sinatra to number one; Longleat Safari Park in Wiltshire opens.

5   Alex Turner is born and Benny Goodman dies; 'Spirit in the Sky' is number one; *The Sun* claims that Freddie Starr ate a hamster.

6   Jarvis Cocker is born and Patsy Cline dies; 'You'll Never Walk Alone' is number one; the Beeching Report decimates the British rail system.

7   Paul Weller is born and Vaughan Williams dies; 'Jailhouse Rock' is number one; the Munich air disaster kills Manchester United players.

8   Joey Ramone dies; So Solid Crew spend '21 Seconds' at number one; Labour minister John Prescott punches a member of the public.

9   Bez is born and Cole Porter dies; 'House of the Rising Sun' is number one; Radio Caroline begins broadcasting.

10 Laura Marling is born and Sammy Davis Jr dies; Kylie is at number one with 'Tears On My Pillow'; Poundland open their first store, in Burton-on-Trent.

11 Dave Grohl is born and Judy Garland dies; 'Something in the Air' tops the chart for Thunderclap Newman; the QEII makes her maiden voyage from Southampton to New York.

12 Adam Faith dies; 'Changes' is at number one for Ozzy and Kelly Osbourne; Roman Abramovich buys Chelsea FC.

13 Matt Bellamy of Muse is born and Jacques Brel dies; 'Three Times a Lady' is number one'; Louise Brown, the world's first IVF baby (or 'test tube baby', as she is called then), is born.

14 John Denver dies; 'Spice Up Your Life' is number one; *Harry Potter and the Philosopher's Stone* is published.

15 Mick Hucknall is born and Eddie Cochran dies; The Shadows' 'Apache' is number one; Harold Pinter's *The Caretaker* opens in London.

BONUS TRACKS

16 Tommy Vance dies; James Blunt's 'You're Beautiful' reaches number one; *Dr Who* returns after an absence of 16 years.

17 Norah Jones is born and Van McCoy of 'The Hustle' fame dies; 'I Don't Like Mondays' is number one for the Boomtown Rats; the IRA murder MP Airey Neave and Earl Mountbatten.

18 Adele is born and Andy Gibb dies; the KLF's 'Doctorin' the Tardis' is number one; Red Nose Day is inaugurated.

19 Donna Summer dies; Jessie J is number one with 'Domino'; Bradley Wiggins is the first British cyclist to win the Tour de France.

20 Michael Stipe is born and George Formby dies; 'You Don't Know' is number one for Helen Shapiro; the contraceptive pill becomes available on the NHS.

21 Chris Martin is born and Bing Crosby dies; 'Silver Lady' is at number one for David Soul; Freddie Laker launches Skytrain.

22 John Lydon is born and Elvis's mum, Gladys, dies; 'Que Sera Sera' is number one for Doris Day; Chancellor Harold Macmillan introduces Premium Bonds in Britain.

23 Eazy-E dies; 'Love Can Build a Bridge' a Comic Relief song by Cher, Chrissie Hynde and Neneh Cherry with Eric Clapton, goes to number one; Manchester United star Eric Cantona kung fu kicks a fan.

24 Malcolm McLaren dies; Bruno Mars is at number one with 'Just the Way You Are'; Ed Milliband becomes Labour Party leader.

25 Ian Dury dies; Britney Spears tops the chart with 'Oops!... I Did It Again'; Tate Modern open on London's South Bank.

26 Dr Dre is born and Nat King Cole dies; 'It's Not Unusual' to find Tom Jones at number one; Ronnie Biggs escapes from Wandsworth Prison.

27 Avril Lavigne is born and Count Basie dies; 'Freedom' is number one for Wham!; Robert Maxwell buys the *Daily Mirror*.

28 Joe Strummer dies; Will Young is at number one with 'Light My Fire'; the Queen Mother dies aged 101.

29 Beck is born and Jimi Hendrix dies; 'Spirit in the Sky' is number one for Norman Greenbaum; the Methodist Church approves the ordination of female ministers.

30 Miley Cyrus is born and Albert King dies; Jimmy Nail has a number one with 'Ain't No Doubt'; Black Wednesday hits the UK stock market.

QUIZ 34

COVER ME

We used to tut at artists who did cover versions, but why? For centuries classical music has seen orchestras recording cover versions of various composers' work. Why shouldn't pop artists do the same? This chapter celebrates the art of the cover version.

Answers: page 488

1   Who had a UK number one in 2001 with 'Somethin' Stupid, originally a duet between Frank Sinatra and his daughter, Nancy?

2   Who released a 2001 covers album called *Strange Little Girls*, comprising songs written by men and re-recorded from a female perspective? The title track, 'Strange Little Girl', was a cover of whose 1982 hit?

3   Elvis and the Beatles were covered on a 2002 double A-side number one single by Gareth Gates and Will Young: which tracks?

4   Which cover by Whitney Houston is the most successful song by a female artist in chart history? Who wrote it?

5   Which band combined with Green Day on a version of 'The Saints Are Coming' in 2006? Who had a minor hit with the original in 1978 off their album *Scared to Dance*?

6   Which 1983 Billy Joel album included the UK number one 'Uptown Girl'? Who gave the song a new lease of life in 2001?

7   Which sixties Nina Simone classic did Elvis Costello cover in 1986? His version of Charles Aznavour's 'She' featured on the soundtrack of which 1999 Richard Curtis rom-com?

8   Which act, originally called Dean Ford and the Gaylords, became the first Scottish group to top the UK singles chart? Which 1968 cover of a Lennon/McCartney song took them there?

9   On a 2007 compilation album to celebrate 40 years of Radio 1, which 1977 David Bowie track did Franz Ferdinand cover?? Which girl group covered Wheatus' 2001 hit 'Teenage Dirtbag'?

10 Who had a Christmas 2001 hit with a covers album called *Swing When You're Winning*? Which Canadian-Italian crooner's Christmas album charted in 2011, 2012 and 2013?

11 'Relight My Fire', recorded with Take That, gave which durable Scottish singer her only UK number one? Which American artist first released the song in 1979, as a follow-up to his 'Instant Replay'?

12 Bruce Springsteen, The Carpenters and the Jacksons have all charted with covers of which 1934 Christmas tune? Which Australian tribute band scored a minor hit with it in 1992?

13 Al Green's ' Take Me to the River' was covered by which US new wave band in 1978? What novelty marketing phenomenon gave his royalties a huge boost with the same song in the late nineties?

14 Eddie Floyd sang 'Knock on Wood' in 1966. Which two artists reached the UK Top 10 in the seventies with the same song?

15 Which two boy bands reached number two with the Bee Gees' 'How Deep Is Your Love' and 'Words'?

BONUS TRACKS

16 Who wrote and recorded the original version of 'Harvest for the World' in 1976? Who took it into the UK Top 10 in 1988?

17 Which artist has won court cases for infringement of copyright or passing off against Frito-lay (PepsiCo), Levi's, Audi and Adam Opel AG (General Motors)? Which song did he cover on a 1988 album of reinterpreted Disney classics?

18 Who had a UK number one with the Lennon/McCartney song 'With a Little Help from My Friends' in 1968? Who reached number four in 1997 with a cover of 'Yesterday'?

19 Whose 1991 take on Elton John's 'Rocket Man' won a 2007 poll in the *Observer* newspaper as the greatest cover version of all time? Which other Elton John song did she cover on the B-side?

20 Whose first big hit was a version of a traditional Irish narrative song, 'Whiskey in the Jar'? Which metal band sang it on their 1998 covers album, *Garage Inc*?

21 *Scratch My Back* was a 2010 covers album released by Peter Gabriel, whose concept was that a future album, *And I'll Scratch Yours*, would feature covers of his own material by the artists whose songs he had covered. Which Bowie song led off *Scratch My Back*? And what did Gabriel do when Bowie declined to reciprocate?

22 Which two artists enjoyed success with single releases of the Elvis Costello songs, 'Girls Talk' and 'Shipbuilding'?

23 Which two cover versions, one a Kinks song, one a Motown hit, gave the Fall their only UK Top 40 hits?

24 CCS's version of which Led Zeppelin song became the theme tune for *Top of the Pops*? Goldbug had a 1996 UK number three: which tune, familiar to cinema regulars, did they mash in with the Zep song?

25 Pet Shop Boys' 'Go West' was a cover of a disco song by which American band? On whose 1996 single 'Hallo Spaceboy' (1996) did Pet Shop Boys provide guest vocals?

26 Which Neil Young song was the debut single for Saint Etienne? What was unusual about it, from their point of view?

27 Bon Iver, Tame Impala, Nick Cave and Erykah Badu are all "fwends" featured on a 2012 covers album by which experimental rock band? Which album did the same band cover in its entirety in 2014?

28 Two artists took the Phil Spector-produced Ronettes hit 'Baby I Love You' to number eight in the UK chart, one in 1973 and one in 1980. Who were they?

29 What was the purpose of the 2012 album *Chimes of Freedom*, whereon 50 international artists covered Bob Dylan songs? Who released an entire album of Dylan covers, *Dylanesque*, in 2007?

30 What are the only two cover versions Adele has included on her three studio albums – one by Bob Dylan and one by The Cure?

QUIZ 35

TABLOID TALES

Rock and roll miscreants both ancient and modern. And remember, kids – it ain't big and it ain't clever. That said, modern music stars don't seem as obsessed with trashing hotels as was once the case – maybe it's the ever-present paparazzi and the fear of getting caught, sometimes literally, with their pants down. Here are 30 questions about some of rock's most notorious misbehavers.

Answers: page 489

1   Which hard-rocking girl band once raffled off their drummer for some post-gig, um, entertainment? On which British TV show did one of them cause a furore by flashing her tuppence at the camera?

2   Who was jailed in 2008 for the false imprisonment and assault of a young Norwegian, Audun Carlsen? Which singer had previously tried to sue this star after he claimed in his autobiography, *Take It Like a Man*, that the pair had a homosexual affair?

3   *See Jungle! See Jungle! Go Join Your Gang Yeah, City All Over!...* Which three words (plus, of course, another exclamation mark) are missing from the end of the title of Bow Wow Wow's debut album? Why was the album the subject of a police investigation?

4   Which 18-year-old future rock and roll star was sent to prison for three years for armed robbery? What offence saw him back in stir for 120 days in 1979?

5   In 1985, *Penthouse* and *Playboy* published seven-year-old nude pictures of which singing star? At which high-profile public performance a few days later did the singer declare, 'I ain't taking shit off today'?

6   Who was sued for $10 million by his own mother, Debbie? And which infamous song did he record about the relationship?

7   Which has so far been the highest-charting Stranglers single, a 1982 UK number two hit about heroin use? Which member of the band served time in prison for possession of drugs?

8   When country star George Jones's wife hid his car keys so the alcoholic singer couldn't leave the house to buy more booze, what did he use instead to take a trip to the shops? And who was the wife in question, also a country singer?

9   Which rock superstar was sentenced to eight months' hard labour in 1969 for getting his todger out on stage in Miami? Why did he never serve the sentence?

10   For what crime was Pete Doherty first jailed in 2003?

11 Which US actor and soap star was Keith Moon's favourite drinking partner when he lived in Los Angeles? And which English actor and boozing legend once said that Moon 'showed me the way to insanity'?

12 The Appleton sisters from All Saints, Nicole and Natalie, have each been married to fellow music stars. Who did they marry? (To get the points, you must pair the husband with the right sister.)

13 Driving without insurance, fraudulent use of a credit card, speeding, larceny, aggravated assault, carrying an unlicensed firearm, fleeing arrest, manslaughter. Of which two of these offences was James Brown never found guilty?

14 Nick Oliveri was arrested in Brazil for performing nude on stage with which band in 2001? Which musician, who also played with Oliveri in Kyuss, is the leader of the band?

15 Which mega-rich star auctioned 20 unused cars in 2001, worth £2 million, and sold the entire contents of his house two years later so he could refurbish it properly? During a 2000 court case, on what did he admit to spending £293,000 in an 18-month period?

BONUS TRACKS

16 Which Britpop hero was sentenced to four months in prison for threatening an airline pilot and hostess? Which other star had airline issues when she kicked up a stink and accused a female security guard of trying to goose her?

17 Tommy Lee was jailed for wife-beating in 1998. With which band is he the long-term drummer? And who was the wife in question?

18 Which eighties glam metal guitarist was arrested for carrying a loaded Beretta on to an aeroplane in 1995? And which young jazz pianist and singer was detained at New York's JFK airport for the same offence in 1992?

19 Which star served with the 3rd Armored Division in Freidberg, West Germany, between 1958 and 1960? Which significant individual did he meet while serving?

20 Which soft porn magazine was guest edited by Shaun Ryder and Bez in 1990? And which 'newspaper' engaged Ryder's writing skills in 1998?

21 Which American singer was arrested in Milwaukee on obscenity charges, apparently for 'simulating masturbation with a sledgehammer'? What was the name of her backing band?

22 Which Jamaican producer destroyed his own studio during a spell when he would only walk backwards? What did he purport to worship during this strange episode?

23 What was the name of the infamous burglary gang who were finally caught after robbing Lindsay Lohan in 2007? For what offence was Lohan herself jailed, apart from her numerous busts for addiction and failure to meet parole commitments?

24 Which 18-year-old did 52-year-old Bill Wyman marry in 1989, after dating her for four years? And who did Wyman's son from his first marriage, now 31, marry in 1993, the same year that Wyman and his wife divorced?

25 On whose TV show did the Sex Pistols earn notoriety with a bit of mild swearing? What was the headline, later pinched as a kind of motto by the band, with which the *Daily Mirror* greeted this 'uproar'?

26 Eddie Fisher, who had a number one single in the US and the UK with 'I'm Walking Behind You' in 1953, became notorious for leaving one film star wife for her best friend. Who were the two women involved?

27 Which rapper hired Farnsworth Bentley, and what was his role?

28 Who was tried (twice) and convicted for the second-degree murder of actress Lana Clarkson in 2003? Which teen comedy film, written by Cameron Crowe and released in 1982, gave Clarkson her first film role, and also provided early exposure for Sean Penn, Nicolas Cage, Phoebe Cates and Jennifer Jason Leigh?

29 Who wasted $50,000 of bail money stumped up by Virgin Records in 1978 by bottling Patti Smith's brother, Todd, in a bar? In which famous New York prison was he detained?

30 Which female rapper served 12 months in 2005 for perjury and conspiracy to pervert the course of justice? For which crime was Lauryn Hill sentenced to three months in jail 2013?

QUIZ 36

ALTERNATIVE JUKEBOX

'The aim of the Alternative Jukebox is to capture BBC 6 Music's alternative spirit, whether classic, cover, niche or unusual' says Chris Hawkins' introduction to the 'Alternative Jukebox page' on the 6 Music website. The Jukebox is updated every year to reflect new trends. It celebrates fresh new music with an independent spirit free from corporate persuasion. Artists managed by Simon Cowell are notable by their absence. This chapter features artists that belong on there.

Answers: page 490

1   Which reggae star sang on Massive Attack's debut album, *Blue Lines*? And who co-wrote and sang on the final track, 'Hymn of the Big Wheel', with him?

2   Which enduring band was fronted for 30 years by Thurston Moore? What was their 1992 Butch Vig-produced eighth album that reached number six in the UK album chart?

3   The cover of Maccabees' fourth album, *Marks to Prove It*, features which south London landmark, a tribute to a famous scientist? What was the album's Mercury-nominated predecessor in 2012?

4   Which city's music scene includes British Sea Power? Which band did Eamon Hamilton form with the White brothers from Electric Soft Parade when he left BSP in 2006?

5   Whose 2016 album was an adaptation of nine Shakespeare sonnets? Which pop superstar provided guest vocals on Sonnet 29?

6   *Midnite Vultures*; MISSING; *Guero*; *The Information*; MISSING; *Morning Phase*. What are the two missing albums from this list of Beck's post-1999 releases?

7   In which year did New Order's 'Blue Monday' first chart in the UK? How many times has it made the Top 20?

8   From which album did New Order take 'Blue Monday'? And who did the revamped 'Acid House Mix' in 1988?

9   Mike Skinner released five albums under which name in the 2000s? What was his sole UK number one?

10 *We're New Here* was a remix album made by Gil Scott-Heron and which young British producer? For which solo album did the latter win a 2016 Grammy award?

11 Whose hit single with a version of 'The Twist' started a 1960 dance craze? Which Brooklyn rap act successfully revived the fad alongside the original artist in 1988?

12 What did Marc Bolan do with his band's name before their fifth album? What was their first UK number one single, in 1971?

13 Whose released *Divers* in 2015? What is her main instrument?

14 Which film gave Iggy Pop's 1977 classic 'Lust for Life' a new lease of life in 1996? Who co-wrote it with Iggy?

15 Which reggae star took 'The Israelites' to number one in the UK in 1968? Which Jimmy Cliff cover hit number two for him two years later?

BONUS TRACKS

16 Smog was the recording alter ego of which US artist? What was the 2013 album (his fifteenth) released under his own name that was a rare chart entry in the UK?

17 Which British band changed their name from Dead Elvis after objections from the Presley estate and used it as the title of their 1999 debut album instead? Who sang on their only UK Top 10 hit, the grunge/dance track 'Aisha'?

18 How is original rock and roller Richard Penniman better known, and what was his 1955 breakthrough single and signature tune?

19 Which 4AD band feature Elena Tonra on guitar and vocals? What was the title of their 2016 second album?

20 What was the Strokes' 2001 debut album called? Who is the band's leader and songwriter?

21 Which groundbreaking German electronic band's fourth album went Top 10 in the UK and US in 1974? What was it called?

22 What sigil (symbol) is the 'official' name of alt-J? What was their Mercury Prize-winning 2012 debut album?

23 Whose 1987 debut album was named after iconic Manchester United footballer George Best? In 1992 the same band released a single each month. Every one reached the UK Top 40, matching whose feat of 12 hit singles in a calendar year?

24 Q: *Are We Not Men?* What was the answer on this 1978 debut album? Two pairs of brothers made up the band: Bob and Gerald Casale and Bob and Mark what?

25 If you were watching Brace Paine play guitar and Hannah Blilie on drums, who was singing? What was the band's breakthrough single?

26 The refrain 'Boom Boom Boom Boom' is associated with which Delta blues guitarist? Which three drinks are cited in the title of another famous song by the same artist?

27 What was the title of the Byrds' debut album, and also the title of the lead track, a Bob Dylan cover? Which other Dylan cover off the album gave them a follow-up hit?

28 Which drum and bass artist was born Clifford Price in 1965? In which 1999 James Bond movie did he play a villainous henchman?

29 Nineties rock band Belly featured singer/guitarist Tanya Donelly; with which other two female-fronted rock acts is she associated?

30 What completes the Belle and Sebastian album titles; 'Fold Your Hands Child, ?????' and 'Girls in Peacetime ???' (the number of question marks indicates the number of missing words).

QUIZ 37

AT THE MOVIES

Film and music have always been inseparable; a soundtrack is an integral part of the movie process. Here are 30 questions on music that has benefited from, or added to, the film in which it was used. Some are questions about movies with music as a theme or subject matter, while others are about soundtracks to popular movies that launched massive hits or acquired a cult following.

Answers: page 491

1 Glen Hansard and Marketa Irglova, who had performed as the Swell Season, starred, composed and played the music for 2007 film *Once*: which song won them an Academy Award for Best Original Song? In which major 1991 film did Hansard play Outspan Foster?

2 What was the name of the fictitious glam rock star played by Jonathan Rhys Meyers in *Velvet Goldmine*? Which artist released the song from whence the film got its title as a 1975 B-side?

3 Which film shot the Righteous Brothers' 'Unchained Melody' back to number one in the UK in late 1990? And how many years had passed since they first charted with the song: 12, 18, or 25?

4 Which Glasgow band recorded the soundtrack to the 2006 movie *Zidane*? What is the origin of their name?

5 Which Mexican-American band provided the soundtrack for *Desperado*, Robert Rodriguez's western starring Antonio Banderas? Which earlier movie about Ritchie Valens gave them their biggest hit?

6 Whose one and only UK number one was 'The One and Only' (1991), taken from the movie *Buddy's Song*, in which he played an aspiring pop star? Who wrote the song?

7 Mike Reno and Ann Wilson's 'Almost Paradise' and Deniece Williams's 'Let's Hear It for the Boy' were hits from the soundtrack of which eighties movie? Which song from the film gave Bonnie Tyler a UK number two?

8 Which film spawned a US number one for B.J. Thomas with 'Raindrops Keep Fallin' On My Head'? Which songwriting duo composed the tune for the movie?

9 The soundtrack to which 1984 film gave Stevie Wonder a UK number two album? What was his big hit single off the album?

10 'All for Love' was a 1993 US number one and UK number two on the back of its use in which remake of a classic swashbuckling tale? It was a collaboration between Bryan Adams, Sting and which other British singer?

11 Will White and Alex Gifford made one album in 1998 under which name? What was the album, which included 'Spybreak!', which featured in *The Matrix*?

12 Which 2002 movie charted the story of Factory Records? Which 2007 film concentrated on the life and death of Ian Curtis?

13 Which 2008 movie spawned a US number one album made up entirely of cover versions of one band's output? And a *Glee* mini-album of cover versions of which artist did the same in 2010?

14 *The Boat That Rocked* (2009) was loosely based on which sixties floating radio station? Who scripted and directed the film?

15 Which movie director, fresh from the success of *Halloween* (1978) directed the 1979 made-for-TV movie biopic of *Elvis*, and who played the singer?

BONUS TRACKS

16 'Everything I Do, I Do It For You' was a huge hit for Bryan Adams on the back of which Kevin Costner film? How long was its record-breaking stint at number one?

17 Wet Wet Wet came within a week of Adams' record with 'Love is All Around' in 1994. Which film gave the song its success, and who had the original hit?

18 Who played fictional jazz trumpeter Bleek Gilliam in the 1990 Spike Lee film, *Mo Better Blues*? Which jazz troupe provided the soundtrack music along with Terence Blanchard?

19 Which Stealers Wheel song enjoyed a second life when it was on the soundtrack to 1992's *Reservoir Dogs*? Bedlam's version of 'Magic Carpet Ride' was also featured: who originally sang the song in 1968?

20 Sasha Gervasi directed the 2008 documentary charting the sorry story of which Canadian heavy metal band? Where does the film begin and end, with two concerts in 1984 and 2007?

21 Which pop superstar played Deena/Diana Ross in 2006 Supremes-based movie *Dreamgirls*? Who won an Academy Award for her portrayal of Effie/Florence Ballard?

22 Who directed the bizarre 1975 film version of Pete Townshend's rock opera, *Tommy*? Who played the Pinball Wizard in the film?

23 What was the 2009 film about a washed-up country star, starring Jeff Bridges? Who played his protégé/rival, Tommy Sweet?

24 Who played the mother of Jimmy B-Rabbit Smith, the Eminem character in 2002 movie *8 Mile*? Which song from the film was number one in the US and UK and won Eminem an Academy Award?

25 What was the 1989 movie directed by Aki Kaurismaki about a fictional Russian band touring the US? After the band became real and grew a huge cult following, what was the name of their 1994 concert movie?

26 Which 2000 film is set in a Chicago record store, Championship Vinyl? Who made his breakthrough movie appearance as slobby store employee Barry?

27 Dick Dale and the Deltones' surf rock gained more fans when 'Misirlou' was included on the soundtrack to which 1994 movie? Who wrote Urge Overkill's 'Girl. You'll Be a Woman Soon' from the same soundtrack?

28 Who starrred as Doughboy Baker in *Boyz n the Hood* (1991)? Who played this star in the 2015 biopic *Straight Outta Compton*?

29 Cadillac Records is a 2008 biopic of which pioneering rock and roll record label? Which rapper appears as guitar hero Chuck Berry?

30 In *This Is Spinal Tap* (1984), what is the title of the doomed album the band are promoting? Who plays the fictional filmmaker Marty Di Bergi?

QUIZ 38

METAL

If you're a hardcore metal fan who bought this book by accident, this quiz will probably be easy-peasy. If you're a day-and-night listener to BBC 6 Music, it may be a little tougher. Still, hang in there: you may well know more of these than you expect. Two sections: some questions on the old wave of heavy rock bands, some on the second wave in the eighties, some on the nineties power metal scene and some on those acts making waves in the 21st century.

Answers: page 492

1   John Petrucci is the much-admired guitarist in which US metal band? What was the band's 2009 album, the first to break the US Top 10?

2   Which Motörhead single and album from 1980 represent the band's commercial peak, with the album reaching number four in the UK and the title track making the Top 20? According to the title of the band's chart-topping 1981 live album, where could the band finally expect to get some kip?

3   Cronos, La Rage, Dante and Mantas have all been members of which metal band? What's the title of their second album from 1982, which eventually came to be used to describe a sub-genre of more extreme metal?

4   *Love, Peace and Fuck* is the debut album by which experimental heavy metal band? And who formed the band, along with Doggen Foster and Kevin 'Kevlar' Bales from Spiritualized?

5   Ritchie Blackmore, Roger Glover, Jon Lord and Ian Paice formed four-fifths of the classic line-up of which heavy band? Who was the vocalist for their most successful period?

6   Who announced their arrival in 2001 by *Sounding the Seventh Trumpet*? Which former Dream Theater drummer stepped in when their drummer, Jimmy 'The Rev' Sullivan, died in 2009?

7   Who released the 1999 live album *S&M*? What does the 'S' signify?

8   Which American rap metal band were chosen by social media activist Jon Morter as the figurehead for a campaign to stop the winner of *The X Factor* from getting the UK Christmas number one in 1999? What was the song that successfully pipped Alexandra Burke to the top?

9   Which American state are Slipknot from? Each member of the band has his own mask – what does percussionist Shawn Crahan wear?

10 Which metal band is made up of Armenian Americans? What are the names of their two 2005 albums that both topped the US charts?

11 Dave Mustaine was the original guitarist with Metallica – which band did he form after leaving the group? Who replaced him in Metallica?

12 Which spandex-bedecked British rockers were behind the classic 1980 album *Wheels of Steel*? Which song of theirs about an appearance at the Monsters of Rock Festival, from their next album, remains their most commercially successful single?

13 Jeff Hannemann, who died in 2011, was a guitarist in which thrash metal band? What was the 1986 album, the band's third, that broke them into rock's top division?

14 Which power metal band was formed by Michael Weikath and Markus Grosskopf in Hamburg in 1984? What's their classic work, released in two parts in 1986 and 1987?

15 Which thrash metal band were named after an infection particularly prevalent in cattle? Who was the band's singer between 1984 and 1992, returning to the fold in 2010?

BONUS TRACKS

16 Kim McAuliffe, Kelly Johnson, Enid Williams and Denise Dufort comprised the classic line-up of the first female British heavy metal band to have mainstream success. What are they called? And what has been their most successful album, a 1981 effort whose title track reached the British Top 40?

17 'Cameltosis', 'Dead Bodies Everywhere' and 'Freak on a Leash' are tracks from which Korn album, which topped the US charts and reached the British Top 10? Which other nu metal singer, the front man of Limp Bizkit, guested on the track 'All in the Family'?

18 In January 1991, which heavy metal act did something that few other metal acts have ever done and topped the British singles chart? Taken from their album *No Prayer for the Dying*, which song reached the summit?

19 Rob Halford is the singer in which Birmingham metal band? What, pretty much uniquely for a metal singer, did Halford do in 1988?

20 *Herzeleid*, *Mutter* and *Rosenrot* are all albums by which German metal band, known for their spectacular live shows? A cover of which Depeche Mode song, sung in English, gave them one of their bigger commercial successes?

21 Who replaced Ozzy Osbourne in Black Sabbath for two albums from 1979? With which other seventies hard rock band was he the singer before joining Sabbath?

22 Chester Bennington, the pretty boy of nu metal, became the lead singer of which band in 1999? What's the name of the debut album the band released the following year?

23 'Ain't My Bitch', 'Hero of the Day' and 'King Nothing' are all tracks from which Metallica album, a departure from the thrash metal style of their first five releases? Which 2003 album, released after a gap of six years, saw the band return to their harder-edged sound?

24 *Chocolate Starfish and the Hot Dog Flavored Water* is the title of a US- and UK-chart-topping album by which nu metal band? Who mans the turntables and arranges the samples for the band?

25 Which Zimbabwe-born producer was in no small way responsible for the rise of Def Leppard, producing their most high-profile albums and co-writing many of their hits? What was the band's breakthrough 1983 album, their second with this producer, that saw them shift towards the radio-friendly sound that brought them enormous success?

26 Brothers Michael and Rudolf Schenker have both found fame separately as guitarists in which two metal bands?

27 What is the significance of the Starchild, the Demon, the Spaceman, the Catman, the Fox and the Wizard? What, in the same context, was *The Elder*?

28 Black Sabbath had two number-one albums in the UK, *Paranoid* in 1970 and *13* in 2013. Apart from Ozzy Osbourne, which two members of the band that played on *Paranoid* also played on *13*?

29 Which band was formed by Dimebag Darrell Abbott and his brother Vinnie Paul in 1981? After that band broke up, the pair formed Damageplan in 2003 – why did this project come to an end?

30 Metallica's eponymous fifth album remains their best seller. What's the opening track? And what's the name of the live album, released two years later, that featured new versions of many of the songs on it?

QUIZ 39

BLUR VS OASIS

Just over 20 years ago, this was British music's big Battle of the Bands. Did you favour the Cockney college charm of Blur, or did you prefer the sweary Mancunian bluster of Oasis? Blur were the more imaginative and experimental of the two acts, but Oasis had a distinct edge brought about in part by their unshatterable self-belief. In recent years, Damon Albarn has remained a touchstone for musical invention, while Noel Gallagher has retained his drive, passion and ability to deliver on stage. The first section of this quiz spotlights Blur and Damon's solo projects, while the second focuses on Oasis and Noel Gallagher's High Flying Birds. See which one nets you the most points – and then you can answer the question above.

Answers: page 493

BLUR

1   Alongside Damon Albarn, who are the three other founding members of Blur? (3)

2   Which independent label signed Blur to their first recording contract? At the time, what was the band's name, which they changed at the label's insistence? (2)

3   What was Blur's first single? (1)

4   What was the one title given to Damon Albarn's two live albums in 2014, featuring tracks from his various projects? At which venue were the albums recorded? (2)

5   Which Blur song follows BBC Radio 4's Shipping Forecast map around Britain? Where, on this journey, did they run into traffic? (2)

6   Which actor provided the Cockney narration on 'Parklife'? (1)

7   What's the title of the first Damon Albarn album to be released under his own name? Which west London neighbour appears on a couple of tracks and is also credited with 'additional production'? (2)

8   Which Blur single pipped Oasis's 'Roll with It' to number one in August 1995? What's the band's only other chart-topping single, released in 1997? (2)

9   Which producer was brought in to record *13*, Blur's sixth album? (1)

10 What's the full title of the 2007 opera co-created by Damon Albarn and based on the Chinese legend of the Monkey King? And what was Albarn's 2011 opera about a famous Elizabethan astronomer, mathematician and mystic? (2)

11 Among Blur's catalogue of singles, what distinction is held by 'Coffee and TV'? The video for the song features an animated object searching for Blur's guitarist: what's the object? (2)

12 Jamie Hewlett, Damon Albarn's main collaborator in Gorillaz, found fame as the co-creator of which comic character? (1)

13 Which singer, hip hop band and actor provided vocals for, respectively, 'Kids with Guns', 'Feel Good Inc' and 'Fire Coming out of the Monkey's Head' on Gorillaz's album *Demon Days*? (3)

14 What's the title of the video documentary about Blur that was released in 2010? And which song was released on a limited-edition single for Record Store Day just a couple of months later? (2)

15 Which American hip hop legend helped Gorillaz introduce us to the world of 'Plastic Beach' at the beginning of the 2010 album of the same name? (1)

16 The Good, the Bad and the Queen saw Damon Albarn collaborate with Tony Allen, Paul Simonon and Simon Tong. Allen was the drummer with which pioneering African musician? Simonon played bass for which prominent punk band? And Tong was the guitarist in which successful Britpop act? (3)

OASIS

17 What name was adopted by Liam Gallagher and the other members of Oasis after Noel left in 2009? (1)

18 What instrument did Mark Feltham of Nine Below Zero contribute to tracks on *Be Here Now* and *Standing on the Shoulder of Giants*? (1)

19 Which Oasis album was voted the greatest record of all time in a 2006 *NME* poll? (1)

20 Alongside the Gallagher brothers, who were the three original members of Oasis that featured on their 1994 debut album? Who later joined the group as drummer, in 1995, and bass player, in 1999? (5)

21 Which Hollywood star is credited with playing slide guitar on 'Fade In-Out', featured on Oasis's third album *Be Here Now*? (1)

22 Who played keyboards on Oasis's *Heathen Chemistry* and later joined Noel Gallagher's High Flying Birds? (1)

23 What was the second album released by Noel Gallagher's High Flying Birds, a UK chart-topper in 2015? (1)

24 Which former Manchester City star features on the cover of *Definitely Maybe*? And which spaghetti Western is playing on the TV? (2)

25 How many studio albums have Oasis released? (1)

26 Name Oasis's eight British number-one singles. (8)

27 What's the title of Oasis's only live album, recorded at Wembley in 2000 and released later the same year? And what's the title of their singles compilation, released in 2010? (2)

28 Which venue staged two huge Oasis concerts in 1996, the biggest crowd (125,000) ever assembled for a single gig? (1)

29 After criticism from Noel Gallagher about the fact that he'd been booked to headline the festival, who opened his 2008 Glastonbury set with 'Wonderwall'? (1)

30 Noel Gallagher has children by both of his wives: what are the ladies' names? And which comedian/actor/broadcaster was the best man at his second wedding? (3)

QUIZ 40

AKA

What is it about rock stars and rappers that they can't be seen using their own name on stage? You can understand Derek Dick wanting to change his name (even if it was to 'Fish'), but what's wrong with being called Damon Gough? The stars have always loved a good pseudonym, and that is what this chapter celebrates. Fifteen straight question, and then a short bonus tracks section asking you to link the pseudonym to the real name.

Answers: page 494

1 Acid House producer Adam Paul Tinley had a massive hit with 'Killer' in 1990 under what moniker? Which singer, born Henry Samuel, provided the vocals, launching his own career in the process?

2 By what name is Stefani Germanotta better known? In which year did 'Just Dance' become her first US and UK number one?

3 If Alecia Moore and Victoria Hesketh were performing a duet, who would we be watching?

4 Under what names do Maxwell Fraser and Ayalah Bentovim play in Faithless?

5 The 'Live Stiffs' Stiff Records Tour of 1977, featured, among others, Declan McManus and Eric Goulden. Under what names did these two artists perform?

6 Which neosoul singer was born Michel Archer in 1974? What name did he give his backing band on his 2014 album, *Brown Sugar*?

7 Which singer was born Deborah Ann Dyer in 1967? Which Britpop-era band did she sing with?

8 What is the stage name of Vincent Furnier? Which sport did he become obsessed with after giving up booze in the seventies?

9 What connects the performer of the musical shows *Bewilderness*, *Tinselworm* and *Dandelion Mind* with Guns N' Roses?

10 Scottish trio John Lawler, Barry Wallace and Gordon McRory are collectively known as what? What is the stage name of drummer Gordon?

11 Carlton D Ridenhour and William Drayton are the main men in hip hop band Public Enemy. Under what names do they perform?

12 Damon Gough released debut album *The Hour of Bewilderbeast* in 2000. Under what name does he record? What was his second album, a soundtrack to a film based on a Nick Hornby book?

13 Which Irish singer was born Christopher John Davison in 1948, in Argentina? What was his huge, mawkish 1986 single?

14 'Dreams' came true for Louise Bobb in 1993: under which name (her middle name) did she reach number one in the UK? And what was her 1999 album and chart-topping title track?

15 What is the stage name of rapper Elliot Gleave? And of Stephen Manderson?

BONUS TRACKS

Which men chose which pseudonyms?

1 Harry Webb; 2 David Evans; 3 Saul Hudson; 4 Raymond Burns; 5 Michael Balzary; 6 Fred Heath; 7 Orville Burrell; 8 Reg Dwight; 9 Chester Burnett; 10 John Ritchie/John Beverly.

a Elton John; b Cliff Richard; c Johnny Kidd; d Shaggy; e The Edge; f Slash; g Captain Sensible h. Sid Vicious; i Flea; j Howlin' Wolf.

Who are these women better known as?

1 Niomi McLean-Daly; 2 Marie Lawrie; 3 Kimberly Jones; 4 Elizabeth Grant; 5 Christa Paffgen; 6 Susan Ballion; 7 Merrill Nisker; 8 Dana Owens; 9 Marianne Elliott-Said; 10 Priscilla White.

a Poly Styrene; b Cilla Black; c Lana Del Rey; d Lulu; e Siouxsie Sioux; f Queen Latifah; g Nico; h Lil' Kim; i Peaches; j Ms Dynamite.

Who are these rappers?

1 Shawn Carter; 2 Tramar Dillard; 3 Dylan Kwabena Mills; 4 Christopher Wallace; 5 Trevor George Smith Jr; 6 William Drayton Jr; 7 James Todd Smith; 8 O'Shea Jackson; 9 Sean Combs; 10 Calvin Broadus.

a Busta Rhymes; b LL Cool-J; c Puff Daddy; d Flo Rida; e Snoop Dogg; f Flava Flav; g Jay Z; h Ice Cube; i Notorious B.I.G; j Dizzee Rascal.

QUIZ 41

WORDS, WORDS, WORDS

There are people who claim that they never listen to the lyrics of a song. They might struggle with this quiz, though it's more straightforward than it might first appear. In these 40 questions, we've taken 40 songs and assumed that their titles are to be taken literally. Based on that assumption, we've created a vaguely cryptic clue hinting at the song title, and included the singer's real first name in it. (Asterisks denote singers who uses different stage names.) You simply have to name the song and the artist. Not there yet? Here's an example: the answer to 'Phil is disappointed that you find him undesirable' would be 'Don't You Want Me' by the Human League. It'll get easier, we promise...

Answers: page 495

1   In which Sandra sees herself as a marionette.

2   In which Florence appears to be advocating Glaswegian osculation.

3   In which Damon and his friends give elliptical advice about artillery fire.

4   In which Robert is underground, missing Duluth and a bit low.

5   In which Chris sings about aeronautical life-saving equipment.

6   In which Michael brackets his indifference to Armageddon.

7   In which Elliot* notes a marked shift in his partner's lovemaking technique.

8   In which Allan comments on the lightweight nature of his sibling.

9   In which Steven sings about reverse schadenfreude.

10 In which Noel, paraphrasing Oscar, writes about crucial laziness.

11 In which Joseph tells 11 stories about Torbay.

12 In which Paul* admits he's continuing to search.

13 In which Steve requests a pick-me-up visit.

14 In which Sia tells David's story of a disintegrating lupus.

15 In which Peter asks about the destination of his mysterious love.

16 In which David, abandoned by Roger but helped by Dick and Nick, temporarily loses his mind in ten chapters.

17 In which Steven* and John call for cooperative kleptomania.

18 In which Raymond, Gerard and Norman tell us about motor racing.

19 In which Paul relates a story written by another man about headgear as a yardstick for domesticity.

20 In which Wayne is positive in triplicate.

BONUS TRACKS

21 In which Robyn* holds a gun to her head.

22 In which Paul, and later Joe, comments on the benefits of cooperation.

23 In which David is a big spanner.

24 In which Alexandria's* desires appear to be confused about the specifics of musical genre.

25 In which Thomas sings about a suspicious robot.

26 In which Andy postulates that human evolution commenced with a dance.

27 In which Desmond assures us it's all about perseverance.

28 In which Michael comments on a young lady's general good health and self-awareness.

29 In which Mary* insists that protestations of sincerity are not compulsory.

30 In which John and his friends are suspiciously insistent about a lack of romance in their work.

31 In which Brian bemoans the emptiness of solitude.

32 In which James (with Justin* helping) tells of his desire for some arboreal pyromania.

33 In which Joseph expresses incredulity at someone's choice of partner.

34 In which Jimmy* expresses a wish to indulge his canine fetish.

35 In which Patrick*, with help from Eric, puts his faith in astrology.

36 In which Ann and Aretha comment on the self-sufficiency of the sorority.

37 In which Mick and friends are concerned about matriarchal lurking.

38 In which Nancy makes some rather obvious statements about footwear.

39 In which James sings Nicky's warning that complicity will have consequences for future generations.

40 In which William, in twelve chapters, tells of conversation with a civil servant.

QUIZ 42

PEOPLE'S PLAYLIST: LIVING THINGS

A themed quiz on animals of all shapes, forms and species in songs, albums and artist names. There are lots of songs about wolves, birds of prey and cats, not so many on hamsters, llamas or koi carp. Go figure. There are 40 questions, and a straight answer is all we need. You only have five minutes, so out with *The Observer Book of Furry Creatures* and on we crack.

Answers: page 496

1   What kind of equestrian company did Jethro Tull keep in 1978?

2   What kind of lion did James Blake bring to *Overgrown*?

3   What did Sting dream of?

4   What was Lloyd Cole & the Commotions' deadly 1984 hit?

5   Who sang about huggin' up a real 'Monkey Man' in 1969?

6   Who repeated the trick a decade later?

7   What was the B-52s' favourite shellfish?

8   Who wore a 'Peacock Suit' in 1997?

9   Who invited us to 'Do the Rat' on the B-side of their second single?

10 Who asked *Why Are You OK* in 2016?

11 How did Steve Miller get to the top of the charts in 1976?

12 Who claimed to have been through the desert on a horse with no name?

13 'Hey hey, mama, said the way you move, gonna make you sweat, gonna make you groove...' Which track?

14 On their debut album, the Detroit Cobras had a choice of 'Mink, Rat or...' What?

15 What was the Byrds' favoured steed?

16 According to the Ramones, and the Trashmen before them, what had everybody heard about?

17 What combination of predator and snake did it for Sinéad O'Connor on her debut album?

18 Which animal was John Lennon on the Beatles' *Magical Mystery Tour*?

19 Who wished they had a photograph of you?

20 Which band sang about 'The Butterfly Collector'?

21 Who were *Lost Souls* in 2000 and visited *Some Cities* in 2005?

22 *I Am a Bird Now*, said who?

23 Which animals provided the Cure with their first Top 10 hit in 1983?

24 What came first for Patti Smith?

25 Who provided *Antidotes* in 2008 and asked *What Went Down* in 2015?

26 Name Prince's avian lachrymosity.

27 How big were the Wonder Stuff?

28 Which friendly Australian animal had an 'Elephant' in 2012?

29 What was Macca's amphibian embarrassment?

30 Who did it *Doggystyle*?

31 Whose love was cool in 2015?

32 Which band sang about things that were fashionable for feline animals?

33 What came with a 'Cherry Tree' for KT Tunstall?

34 Which avian band was formed by Gary Louris and Marc Olson?

35 When Elton John and Suzie were young, what did they do?

36 Which hybrid animal took the Everly Brothers to the top of the charts?

37 On which album did Duran Duran form the 'Union of the Snake'?

38 Which bird was honoured in the title of the Stranglers' fourth album?

39 What was Elvis' tautological canine?

40 What kind of eyes did Mumford & Sons have on *Wilder Mind*?

QUIZ 43

SONGWRITERS

Singer-songwriters have come back into fashion of late, though most are indistinguishable and earnest men with scruffy beards whining about getting dumped. This quiz isn't really about them, though (though one or two might match that description...). Instead, here are 30 questions about the names in brackets below the titles – the women and men who write the songs.

Answers: page 497

1   What's the title of Anohni's 2016 album, the first released under the artist's new identity? Under what name does Ross Birchard, who wrote and produced a number of the tracks on the album, ply his trade?

2   Whose first solo album, *Yr Atal Genhedlaeth* (2005), was sung entirely in Welsh? What's the name of his 2014 effort, accompanied by a film of the same name that followed in the footsteps of the Welsh explorer John Evans?

3   Who were the songwriting duo behind the success of Abba? (Full names for the points.)

4   Who wrote the country hits 'Galveston' and 'Wichita Lineman' for Glen Campbell? Which psychedelic smash had he previously written for the 5th Dimension?

5   *Car*, *Scratch*, *Melt* and *Security* – what are they?

6   Which discarded Beach Boys project did Brian Wilson revisit on his sixth solo album, released in 2004? Which lyricist, who had been involved in the original project, collaborated with Wilson on it?

7   Who wrote 'Save the Last Dance for Me' for the Drifters, 'Suspicion' for Elvis Presley and 'Can't Get Used to Losing You' for Andy Williams? Which band had a UK number three hit with the latter song in 1983?

8   *Before These Crowded Street, Everyday, Busted Stuff, Stand Up, Big Whiskey and the GrooGrux King* and *Away from the World* all topped the US albums chart for which band, who have never even made the UK Top 50? What unique record do the six chart-toppers hold?

9   Which songwriter and composer was the subject of Brian Wilson's 2010 solo album? And which Randy Newman song from *Toy Story* kicked off Wilson's next album, a reimagining of classic Disney songs?

10   Who wrote the classic and much-covered ballad 'Because the Night'?

11   Who was a *Supposed Former Infatuation Junkie* in 1998? And who joined her to co-headline the Five-and-a-Half Weeks Tour while promoting her own album *To Venus and Back*?

12 *Running on Empty* (1977) remains, by some distance, the bestselling album by which American singer-songwriter? Which old soul song by Maurice Williams did he cover for the album's final track?

13 Who wrote the Julie Covington hit 'Don't Cry for Me, Argentina'? Who sang the song in the original stage version of *Evita* after Covington turned down the role?

14 Jeff Buckley recorded an acclaimed version of the song 'Hallelujah'. Who wrote it? And whose version of the song featured on the soundtrack to *Shrek*, despite not being the recording used in the film?

15 What's the title of the 1993 single and album that gave Billy Joel his last big international hit? Which song about an itinerant lounge singer, also the title track to one of his albums, gave him his commercial breakthrough?

BONUS TRACKS

16 Which duo wrote the 1967 classic 'The Look of Love', a hit for Dusty Springfield? Who nicked the title for a track on their 1982 album *The Lexicon of Love*?

17 Named after the Elvis hit they wrote, *Hound Dog* is the title of the 2009 autobiography by which songwriting pair? And for which band did they write a string of hits in the late fifties and early sixties, including 'Charlie Brown', 'Yakety Yak' and 'Poison Ivy'?

18 Which 1998 David Gray album sold slowly at first but ended up shifting three million copies in the UK? A nine-minute version of which Soft Cell song closes the album?

19 Who offered advice for boys on his 1979 single 'It's Different for Girls'? What's the title of his 1982 album that features his other UK Top 10 single, 'Steppin' Out'?

20 Which downbeat folk-blues classic by Bonnie Dobson has been covered by Tim Rose, Jeff Beck, Robert Plant and the National? Which Californian psychedelic band adopted the song as a signature tune?

21 Elton John didn't have a UK number one single on his own until 1990. Paired with 'Healing Hands' on a double A-side, which song finally took him to the top? Which lyricist, who has worked with John for much of his career, wrote the words?

22 Which song connects American band Grand Funk Railroad to Kylie Minogue? And who wrote it?

23 Muslim singer-songwriter Yusuf Islam performed under which name before his conversion in 1978? What has been his biggest hit in the UK, reaching number two in 1967?

24 *In Between Dreams* became the first Jack Johnson album to top the UK charts in 2005. His next two albums accomplished the same feat – what are they called?

25 Which Irish singer and songwriter supplied female vocals to Damien Rice's album *O*? What was Rice's follow-up album, which reached number four?

26 What has been by far the most successful album of Rufus Wainwright's career to date, reaching number two in the UK and number 23 in the US in 2007? Which father of a friend played guitar on five of the album's 12 tracks?

27 Who looked at love from 'Both Sides Now' in the charts in 1967? Who wrote the song and recorded it two years later on her album *Clouds*?

28 Before his first album, *Every Kingdom,* who released EPs called *Games in the Dark* and *These Waters*? What's the name of his UK chart-topping follow-up album, released in 2014?

29 In Don McLean's 'American Pie', which month made the singer shiver? And from whom did the Jester borrow a coat before singing for the King and Queen?

30 What was Elvis Costello's first UK Top 20 single? And what was 'she' doing while they were dragging the lake?

QUIZ 44

NAME THE BAND #2

As with Quiz 7, we give you the band members and you give us the band. However, there is a catch this time – a key member of the group is missing, and must be identified along with the band. Just to make it harder, it's the most famous one.

Answers: page 498

1   Kelly Rowland, Michelle Williams

2   Jerry Augustyniak, Bob Buck, Dennis Drew, Steve Gustafson, John Lombardo

3   Will Farquharson, Kyle Simmons, Chris Wood

4   Lars-Olof Johansson, Bengt Lagerberg, Magnus Sveningsson, Peter Svensson

5   Bill Berry, Peter Buck, Mike Mills

6   Bob Hardy, Nick McCarthy, Paul Thomson.

7   David Johansen, Killer Kane, Jerry Nolan, Sylvain Sylvain

8   Robin Goodridge, Dave Parsons, Nigel Pulsford

9   David Boulter, Mark Colwill, Neil Fraser, Dickon Hinchcliffe, Alistair Macaulay

10 Guy Berryman, Johnny Buckland, Will Champion

11 Nikolai Fraiture, Albert Hammond Jr, Fabrizio Moretti, Nick Valensi.

12 Zal Cleminson, Chris Glen, Eddie McKenna, Hugh McKenna

13 Chet, Knuckles, Koool G Murder, P-Boo

14 Phil Calvert, Mick Harvey, Rowland S Howard, Tracy Pew

15 Gary Beers, Andrew, Jon and Tim Farriss, Kirk Pengilly

BONUS TRACKS

16 Verden Allen, Dale Griffin, Mick Ralphs, Pete Overend Watts

17 Pete Briquette, Gerry Cott, Simon Crowe, Johnny Fingers, Garry Roberts

18 Paul Heard, Mike Pickering, Shovell

19 Compton Amanor, Charley Anderson, Charley H Bembridge, Desmond Brown, Neol Davies, Gaps Hendrickson

20 Jimmy Chamberlin, James Iha, D'arcy Wretzky

21 Wes Borland, DJ Lethal, John Otto, Sam Rivers

22 Mark Andes, Denny Carmassi, Howard Leese, Ann Wilson

23 Emmy-Kate Montrose, Marie du Santiago, Johnny X

24 Gota, Heitor TP, Tim Kellett, Ian Kirkham, Fritz McIntyre, Shaun Ward

25 Ted Dwane, Ben Lovett, Winston Marshall

26 Olly Betts, Toby Butler, Luke Ford, Dan Higgins

27 Andy Cox, Everett Morton, Saxa, David Steele, Dave Wakeling

28 Pal Jones, Owen Powell, Aled Richards, Mark Roberts

29 Ron Blair, Mike Campbell, Stan Lynch, Benmont Tench

30 Dave Keuning, Mark Stoermer, Ronnie Vanucci Jr

QUIZ 45

EVERYBODY DANCE

Woo-hoo, clap your hands. Dancing to popular music is rarely an edifying spectacle. Maybe that's why Ballroom and Latin have made such a strong comeback – watching people dance properly reminds us it is an art form more honoured in the breach than the observance.

Here is a straight quiz on foot-tappers and hip-shakers: artists and songs that make you get up on your feet, dance to the beat and strut your funky stuff. Get your dancing shoes on.

Answers: page 499

1   Which famous Manchester nightclub of the late eighties and early ninetines was an integral part of the northwest music scene? Which band were part owners of the club?

2   Fatboy Slim's 'Going Out of My Head' sampled the guitar riff and vocals from a cover of which Who song? Which 1996 Fatboy album was the single taken from?

3   The Blue Notes, then Thelma Houston, then the Communards; what's the song? Which 1977 Baccara hit pinched its bassline?

4   'Don't Call Me Baby' went number one in the UK after doing well on the club circuit around the millennium. Who were the band, and where were they from?

5   Whose work on Happy Mondays remixes led to him producing their 1990 album, *Pills 'n' Thrills and Bellyaches*? What divine London dance club lies in the arches under Charing Cross station?

6   Who co-wrote Scissor Sisters' only UK number one, 'I Don't Feel Like Dancin'', with the band? On which album did the song feature?

7   'More Than a Woman' (Tavares), 'Boogie Shoes' (K.C. and the Sunshine Band) and 'Disco Inferno' (the Trammps) all owe some of their success to which seventies soundtrack? Which song off the same album gave Yvonne Elliman a US number one?

8   Who helped with the mixing and added vocals to the 2016 New Order track 'Superheated'? And who sang on 'Tutti Frutti' and 'People on the High Line'?

9   The Prodigy hit their zenith in 1996 with the album *The Fat of the Land*. Which two number one singles did it yield?

10   American dance act The Outhere Brothers had two UK number ones in 1995. What were they?

11   One of the first bands to use remixes and reinterpretations as extra album tracks, the PetShop Boys also released four albums of such remixes. What

generic title did they use for them? And what was different about the final one?

12 Flo Rida's 'Good Feeling' (2012) sampled the same 1962 Etta James song as which hit by Avicii from the previous year? His previous biggest hit heavily sampled 'You Spin Me Round (Like a Record)' – who sang that?

13 Which French band's sing-a-long hit 'D.I.S.C.O.' reached number two in Britain in 1980? Lipps Inc had their only UK hit the same year with which pop-funk number?

14 Under a stage name, Jason Cheetham fronts which funky UK band? What was the title of their 1993 number one debut album?

15 What were David Guetta's two club hits with Australian singer Sia?

BONUS TRACKS

16 Which soul singer had a UK Top 10 hit with 'Reet Petite' in 1957, and a number one when it was re-released in 1986? Who is the former Scottish darts player forever linked to him in some people's minds?

17 What was the hit single that ensured the success of Bastille's 2014 debut album, *Bad Blood*? The follow up, 'Laura Palmer', took its title from a character in which cult TV series?

18 What were the two early nineties chart-topping singles by Snap!, the German Eurodance/techno combo?

19 Who created disco, according to his first (2007) album? According to the first single off this album, when was it acceptable?

20 Róisín Murphy emerged in the 1990s as part of which dance pop duo? What was her third solo album from 2015 that earned a Mercury Prize nomination?

21 Which DJ/producer had a hit with a dance version of Samuel Barber›s *Adagio for Strings* in 2005? Who had a hit with it ten years earlier with the help of a strong dance remix by Ferry Corsten?

22 'Louder' and 'Hot Right Now' were 2011 number ones for which dubstep DJ and producer? Who sang on 'Hot Right Now'?

23 Who added '(For My Love)' to the title of their 1984 single 'Jump' to avoid confusion with Van Halen? What emotion did they express the year before, and again (on re-release) later in 1984, in a song which became their showstopper?

24 Which vocalist sang at least one track on each of the six studio albums by Faithless? What is her other strong connection to the band?

25 Which Belgian-born producer and mixer teamed up with New Zealand singer Kimbra on the best selling single of 2012? What was the song, a number one for five weeks?

26 What dance move did Shalamar's Jeffrey Daniels do on *Top of the Pops* in 1982 during 'A Night to Remember', a year before a musical legend made it his own? What was Shalamar's equally successful follow-up single?

27 Who had a hit with 'Danger! High Voltage' in 2003? Which Queen song did they release as a single in 2004?

28 Whose headline appearance at Glastonbury in 1994 scotched the idea that electronic dance bands couldn't work live? What is the surname of the band's brothers, Paul and Philip?

29 Gwen Dickey was the singer in which seventies and eighties soul/funk band? Which 1976 Richard Pryor comedy gave them a US number one?

30 Diana Ross's tenth solo studio album, entitled simply *diana* (note that lower case) was a career revamp in a disco style masterminded by which production team? What was the lead single, a US number one?

QUIZ 46

ALL MY COLOURS

Colour has infused pretty much every artist's work. Prince's car would have been much less interesting had it just been a *little corvette* (and it wouldn't have scanned). And the White Stripes would never have found fame and fortune if they were just called the Stripes, surely? Hence this colourful quiz.

The first part of the quiz is 15 straight two-part questions. The second part is an identification game. We give you three tracks off an album and you have to give us the artist and album title.

Answers: page 500

1   Which delicate colour gave Procol Harum their only UK number one in 1967? In which 1991 film does a priest admonish a young organist for getting the words to the song wrong as he practices it on the church organ?

2   Who had a minor hit with 'Pretty in Pink' in 1981? Who starred in the lead female role in the John Hughes film that took the song's name as its title and made it chart far higher?

3   For Prince, the rain was this colour – what was for Hendri? And which legendary 1967 rock festival did he showcase the song at?

4   What was Chuck Berry's B-side to 'Too Much Monkey Business', written after he saw cops arrest a Hispanic man for no reason? Who wrote a 1967 classic about an identically endowed girl?

5   '5AM' and 'Crying for No Reason' were hit singles off which 2014 number one album by which London singer?

6   What is the correct title of the Beatles' album generally known as the *White Album*? Which is the only Beatles album to have a colour in its actual title?

7   'Change Gonna Come', 'Wonderful World' and a cool version of the Rolling Stones' 'Satisfaction' are all on which classic 1967 soul album? Which other soul singer wrote the first two songs?

8   Who, respectively, were *Back in Black* in 1980 and *Back to Black* in 2006?

9   Under what name does Alecia Moore usually record? And under what name did she release an album with Dallas Green?

10 Who had a 2011 number one with 'Read All About It'? Who sang guest vocals on the song?

11 What colour was Dorothy Moore's world turned in 1976? Who had a big country hit with the same Bob Montgomery song in 1967?

12 Who had a top ten UK hit with 'Fade to Grey' in 1980? Which prominent eighties pop star co-wrote and produced the song?

13 *To Lose My Life* was the 2009 UK number one debut album by which London band? What was the title of their 2011 follow-up?

14 Which two Davids had hit singles with 'Silver Lady' (1977) and 'Silver Dream Machine' (1980)?

15 Which 1941 song was popularised during the Second World War by Vera Lynn? Who released a version as the B-side to their cover of 'Unchained Melody', the best-selling single of 1995?

BONUS TRACKS

Identify the artist and album from the following tracks.

16 'Turn to Stone'; 'Mr Blue Sky'; 'Wild West Hero' (1977)

17 'Give Me a Reason', 'Irresistible', 'Breathless' (2000)

18 'Nightblindness', 'Say Hello Wave Goodbye', 'Please Forgive Me' (1998)

19 'Fight Test', 'Ego Tripping at the Gates of Hell', 'Do You Realize??' (2002)

20 'Stormkeeper', 'Miss Me Blind', 'Karma Chameleon' (1983)

21 'Bennie and the Jets', 'Saturday Night's Alright for Fighting', 'Candle in the Wind' (1973)

22 'Space Dog', 'Past the Mission', 'Cornflake Girl' (1994)

23 'Bodysnatchers', 'House of Cards', 'Jigsaw Falling Into Place' (2007)

24 'Conversation 16', 'Anyone's Ghost', 'Bloodbuzz Ohio' (2010)

25 'Long and Lost', 'Queen of Peace', 'Ship to Wreck' (2015)

26 'Tank', 'Threatened,' 'Nice 'n' Sleazy' (1978)

27 'Why Don't You Love Me Anymore?', 'Sensitive New Age Guy', 'GMF' (2013)

28 'The Last Time', 'I Knew You Were Trouble', 'State of Grace' (2012)

29 'The Song of Solomon,' 'Top of the City', 'Rubberband Girl' (1993)

30 'World Leader Pretend', 'Stand', 'Orange Crush' (1998)

QUIZ 47

SUNDAY SERVICE WITH JARVIS

Jarvis Cocker has an eclectic approach to his radio show, rarely sticking to a formula and eschewing regular features in favour of whatever is on his mind. So, in equally whimsical fashion, here are 15 questions on a vaguely religious theme for Sunday Service.

The second set of questions concerns Jarvis himself. Pulp were never dull and often entertainingly spiky. Cocker himself has remained an interesting observer on the music scene and life in general. He retains a rock and roll spirit without self-destructive excess. He may not thank us for saying this, but he may even be a national treasure.

Answers: page 500

1   What connects Donny Osmond and Brandon Flowers of the Killers? Which Atlanta-born female soul legend could be added to this strand?

2   Who asked 'What if God was one of us?' in 1995? What was her debut album that it came off?

3   Which Madonna song begins with the singer uttering the word 'God'? Which company cancelled a deal with Madonna after Christian groups in the US panned them for using the song in an ad?

4   'Jesus died for somebody's sins but not mine …' recites Patti Smith at the beginning of which cover from her album *Horses*? Who wrote the original song?

5   What, respectively, were Tom Waits's and Depeche Mode's versions of Jesus?

6   In which Beatles song did Mother Mary come to the singer in times of trouble? What did she speak?

7   Where is Heaven, according to Belinda Carlisle? And how far does Eddie Cochran have to go to get there?

8   Who declared that he had forgiven Jesus in 2004? And what fact about Christ did Bruce Springsteen regurgitate on his 2005 album *Devils and Dust*?

9   Under which name did three members of R.E.M. release an album with Warren Zevon in 1990? Which Prince song did they put out as a single?

10 Who took 'My Sweet Lord' to the top of the UK singles chart in 1970 and 2002? What prompted the second chart entry?

11 'Jesus Doesn't Want Me for a Sunbeam' appeaed on which famous 1994 live album? Which Scottish band recorded the original song (with 'Wants', not 'Doesn't Want') for a 1987 EP?

12 Whose 2009 album *The Life of the World to Come* took its song titles and topics from passages in the bible? And what type of bible were Arcade Fire reading in 2007?

13 Which two major British acts released albums called *Faith* in the 1980s?

14 Who had a UK number four in 1968 with the Bacharach and David song 'I Say A Little Prayer'? Who went two places higher with 'Save a Prayer' in 1982?

15 Frank Sinatra liked to belt out 'Get me to the Church on Time': for which musical was the song written? Which David Bowie song uses the line in its chorus?

BONUS TRACKS

16 Who worked with Jarvis on 'Sliding Through Life on Charm' on her 2002 album *Kissin Time*? Which song from *West Side Story* did they sing together on her later 2008 album *Easy Come, Easy Go*?

17 Which annual London festival did Jarvis curate in 2007? Which 6 Music colleague of Jarvis's curated it in 2016?

18 When Jarvis took a break from 6 Music in 2014, who took over his show on a semi-permanent basis? What time does the show start?

19 Which future 6 Music DJ described 1991 Pulp single 'My Legendary Girlfriend' as a 'throbbing ferment of nightclub soul and teen opera' in the *NME*? It was the first from which album?

20 Which key member of Pulp left the band between *Different Class* and *This is Hardcore*? Mark Webber, who took over guitar duties, was formerly connected to the band in what capacity?

21 What was the name of the band fronted by Jarvis who appeared at a Hogwarts Ball in *Harry Potter and the Goblet of Fire*? Members of which other British group made up much of the backing band?

22 In Pulp's 'Common People', what did 'she' study at St Martin's College? And where did he take her for their first date?

23 Which Pulp album features the songs 'Seductive Barry', 'The Fear' and 'Party Hard'? What was the lead single from the album?

24 What was on the other side of a Pulp double-A side single with 'Sorted for E's and Whizz'? And which newspaper got their knickers in a twist over the single?

25 The video to which Pulp song featured various well-known figures remembering losing their virginity? Which of the following did NOT appear: Reeves and Mortimer, John Peel, Alison Steadman, Jo Whiley?

26 What was the tongue-in-cheek title of the last Pulp single fom the original incarnation of the band in 2002? Whose cover of 'Disco 2000' appeared on the second CD of the single?

27 In 2008 Jarvis released a version of Heaven 17's 'Temptation'. Who sang on the track with him? What other obvious connection did Heaven 17 have with Jarvis Cocker?

28 'Don't Let Him Waste Your Time' and 'Baby's Coming Back to Me' were both on Jarvis's self-named 2006 debut solo album: which veteran singer had he let use both tracks on her own album two years earlier? Which Sheffield musician played guitar on most of the tracks on *Jarvis*?

29 Which major label released all the Pulp albums from their halcyon years? On which famous indie label did he release his solo works?

30 On Jarvis's 2009 album *Further Complications,* the singer stated he had never said he was... what? What sort of blues did he essay on this album?

QUIZ 48

CLASSIC ALBUMS #3:
THE EIGHTIES

The same routine as before. You get three tracks from an album – these are all from the eighties – and think of the name of the album and the name of the artist who recorded it.

Option, again: if you are reading the quizzes out loud, try giving the quizzers two tracks – if they can identify the album from these, they get both points. If they need the third track, which is usually the charm (the big single or stand-out track), then they just get one. You know the drill.

Answers: page 501

1   'Two Hearts Beat As One'; 'New Year's Day'; 'Sunday Bloody Sunday' (1983)

2   'The Yo Yo Man'; 'Seven Seas'; 'The Killing Moon' (1984)

3   'Fat Lady Wrestlers'; 'Lazyitis'; 'Mad Cyril' (1988)

4   'Wave of Mutilation'; 'Monkey Gone to Heaven'; 'Debaser '(1989)

5   'The Lady Don't Mind'; 'Road to Nowhere'; 'And She Was' (1985)

6   'Cold'; 'Siamese Twins'; 'The Hanging Garden' (1982)

7   'I'm Losing You'; 'Watching the Wheels'; '(Just Like) Starting Over' (1980)

8   'One More Chance'; 'King's Cross'; 'It's a Sin' (1987)

9   'Where's the Party?'; 'La Isla Bonita'; 'Papa Don't Preach' (1986)

10 'Scream Like a Baby'; 'Up the Hill Backwards'; 'Fashion' (1980)

11 'Mr Disco'; 'Round & Round'; 'Fine Time' (1989)

12 'Mr Brownstone'; 'My Michelle'; 'Sweet Child o' Mine' (1987)

13 'Walking in Your Footsteps'; 'King of Pain'; 'Every Breath You Take' (1983)

14 'Potholes in My Lawn'; 'Me Myself and I'; 'Magic Number' (1989)

15 'Give the Dog a Bone'; 'Rock and Roll ain't Noise Pollution'; 'Shoot to Thrill' (1980)

BONUS TRACKS

16 'The Flowers of Guatemala'; 'Begin the Begin'; 'Cuyahoga' (1986)

17 'Geisha Boys and Temple Girls'; 'The Height of the Fighting'; '(We Don't Need This) Fascist Groove Thing' (1981)

18 'To Have and to Hold'; 'Strangelove'; 'Never Let Me Down Again' (1987)

19 'Children of the Damned'; 'Hallowed Be Thy Name'; 'Run to the Hills' (1982)

20 'Don't Shoot Shotgun'; 'Rocket'; 'Pour Some Sugar On Me' (1987)

21 'Winter Kills'; 'I Before E Except After C'; 'Only You' (1982)

22 'Air of December'; 'Circle'; 'What I Am' (1988)

23 'African Dance'; 'Jazzie's Groove'; 'Back To Life' (1989)

24 'Arrogance Gave Him Up'; 'Gloomy Sunday'; 'Party Fears Two' (1982)

25 'The Sick Bed of Cuchulainn'; 'Dirty Old Town'; 'A Pair of Brown Eyes' (1985)

26 'Chameleon Day'; 'Happiness Is Easy'; 'Life's What You Make It' (1985)

27 'Aloha from Hell'; 'How Far Can Too Far Go?'; 'Can Your Pussy Do the Dog?' (1986)

28 'Shore Leave'; 'Gin Soaked Boy'; 16 'Shells from a Thirty-Ought-Six' (1983)

29 'Kissing a Fool'; 'Father Figure'; 'I Want Your Sex' (1987)

30 'Driven Like the Snow'; 'Lucretia My Reflection', 'This Corrosion' (1987)

QUIZ 49

MADONNA

She emerged in the eighties as a saucy siren and has bestraddled the pop world like a peroxide colossus ever since. You need a special kind of determination to remain on top of music and all of pop's trends for more than 30 years – but then, Madonna has never exactly lacked for determination. Two parts to this quiz: the first on Madonna herself, the second on blonde singers who have taken her as an inspiration.

Answers: page 502

1 Who wrote Madonna's massive 2000 hit 'American Pie'? For which film starring herself and Rupert Everett did she record her version?

2 Which film actor did Madonna divorce in 1989? Which director did she marry in a lavish ceremony in 2000?

3 Madonna whipped up a media frenzy by kissing which singer at the 2003 MTV awards? Who else did she snog moments later?

4 Which Parisian producer and DJ collaborated with Madonna on her 2000 album *Music*? The Guy Ritchie-directed video for which single was banned by some outlets for its violent content?

5 What is the name of the record label founded by Madonna in 1992 together with Time Warner? Which Canadian star's 16 x platinum third album, released in 1995, became its biggest success outside of Madonna's own releases?

6 Madonna's 1985 UK number one 'Into the Groove' was taken from which movie in which she appeared? Who took the lead role?

7 Which New York DJ did Madonna date and bring in to mix her second single, 1983's 'Burning Up'? What was her next single – her big breakthrough hit?

8 What was Madonna's first US number one single? How about in the UK?

9 What was Madonna wearing on her head on the cover for her 2000 album, *Music*? What was the name of the tour that promoted this album?

10 What was the subject matter of the 2011-12 movie *W.E.* directed by Madonna? Which song did she write especially for the film and later include on her 2012 album, *MDNA*?

11 What album of jazz and swing numbers did Madonna release as the soundtrack to 1990's *Dick Tracy*? Who was her co-star in the film who duetted on a couple of numbers?

12 After 1990's *Vogue*, Madonna had to wait another eight years for her next UK number one: what was it? Which well-known DJ and producer worked on this track?

13 Which two guys, a pop star and a rapper/producer, appeared on '4 Minutes', a hit single off *Hot Candy* (2008)?

14 Which album did Madonna release simultaneously with her book *Sex*? What erotic thriller did she star in the following year?

15 Which 1999 film soundtrack gave Madonna a US number one with 'Beautiful Stranger'? Which movie, in which she starred, led to two UK Top 10 singles in 1997?

BONUS TRACKS

16 Which blonde singer contributed guest vocals to will.i.am's 2012 UK number one 'Scream and Shout'? And whose 2011 single 'S&M' did she also feature on?

17 What band launched the career of Gwen Stefani? What was the title of her third solo album, which topped the US chart in 2016?

18 Christina Aguilera's 2002 album, *Stripped*, sold 13 million copies worldwide. What was the name of her 2006 follow-up? Which huge 2011 Maroon 5 single did she guest on?

19 What is Pink's only UK number one album (released in 2008)? What shouty single off it went to number one?

20 What 1986 title track from Cyndi Lauper's second album was a US number one? Which Marvin Gaye song did she cover on the album?

21 Jenny Frost joined girl group Atomic Kitten in 2001, replacing which tabloid staple? Which TV programme (it coined the term *makeunder*) did Frost present from 2008 to 2011?

22 Who made up the quartet in girl group All Saints alongside the blonde Appleton sisters?

23 Whose 2009 debut *Hands* reached number five in the UK album chart? In which electronic three-piece did she begin her recording career?

24 Which blonde singer appeared on Tinchy Stryder's 2012 single 'Bright Lights'? What was her debut single, a UK number one when she was just 18 in 2009?

25 By what name is New Zealand singer-songwriter Pip Brown better known? Who was the female lead in the 1985 film from which she took her stage name?

These last five questions are all about Lady Gaga, who it is probably fair to call the 21st century Madonna.

26 Lady Gaga's 2009 single 'Telephone' featured which R&B superstar? For which other blonde pop star was the song initially written?

27 When did Gaga play a seven-show residency at the New York's Roseland Ballroom right before it closed down? Which famous street was it on?

28 How did Gaga dress at 2010's MTV Music Video Awards? What did that make her, according to the Smiths in 1985?

29 Who collaborated with Gaga on 2015 album *Cheek to Cheek*? What song did they record together on his 2011 album *Duets II*?

30 Gaga won a 2016 Golden Globe for her performances in the fifth season of which American TV series? What charitable organisation did she set up in 2012?

QUIZ 50

PUNK II

This quiz spotlights the heyday of punk rock in the late seventies, when a handful of young bands blew open the sterile cartel that was strangling rock and roll. It started with Johnny snarling, 'I am an anti-Christ', and finished with the Jam and Blondie dominating the charts. Politically, these were grievous days of rancour and hardship – but musically, they were some of the best of times. Quiz-wise, it's the same old, same old: 30 straight questions, all two-parters.

Answers: page 503

1   'Boredom' became a punk anthem after it appeared on which collectible EP
     released by Buzzcocks in 1977? Who was the band's singer at the time, though
     he left before their debut album saw the light of day?

2   Viv Albertine was the Australian guitarist in which all-female punk band?
     What very clean stage name did their Spanish-born drummer Paloma Romero
     adopt?

3   Pauline Murray was the lead singer of Penetration. What's the title of their
     classic debut single? And which band provided the backing for Murray after
     Penetration broke up?

4   Which band sang 'Top of the Pops' on *Top of the Pops*? Which Sweet song did
     they cover as a live showstopper?

5   Which two singles, the titles of which both contain the then-inflammatory F
     word, did the Dead Kennedys release in 1981 between their first two albums?

6   *Fulham Fallout* was the first album by which punk band, who are still active
     today? An anarchic reworking of which Phil Spector sixties classic featured on
     the album and became a live favourite?

7   Which Sex Pistol produced Bananarama's debut album *Deep Sea Skiving*? And
     which Pistol joined the Damned for 1995's *Not of this Earth*?

8   Which still-active band fronted by Chris Bailey were the premier act on the
     Australian punk rock scene? What was their only single to make the UK
     charts?

9   Which anarchist band ran into problems when their record pressing plant
     refused to press 'Asylum', the opening track on their debut album, and left a
     two-minute gap in its place? What's the title of their third album, on which
     Eve Libertine and Joy de Vivre replaced Steve Ignorant on vocals?

10   Which band advised us to 'clean your teeth ten times a day, scrub away, scrub
     away, scrub away the SR way'? At whom was the advice aimed, according to
     the title of both the song and the album from which it was taken?

11 Fronted by the ill-fated Malcolm Owen, who died of a heroin overdose aged 26, which band first made the charts with 'Babylon's Burning'? What was their biggest hit, a comment on the skinhead following of the emerging ska bands?

12 'Some people think little girls should be seen and not heard. But I think...' What did she think? And who was she?

13 *Teenage Warning* is the title of both the debut album and a UK Top 30 single by which political punk band from the North East? Which Durham figure, who died controversially in police custody in 1976, was the subject of their first single?

14 Which Ramones album contained the dopey punk anthems 'Cretin Hop' and 'Teenage Lobotomy'? And which Searchers song did they cover on their next album, *Road to Ruin*?

15 Which song from *Machine Gun Etiquette* gave the Damned their first UK Top 20 hit? And which Barry Ryan song gave them their only Top 10 entry in 1986?

BONUS TRACKS

16 In 1977, who became the first punk or new wave band to appear on *Top of the Pops* when they performed 'Lookin' After Number One' on the show? What became their first UK number one hit the following year?

17 What was the Sex Pistols' first single? And what was the title of their only studio album?

18 Whose first 1977 album was so good they named it three times? What's the opening track, also so good they named it thrice?

19 Which controversial single hit the charts on 3 June 1977? Which artist, hugely popular throughout the seventies, kept it off the UK number one spot amid allegations that the chart was being rigged?

20 Who were the 'Hersham Boys'? And what was their first UK Top 10 single, a foot-stomping sing-a-long?

21 Who had a hit in 1979 with a punk version of the theme tune to *The Banana Splits*? Which Christmas carol had they butchered for a seasonal single the previous year?

22 Penetration took their name from a song by which band, hugely influential on the punk scene? What's the title of their second album, a follow-up to the brilliant *Moving Targets*?

23 What were the Clash bored with on their first album? And where did they get lost on *London Calling*?

24 Who sang vocals on the Sex Pistols' hit 'No One Is Innocent', released after Johnny Rotten had left the group? And which Eddie Cochran song was their next hit, credited to Sid Vicious backed by the Pistols?

25 Jake Burns sounded like he had been gargling broken glass – with which Irish punk band was he the singer? What's the title of their politically charged debut album?

26 Who was the original bass player with the Damned, still playing with the group today as their guitarist? What is his signature headgear?

27 Eugene Reynolds and Fay Fife were the dual vocalists of which comic book Scottish punk band? What was their tempestuous debut single, released in 1977?

28 *Damaged* is the 1981 debut by which American hardcore band? Which much-covered song did they release as a single the same year?

29 Who released the self-deprecating single 'One Chord Wonders' in 1977? What's the title of their signature song, a paradigm for the entire punk movement?

30 What are the titles of the two UK Top 20 albums released by Buzzcocks in 1978?

QUIZ 51

RAP & HIP HOP

Some of the most dynamic, powerful and politically engaged music of recent years has come from the hip hop fraternity – but so, too, have some of pop's most infectious singles. This two-part quiz looks at both these sides of the hip hop coin, from homegrown talent to West Coast rap, and almost everything in between...

Answers: page 504

1   'U Can't Touch This' and 'Have You Seen Her' were hit singles in 1990 for which rapper, one of the first to deliberately try to cross over into the pop market? What was his signature fashion feature, showcased in his energetic dance routines?

2   Working alongside Jazzy Jeff, what's the real name of the Fresh Prince? And what was their number one hit together?

3   Under what name did Daz Dillinger and Kurupt appear on both Dr Dre's and Snoop Dogg's debut albums? What's the title of their own debut album, released in 1995?

4   Which British female artist was sampled on Eminem's 2000 hit, 'Stan'? 'Thank You', the featured track, first appeared on which 1999 album?

5   'Purple Pills', 'How Come' and 'Shit on You' are all singles by which rap collective, which counts Eminem as a member? The group have significantly reduced their output since which member of the band died in 2006?

6   Who was a college dropout in 2005? Despite this, what did he achieve two years later?

7   Whose album *Licensed to Ill* was one of the biggest-selling albums of 1986? Which artist, then still a relative newcomer herself, gave the band a helping hand when she invited them to be her support act on her 1985 tour?

8   Who had three singles 'Candy Shop', 'Disco Inferno' and 'How We Do' in the US top five in the same week, the first solo artist to achieve this? Which album was the only UK No1 hit for this artist?

9   Which nineties hip hop act from Queens was led by rappers Q-Tip and Phife Dawg, with Ali Shaheed Muhammad as producer? What was the name of the 1996 album that broke the band in the UK?

10 After adopting Rastafarianism in his early forties, which rapper released a reggae album called *Reincarnated* in 2013? Under what name did he release it?

11 Whose first album *1 Polish, 2 Biscuits and a Fish Sandwich* yielded two British number-one singles, 'Don't Stop (Wiggle Wiggle)' and 'Boom Boom Boom'? What's the name of their greatest-hits compilation?

12 What was the original name given to Public Enemy's production team? And who was the group's DJ until 1999, when he was replaced by DJ Lord?

13 Who did Kanye West marry in May 2014? With which distinctly non-hip hop star did Kanye collaborate on the songs 'Only One' and 'FourFiveSeconds'?

14 'Bad Meets Evil' is a collaboration between Eminem and which other rapper? What's the name of their 2011 EP, which topped the US chart and reached the British Top 10?

15 Released in 2000, *Country Grammar* is the bestselling album by which Texan rapper? Who guested on his 2002 single 'Dilemma', a British and American number one?

BONUS TRACKS

16 Which British hip hop artist made his debut in 1999 with *Brand New Second Hand*? What's the anthemic single from his second album *Run Come Save Me*, in which the singer describes himself as 'Scum of the earth/His worth was nil until he gained the skill of tongues'?

17 What's the faintly paranoid title of Tupac Shakur's third album, his first to top the US charts? Which track from the follow-up, *All Eyez on Me*, gave 2Pac and his collaborator Dr Dre their first American number one?

18 Who had a number one in 1995 in most major music territories with 'Gangsta's Paradise'? On which British reality TV programme did he appear in 2009?

19 On which classic 1988 album, by which short-lived Californian act, is the title track followed by 'Fuck Tha Police' and 'Gangsta Gangsta'?

20 Jay Z's 2010 album was inspired by and shared a title with which 2007 Ridley Scott film? Which other movie inspired a 2002 hit single by Jay Z featuring Beyoncé, taken from Jay Z's album *The Blueprint 2*?

21 What was the name of the alter ego that Eminem featured on his first major label album? And which two albums, released in 2000 and 2013, saw the rapper revert to his given name?

22 Who wanted to *Thank Us Later* in 2010, then advised us to *Take Care* a year after that? What did the same artist want us to listen to in 2016?

23 Sen Dog, B-Real and DJ Muggs found success in the nineties as which West Coast rap band? How, culturally, were they different from most big rap acts of the same era?

24 Which two high-profile rappers were shot and killed in drive-by shootings in September 1996 and March 1997, the height of the hip hop feuds?

25 Who had a British number one alongside Faith Evans with 'I'll Be Missing You' in 1997? And which band's earlier hit did it rework?

26 Who attacked his former NWA bandmates in the notorious rap 'No Vaseline', which appears on his second album *Death Certificate*? What's the title of the 1992 follow-up, the artist's only American number-one album?

27 Which two singles, one a collaboration with Kanye West and Rihanna, the other a homage to New York featuring Alicia Keys, helped to turn Jay Z's 2009 album *The Blueprint 3* into a worldwide hit?

28 What followed *The Eminem Show* (2002)? And what came after *Relapse* (2009)?

29 Who guested on the Drake singles 'Take Care' (2012) and 'Too Good' (2016)? And on which 2010 single by this artist, a number one in the UK and the US, did Drake provide guest vocals?

30 Which band's first five albums were entitled *Club Classics* Volumes I to V? In what way was Volume IV different?

QUIZ 52

PEOPLE'S PLAYLIST:
DATE STAMP

Another fantasy playlist, this time themed around days and dates. It's a little tricky, as the theme has different aspects to it, but just try to keep in mind that somewhere in there will be something linked to time and how we measure it. There are 40 fast questions: keep your answers concise and try to limit yourself to five minutes for the quiz. You can always cheat a bit if you're still on Number 12.

Answers: page 504

1   Which song topped the indie charts for 13 consecutive weeks in 1983?

2   Who were 'Living After Midnight' in 1980?

3   What did Kasabian erase from memory on *Velociraptor!*?

4   What came before 'Everything After' for Counting Crows?

5   Whose debut album was called *Tuesday Night Music Club*?

6   What was Patti Smith's year on her 1997 album *Peace and Noise*?

7   Who got his first real six-string in the 'Summer of '69'?

8   For how long did Bloc Party declare they would keep going in 2005?

9   Who had a UK Top 30 hit in 1984 with a cover of Abba's 'The Day Before You Came'?

10 Matthew Healy is the lead singer in which dated band?

11 Who were in love on Friday in 1992?

12 David Gavurin and Harriet Wheeler have taken an indefinite sabbatical in order to bring up their children. With which band did they previously enjoy success?

13 What was the second British number one to be taken from Blondie's *Parallel Lines*?

14 Who released an album and toured a live show presenting *1,000 Years of Popular Music*?

15 According to their second single, what time of day does it for Arctic Monkeys?

16 Who sang about just another 'Manic Monday'?

17 To what was Coldplay's 2016 hymn dedicated?

18 Who were in the British Top 10 at precisely '12:51' in 2003?

19 What has been Hazel O'Connor's biggest UK hit?

20 Who warned us that 'Anything Can Happen in the Next Half Hour' in 2007?

21 'The '59 Sound' was the debut single and first major label album by which New Jersey band?

22 Who was working the 'Midnight Shift' in 1956?

23 Which night was 'Alright for Fighting', according to Elton John?

24 What was Paul McCartney's first solo single?

25 Who recorded a cover of Zager & Evans' 'In the Year 2525' on his 2009 album *My Way*?

26 After which month did U2 name their second album?

27 How and when did Editors release their third album in 2009?

28 Which Easybeats song did David Bowie have on his mind on 1973's *Pin Ups*?

29 When did the Kings of Leon want us to 'Come Around' on their fifth album?

30 Which female singer had a hit with a cover of the Rolling Stones' Ruby Tuesday?

31 Who identified 'Time' as the 'Clock of the Heart' in 1982?

32 Which year was Scottish singer-songwriter Al Stewart singing about in 1976?

33 What year was it for Prince in 1982?

34 In 2008, where did Mark Lanegan and Isobel Campbell spend their Sunday?

35 What 'never happened at all' for the Undertones in 1980?

36 What daily phenomenon did Example want to witness on the first single from his album *Won't Go Quietly*?

37 Which Britpop band did she leave on a Friday?

38 Who sang about 'Thursday' on their 2013 album *Electric*?

39 Which Scottish band wished us 'Happy Birthday' in 1981?

40 How was Robbie Williams two years early in 1998?

QUIZ 53

KEEP IT IN THE FAMILY

Brothers and sisters, fathers and daughters, mothers and sons. Just as plenty of families have made waves throughout rock and roll history, so the family has been the subject of obsession and reflection for many a singer and songwriter. This quiz comes in two parts: the first features 15 questions about siblings, parents and children in rock and roll, while the second is a quickfire burst of questions on songs or bands with a familial reference. You'll figure it out.

Answers: page 505

1 Which two brothers play in Spandau Ballet?

2 Twin sisters Kelley and Kim Deal shared guitar duties in which nineties rock band? What's the title of the band's second album, their only UK Top10 hit?

3 Karen Carpenter died in 1983 aged only 32 from complications associated with which disorder? As well as singing, what was Karen's role in the band?

4 Which celebrity couple had a daughter named Blue Ivy Carter in 2012?

5 Over the last 30 years, two high-profile Scottish bands have had a pair of brothers called Reid at the core. Which bands?

6 Who are the brothers at the heart of Arcade Fire? And which band member is married to the elder of the two brothers?

7 Two pairs of siblings, the Stodarts (Romeo and Mchele) and the Gannons (Sean and Angela), make up which indie rock band? Which single gave the group their first UK hit in 2005?

8 Which two rock stars are the fathers of Chrissie Hynde's daughters, Natalie and Yasmin?

9 Rufus Wainwright is the son of folk singer Loudon Wainwright III and which Canadian singer, one of a famous pair? In 2006, Rufus performed a series of shows in celebration of which Hollywood star?

10 Eliza Carthy is the fiddle-playing folk daughter of Martin Carthy and which other lauded folk singer? What's the title of the Anglo-American album Eliza made with Tim Eriksen in 2015?

11 Paul Simon has been married three times, the second and third times to an actress and a singer respectively. Who?

12 Who were Brian Wilson's two brothers in the Beach Boys? How is Mike Love related to the Wilsons?

13 Which band is made up of four siblings called Andrea, Caroline, Sharon and Jim? Released in 1997, what has been their biggest-selling album so far?

14 Brothers Caleb, Nathan and Jared, plus cousin Matthew on guitar, are the members of which group? From which US city, more commonly associated with country music, do they hail?

15 What are the names of Madonna's eldest two children, a girl by her first husband and a boy by her second?

BONUS TRACKS

16 Which brotherly group had a worldwide hit in the seventies with 'If I Said You Had a Beautiful Body Would You Hold It Against Me'?

17 Jake Shears and Ana Matronic sing in which New York pop band?

18 Who sang about 'The Blower's Daughter' on his debut album, O?

19 Who was doin' it for herself alongside Annie Lennox on the Eurythmics' 'Sisters Are Doin' It for Themselves'?

20 Who wrote about a 'Mother and Child Reunion' in 1972?

21 Who sang about being a 'Coal Miner's Daughter'?

22 Who were *Hormonally Yours* in 1992, an album that contained their big hit 'Stay'?

23 *No Depression*, a magazine covering the Americana scene, takes its name from the 1990 debut album by which band?

24 Which goth group used a drum machine called Doktor Avalanche, the only permanent member of the band along with singer Andrew Eldritch?

25 Which of the original Felice Brothers left the band and formed the Duke and the King?

26 In 2010, *Brothers* was the breakthrough album for which blues-rock duo?

27 On which album did David Bowie sing about 'The Bewlay Brothers' in 1971?

28 'Oh Sister' closes side one of which classic Dylan album, released in 1976?

29 Which band did Blaine Harrison form with his dad while still at school, going on to release their first album, *Making Dens*, in 2006?

30 *Cadenza* and *O Shudder* are the 2011 and 2015 albums by which British art-rock band?

31 *Fear Fun* (2012) was the first album to be released by Josh Tillman under which alter ego?

32 *Beauty Queen Sister* is the 13th studio album by which country rock duo, standard-bearers for the LGBT scene in rock for over 20 years?

33 According to their 1971 hit, who was the brother of Free singer Paul Rodgers?

34 Released in 2001, *Motherland* is the third solo album by which American singer-songwriter?

35 Which neo-classical bluegrass band reached the US Top 40 with their 2015 album *The Phosphorescent Blues*?

36 Bobby Hatfield and Billy Medley sang as which 'brothers'?

37 What's the title of the 1966 Rolling Stones single about a housewife on tranquilisers?

38 'Money for Nothing' and 'Walk of Life' first appeared on which Dire Straits album?

39 'Cousins' was the lead-off single from which band's second album, *Contra*, released in January 2010?

40 'Big Brother' is the closing track on which Kanye West album?

41 Which Scottish post-punk band of this century acquired a cult following with their second album *The Repulsion Box*?

42 *White Men Are Black Men Too*, according to whom in 2015?

43 *Gold Mother* is the 1990 album by which much-loved indie band?

44 What's the title of Daughter's debut album, which features ten tracks that all have single-word titles?

45 Which singer formed his own Brotherhood after the dissolution of the Black Crowes?

QUIZ 54

BRITPOP

Almost every new band who emerged in the UK during the nineties was deemed to be part of the Britpop movement, and not everyone enjoyed being pigeonholed. If it had a reliable definition, Britpop could be said to have encompassed bands who paid some kind of homage to the guitar music of yesteryear, whether Stonesy blues-rock, Who-like R&B, Byrdsian jingle-jangle or trippy, Love-like psychedelia. Much of it was derivative, but many Britpop acts gave the old sounds a new twist. These two sections contain 'No Surprises' – that was by Radiohead and they come later...

Answers: page 506

1   Which two eighties stars joined forces to release three albums under the moniker Electronic?

2   Crispin Hunt was the singer in which Britpop band, who enjoyed success with their albums *The Sun Is Often Out* and *Mobile Home*? Who was their lead guitarist, nominated for the Mercury Music Prize in 2007 for *Coles Corner*?

3   With which two bands is John Power associated, the first as bass player and backing vocalist in the late eighties and the second as singer, songwriter and guitarist in the nineties?

4   'As Good as It Gets' is the title of both a UK Top 30 single and a 2001 best-of compilation by which nineties pop band? What's the title of their 1995 debut album, which helped the group win the first NME New Act of the Year award?

5   Which album followed *A Storm in Heaven* (1993) and *A Northern Soul* (1995)? Which single from it borrowed a riff from a string arrangement of 'The Last Time' by the Rolling Stones?

6   Coldplay had to wait eight years for their first British number one single – but which song, the first single from their album *A Rush of Blood to the Head*, made number two in 2002? And which former *Pop Idol* finalist kept them off the top with 'Colourblind'?

7   Lee Mavers was the leader of which late eighties indie band? What was the single that gave the band their only UK Top 20 hit?

8   What's the chaotic, 13-minute single by Flowered Up that seemed to encapsulate the party-till-you-drop atmosphere of the early nineties rave rock scene? What was the surname of brothers Liam and Joe, who were the core of the band?

9   Which Britpop band reached their *Maximum High* in 1996? Which single from the previous year gave the band their biggest hit?

10 In what way did *The X-Files* contribute to the success of Welsh band Catatonia in the 1990s? What's the title of their second album, a British number one on the back of two successful singles?

11 Who were 'Caught by the Fuzz' in 1994? And what's the title of the group's debut album on which the single appears?

12 Who brought *1977* to 1995? And which film from the former year was strongly referenced on the album?

13 Which member of Blur helped write 'Vindaloo', the 1998 England World Cup song? Which actor and comedian wrote the lyrics and sang/spoke the words?

14 Which band topped the British albums chart with the mononymically-titled *K* in 1996? Which scion of an acting family still serves as the band's frontman?

15 Who co-wrote Suede's early hits with guitarist Bernard Butler? Under which name did the duo revive their partnership for a one-off album in 2005?

BONUS TRACKS

16 What connects John Wayne to the Britpop band behind *This World and Body* (1996)? Phil Cunningham, the band's guitarist, joined which other band in 2001 and remains a permanent member?

17 Which member connects the Stone Roses with Primal Scream? And which sporting passion connects him to the Gallagher brothers?

18 Up to 2016, what have been Coldplay's two British number one singles?

19 Which band, who found success in the nineties after a decade of struggle, began their career with 'Arabicus' as a prefix to their name? And what's the title of their 1983 debut album?

20 In 1995, whose debut album was *Smart* enough to reach the British Top 10? What facetious name was given to the less vocal members of the band?

21 What were the two UK Top 10 singles taken from Happy Mondays' 1990 album *Pills 'n' Thrills and Bellyaches*?

22 Which very positive single took Bernard Butler into the Top 10 after he left Suede? Which singer was co-credited on it?

23 What's the title of the Stone Roses' long-awaited second album? Which track was released as the first single, giving the band their biggest hit?

24 Who had a hit with 'This Is How It Feels' in 1990? Which young guitar technician with the band went on to achieve a level of success his former employers never came close to matching?

25 Which band was fronted by Justine Frischmann? With which other artist did Frischmann have a long-standing relationship?

26 Which Welsh band were the first to sign to Richard Branson's V2 label, making their debut with 'Local Boy in the Photograph'? Who is still the band's songwriter, singer and leader?

27 Which Britpop latecomers first entered the Top 20 in 1996 with 'Stripper Vicar', the third in a series of numbered EPs? What's the title of their debut album that followed in 1996, topping the British charts?

28 Lou Reed, Snoop Dogg, De La Soul, Mark E Smith and Mick Jones all appeared on which 2010 album by Damon Albarn's Gorillaz? Which soul legend appeared alongside Mos Def on the single 'Stylo'?

29 In 1995, Robson & Jerome's number one singles 'Unchained Melody' and 'I Believe' ensured that two Britpop classics only reached number two. Which songs by Pulp and Oasis suffered at the hands of the winsome twosome?

30 *Unfinished Monkey Business* is the 1998 debut solo album by which singer? Who provided vocals on his 2007 single 'Illegal Attacks'?

QUIZ 55

SOUL DIVAS

Lots of throat lozenges, lots of lemon and honey, now work those vocal chords, lady! Here is a section on the full-voiced women of the world of R&B. High notes and hissy fits abound. OK, you don't hear too much of this stuff on 6 Music, but you need to know your history...

Answers: page 507

1   What was Janet Jackson's 2015 comeback album? What is the nickname of James Harris III, who, along with Trevor Lewis, helped to write most of the album (and many of her previous hits)?

2   Which BRIT School graduate singer shaved her head for Red Nose Day 2012? How did her 2011 debut single suggest we should 'do it'?

3   Anita, Bonnie, June, Ruth and extended family members Issa and Sadako have all been in which singing group? Which Bruce Springsteen song gave them their first US Top 10 single in 1979?

4   *What's the 411?* Whose debut album was that – and what was her album in 1997, five years later, which was a US number one?

5   Who recorded a number of jazz and swing standards for the 1999 film *Swing*, in which she starred? What was her sole UK number one single (1989)?

6   Who sang with Rip, Rig + Panic in the early eighties? What was the title of her 1989 debut solo album?

7   Which are the only three singles to spend more than seven weeks at number one in Britain since the millennium?

8   On which two US number one singles has Rihanna collaborated with Eminem?

9   What was Gabrielle's number one debut single of 1993? Which boy band sang with her on the 1996 hit 'If You Ever'?

10 LaTavia Roberson, LeToya Luckett and Farrah Franklin were all early members of which band? Which other former member has sold over 100 million records as a solo artist?

11 Who was the world's best-selling artist in the 1990s? With whom did she collaborate on 'One Sweet Day', which spent a record 16 weeks at number one in the US?

12 Whose 2013 debut album *Sing to the Moon* (2013) earned her a Mercury nomination? What variation on the same album was released the following year?

13 Natalie Renee McIntyre's debut album was 1999's *On How Life Is*; what is her stage name? And what 2001 follow-up topped the UK chart?

14 Who is the second biggest-selling *X Factor* alumnus after One Direction? What was the title of her 2007 debut album?

15 Whose video for her 'Window Seat' single showed the singer stripping naked on the empty streets of Dallas? What titles were her 'state of America' albums of 2008 and 2010 released under?

BONUS TRACKS

16 Whose *The Breakthrough* album of 2005 featured tracks recorded with 50 Cent, will.i.am, U2 and Jay-Z? What was the U2 song, which became her biggest UK single?

17 What are Beyoncé's two UK number one singles on which Jay-Z appears as a guest vocalist?

18 Which group's original line-up was Terry Ellis, Cindy Herron, Maxine Jones and Dawn Robinson? What did they call their hugely successful second album?

19 What train gave Gladys Knight and the Pips their first UK Top 10 single in 1973? Which Bond movie gave Gladys her first solo UK Top 20 single, 16 years later?

20 Which singer and pianist's 1990 album *Circle of One* topped the UK chart? Which British band 'discovered' her and showcased her talent on their *Seeds of Love* album?

21 Born Michelle Wallen, which UK singer's most successful album was her 1988 debut, *So Good*? Which BBC makeover and fashion show did she present in 2006 and 2007?

22 What was Diana Ross's 1985 UK number one single? Which tremulous superstars wrote it and sang backing vocals?

23 Whose self-named 1993 album and 1996 follow-up *Secrets* both went eight-times platinum in the US? Which single then became the second-biggest selling of all time by a female artist?

24 What were the sole UK Top 10 hits for soul singers Anita Ward (1979) and Stacy Lattislaw (1980)?

25 Which soul singer sang soprano on Stevie Wonder's *Fulfillingness' First Finale* album then had a 1976 solo hit with 'Free'? Two years later, she sang 'Too Much, Too Little, Too Late' with which crooner?

26 *Como Ama una Mujer* was the fifth (and first Spanish language) album by which US superstar in 2007? Her breakthrough film role came in 1997: which late Latin singer was it a biopic of?

27 Who sang 'Street Life' in 1979, the sole crossover chart hit for US jazz band the Crusaders? Which 1997 Tarantino movie featured a faster version of the song by the same singer?

28 Which 1993 album was the only UK number one for Janet Jackson? (Write down the answer – for two points, the idiosyncratic styling needs to be perfect).

29 Under what name does Helen Folasade Adu perform? What was the title of her 1984 debut album?

30 T-Boz Watkins & Chilli Thomas are the two remaining members of which hip hop trio? Which third member died in a 2002 car crash, aged 30?

QUIZ 56

THE NUMBERS GAME #2

You remember Quiz 23? This works the same. Question one requires one answer, question two requires two, right up to question ten, which requires ten. (As before, we have a 'bonus' question, 5a, to help the numbers to even out)

Answers: page 507

1   The Eagles, so huge in the US, never matched that success in the UK. What was their only UK Top 10 single, in 1977?

2   What were the Chemical Brothers two number one singles?

3   What were Manfred Mann's three number ones, including their Dylan cover?

4   Name T. Rex's four UK number ones.

5   Between 1999 and 2007 Stereophonics released five albums, all of which went number one. Name them.

5a Who were the five original members of Take That?

6   What are PiL's six Top 30 singles to date?

7   What were David Bowie's five UK number one singles? Two were collaborations with other artists, whom you must name to collect all the points.

8   *Uno!*, *Dos!* and *Tré!* were the ninth, tenth and eleventh Green Day albums when released in consecutive months in 2012. What were the first eight?

9   Can you name all nine wives of the four main members of the Beatles?

10 Name the ten acts who spent the most weeks on the UK chart in the seventies. Clues: there are six solo artists, two bands and two artists who are a bit of both. There are two Americans and seven British acts. There are two acts with a recognisable female presence and three of the artists (or their star turns) are deceased.

QUIZ 57

MAKING MUSIC

Another two-part quiz. Part one takes on a variety of topics relating to musicians, their equipment and the process of making a record. Part two, by contrast, is a quick quiz about transient, pointless but often commercially lucrative music awards. As usual, there are 15 questions in each section.

Answers: page 508

1 Who was the drummer in the Beatles from 1960 to 1962, leaving before Beatlemania? With which band did Chad Channing have a similar experience, vacating the drummer's seat before his bandmates made it big?

2 Which session drummer, briefly a member of the Joe Meek-produced band the Tornados, played on no fewer than 44 UK number one singles? Which up-and-coming-at-the-time actor-presenter, now a huge star, played him in *Telstar*, a film about Meek's career?

3 Which fashion designer pioneered the punk look in the seventies? Which band was apparently 'invented' in 1980 by Malcolm McLaren partly to promote her fashions?

4 A mix tape was the term originally given to a home-made cassette (or, later, a CD) that one might make for a friend. What does the term represent in today's hip hop world?

5 Designed to promote independent music shops, which event takes place in mid-April every year? Which band served as the event's ambassador in 2016, releasing a live LP recorded in Paris in aid of the victims of the 2015 terrorist attacks?

6 'I Heard It through the Grapevine' (Marvin Gaye, 1985), 'Wonderful World' (Sam Cooke, 1985), 'Stand by Me' (Ben E King, 1987), 'When a Man Loves a Woman' (Percy Sledge, 1987), 'C'mon Everybody' (Eddie Cochran, 1988), 'Mannish Boy' (Muddy Waters, 1988), 'Be My Baby' (the Ronettes, 1989) and 'Nobody Home' (BB King, 1989). What's the connection?

7 What brand and model of guitar did Jimi Hendrix favour? Developed in the sixties, which effects pedal favoured by Hendrix also defines the opening of Isaac Hayes' 'Theme from *Shaft*'?

8 Which album by which artist was described as follows in *Mojo* magazine upon its release in 2005: '[It] finds her at very best, where daring conceits... emotional nudism and neoclassical sonics culminated in a mood-altering crypto-Balearic tranceathon.'

9   Who hosted a rock show every Friday on BBC 6 Music from 2002 to 2010? His last show was a tribute to which former Rainbow vocalist, who died in 2010?

10 Led by Storm Thorgerson, which design company created the sleeves for such albums as Floyd's *Dark Side of the Moon*, 10cc's *Sheet Music*, Led Zeppelin's *Houses of the Holy* and Genesis's *The Lamb Lies Down on Broadway*? The company's album cover for *Force It* was particularly controversial – but for which band was it designed?

11 Which two of these guitarists does not or did not play left-handed: Ritchie Blackmore, Kurt Cobain, Jimi Hendrix, Tony Iommi, Paul McCartney and Jack White?

12 Which singer learned to dance from modern artiste Lindsay Kemp and appeared in a Lyons Maid commercial while trying to make his way as a recording artist? Originally released in 1967, which novelty song of his found its way to number six after he'd had his first number one hit?

13 The Korg PS-3300, the ARP Odyssey and the Yamaha GX-1 are all early examples of what type of instrument? Which smaller version from the same family was produced between 1970 and 1981 and was widely used in live performances?

14 What are Blackie, Brownie, the Fool and Lucy? Who was given Lucy as a gift in 1968?

15 What's the name of the small pair of cymbals that sit one above the other on a stand, and are operated by a foot pedal? Whose use of the Ludwig drum kit on an American TV show helped make it make the most popular type of drum kit in the sixties?

BONUS TRACKS

16 The Brit Awards were broadcast live for the first time in 1989. Which presenters, a rock star and a Page 3 model, had a nightmare with the autocue and presided over what became a laughing stock both within and outside the industry?

17 In the 21st century, two artists have won the Brit Award for Best British Female Solo on two occasions. Who won in 2002 and 2004? And who followed suit in 2012 and 2016?

18 Who hijacked the Brits in 1992, firing a machine gun (loaded with blanks) into the audience, announcing their retirement from the music industry, dispatching a motorcycle courier to collect their award and sending a dead sheep to the after-show party? Which hardcore band did they persuade to open the show with them?

19 Which annual entertainment was invented by Marcel Bezençon in 1956? And who described it as a 'monument to magnificent foolishness'?

20 Which politician was soaked by a member of Chumbawamba at the Brits in 1998? Ten years later, which comedian and presenter was shoved out of the way and accused of being drunk by Sharon Osbourne when he struggled with a faulty autocue?

21 Which pop star hit the headlines when he wiggled his bum behind Michael Jackson while the King of Pop was performing at the 1996 Brits? Which song was Jackson singing at the time?

22 What piece of iconic clothing, which later sold at auction for nearly £50,000, did Geri Halliwell first wear at the Brits in 1997? And who used the ceremony in 2014 to send a message, read by Kate Moss, that encouraged Scotland to vote to stay in the UK?

23 Who is the only one of these four acts to have won a Grammy Award: Guns n' Roses, Led Zeppelin, REM and Sting? And who is the only member of this

quartet never to have won a Grammy: Bruce Springsteen, Bob Dylan, David Bowie and George Michael?

24 Chuck Berry, James Brown and Ray Charles were among the first members inducted into which new 'society' on 23 January 1986? In which US state are the organisation's headquarters?

25 Who won the *NME*'s Dickhead of the Year award between 1997 and 1999 (in 1997, it was awarded to the Arse of the Year)? To which more wholesome title was it changed over the next few years, when Robbie Williams was a regular winner?

26-30 For these last five questions, we'll list five nominees for the Mercury Music Prize from a particular year. Tell us the year – and tell us which of these acts won the award.

26 *19* by Adele, *Do You Like Rock Music?* by British Sea Power, *The Seldom Seen Kid* by Elbow, *Stainless Style* by Neon Neon and *In Rainbows* by Radiohead.

27 *A Rush of Blood to the Head* by Coldplay, *Permission to Land* by the Darkness, *Boy in da Corner* by Dizzee Rascal, *So Much for the City* by the Thrills and *Quixotic* by Martina Topley-Bird.

28 *Rafi's Revenge* by Asian Dub Foundation, *International Velvet* by Catatonia, *Bring It On* by Gomez, *This Is Hardcore* by Pulp and *Life thru a Lens* by Robbie Williams.

29 *The Sea* by Corinne Bailey Rae, *Tongue n' Cheek* by Dizzee Rascal, *Sky At Night* by I Am Kloot, *Sigh No More* by Mumford & Sons and *xx* by The xx.

30 *Wake Up!* by the Boo Radleys, *Leftism* by Leftfield, *Days Like This* by Van Morrison, *Dummy* by Portishead and *Maxinquaye* by Tricky.

QUIZ 58

PEOPLE'S PLAYLIST: OUT OF TOWN

Rock bands and musicians are generally pretty urban creatures – perhaps they need people around them, both to give them something to write about and to provide an audience to listen to what they do. Here's a playlist based around those times that musicians reflect on the natural world outside the metropolis: walking through the woods, rubbing your toes in the sand, skinny-dipping under the waterfall. You know the sort of thing. Keep it brief and don't come up for air unless you really have to. Five minutes and you're almost there, as the Stranglers once said.

Answers: page 508

1 Which natural phenomenon did the Killers observe on *Sam's Town*?

2 Where did Toyah see 'Thunder' in 1981?

3 Who sang about a 'Waterfall' on their 1989 debut album?

4 Who went 'River Deep – Mountain High' in 1966?

5 Who was in the 'Same Trailer' but a 'Different Park' in 2013?

6 *Big Hits (High Tide and Green Grass)* was the first compilation released by which major rock band in 1966?

7 Who twisted the title of that album in their country-rock classic from 1975, 'Green Grass and High Tides', a ten-minute track that out-Skynyrds Lynyrd Skynyrd?

8 Who wanted *Room to Roam* in 1990 and were *A Rock in the Weary Land* ten years later?

9 *High Land, Hard Rain* is the debut album by which tuneful eighties band?

10 Who, in 1968, set themselves up as *The Village Green Preservation Society*?

11 Kate Bush's 'Flower of the Mountain' is a reworking of which title track from an earlier Bush album?

12 Who claimed they could 'Hear the Grass Grow' in 1967?

13 Who felt the 'Ocean Spray' in 2001?

14 Who were in the 'Warm Foothills' on their second album in 2014?

15 Which Irish indie folk band's 2010 debut *Becoming a Jackal* was nominated for the Mercury Music Prize?

16 Who sang to us 'From a Mountain in the Middle of the Cabins' on their 2008 album *Pretty. Odd*?

17 Wht's the title of My Morning Jacket's 2015 album, their first for four years?

18 Whose signature tune was the 1971 composition 'Take Me Home, Country Roads'?

19 Who took the same song into the UK Top 20 in 1973?

20 Who offered us some 'Country Feedback' on their 1991 album *Out of Time*?

21 What did 'Every Teardrop' become on Coldplay's *Mylo Xyloto*?

22 Whose fourth album, released in 1974, was *Country Life*?

23 Who did a 'Misty Mountain Hop' on their fourth album?

24 *The Place I Left Behind* (2011) and *Jubilee* (2013) are critically acclaimed albums by which Canadian alt.country band?

25 Which Liverpool band were sailing on the 'Seven Seas' in 1984?

26 Which album was Pink Floyd's farewell in 2014?

27 Who promised us *Tomorrow the Green Grass* on their 1995 album, the follow-up to their acclaimed *Hollywood Town Hall*?

28 What was the first single to be taken from Biffy Clyro's 2008 album *Only Revolutions*?

29 Which Scottish rock band went to *The Remote Part* in 2002?

30 What was the only UK Top 10 single for the Skids?

31 Who followed the 'Rocky Mountain Way' in 1973?

32 Which London waterway did Adele sing about on *25*?

33 Whose 1969 album *Green River* contains the band's best-known song, 'Bad Moon Rising'?

34 Which British chart-topping album from 2012, which has gone on to sell over two million copies, includes songs called 'Mountains' and 'River'?

35 Which Canadian rockers had a *Wilderness Heart* in 2010?

36 Which song on U2's album *The Joshua Tree* was dedicated to a former Maori roadie killed in a car crash?

37 What were 'back in Louisiana, about a mile from Texarkana'?

38 Which topographical feature gave Boney M the biggest-selling single of 1978?

39 Which UK country band were 'Brave' in 2015?

40 Which heavy rock band urged us to 'Run to the Hills' in 1982?

QUIZ 59

NIRVANA

They lasted only seven years and made just three studio albums, but Nirvana made an impact that went far beyond their home city of Seattle. Part one of this quiz focuses on the band, and on those heady, rowdy days before it all went horribly wrong. It's followed by a name-the-album quiz that spotlights 15 bands who all have some connection to the grunge scene.

Answers: page 509

1 Along with Kurt Cobain, who was the other founding member of Nirvana? What was the unpleasant band name they originally chose?

2 Which independent Seattle label released Nirvana's first album *Bleach*? Roughly how much did it cost to record?

3 What role did Dave Grohl play in Nirvana? What's the name of the supergroup he formed with ex-Led Zeppelin bass player John Paul Jones and Josh Homme of Queens of the Stone Age?

4 Which Shocking Blue song did Nirvana cover for their debut single? And what was their second, a blistering number released between their first and second LPs?

5 Which song from *Bleach* was reworked for the release of the 1993 album *MTV Unplugged in New York*, and was the only track from the album released as a single? On the album, Nirvana were joined by two members of which band, singing two of their songs during the set?

6 'Smells Like Teen Spirit' is the opening track from the album *Nevermind*. Which two tracks follow it?

7 In which year did Kurt Cobain and Courtney Love get married? What's the name of their daughter, born a few months later?

8 What's the title of Nirvana's third album? Which producer was brought in specifically to give it a hardcore edge?

9 What was the title of Nirvana's live electric album, released two years after Kurt Cobain's death? Why was it so named?

10 Which band did Dave Grohl form after Nirvana? What was their debut single, a UK Top 10 hit that did nothing in the US?

11 Butch Vig, who produced *Nevermind*, formed Garbage in 1993. What's his musical role in the band? Which Scottish singer is the group's frontwoman?

12 Garbage's hit single '#1 Crush' appeared on the soundtrack to which Baz Luhrmann film? For which 1999 James Bond movie did the band provide the theme tune?

13 Released in 2002, eight years after Cobain's death, what was Nirvana's final single? Which cover of a David Bowie song, originally released on *MTV Unplugged in New York*, is the only cover to appear on the 2002 best-of compilation *Nirvana*?

14 Whose debut album, dating from 1991, was *Pretty on the Inside*? What was their connection to Nirvana?

15 Who directed the 2005 film *Last Days*, a fictionalised account of the end of Cobain's life? Under what title did an edited version of Cobain's diaries appear in 2002?

BONUS TRACKS

Here are tracks from 15 albums – they're not all grunge, but they've all helped to define the grunge sound. Simply identify the band and the album title.

16 'Where Is My Mind?', 'Bone Machine' and 'Cactus' (1988).

17 'The Trick Is to Keep Breathing', 'Special' and 'I Think I'm Paranoid' (1998).

18 'Wargasm', 'Everglade' and 'Pretend We're Dead' (1992).

19 'Bright Yellow Gun', 'Snakeface' and 'No Way in Hell' (1995).

20 'Immortality', 'Tremor Christ' and 'Spin the Black Circle' (1994).

21 'The Day I Tried to Live', 'My Wave' and 'Black Hole Sun' (1994).

22 'Standing on the Edge', 'The Turning' and 'Orange Airplane' (1986).

23 'Very Ape', 'Scentless Apprentice' and 'Heart-Shaped Box' (1993).

24 'Sedan Delivery', 'Powderfinger' and 'Hey Hey, My My (Into the Black)' (1979).

25 'Pokin' Around', 'Broken Hands' and 'Generation Genocide' (1991).

26 'Porkfist', 'Forever Means' and 'Swallow My Pride' (1988).

27 'On the Brink', 'Yeah Right' and 'Feel the Pain' (1994).

28 'These Days', 'Arlandria' and 'Bridge Burning' (2011).

29 '1979', 'Tonight, Tonight' and 'Bullet with Butterfly Wings' (1995).

30 'Hoover Dam', 'The Act We Act' and 'If I Can't Change Your Mind' (1992).

QUIZ 60

A SONG FOR GUY

Guy Garvey's Finest Hour is actually two, recurring every Sunday afternoon. Guy has lots of features, and often has a theme for the show, around which he weaves his musical choices and personal reflections.

There is a running feature through the show (with a playlist to match on the 6 Music website) called A Song for Guy, in which listeners submit songs they think he would like, could sing or might help in some other, more mysterious way. The artists in this quiz reflect that playlist. We've finished off with a handful of questions about the man himself.

Answers: page 510

1 Which Tom Waits' song was used as the theme tune for the HBO drama series *The Wire*? Which singer, who also acted in the show, supplied the version of the song used for the fifth and final season?

2 *Rabbit Fur Coat* (2006) was Jenny Lewis's debut solo album: with which band did she previously record? Who is her boyfriend, with whom she recorded a 2010 album. *Jenny & Johnny*?

3 Which band, fronted by Andy Fairweather-Low's lilting falsetto, had a UK number one with '(If Paradise Is) Half As Nice' in 1969? Which famous golf course has a tricky three-hole stretch with the same name?

4 Under what name does Sam Beam usually record? Who collaborated with him on 2016 album *Love Letter for Fire*, a series of intimate duets released under his own name?

5 Which 1973 song in a retro rock and roll style from *Don't Shoot Me, I'm Only the Piano Player* gave Elton John his first US number one? Who wrote the lyrics, as he did for all Elton's hits of that era?

6 Henry Binns and Sam Hardaker, two studio techs, formed which chill-out band? Which Australian singer provided vocals on their two most successful albums, *When It Falls* (2004) and *The Garden* (2006)?

7 Which song, with a pseudo-classical title, gave ELO their first hit single? Which song from a movie soundtrack gave them their only UK number one, in conjunction with Olivia Newton-John?

8 Who was Don Van Vliet and what did he call his entourage?

9 Which American star won the Brit award for best international solo artist from 1998-000? Which 1997 album launched him onto the A-list?

10 Who, according to the Kinks in 1970, 'walked like a woman and talked like a man'? What was the follow-up single from the same album, their final UK Top 10 hit?

11 Which band is fronted by sharply dressed New Yorker Hamilton Leithauser? What is their live show-stopper, a 2004 single from their album *Bows + Arrows*?

12 'Chestnut Mare' was written for a planned musical, but was instead released as a 1970 single by which country-rock band? Who provided the distinctive vocals?

13 *Emotional Mugger* (2016) was the eighth album release in eight years by which prolific American indie musician? What is the harder-edged side-project he began in 2013 with guitarist Charles Moothart?

14 Which new waver released *Almost Blue*, a collection of country covers, in 1981? Which Jerry Chesnut song gave him a UK Top 10 hit?

15 Win Butler and Regine Chassagne are the husband-and-wife team in which band? Their 2004 debut album, *Funeral*, was the first album to hit the charts off which independent label?

BONUS TRACKS

16 Who was the *Jesus of Cool*, according to his 1978 debut album? Which band did he form in the late seventies with Dave Edmunds, Billy Bremner and Terry Williams?

17 'I Can Help' (1974) was the only mainstream hit for which country singer, even reaching number one in America? Which Elvis' song did he cover as a follow-up the next year

18 Who declared they were from 'a land own under' as they went to number one in the US, the UK and their native Australia? What was their debut album, which was also a worldwide number one?

19 Who was the vocalist and a guitarist in the nineties indie band Red House Painters? What is the main band name under which he has recorded this century?

20 Which band, now based in Brooklyn, has the Dessner brothers playing guitars and keyboards and the Devendorf brothers as the rhythm sections? Who adds the broody vocals?

21 Which mellow pop band's second album, in 2003, was *Ether Song*? Which single off this album gave them their first UK Top 10 hit?

22 What is the stage name of American singer Chan Marshall? Which 2006 album was her commercial breakthrough?

23 Alun Woodward, Emma Pollock, Stewart Henderson and Paul Savage made up this critically acclaimed band who put out *The Great Eastern* in 2000. Who were they, and which country were they from?

24 What was the New Zealand band formed by Tim Finn and Phil Judd in 1972? And in which band, formed in Melbourne in 1985, did Tim Finn joing his brother Neil in 1990?

25 Which Canadian singer-songwriter scored a breakthrough with her third album, *The Reminder*, in 2007? With which band, that included her friend Bernard Canning, did she tour in the early 2000s?

Our last 5 questions are more A Song *About* Guy – about Guy Garvey and his band

26 Which town near Manchester was the birthplace of Guy Garvey?

27 What prestigious songwriting award did Elbow's 'One Day Like This' win in 2009? Which major sporting event made use of the song in 2012?

28 What is the surname of the brothers, Craig and Mark, in Elbow? What role in the band was played by Richard Jupp, who departed in 2016?

29 The title of the Elbow album *The Seldom Seen Kid* was a line in which single off the album? And which single off *Leaders of the Free World* has the line 'St Peter in satin, he's like Buddha with mace?'

30 What was Elbow's 2001debut album? And what riff on this title did they use for their 2012 collection of B-sides?

QUIZ 61

NEW WAVE

A lot of the bands who benefited from the punk explosion at the end of the seventies weren't punk bands at all. Artists such as Elvis Costello weren't banging out two-chord tracks about being on the dole – but the rapid growth in independent labels and the subsequent frenzy as major labels tried to claim back their unrighteous hegemony gave opportunities to a host of musicians who had been struggling to get airplay. So 'new wave' was coined as a catch-all style: sharing an independent spirit with the punks, but choosing different subject matte and often a very different method of delivery. For a more recent parallel, think Radiohead rising up on the back of Britpop. Here we go: 30 questions in two equal parts.

Answers: page 511

1   Who sang the archetypal song about 'Sex & Drugs & Rock and Roll'? The B-side was a song called 'Razzle in My Pocket' – what was 'Razzle'?

2   Which murderous single from 77, the first Talking Heads album, helped to bring the band their first taste of cult success? Which song from their fourth album *Remain in Light* gave them their first UK Top 20 hit in 1981?

3   'Take Me, I'm Yours' was the first single by which group, who formed in London in the late seventies? Who started his career as the band's keyboard player?

4   *Why Don't You Kill Yourself?* is the blackly humorous title of a 2004 compilation of music by which new wave band, bringing together the three albums they released between 1978 and 1980? What's the title of their third album, which contains the track that gave its name to the compilation?

5   Who joined Talking Heads from the Modern Lovers, another New York new wave band, in the early seventies? Who went on to lead the Modern Lovers into the UK Top 5 with 'Egyptian Reggae' in 1977?

6   What was the 1975 debut single by Television? What was the second single from their debut album, which gave the band their biggest UK hit?

7   Who was the lead singer and guitarist in the Stranglers from 1974 until 1990? Who has filled the same role for the band since 2000?

8   Which two singles took Nick Lowe into the British Top 10?

9   What was the only cover version to appear on any of the eight Talking Heads studio albums? Featuring the singles 'Road to Nowhere' and 'And She Was', which album took the band into the Top 10 of the UK albums chart for the first time?

10 Who are the two main songwriters in Squeeze, who both contribute vocals and guitar to the band?

11 Which mod band included a cover of the theme from the 1960s TV show *Batman* on their debut album? What was the album called?

12　Magazine, Visage, Siouxsie & the Banshees and Public Image Ltd all feature on the CV of which pioneering guitarist? What's the title of the debut single by Magazine on which he announced himself to the world with a searing guitar solo?

13　What was the debut single by cult new wave band Devo, which also appeared on their *B Stiff* EP? Which jerky cover of a Rolling Stones song appeared on the same collection?

14　The Clash never reached the UK Top 10 until a 1991 e-release of which track from *Combat Rock* shot to number one on the back of a Levi's ad? Although two other albums got higher in the charts, what has been their biggest-selling album?

15　What was new in the title of Ian Dury & the Blockheads' debut album in 1977? What mock title did Dury give himself in a controversial single four years later, written as a protest against what the singer saw as the patronising International Year of Disabled Persons?

BONUS TRACKS

16 Apart from 'I Only Want to Be with You', what was the Tourists' only other UK Top 10 hit? Which group did two members go on to form after the Tourists had broken up?

17 Where didn't Elvis Costello want to go? And what did 'The Angels Wanna Wear'?

18 Which single from *Plastic Letters* gave Blondie their first British hit, reaching number two in 1978? Incorporating elements of disco into their new wave sound, what became their first UK number one a year later?

19 Which American landmark lent its title to the first major UK single release by XTC in 1978? And what became their first British Top 10 hit four years later?

20 John Foxx was the leader of the seventies incarnation of which band, who went on to enjoy great success in the eighties? Who replaced him and helped move the band towards a smoother, more commercial sound?

21 Which seven-and-a-half minute track closed *Rattus Norvegicus*, the Stranglers' debut album, and showed that while their aesthetic may have been punk, their sound was far ahead of the game? What was their debut single, which featured a Welsh miner named Eric Clarke playing the saxophone?

22 Who was the keyboard player in the Attractions, Elvis Costello's backing band for much of the first half of his career? Which instrument did Costello play himself?

23 Who enjoyed chart success with the 1979 re-release of his first single 'Is She Really Going Out with Him'? What was the singer (or stand-in model) wearing on the cover of *Look Sharp!*, his debut album?

24 What's the title of Elvis Costello's fourth album, an exploration of sixties soul sounds and ska beats? Which song from the album, also a single, had originally been recorded by soul duo Sam & Dave?

25 Which Blondie single was a cover of a track by the Nerves, an influential pop-punk band from the mid-seventies? What's the other cover on *Parallel Lines*, a straight reworking of a Buddy Holly song?

26 Which band's second album included a 14-minute version of the Lord's Prayer? What's the title of their debut album, which combined basic punk thrash with startlingly sophisticated sounds?

27 Whose single 'The Sound of the Suburbs' was used as the title for a big-selling punk compilation some years later? Taking his surname from a British supermarket chain, who was the band's singer?

28 Who was the tremolo-voiced original singer with Ulster punk band the Undertones? What's the title of the opening song on their second album *Hypnotised*, an acknowledgement of the fluffy nature of their lyrics and a spoof of the Talking Heads' album title *More Songs about Buildings and Food*?

29 What were the adopted 'Ramones' names of the band's three main drummers? Which drummer, best known for his work with Blondie, played two gigs with the band as a stand-in under the name Elvis Ramone?

30 *How Could Hell Be Any Worse?* is the debut album by which American pop-punk band? Who has been the band's singer and mainstay for all 16 of their albums?

QUIZ 62

CLASSIC ALBUMS #4:
THE NINETIES

The decade of grunge and Britpop, but also the time of Take That and the Spice Girls. It's the usual caper with the albums quizzes, where you get three tracks and must name the album and artist.

Once again: if you are reading the quizzes out loud, try giving the quizzers two tracks – if they can identify the album from two they get both points, if they need the third track, which is usually the charm (the big single or stand out track), then they just get one.

Answers: page 512

1   'She's So Strange'; 'Driftwood'; 'Why Does It Always Rain On Me?' (1999)

2   'Daysleeper'; 'Lotus'; 'Hope' (1998)

3   'Kaleidoscope'; 'Polar Bear'; 'Vapour Trail' (1990)

4   'Take the Long Way Home'; 'Hem of His Garment'; 'God is a DJ' (1998)

5   'Save Me'; 'Dirty Water'; 'Sometimes Always' (1994)

6   '911 is a Joke'; 'Leave This off Your Fuckin' Charts'; 'Burn Hollywood Burn' (1990)

7   'Talula'; 'Caught a Lite Sneeze'; 'Professional Widow' (1996)

8   'Classic Girl'; 'Stop!'; 'Been Caught Stealing' (1990)

9   'Pretty Penny'; 'Big Empty'; 'Interstate Love Song' (1994)

10 'Five Man Army'; 'Safe from Harm'; 'Unfinished Symphony' (1991)

11 'Magician (Internally)'; 'Dorita (The Spirit)'; 'Gassed and Stoked (Loss)' (1992)

12 'Drive Time', 'Sight for Sore Eyes', 'Search for the Hero' (1994)

13 'Rotterdam;' 'Corduroy'; 'Dalliance' (1991)

14 'Allison Road'; 'Found Out About You'; 'Hey Jealousy' (1993)

15 'Playing with Fire'; 'Ground Level', 'Step It Up' (1992)

BONUS TRACKS

16 'Spooky'; 'Ruined in a Day'; 'Regret' (1993)

17 'This is How I Disappear'; 'I Don't Love You'; 'Famous Last Words' (2006)

18 'The Campaign for Real Rock'; 'Make Me Feel Again'; 'A Girl Like You' (1994)

19 'The Kids'; 'Stillness in Time'; 'Half the Man' (1994)

20 'Dance of the Stars'; 'Live the Dream'; 'Free Me' (1997)

21 'Buried Bones', 'Rented Rooms', 'Bathtime' (1997)

22 'Hand on the Glock'; 'When the Shit Goes Down'; 'Insane in the Brain' (1993)

23 'Bubble Gum Years'; 'Whippin' Piccadilly'; 'Get Myself Arrested' (1998)

24 'Junk of the Heart'; 'Erase/Rewind'; 'My Favourite Game' (1998)

25 'Not Sorry'; 'Dreams'; 'Linger' (1993)

26 'Every Ghetto, Every City'; 'Ex-Factor'; 'Doo-Wop (That Thing)' (1998)

27 'Broken Heart'; 'Electricity'; 'I Think I'm in Love' (1997)

28 'Love is Blindness'; 'The Fly'; 'Even Better than the Real Thing' (1991)

29 'Hudson Line'; 'Goddess On a Hiway'; 'Holes' (1998)

30 'The Certainty of Chance'; 'Generation Sex'; 'National Express' (1998)

QUIZ 63

LIVE AND DANGEROUS

And right now... right now... right now it's time to... kick out the jams, motherfuckers! screamed Rob Tyner as the MC5s took to the stage in 1969. Not every live show can be as flat-out incendiary as Detroit's finest but a great gig is still one of life's most intense pleasures – and ever more important to the music industry as record sales plummet..

So here goes for 30 questions on live shows, classic concerts, live music on TV, major events and all that rock and roll.

Answers: page 513

1 What was the 1976 live album by Led Zeppelin (actually the soundtrack to a concert film of the same name)? Which twelve-and-a-half-minute track was mainly an interminable drum solo?

2 *Stop Making Sense* was a concert movie about which New York band? Which Academy Award-winning director made it?

3 What was the title of Pet Shop Boys' first live CD, a set they played for the BBC at the Mermaid Theatre in 2006? Who guested and sang 'Jealousy'?

4 Before *Later ...with Jools Holland* launched on the BBC, he hosted a rather more anarchic music show on Channel 4. What was it? And with which band did he start his career?

5 Which rockabilly classic was Eddie Cochran's only US Top 10 hit? Who did a memorable live version of it on a classic 1970 live album?

6 Who was the main character, played by Bob Geldof, in the film version of Pink Floyd's *The Wall*? Where did Roger Waters lead an all-star cast in a live version of this epic in 1990?

7 After the Coldstream Guards played 'God Save the Queen' at the Wembley Live Aid in 1985, who played the first set? With which fitting song did they open proceedings?

8 Madonna has played ten world tours: The Virgin, Who's That Girl?, MISSING, The Girlie Show, Drowned World, Re-invention, Confessions, MISSING, MDNA, Rebel Heart. Can you name the two missing from the list?

9 Who, in 1991, was the first artist to release a session recorded for *MTV Unplugged* as a live album? When Robert Plant and Jimmy Page did so, what alternative title did they use?

10 Which band's song 'Free Nelson Mandela' led to the 1988 Nelson Mandela seventieth Birthday Tribute concert at Wembley? Which US TV network screened it but erased any mention of Nelson Mandela or apartheid?

11 Whose 1996 reunion tour, and subsequent live album, was called *Hell Freezes Over*? What was the title of their comeback album 13 years later, together with an ensuing final tour?

12 *James Brown Live at the Apollo,* recorded in 1962 and released in 1963, is a classic live album – but where is the Apollo? Which Brown lyric does manager Jimmy Rabbitte comically appropriate to try to inspire the band in 1992 movie *The Commitments*?

13 At which band's gig did Islamic terrorists murder 89 people at a Paris venue in November 2015? What was the name of the venue?

14 What was the name of the 1992 tour organised by the Jesus and Mary Chain? Which Britpop heroes-in-waiting were bottom of the bill below the Mary Chain, Dinosaur Jr and My Bloody Valentine?

15 Which song took up the whole fourth side of Marvin Gaye's 1977 double album *Live at the London Palladium*? Who performed a medley of his best known duets with him?

BONUS TRACKS

16 Where was The Who's famous live album recorded on Valentine's Day 1970? Where was a second gig recorded the next evening, which was included on a 40th anniversary edition of the album in 2010?

17 On 12th July 1985, Live Aid was broadcast from London and which US city? Who was the co-founder alongside Bob Geldof?

18 What was the name of Bob Dylan's famous two-part tour of 1975/76 Which female singer and former lover accompanied him?

19 Whick punk rock icon played a tour for anarchist group Class War in 1988? What was the tour called?

20 At which major sporting event did Diana Ross miss the target in 1994? Who didn't do much better while introducing her?

21 Who invited strippers to perform with them at an open-air gig in London's Battersea Park in 1979? To which track did they gyrate and disrobe?

22 Which major live event took place in cities across the world on 1 July 2005? Which band performed 'Sgt. Pepper's Lonely Hearts Club Band' with Paul McCartney?

23 Which reggae band beloved of John Peel were *Live at the Counter Eurovision* in Belgium in 1979? What was unusual about the release of this live album in terms of their career?

24 Who made a classic mostly-live 1979 album called *Rust Never Sleeps?* Which song features twice on it?

25 When Rod Stewart mimed to 'Maggie May' on Top of the Pops in 1971, who pretended to play the mandolin? 'Maggie May' was originally the single's B-side, but received more airplay than the purported A-side: what was it?

26 The Last Waltz was a valedictory concert held on Thanksgiving Day 1976 by which band? Who directed the movie of the concert?

27 The Buzzards and The Peacocks. Explain.

28 Bill Graham was the American promoter behind the famous music venues Fillmore East and Fillmore West. In which two cities were the venues located?

29 Where did Dylan record a 1979 live album in a rock style that upset some fans and critics? Which West Coast band accompanied Dylan on another tour and live album ten years later?

30 Who performed a famous reunion concert in Central Park in 1982 (it was released as a live album)? Which song from the movie *The Graduate* opened the set?

QUIZ 64

FOLK MUSIC

It isn't all 'hey-nonny-nonny', you know. The word 'folk' now covers a multitude of styles, from traditional songs played on old instruments to roustabout rock-tinged music. There's a definite transatlantic difference – British and American folk-influenced music each has a unique flavour. In modern times, folk has crossed over much more noticeably than in previous decades – Mumford & Son, Fleet Foxes and the Shins are just three acts who have taken folk-influenced and acoustic music in different directions. Here are 30 questions covering folk and folk-inspired artists past and present, traditional and modern, acoustic and fully amped-up.

Answers: page 514

1 Richard Thompson started out as the guitarist in which sixties folk rock band? Who was the band's fiddle player from 1969 until 1984?

2 Who briefly replaced Shane MacGowan as lead singer with the Pogues when MacGowan was sacked in 1990? Who took over in 1991, holding the role until the band's break-up in 1996?

3 First recorded in 1969, 'Streets of London' became a UK hit five years later. Who wrote it? And who released an anarchic punk version of the song as their debut single in 1981?

4 *Mermaid Avenue* featured new settings of (mostly unpublished) lyrics by which songwriter? Which alt.country band teamed up with Billy Bragg on the project?

5 The UK's biggest folk festival is held every year at Cherry Hinton Hall near which major city? Where do Fairport Convention host an annual festival every August?

6 Laura Marling was once briefly a member of which folk rock band fronted by Charlie Fink, then her boyfriend? Who played percussion on Marling's first two solo albums?

7 World Party is led by which musician and songwriter? Which band did he leave in 1986 to form the group?

8 Father John Misty is the alter ego for which contemporary indie folk artist? In which band was he previously the drummer?

9 Released in 1975, *Diamonds and Rust* was an album of mainly covers by which American singer-songwriter, best known for her output in the sixties? Who apparently was the subject of the title track, one of three songs on the album that she wrote herself?

10 Whose 1990 song 'I Useta Lover' is one of the biggest-selling singles in Irish history? In the song, what does the singer do in church one Christmas Eve to try and impress his girl?

11 *Barton Hollow* is the debut album by which modern folk duo? Their second album, released in 2013, features a pared-back cover of 'Disarm' by which nineties grunge band?

12 Whose 2011 album *You Can't Teach an Old Dog New Tricks* features John Paul Jones of Led Zeppelin on a few tracks? How much did this artist begin with, according to the title of his 2008 album, and how much has he still got?

13 *The Hissing of Summer Lawns* and *Chalk Mark in a Rain Storm* are typically poetic album titles from which Canadian singer-songwriter? In her late sixties and early seventies heyday, she had one UK Top 20 single – what was it?

14 Who is the leader of the Waterboys? Which poet, a huge influence, was the inspiration for the band's 2011 album?

15 *Blue Horse*, *Chinatown* and *Hello Love* were the three albums made by which Canadian folk trio? Which member of the band released a solo album in 2014 called *Indian Ocean*, which featured Al Green's guitarist Mabon 'Teenie' Hodges?

BONUS TRACKS

16 Which 1988 song from her eponymous debut LP gave Tracy Chapman her only UK Top 10 single? Her performance at which London concert gave the song a huge leg up the charts?

17 Which Oxford indie folk band take their name from a town in the Hebrides? What's the title of their 2010 debut album, a UK Top 20 hit?

18 Which TV theme tune gave Irish folk band Clannad their British commercial breakthrough when it entered the Top 10 in 1983? *Legend* gave the band their first British Top 20 album the following year – for which TV series did it serve as the soundtrack?

19 *I Want to See the Bright Lights Tonight* was the first album co-credited to which husband-and-wife folk duo? What's the title of the final album they recorded together, released in 1982 at a time when their relationship was falling apart?

20 'Tell her to make me a cambric shirt' is a line from which famous traditional song? Who released it as the first single from their 1966 album *Parsley, Sage, Rosemary and Thyme*?

21 Where were Christy Moore's 1994 and 2006 live albums recorded? Which song, the title track of a 1984 album and something of a signature tune, did he play live on stage with Coldplay in 2011?

22 *The First of a Million Kisses* is the only album recorded by which British folk pop group? The band launched the career of which enduring Scottish singer-songwriter?

23 In 2015, at the age of 66, Richard Thompson entered the UK top 10 for the first time with which album? Which alt.country star, the singer and guitarist with Wilco, produced the record?

24 A memorial to which singer-songwriter, who died in relative obscurity at the age of 26 in 1974, can be found at Tamworth-in-Arden in Warwickshire?

What's the name of his second album, released in 1971, which has seen him posthumously recognised as a major figure in acoustic music?

25 Which Portland, Oregon band are named after an unsuccessful military uprising in Russia in the 1820s? What's the name of their 2011 album, their first American number one?

26 Maddy Prior has been the singer of which folk band for the majority of their 47-year lifespan? What became their only UK Top 10 hit in 1975?

27 The Rails consist of James Walbourne and his wife Kami, the daughter of which folk-rock legends? Which other modern folk star played fiddle on their 2014 debut album *Fair Warning*?

28 Who wrote 'The First Time Ever I Saw Your Face' for his wife-to-be, Peggy Seeger? Which pop singer was his daughter?

29 Championed by BBC Radio 2, which singer's albums *Regardless* and *Ghosts and Graffiti* have both made the UK Top 40? Her 2011 album, *Don't Stop Singing*, featured the singer setting words by which late folk rock singer to new melodies?

30 Liam Ó Maonlaí and Fiachna Ó Braonáin are the two former buskers who formed which successful folk-rock band? Taken from their 1988 debut album *People*, which Top 20 single helped popularise the band in Britain?

QUIZ 65

FREAK ZONE

Stuart Maconie's Freak Zone is the show, broadcast on Sunday evenings, for those who like their music on the esoteric side. It features all kinds of sonic weirdness, with feedback, distortion, experimentation and general craziness the order of the evening. If you want it even more out there, stay up until midnight and explore the Freakier Zone.

There is a playlist on the 6 Music website that lists some of the bizarre offerings featured on the show. This quiz borrows heavily from there, but not just from there. So, here we go into music's twilight zone...

Answers: page 515

1   What was the debut solo album by Syd Barrett in 1970? Which legendary rock photographer, then still a relative novice, took the cover shot of Barrett in his Earl's Court flat?

2   *Live at the Witch Trials* (1979) was the first of (to date) 30 studio albums by which post-punk band? Their 1988 album *I Am Kurious Oranj* accompanied what?

3   On which Caravan album did an eight-part suite, *Nine Feet Underground*, take up the entire second side of vinyl? Who is the band's singer and guitarist?

4   Who released a series of albums in 1973 and 1974 featuring, among others, Yoni the witch and the Pothead Pixies? Who was the founder member of the band who left in 1975 after a force field 'refused to let him go on stage'?

5   Brothers Michael and Marcus Eoin Sanderson make up which electronic band? What was their 2013 album, released after a series of cryptic codes were issued via different media opening access to a website trailing the new material?

6   Indie experimentalists Cabaret Voltaire took their name from a Zurich nightclub associated with which artistic movement? Founder member Chris Wilson, is also a sound recordist specialising in which area?

7   David Thomas is the sole constant member and singer of which veteran US arty band? Which of these backing bands has NOT been credited on any of his many side projects: His Legs, Two Pale Boys, the Wooden Birds or the Dirty Carrots?

8   Who has collaborated with Ryuichi Sakamoto, Robert Fripp and performance artist Russell Mills? With which band did he release five electronic post-punk albums between 1978 and 1981?

9   Robert Fripp first made waves as the guitarist in which band? Who was the former college friend recruited to sing and play bass on their first two albums?

10 Which performance art/rock band have a penchant for eyeball masks? Who is their main singer?

11 In the 1995 single 'Hyperballad', what did Björk admit to throwing off the top of a mountain? Earlier in the same year, what cover version gave her her biggest British chart hit?

12 What happened when Spiritualized drummer Kev Bales teamed up with Nottingham-based artist Wolfgang Buttress? (extra point for a bit of detail)

13 Which band sing many of their songs in Vonlenska, a language with no words, only sounds? What is their native tongue?

14 Which actor released a 1968 album called *The Transformed Man*, including extracts from Shakespeare and recitals of the words of pop songs? What is the Bowie-influenced title of his 2011 offering of songs on a space theme?

15 In 1971, avant-garde composer Gavin Bryars made 'Jesus' Blood Never Failed Me Yet' around a vocal by a singing tramp. What instrument does Bryars play? Which mordant songwriter sang the tramp's part in a later remake?

BONUS TRACKS

16 Which female performance artist had a surprise number two hit in Britain in 1981 with minimalist electronic piece 'O Superman'? The track's full title referenced which classical composer, from whose opera *Le Cid* she borrowed themes for the song?

17 Nico was a German singer and model best remembered for her work with which avant-garde band? Which former bandmate supplied most of the musical arrangements and production for her solo albums?

18 What was the name of Frank Zappa's backing band? And which creatures ripped his flesh in one of his album titles?

19 Mary Hansen was killed in a cycling accident in London in 2002. Of which alternative nineties band was she a member? What was the land of her birth?

20 Which band set excerpts from public information films to a musical background? Alongside multi-intrumentalist J Willgoose Esq, who is the other permanent member, playing drums and percussion?

21 Which band from Carmarthen released nine studio albums between 1992 and 2003 (the most successful was 1997's *Barafundle*) and often sang in Welsh? Who was the band's singer and keyboard player who has since recorded 11 solo albums?

22 What was Siouxsie Sioux's side-project, releasing four albums from *Feast* in 1983 to *Hai* in 2003? Which other member of the Banshees was her collaborator?

23 What was the name of Faith No More singer Mike Patton's side-project, also featuring Trey Spruance and Trevor Dunn? Which 2012 thriller starring Bradley Cooper and Ryan Gosling did Patton write the musical score for?

24 *Symphony No 1* was a classical piece that earned a Grammy for which English singer-songwriter and composer? Which technically skilled guitarist, formerly one of Frank Zappa's bandmates, did he use on the record?

25 Which prog rock band toured with a full orchestra, and Budgie on drums, to promote fourth album *Piramida* in 2012? Where are they from?

26 Which industrial art-rock band played in North Korea in 2015? Their name is the German name for their home city: which city?

27 Godley & Crème enjoyed success as an experimental duo after leaving which pop-rock band in 1976? In which medium did the duo become active and could claim to be pioneers in the eighties?

28 Which French actress duetted with Serge Gainsbourg on 'Bonnie and Clyde' in 1968? Who recorded the saucy 'Je t'aime ... moi non plus' with him the following year and saw it go to number one in the UK despite being banned by the BBC?

29 In 1996, which Chicago post-rock band's second album was called *Millions Now Living Will Never Die*? Its title references a belief of followers of which Christian denomination?

30 Which Edgar Allan Poe short story was adapted into a rock opera by Peter Hamill and Chris Judge Smith in 1991, with Lene Lovich in the lead role? What is the name of the prog rock band that Hammill and Judge Smith reformed in 2005?

QUIZ 66

THOSE WHO DIED YOUNG

Rock and roll history contains many tragic tales of artists who died young and didn't survive to fully enjoy the fruits of their successes. So much money at such a young age, often surrounded by sycophants and leeches, and the lifestyle the industry threw at them. Here are two sections on some of those who didn't stay the course. And not all of them were 27.

Answers: page 516

1   Which flamboyant sixties singer was known as the Lizard King? In which city was he found dead in the bath in 1971?

2   Which band's drummer, Rick Allen, survived a car accident and the loss of an arm to continue his career? Which guitarist from the same band was less fortunate and died of alcohol poisoning in 1991?

3   Who was shot dead by his father on the eve of his 45th birthday in 1984? What was his last UK Top 10 single, a hit two years before his death?

4   Fred Durst, frontman of Limp Bizkit, has two musical icons tattooed on his chest. One died in 1977, the other in 1994. Who are they?

5   Ronnie van Zant and Steve Gaines died in a plane crash in 1977. Which band were they in? What was the inappropriately named (for these two, at least) album that the band had released only weeks earlier?

6   Drummer Robbie McIntosh died of a heroin overdose in 1974. With which white soul band did he play? And what was the band's biggest hit, a 1974 instrumental that topped the singles chart in the US?

7   Who died in Barnes, West London, in 1977 when a car driven by his girlfriend hit a tree? Which of his songs returned to the British Top 20 in 1991 after the release of a best-of compilation?

8   Who was killed as he returned to his New York apartment late in the evening of 8 December 1980? Who was responsible for his murder?

9   Which band lost two original members, James Honeyman-Scott and Pete Farndon, in 1982 and 1983 respectively? (Farndon had already been fired from the band for excessive drug abuse.) What was the single that the two remaining members of the band released in 1982 and dedicated to Honeyman-Scott?

10 Terry Kath died in an accident in 1978. With which band was he a singer and the main guitarist? How did he die?

11 Which UK folk-rocker died in 1974 aged 26 but remained largely unrecognised until the nineties? What's the name of his third and final album, released in 1972?

12 In April 1960, which rock and roller died at the age of just 21 from injuries suffered in a motor accident? Along with his girlfriend Sharon Sheeley, who co-wrote the song 'Somethin' Else' with him, which other rock and roll singer survived the crash?

13 Folk singer Sandy Denny died aged 31 in 1978 from a brain haemorrhage. With which two high-profile folk bands did she sing in the sixties?

14 Fred 'Sonic' Smith died in 1994, aged 45. Who was left a widow? With which garage rock band had Smith played bass in the late sixties?

15 Which female singer-songwriter died when she was hit by a powerboat in Mexico in 2000? To which music producer had she previously been married?

BONUS TRACKS

16 Phil Lynott, who died in 1986, was best known as the frontman for which band? As well as being the band's lead vocalist, which instrument did he play?

17 Which singing duo was shattered in 1990 by the loss of one of the sisters to cancer at the age of 23? What was their only UK number one, a Stock/Aitken/Waterman-produced single from 1987?

18 Who was found hanging in a hotel room in Sydney in November 1997 (coroner's verdict: suicide)? Who was the mother of his child, who herself died three years later of a drug overdose?

19 Which two rock legends, both aged 27, died in 1970 within three weeks of each other?

20 A plane crash led to 3 February 1959 being referred to as 'the day the music died', because three prominent stars lost their lives. Along with Buddy Holly, who was killed in the crash?

21 Little Feat disbanded just before their mainstay and principal songwriter died of a heart attack at 34. What was his name? And what's the title of the band's best known album, released in 1973?

22 Which singer survived an attempt on his life two days before a concert in Jamaica in 1976, but died four years later of a brain tumour? Which former colleague of his was murdered in 1987 when armed robbers broke into his home and tried to extort money from him?

23 Best known for his work with Free, which guitarist died from a drug overdose in 1976 at the age of just 25? What was the name of the band he'd formed on Free's demise three years earlier?

24 '(Sittin' on the) Dock of the Bay' by Otis Redding was the first posthumous US number one single. What was the second, a hit for Janis Joplin in 1971? And who wrote the song, which had previously been released as a single by country singer Roger Miller?

25 What was the name of the Who's wild child drummer who died in 1978? What part did he play in the film version of the band's rock opera *Tommy*?

26 It reached number 149 in the US and didn't chart in the UK, but *Grace*, released in 1994, is now regarded as a classic album. Who released it? How did the singer meet an untimely end in 1997, aged just 30?

27 Which Rolling Stone drowned after a barbiturate-fuelled midnight swim in 1969? Who replaced him on guitar?

28 *Songbird* was a posthumously released compilation album from 1998 by which American singer? Who wrote the song from which the album took its title?

29 Which Brooklyn-born R&B singer was killed in a plane crash in the Bahamas in 2001, aged 22? Which R&B singer is she alleged to have secretly married in 1994?

30 Who died shortly after being charged with the murder of his girlfriend, Nancy Spungeon? What was the title of the cynical solo live album released a few months after his death?

QUIZ 67

THE ROLLING STONES

Another quiz about the dinosaurs, the bands who now sell out the football stadiums that not even their football teams can fill. That said, most of these behemoth bands started from small acorns: Green Day were an indie punk band and REM were the darlings of the American alternative scene, and it took them years to take the jump to 50,000-capacity outdoor summer shows. The quiz is in three quick parts: one on the Rolling Stones and one on a number of other big acts, ending with a name-the-album quickfire round.

Answers: page 517

1 Which Rolling Stones album had a large cake on the cover? And which featured a rampant silver lion?

2 The original cover of which Stones album featured a real zip? What was inscribed on the belt buckle on the version released in the Soviet Union?

3 Since *Goat's Head Soup* in 1983, only two Stones albums have topped the UK charts. Which two?

4 Billy Preston, Nicky Hopkins and Ian McLagan all provided which type of support to the Stones? And what's the name of the singer, a fan favourite, who's toured with the band since 1989?

5 What were the first solo albums by Mick Jagger (1985) and Keith Richards (1988)?

6 A cover of which Chuck Berry song was the Stones' first single, released in 1963? On the band's first album, what was the significance of the song 'Tell Me'?

7 Taken from *Emotional Rescue* and released in 1981, what was the Stones' most recent UK Top 10 single? Featuring a gorilla on the cover, what's the title of the career retrospective released in 2012 to celebrate 50 years in the business?

8 Which song written by Bobby and Shirley Womack gave the band their first British number one in 1964? And which was the most recent of their singles to hit number one in the UK, back in the summer of 1969?

9 Released in 1978, which was the first Stones album to feature Ronnie Wood as a full band member? Which Temptations song did they cover on it?

10 What was the title of the Stones' classic 1970 live album that went straight to number one in the UK, a first for a live LP? At which famous New York venue were most of the takes recorded over two nights in November 1969?

BONUS TRACK 1

11 Which Green Day album from 2004 was their first to top the US and UK charts? What's the second track on the album, a nine-minute suite in five sections?

12 Which single from *Document* gave REM their big commercial breakthrough? And what's the title of the 1991 album that topped the charts in both the US and the UK?

13 Released in 2005, what was the first Coldplay album to top the albums chart in the UK and the US? All of the band's albums since have emulated this feat except *A Head Full of Dreams* in 2015, which only made number two in the US. Which British artist kept the album from number one?

14 The title of Mumford & Sons' debut album, and some lyrics on the title track, reference which playwright? How many weeks had it been on the UK albums chart before it reached its peak position of number two? (Get within ten weeks to score one point.)

15 What was the first album released by Manic Street Preachers after the disappearance of guitarist and lyricist Richey Edwards in 1995? Who took over responsibility for the band's lyrics?

16 Which Coldplay album is a concept album set in the world of Silencia? 'Ghost Stories' is believed to chart Chris Martin's split from his actress wife: who is she?

17 Alongside the rhythm section of Mike Mills and Bill Berry, who were the other two founding members of REM?

18 Whose love did Manic Street Preachers sing about on a single from their *Lifeblood* album? And what were we told about love on the 2007 follow-up, *Send Away the Tigers*?

19 What was the first single to be taken from Green Day's 1995 album *Insomniac*, telling of the metabolistic effects of methamphetamine? What

was the rather mellower acoustic song that the band released as a single from *Nimrod* in 1997?

20 What's the title of the final REM album, released in 2011? And what's the career retrospective that the band released after announcing their retirement?

BONUS TRACK 2

In the following lists of four tracks, three are from the same album, while the fourth is from a different record by the same band. Name the album and spot the odd one out.

21 'Crush with Eyeliner', 'Everybody Hurts', 'Nightswimming' and 'The Sidewinder Sleeps Tonight' (REM, 1992).

22 'Enter Sandman', 'Eye of the Beholder', 'Harvester of Sorrow' and 'One' (Metallica, 1988).

23 'Clocks', 'God Put a Smile upon Your Face', 'The Scientist' and 'Yellow' (Coldplay, 2002).

24 'Kicked in the Teeth', 'Riff Raff', 'Rock 'n' Roll Damnation' and 'Touch Too Much' (AC/DC, 1978).

25 'Broken Crown', 'Dust Bowl Dance', 'I Will Wait' and 'Lover of the Light' (Mumford & Sons, 2012).

26 'Angie', 'Rocks Off', 'Shine a Light' and 'Tumbling Dice' (The Rolling Stones, 1972).

27 'Charlie', 'Dosed', 'Slow Cheetah' and 'Snow (Hey Oh)' (Red Hot Chili Peppers, 2006).

28 'The Doberman', 'Goodbye Kiss', 'Me Plus One' and 'Shoot the Runner' (Kasabian, 2006).

29 'Basket Case', 'Longview', 'Nice Guys Finish Last' and 'When I Come Around' (Green Day, 1994).

30 'Intense Humming of Evil', 'Motorcycle Emptiness', 'Revol' and 'She Is Suffering' (Manic Street Preachers, 1994).

QUIZ 68

PRODUCERS & LABELS

The great facilitators: those who help the music get made, and those who help pay for it and get it out to the public. Producers have become an increasingly high-profile breed, sometimes receiving credits alongside the artist and often helping to write as well as record the material. Some producers, such as Mark Ronson and Danger Mouse, have even become *de facto* artists who also happen to produce as well. Alongside questions about some of the world's leading producers, this quiz also spotlights some of the most notable record labels, past and present.

Answers: page 518

1 Now part of the Beggars group, which independent label was founded by Peter Kent and Ivo Watts-Russell in 1980? Which musical collective was formed by Watts-Russell in 1983 to showcase some of the label's talent?

2 For which famous soul label were the keyboard player Booker T and his band the house session musicians? What colour were their onions?

3 Who provided the glossy production for John Lennon's album *Imagine*? And which Lennon hit, not from this album, featured a group of children called the Harlem Community Choir?

4 Founded by Bruce Pavitt in 1986, which label released the first records by Nirvana and Soundgarden? In which American city is it based?

5 Who wrote and produced the ten-minute epic 'Bat out of Hell' for Meat Loaf? And who played the revved-up lead guitar part?

6 Which independent record label released the first Suede album in 1993? Many of their assets were later transferred to another London indie imprint, who launched the careers of the Sugarcubes and Alabama 3: which label?

7 What connects 'Baby, I Love You' by the Ronettes, 'You've Lost that Lovin' Feeling' by the Righteous Brothers and 'My Sweet Lord' by George Harrison? Which Beatles single, their last US number one, could be added to the list?

8 Which Jamaican producer worked at the Black Ark, where he produced records for the Heptones, the Wailers, Max Romeo and many others? What's the title of the famous three-CD box set of his work, released in 1997?

9 U2 have been signed to which record label for their entre career? Which of their albums was the first to top the chart in both the US and the UK?

10 Who helped kick Adele's career into another gear when he wrote and recorded 'Rolling in the Deep' with the singer in two days? In 2011, he produced *Ceremonials*, the second album by which act?

11 Which DJ co-produced (with Steve Osborne) the Happy Mondays album *Pills 'n' Thrills and Bellyaches* in 1990? Which record label had he set up the previous year?

12 Who received production credits and added some backing vocals on all but four tracks on *Humbug*, Arctic Monkeys' third album? Which member of Simian Mobile Disco produced the other four tracks, then went on to work with the band on their next two albums?

13 Who set up Creation Records in 1983, going on to release records by the likes of the Jesus & Mary Chain, Primal Scream and Oasis? Which label did he set up after Creation was dissolved in 1999?

14 Who produced the first album, and all the band's major hits, for Frankie Goes to Hollywood? What was the record label he co-founded with Jill Sinclair and Paul Morley?

15 Which famous label was started by record store owner Geoff Travis in the late seventies? After it fell into receivership, which other indie label and distributor purchased the company from Sanctuary Records in 2007?

BONUS TRACKS

16 Who worked as an engineer on some of the early records by the Smiths, and was then credited as co-producer on the band's album *Strangeways, Here We Come*? Which classic Britpop album did he produce for release on the Food label in 1994?

17 What is the trade name of the Norwegian songwriting and production duo Tor Hermansen and Mikkel Eriksen? For which bestselling artist did they help to create a run of four consecutive American number ones?

18 Which entrepreneur became the manager of the Beatles, helping them to land their first recording contract? To which label did EMI assign the band?

19 Which label was started in Manchester in 1978, and went on release records by groups such as Joy Division and the Happy Mondays? Along with Alan Erasmus and Rob Gretton, who was the driving force behind the label?

20 Which professional footballer founded a small label called 2 Wikid? With which singer did he enter into a legal dispute in 2004, after the singer attempted to release an album under his own steam despite allegedly being under contract to 2 Wikid?

21 Which two big hitters, one a Canadian guitarist and the other a British keyboard player, shared producing duties on U2's *Achtung Baby*?

22 Whose production output includes most of David Bowie and Marc Bolan's work, some Thin Lizzy records and a 2006 album by Morrissey? Which band, fronted by Pete Ham and touted as the 'new Beatles', hired him to produce their first album, *Magic Christian Music*?

23 Which label unsigned the Sex Pistols after a notorious TV appearance by the group, and went on to become the subject of the band's ire on their debut album? Which label actually released the record?

24 Which independent label has released all five Arctic Monkeys albums? In which city did the band start out?

25 Which record label was founded by the Wailers in 1965? Which major label distributed the music internationally?

26 What was the name of the label for which Dr Dre produced his own and Snoop Dogg's debut albums? Which co-founder of the label eventually filed for its bankruptcy in 2006, and is now awaiting trial on hit-and-run murder charges over an incident in 2015?

27 With which record label is producer and mogul Chris Blackwell most closely associated? In 1989, by which time it had become the world's biggest independent imprint, the label was sold to which major record company?

28 Which label, whose roster includes Beach House, the Low Anthem and John Grant, won Independent Label of the Year in 2010, 2012, 2014 and 2016? The label was founded by two former members of which Scottish indie band?

29 The compilation series *Now! That's What I Call Music* was launched in the UK in which year? (Two points if you get the year spot on, one point for two years either side.)

30 Who produced the first four Elvis Costello albums? Which of these albums remains Costello's biggest seller?

QUIZ 69

SWEET SOUL MUSIC

Atlantic, Philadelphia, soul, R&B, funk – if this is your bag, this is your quiz. Come on, let's groove tonight and share the spice of life, as Earth, Wind & Fire once urged us. The first section is a chain, so one question leads on to the next – it can be a help, or a hindrance. Part two is 15 straight questions on soul greats.

Answers: page 519

1   Who, appropriately, were the first band to release an album on Neal Sugarman and Gabriel Roth's new label, Daptone, in 2002? The label's house band and recording studios were used by which ill-fated star for a classic 2006 album?

2   Mark Ronson had a hit under his own name in late 2014 with 'Uptown Funk'; which American pop singer guested as vocalist? Ronson borrowed heavily from the 'Minneapolis sound' first developed by which major artist in the late seventies and eighties?

3   (2b)'s 1990 number one album featured a track that was also the name of the artist's backing band; what was it called? At which London venue did he play a 21-night residency called the Earth Tour in 2007?

4   Maceo Parker is a jazz-funk bandleader and a majestic player of which instrument? And with which soul legend did Parker cut his funky teeth in his backing band?

5   (4b)'s original backing ban was the Famous Flames; what was the band he used from 1970 onwards called? And who was the bass player who played with them for a year before moving on to create a unique sound alongside George Clinton in the P-Funk collective?

6   Which 1978 club classic by Funkadelic featured chanted lines such as 'Feet don't fail me now!'? The other half of P-Funk, Parliament had only one US Top 20 single. The title was 'Give Up the Funk (____ the ____ off the _____)' – which words are missing from the brackets?

7   The song in (6b) featured in the funk episode of US TV show *Glee*; which Rufus hit (written by Stevie Wonder) was used as a seduction number in the same show? Who was the lead singer of Rufus who enjoyed as much success in her later solo career?

8   (7b)'s biggest selling single, 'I Feel For You' features an introductory rap by which pioneer of that genre? What was the name of his band, who hit big with 'The Message' and 'White Lines (Don't Do It)?'

9   What was Stevie Wonder's contribution to the success of 'I Feel For You'? His last US number one solo single, 'Part Time Lover', featured backing vocals by Luther Vandross and which of the two vocalists in Earth, Wind & Fire?

10 What, in 1978, was the first UK Top 10 single for Earth, Wind & Fire? That band's Maurice White also produced many hits by female singing group the Emotions – what was their 1977 US number one?

11 Stax Records executive Al Bell also worked with the Emotions. For which band did he produce big hits 'Respect Yourself' and 'I'll Take You There' (which he also wrote)? With which influential funk star did this act collaborate on the soundtracks for two Sidney Poitier-directed films, *Let's Do It Again* and *A Piece of the Action*?

12 (11b) already had a pedigree in movies with his brilliant, socially conscious soundtrack to which 1972 blaxploitation thriller? What was the name of the group with which he started his career, and with whom he recorded the influential 1965 hit, 'People Get Ready'?

13 (11b)'s label was distributed by the Buddah organisation, as was T-Neck records, a label set up and owned by which former Tamla vocal group turned funk-soul band? Their biggest single was 'This Old Heart of Mine' – who covered it and had a UK number four single in 1975?

14 In the early sixties, (13) showcased a talented young guitarist, featuring him on a couple of singles on T-Neck: who was he? With which soul legend did he share an album (they had a side each) of performances from the legendary Monterey Pop Festival?

15 Hailed as the 21st Century (14b), who released his debut album *No Time for Dreaming in 2011*, aged 63? Which soul revival label released the album and launched the career of this 'new' star?

BONUS TRACKS

16 Who were *Searching for the Young Soul Rebels* in 1980? And who was their lead singer?

17 The Best Disco in the World, according to *Billboard* magazine, closed its doors in 1981. Where in northern England was it, and with which type of music is it forever associated?

18 'Endless Love' was a number one for Lionel Richie and Diana Ross in 1981. Who took the song back up the charts in 1994?

19 *The Jazz Soul of Little Stevie* was Stevie Wonder's debut album in 1962. How old was he? 'Fingertips', from the album, was his first US number one single in 1963. His next, in 1972, came from *Talking Book* – what was it?

20 'Bag Lady' from the album *Mama's Gun*, was the first US Top 10 single by which neo-soul singer? Which rapper is the father of her child, born in 1997?

21 'You Send Me' (1957) was a US number one, arguably the first modern soul record to be a major hit: who wrote and recorded the song? Which George Gershwin song was on the B-side?

22 *Brown Sugar* was the debut album in 1995, and *Black Messiah* the hugely anticipated comeback in 2014. Who is the artist, and what was the 2000 album that went to number one in the US?

23 Which Bobby Womack song did Quentin Tarantino use to open his 1997 film, *Jackie Brown*? Whose widow, Barbara, did the 21-year-old Womack marry in 1965, three months after her husband's death?

24 What was the only UK Top 10 hit for Womack & Womack (1988)? Which British band covered it on the bonus disc of their self-named 2009 debut album?

25 In 1987 two soul singers in their late forties, Percy Sledge and Ben E King, were number one and number two in the UK singles chart on the back of a movie and a hugely popular Levi's commercial. What were the two songs?

26 Who sang lead vocals on the Drifters' 1962 US number one 'Save the Last Dance for Me'? Which other Drifters' hit, about not paying attention in the cinema reached number two in Britain in 1974 with vocals by Johnny Moore, who became the band's main singer?

27 Which song from her 1985 album *Who's Zoomin' Who?* took Aretha Franklin into the US Top 10 for the first time since 1973? Which seminal music-based 1980 movie, starring John Belushi, did she make a cameo appearance?

28 The Miracles had a string of hits before changing their name to highlight the skills of which songwriter and singer? What was their biggest hit, a number one on both sides of the Atlantic?

29 What was the Miracles first UK Top 10 single, from 1965? And what was their biggest hit with new singer Billy Griffin, with a new, more disco-oriented sound (1975)?

30 Which barefoot British soul singer released her first album at 16 and had seven full studio albums out before her thirtieth birthday? What was the name of the short-lived supergroup she formed along with Dave Stewart, Mick Jagger, Damian Marley and Indian composer AR Rahman?

QUIZ 70

NAME THE BAND #3

We're here again. As with quizzes 7 and 44, we give you the band members and you identify the band. Remember, these are not all of the members who ever played in a band, just classic line-ups from a particular album or at a particular time. There is a cross section of old and new; rock, pop and soul.

Answes: page 519

1   Frank Beard, Billy Gibbons, Dusty Hill

2   Aaron Burtch, Tim Dryden, Jim Fairchild, Kevin Garcia, Jason Lytle

3   Barry Adamson, Howard Devoto, John Doyle, Dave Formula, John McGeoch

4   Noel and Padraig Duggan, Ciaran, Moya and Pol Brennan

5   Rob Allen, Billy McCarthy, Eric Sanderson

6   Dave Alexander, Ron and Scott Asheton, Iggy Pop

7   Graeme Douglas, Paul Gray, Dave Higgs, Barrie Masters, Steve Nicol

8   Dave Best, Matt Bowman, Oliver Main, Jimmy Naylor, Ryan Wilson

9   Lauryn Hill, Wyclef Jean, Pras Michel

10 Brian Connolly, Steve Priest, Andy Scott, Mick Tucker

11 Dan Gillespie-Sells, Richard Jones, Kevin Jeremiah, Ciaran Jeremiah, Paul Stewart

12 Norman Blake, Gerard Love, Francis MacDonald, Raymond McGinley

13 Roy Bittan, Danny Federici, Garry Tallent, Steven van Zandt, Max Weinberg

14 Tom Fletcher, Danny Jones, Harry Judd, Dougie Poynter

15 Paul Banks, Carlos Dengler, Sam Fogarino, Daniel Kessler.

16 Ralph Molina, Frank Sampedro, Billy Talbot

17 Travis Barker, Tom DeLonge, Mark Hoppus, Scott Raynor

18 Robin Pecknold, Skyler Skjelset, Josh Tillman, Christian Wargo, Casey Westcott.

19 Henry Famborough, Billy Henderson, Pervis Jackson, Bobby Smith, Philippé Wynne

20 Bob Bryar, Frank Iero, Ray Toro, Gerard Way, Mikey Way

21 Richie Furay; Dewey Martin; Bruce Palmer; Stephen Stills; Neil Young

22 Sheila Ferguson, Fayette Pinkney, Valerie Holiday

23 Karl Hyde, Rick Smith

24 Dave, Maseo, Posdnuos

25 Johnny Echols, Ken Forssi, Bryan MacLean, Michael Stuart

26 Jimi Chambers, Jonathan Donahue, Dave Fridmann, Grasshopper, Adam Snyder, Suzanne Thorpe

27 Eric Avery, Perry Farrell, Dave Navarro, Stephen Perkins

28 Allan Clarke, Bobby Elliott, Eric Haydock, Tony Hicks, Graham Nash

29 Justine Frischmann, Annie Holland, Donna Matthews, Justin Welch

30 Rick Danko, Levon Helm, Garth Hudson, Richard Manuel, Robbie Robertson

BONUS TRACKS

31 Jim Capaldi, Steve Winwood, Chris Wood

32 Andy Bell, Laurence Colbert, Mark Gardener, Steve Queralt

33 Boz Burrell, Simon Kirke, Mick Ralphs, Paul Rodgers

34 Steve Cropper, Duck Dunn, Al Jackson, Booker T Jones

35 Paul Court, Steve Dullaghan, Tracy Tracy, Tig Williams

36 Petey Dammit, Brigid Dawson, John Dwyer, Mike Shoun

37 Chris Acland, Emma Anderson, Mike Berenyi, Steve Rippon

38 Kevin Cadogan, Brad Hargreaves, Stephan Jenkins; Arion Salazar

39 Nels Cline, Mikael Jorgensen, Glenn Kotche, Pat Sansone, John Stirratt, Jeff Tweedy

40 Faris Badwan, Tom Cowan, Joshua Hayward, Joseph Spurgeon, Rhys Webb

41 Charlotte Caffey, Belinda Carlisle, Gina Schock, Kathy Valentine, Jane Wiedlin

42 Andy Hurley, Patrick Stump, Joe Trohman, Pete Wentz

43 Iain Cook, Martin Doherty, Lauren Mayberry

44 Carol Colman, August Darnell, Cora Daye, Adriana Kaegi, Coati Mundi, Jimmy Rippetoe, Peter Schott

45 Bobby Drake, Craig Finn, Tad Kubler, Franz Nicolay, Galen Polivka

46 Guy Lawrence, Howard Lawrence

47 John Ashton, Richard Butler, Tim Butler, Vince Ely, Duncan Kilburn, Roger Morris

48 Christopher Chartrand, Alice Glass, Ethan Kath

49 Kelcey Ayer, Nik Ewing, Matt Frazier, Ryan Hahn, Taylor Rice

50 Brinsley Forde, Drummy Zeb Gaye, Dee Griffiths, Ras Oban, Gad Robinson

51 Anthony Burulcich, John Conway, Sam Endicott, Mike Hindert, Michael Zakarin

52 Nadine Coyle, Sarah Harding, Nicola Roberts, Cheryl Tweedy, Kimberley Walsh

53 Charlie Burchill, Derek Forbes, Mel Gaynor, Jim Kerr, Michael McNeil

54 Bruce Foxton, Mark Brzezicki, Russell Hastings

55 James Eller, Matt Johnson, Johnny Marr, David Palmer

56 Tom Bailey, Alannah Currie, Joe Leeway

57 Stephanie Bailey, Christian Bland, Jake Garcia, Kyle Hunt, Alex Maas

58 Les Holroyd, John Lees, Mel Pritchard, Woolly Wolstenholme

59 Dennis Duck, Karl Precoda, Kendra Smith, Steve Wynn

60 Ben Johnston, James Johnston, Simon Neil

QUIZ 71

THE SWINGING SIXTIES

The fifties was when rock and roll music began – but the sixties was when
the industry really started, a period when people realised that music was
something that could be exploited for corporate benefit and sullied by
bloated contracts and rampant egos. It was the beginning of rock music
as we know it, but also the death of its innocence. Here are 30 questions
on this most storied of decades.

Answers: page 520

1   Mitch Mitchell and Noel Redding were the rhythm section of which sixties trio? Chas Chandler, the band's manager, had formerly been the bass player in which blues-rock band fronted by Eric Burdon?

2   Who had a British number one with 'Keep on Running' in 1965? Along with the man who gave the group its name, which two brothers featured in the band?

3   Who reached the UK Top 10 with 'Friday on My Mind' in 1966? Which country were the band from?

4   In 1962, Phil Spector and his production team had their first American number one single with 'He's a Rebel'. To which girl group was the single attributed? But who actually sang the lead vocal?

5   At which famous Liverpool club did the Beatles play many of their early gigs? Which Dutch prog rock band were the last act to play at the venue before it closed in 1973?

6   There was no one called Dave Clark in the Dave Clark Five – true or false? Boasting a rousing, football-chant chorus, what was their first British number one in 1964?

7   Whose version of 'House of the Rising Sun' reached number one in the UK and became the band's signature song? Which American group took a harder-edged version of the song into the British and American Top 10 in 1970?

8   Who was the lead singer with Jefferson Airplane? And which band did she form after the group broke up?

9   Which future BBC radio DJ did Mike d'Abo replace when he became the singer with Manfred Mann in 1966? Jack Bruce briefly played bass for Manfred Mann around the same time, before leaving to form which band?

10 The Beach Boys had only two British number one singles. What were they?

11 *My People Were _____ and Had _____ in Their Hair... But Now They're Content to Wear _____ On Their _____.* Fill in the missing words from the rather long-winded title of Tyrannosaurus Rex's first album.

12 'It's Not Unusual' shot which hip-swinging sex bomb to the top of the UK charts in 1965? Which ballad provided him with his only other British number one the following year?

13 Formed by Dick Taylor and Phil May in the early sixties, which band earned a reputation for their wild behaviour – which included one incident that saw them set fire to a bag of crayfish on a flight in New Zealand? With which band had Taylor previously played bass before leaving to study at art college?

14 'Baby, Please Don't Go' was the first hit single for which Northern Irish R&B band in 1964? Their singer later launched a successful solo career – what's his name?

15 The Tremeloes first hit number one with a cover of 'Do You Love Me', originally recorded by the Contours. What was their only other chart-topper, released in 1967? And who was the band's singer?

BONUS TRACKS

16 Which founder member of Pink Floyd left the band in 1968 with acute mental health problems? Who took over vocal duties, having joined as a second guitarist in December the previous year?

17 Who had a UK number one with 'Yeh Yeh' in 1964? What was the name of his backing band?

18 Which folk quartet had a hit with the title track from the soundtrack of the 1966 film *Georgy Girl*? Who was the band's wholesome lead singer?

19 Who was the founder, singer and main songwriter in the sixties guitar band Love, seen by some critics as archetypal of the sound of the Summer of Love? Speaking of the Summer of Love, which year was it?

20 Which 1964 single took the Kinks to the top of the UK charts for the first time? Who was the band's singer and primary songwriter?

21 How many studio albums did the Kinks release in their 30-year career? (Two points if you're spot on, one point if you're within three of the correct answer.)

22 Which sixties heartthrob got Mary Whitehouse in a lather when he split his trousers on stage at the ABC in Croydon? What was his first British hit, reaching number three in 1964 after he appeared on a TV special with the Beatles?

23 What could the Move hear near the top of the charts in 1967? And what were they sitting watching later that year?

24 During the sixties, 'I'm Alive' was the only British number one for which successful UK band? Which song of theirs hit the top of the chart 23 years later on the back of its use in a lager commercial, setting a record for the biggest gap between number-one hits?

25 For which band was it 'All or Nothing' at the top of the charts in 1966? According to another hit from 1968, what was their favourite day of the week?

26　Michael Nesmith and Davy Jones, both born on 29 December, were also both members of which pop group? Which film director, whose movies include *Five Easy Pieces* and the remake of *The Postman Always Rings Twice*, co-created the group for an American TV series?

27　Which Merseybeat band was formed by John McNally and Mike Pender? Which Jackie DeShannon song sewed up the British number-one slot for them in 1964?

28　Christine McVie joined Fleetwood Mac from blues band Chicken Shack while she was still using which name from before her marriage? What was the title of the UK Top 20 hit she scored with Chicken Shack, adding her trademark smoky vocals to a cover of a soul classic?

29　Whose 1967 debut album included the psychedelic classic 'Light My Fire', their first successful single in the UK? What's the title of the follow-up album, which ends with the haunting 'When the Music's Over'?

30　Jeff Beck, Eric Clapton and Jimmy Page all played guitar in which early sixties R&B group? They never played together, as Clapton left before the others arrived – which band did he join?

THE CHAIN

The Chain is officially the longest listener-generated thematically linked sequence of musically based items on the radio. As all regular 6 Music listeners will know, it is a Radcliffe and Maconie feature whereby listeners connect one track to another, and the next listener picks up where the last one left off and continues the connected sequence.

This quiz is simple: two sets of 30 questions, which make up one chain of 60 connected answers. The chain closes at the end as the answer to 60 refers back to the first question.

Answers: page 521

1 Who played the stylish picked guitar on Bob Dylan's 1979 Christian album *Slow Train Coming*?

2 What was the 1984 comeback album that relaunched the career of Tina Turner?

3 What was the opening track on that album, reputed to be reflective of Tina's notion that she was an Egyptian ruler in a previous life?

4 Which album gave Queen their first UK number one?

5 And which song from the album gave them similar success in the singles' charts?

6 What was the Dandy Warhols' only UK Top 10 single, in 2000?

7 Whose self-named 1967 debut album featured a picture of a banana, painted by Andy Warhol, on the cover?

8 Who was that band's primary songwriter, having a hand in all the tracks on that debut?

9 With which band did this artist collaborate on the 2011 album *Lulu*, the last he made before his death in 2013?

10 The fourth single from that band's *...And Justice for All* album became a concert standard and was also a Grammy winner for best metal song. What is the song?

11 U2 released a song with the same title on their 1991 album, *Achtung Baby*. Who covered it on the third volume of his *American* Recordings series in 2000?

12 Who was the American producer and founder of Def Jam records behind this series of recordings?

13 For which band did he produce a number of albums through the peak of their career, including the 1999 breakthrough *Californication*?

14 In a break with this arrangement, the band's 2016 album was producd by which member of pop-dance act Gnarls Barkley?

15 What was this duo's massive selling hit worldwide in 2006?

16 Who had a hit in 1962 with a Willie Nelson-penned song with the same title?

17 What was the title of this singer's hit that became the title of a biopic made about her life, starring Jessica Lange?

18 Which British band had a big hit with the same title in 1983?

19 The Eurythmics drummer is also an integral part of Blondie: what is his name?

20 Blondie had a big hit with 'The Tide Is High'. Which girl band did the same in 2002?

21 What is the derivation of the title of the OMD hit 'Enola Gay'?

22 Whose 1979 single, 'Nuclear Device', was a dig at the right-wing Governor of Queensland, Australia at the time, Joh Bjelke-Petersen?

23 The same band released an excellent cover of the Bacharach and David song 'Walk On By' in 1978: who had the original hit with this song?

24 And who composed her biggest UK hit, 'Heartbreaker' (1982)?

25 Why was 'Jive Talkin'' the odd track out on the multi-million-selling *Saturday Night Fever* soundtrack?

26 Who wrote the title track to the following year's musical sensation, *Grease*?

27 And who sang it?

28 Which Beatles' song was at number one in the UK for five weeks from November until late December 1963?

29 Who replaced the Beatles at the top early the following year with their first number one, 'Glad All Over'?

30 When that band were inducted into the Rock and Roll Hall of Fame in 2008, which of their hits did Joan Jett sing, having recorded it on a 1981 album and used it as a live staple?

BONUS TRACKS

31 What was the title of that Joan Jett album and also her chart-topping single off it, comfortably her biggest hit?

32 Who covered this song on her second album and also sang it in her 2002 showcase movie, *Crossroads*?

33 Which singer-guitarist had a 1991 hit with the song 'Girlfriend', and also featured in *Crossroads*?

34 He has released three albums of cover versions recorded with Susanna Hoffs, formerly the singer in which successful all-girl pop rock band?

35 What was this band's first US number one single, whose title implied ambulatory cultural appropriation?

36 What was the biggest UK hit for quirky American new wave artist Jonathan Richman?

37 On which album did the Sex Pistols release a version of Richman's classic track, 'Roadrunner'?

38 The film to which that Pistols' album was an accompaniment was directed by Julien Temple. Which English R&B band were the subject of his 2009 documentary, *Oil City Confidential*?

39 Who was the band's original guitarist before he left to pursue a solo career that included a 2014 hit album with Roger Daltrey?

40 Daltrey starred in the 1975 rock opera *Tommy*, directed by Ken Russell and based on whose songs?

41 This songwriter's second rock opera (not including a shelved project) was made into a 1979 film directed by Franc Roddam and starring which young actor as a disaffected mod?

42 Who co-starred as the Ace Face, bellboy by day, coolest of the mods by night?

43 He sang with a band who had great success with their second album, *Regatta de Blanc*: what was the lead single that gave them their first UK number one?

44 *Regatta de Blanc* translates as White Reggae (sort of). Which band, playing exactly that, released their debut album, *Signing Off*, in 1980?

45 Which Elvis Presley song gave this band a UK number one in 1993 and gave their career a second lease of life?

46 What was the title of the last album Elvis released before his death in 1977?

47 *On the Threshold of a Dream* (1969) gave which prog rock band their first UK number one album?

48 The band's singer (or one of them), Justin Hayward, had a hit with the song 'Forever Autumn': from which musical project was it taken?

49 Who played the ill-fated Parson Nathaniel on the original 1978 album?

50 Which friend of his played guitar on the 1979 album *Black Rose: A Rock Legend* and also collaborated on the single 'Parisienne Walkways' off his own album *Back on the Streets*?

51 That artist's 1995 album, *Blues for Greeny*, was a tribute to which major influence on his career?

52 Hanging around their necks, what was the UK number one that this guitarist and singer's band recorded in 1968?

53 Apart from a re-release of that single, this band didn't reach the UK Top 30 again until 'Dreams' in 1977. Which member of their new line-up wrote and sang this song?

54 When this singer released her first solo album, who co-wrote and duetted on the lead-off single, 'Stop Draggin' My Heart Around'?

55 Paul Michael Glaser (*Starsky and Hutch*) made a film in 1986 called *Band of the Hand*, a crime caper originally pitched as a TV series. Who recorded the title song for the soundtrack, with (54) and his band backing him?

56 Both (54) and (55) were members of which late eighties supergroup?

57 Which 1990 hit film used the title of a signature tune of another member of this supergroup?

58 The lead actress from this film appeared in a similarly successful British romantic comedy in 1999, featuring songs from Bill Withers, Elvis Costello and Ronan Keating on the soundtrack: which film?

59 What was the name of the one-off band whose only album, *Missing ... Presumed Having a Good Time* (1990) reached number two in the UK album chart?

60 This band played 'When It Comes To You' on their tour, a song which appeared on *On Every Street* in 1991, the last album by which English rock band?

QUIZ 73

CULT BANDS

You know the ones: the bands you've never heard of who sell out every gig in about two minutes flat. The bands whose names are tattooed on the wrists of the weird kids at school. The bands whose names appear on the T-shirts worn by the guy down the street who everyone thinks is a serial killer. The bands you finally get to see at *End of the Road* and think: 'F*** me, they're brilliant.' Here are two sections of straight questions – but very definitely not straight answers.

Answers: page 522

1 John Darnielle is the main songwriter and performer in which cult US indie band? What's the subject matter of their 2015 album *Beat the Champ*?

2 Which electronic production team have produced three albums of artists covering other people's songs called *Music of Quality and Distinction*? What was the subtitle and subtext of the third release, which came out in 2013?

3 Released in 1972, *#1 Record* was the first album by which Memphis guitar band fronted by Alex Chilton? Chilton had first found fame in which band, who had a big hit with *The Letter* in 1967?

4 Tim Friese-Greene acted as producer and co-writer for much of the output by which eighties band? Who was the band's frontman, singer and main songwriter, who subsequently retired from the music industry to spend more time with his family?

5 Whose steadfastly uncommercial career spans 16 studio albums, from 1982's *Closing Time* to 2011's *Bad as Me*? Which Grammy-winning 1999 release gave him his first UK top ten album?

6 Which 1980s proto hip hop funk band is made up of David Weiss and Don Fagenson? Which Temptations song gave them a UK Top 20 hit?

7 Led by Robert Pollard, which band have released over 20 albums since 1987 to massive acclaim but little commercial success? What name have they given to a series of four box sets, each containing four CDs and 100 tracks of unreleased material?

8 Luke Haines was the singer and songwriter in the Auteurs. Under what name, taken from a seventies radical militant organisation, did he release a solo album in 1996? What was the side project he formed with John Moore and Sarah Nixey, reaching the Top 20 with 'The Facts of Life'?

9 Mark Linkous, who committed suicide in 2010, was the frontman and songwriter for which American band? What was the name of their last album, made with multiple collaborators and produced with Danger Mouse?

10 What is the name of the band formed by Dean Wareham after the break-up of Galaxie 500? Which guitarist, a huge influence on them, joined the band on their third album, *Penthouse*?

11 Who is the only permanent member of Spiritualized? What's the name of the band he previously formed in 1982 with Pete Kember, developing the experimental guitar sound that later characterised Spiritualized's output?

12 Gordon Gano and Brian Ritchie have been at the helm of the various line-ups of which American indie band? Which cult song of theirs found a new lease of life when it was re-recorded for the movie *Grosse Point Blank*?

13 Which Australian band acquired a cult following and had a Top 10 hit with their debut album, *Since I Left You*, in 2001? What's the name of the follow-up album, released a full 15 years later in July 2016?

14 *Isn't Anything* is an album of noisy, effects-saturated guitar rock by which experimental Anglo-Irish band? Which record label removed them from their roster after their second album, *Loveless*, went way over budget and failed to match its terrific reviews with commercial success?

15 Fee Waybill is the demonic stage presence of which cabaret-cum-punk band, formed in the mid seventies? What has been their only UK Top 30 hit, reaching number 28 in 1977?

BONUS TRACKS

16 Alison Statton is the breathy, emotionless voice of which cult band, who formed in the late seventies and have recently got back together? What's the title of the band's only album, a genuine cult classic?

17 'The alcohol loves you, while...' Doing what, according to the Associates' biggest hit, 'Party Fears Two'? Who was the band's lead singer, who committed suicide in 1997 two months before his 40th birthday?

18 What was the debut single by the Talking Heads spin-off Tom Tom Club in 1981, a cult club classic? 'Under the Boardwalk', the second single from their debut album, was a cover of a 1964 hit by which American vocal group?

19 Cindy Wilson and Kate Pierson are the bouffant-haired singers in which classic band? Who's the group's male singer, who often delivers songs with Wilson and Pierson in a call-and-response style?

20 Charles Thompson is the real name of which influential singer, songwriter and guitarist? What's the name of his best-known band, co-founded with Joey Santiago when they were students at the University of Massachusetts?

21 Which Leeds-based indie act, pushed by John Peel when they emerged, released their debut album, *When in Rome, Kill Me*, in 1989? Named after their highest-charting single, what's the title of their compilation, released in 2006?

22 Ed Droste and Daniel Rossen share singing duties and play guitar in which chilled-out American rock band? What was their breakthrough album, which hit the UK charts in 2009?

23 Which Newport trio advertised their presence as *The Big 3* on the title of their debut album? And what was their cult debut single, named after a string of convenience stores?

24 The band Portishead took their name from an area to the south-west of which large British city? What's the name of their lead singr?

25 What was the debut single, an acid house cult classic, by A Guy Called Gerald? Performing as Derek and Clive, which two comedians are sampled on the record?

26 Under what name does Vini Reilly usually record, often with drummer Bruce Mitchell? On which Mancunian's debut solo album did Reilly play guitar in 1988?

27 Which singer composed the orchestral arrangements for Sarah Brightman's 2003 album *Harem*? What's the name of the band he's fronted for nearly 40 years?

28 Which TV drama made a hit out of eighties anthem 'Don't Stop Believin'' by Journey? And what's the title of the show's main theme, performed by London's Alabama 3?

29 Greg Saunier is the last original member still playing with which experimental US band, a cult favourite for 20 years? With which Madonna hit does their 2014 album share a title (but little else)?

30 Inspired by the familial roots of guitarist Peter Solowka, which band recorded sessions of Ukrainian folk music for John Peel's radio show? What was the unsurprising name of the new band formed by Solowka when he left the group in 1991?

QUIZ 74

THE BOSS

Over the last 40 years, Bruce Springsteen has been arguably the most potent chronicler of the broken American dream. An ardent opponent of corporate unfairness, a passionate voice for equal opportunities and a hard worker who plays three-and-a-half-hour concerts because he thinks fans should be rewarded for shelling out, he does seem to be a preposterously decent guy as well as a wealthy and successful one. You know you've made it when the President of the United States addresses an audience and says, as Obama did, 'I may be the President, but he's the Boss.' This one's in three parts: straight questions, a lyric quiz and a spot-the-album challenge.

Answers: page 523

1 Which 1982 album was made on a four-track recorder at Springsteen's home? Which song, made famous on his next non-acoustic album, was recorded during these sessions and was eventually released in 1998 on the *Tracks* box set?

2 Who was the actress Springsteen married in 1985? Three years later, which album charted the turmoil and eventual break-up of the marriage?

3 Which song won Springsteen an Oscar in 1994? Released the following year, which mainly acoustic album was inspired by a John Steinbeck novel?

4 How many channels were on Springsteen's TV on *Human Touch*? Which companion album was released on the same day as *Human Touch* in 1992?

5 Amadou Diallo, an unarmed immigrant shot dead by four armed plain-clothes NYPD officers in 1999, was the subject of which Springsteen song, which he premiered at his 2000 reunion concerts with the E Street Band? On which album did a re-recorded version of the song eventually appear?

6 Which radical folk singer's work was the subject of a 2006 Springsteen album? Where did Springsteen record a live album featuring these songs, which was released the following year?

7 What's the title of Springsteen's 2009 album, dedicated to the E Street Band's late organ player Danny Federici? What was the name of the outlaw on it?

8 In which TV show did Springsteen make his acting debut in 2014? And what's the title of his directorial debut, a short film made the same year to accompany a track from his most recent album?

9 When Springsteen played in London's Hyde Park in 2012, the authorities cut the power while he was on stage performing with which British musical royalty? The unwelcome interruption meant that the audience didn't get to hear the final track, which would have been a tribute to which recently deceased member of the E Street Band?

10 Which of Springsteen's backing singers is the mother of his three children? At what sport did his daughter Jessica represent the USA in 2014?

BONUS TRACK 1

Fill in the missing lyrics to the following songs – the numbers in brackets represent the number of missing words.

11 'The highway's jammed with broken heroes ...' ('Born to Run' – 6)

12 'Put your make-up on ... And meet me tonight in Atlantic City' ('Atlantic City' – 5)

13 'But when I see you walkin' with him ... I wish I were blind' ('I Wish I Were Blind' – 4)

14 'No wedding day smiles, no walk down the aisle ...' ('The River' – 5)

15 'Sent me off to a foreign land, to go and ...' ('Born in the USA' – 4)

16 'Well my daddy worked the furnaces, kept 'em ...' ('Youngstown' – 3)

17 'I want a kiss from your lips, I want ... Woke up this morning to an empty sky' ('Empty Sky' – 5)

18 'Lights out tonight ...' ('Badlands' – 4)

19 'At night I wake up with the sheets soaking wet, and a ...' ('I'm on Fire' – 9)

20 'Mister state trooper, ...' ('State Trooper' – 4)

BONUS TRACK 2

In these lists of four tracks, three are from the same Springsteen album, while the fourth is a red herring from a different record. Name the album and spot the odd one out.

21 'Badlands', 'Factory', 'Prove It All Night' and 'State Trooper'.

22 'Death to My Hometown', 'Hunter of Invisible Game', 'This Depression' and 'We Take Care of Our Own'.

23 'Dancing in the Dark', 'Glory Days', 'Hungry Heart' and 'I'm on Fire'.

24 'Long Walk Home', 'Maria's Bed', 'Radio Nowhere' and 'Your Own Worst Enemy'.

25 'Kitty's Back, 'Mary Queen of Arkansas', 'Rosalita (Come Out Tonight)' and 'Wild Billy's Circus Story'.

26 'Brilliant Disguise', 'If I Should Fall Behind', 'Tougher than the Rest' and 'Walk Like a Man'.

27 'Adam Raised a Cain', 'Fire', 'Outside Looking In' and 'Rendezvous'.

28 'Atlantic City', 'Highway Patrolman', 'Reason to Believe' and 'Youngstown'.

29 'Backstreets', 'Jungleland', 'New York City Serenade' and 'Tenth Avenue Freeze-Out'.

30 'Empty Sky', 'The Fuse', 'My Best Was Never Good Enough' and 'My City of Ruins'.

QUIZ 75

PEOPLE'S PLAYLIST: YOU SEXY THING

Here are 40 songs, some explicit and some merely suggestive, that detail or imply the act of love... or at least the prospect of it. Yes, it's a quiz devoted to intimations of the beast with two backs... Let's talk about sex, baby.

Answers: page 524

1   Which US married couple asked each other to 'Do That to Me One More Time' in 1979?

2   And who moaned her way through the highly suggestive 'Love to Love You Baby four years earlier'?

3   Which unlikely sex symbol professed that he 'Can't Get Enough of Your Love, Babe' in 1974?

4   On which single, a cover of a 1975 hit for Labelle, did All Saints wonder – in French – whether we might like to join them in bed?

5   Which French band took a 'Sexy Boy' into the UK Top 20 in 1998?

6   Which band were named after a steam-powered dildo in William Burrough's *Naked Lunch*?

7   Who went 'Up the Neck' on their first album, and sang about 'The Adultress' on their second?

8   Who provided the sexy noises and giggling at the end of the Rod Stewart hit 'Tonight's the Night'?

9   Who exhorted us to 'Get Up' because he felt 'Like Being a Sex Machine'?

10 'Sexcrime' was a hit for the Eurythmics from which movie starring John Hurt?

11 Who was the object of Jimi Hendrix's attention on the first track of *Are You Experienced*?

12 Who sang about 'Hanky Panky' in 1990?

13 According to PJ Harvey, what do the whores do 'While the Hustlers Whore'?

14 Who was *Lovesexy* in 1988?

15 Who alone could 'quench this thirst' for Gregory Isaacs?

16 Who was 'Sexed Up' and 'Tripping' in the 21st century?

17 Who didn't have to put out the red light, as far as the Police were concerned?

18 And who referenced the song in a line from their single 'When the Sun Goes Down'?

19 Where did Dylan want his friend to 'Lay Lady Lay'?

20 What am I, if 'I won't work for nobody but you'?

21 Who sang 'Don't Wake the Scarecrow', a bleak tale of a rural American brothel?

22 Who wanted your sex on the *Beverly Hills Cop II* soundtrack?

23 What's the title of US rapper K7's dirty hit from 1994?

24 'Where you from, you sexy thing?' Who asked the question?

25 'The bed is on fire with passionate love, the neighbours complain about the noises above.' Which band?

26 Who suggested 'Let's Get It On' on his 1973 album of the same name?

27 Where did T-Spoon make out in their 1997 European hit?

28 Who wanted to 'Rock Your Body'?

29 In *This Is Spinal Tap*, Nigel Tufnel (played by Christopher Guest) plays the first few chords of a new ballad on the piano and then reveals the title to be – what?

30 Who sang 'X Offender', a song about a crush on a policeman?

31 What saucy request did the 1975 make on their second album *I Like It When You Sleep, for You Are So Beautiful Yet So Unaware of It*?

32 And who admitted that 'I Love a Man in Uniform'?

33 Whose had a hit with 'Sex on Fire' in 2008?

34 Who wanted to talk about sex in 1991?

35 What kind of sex did Japan sing about in 1981?

36 Who was a 'Sexy MF' in 1992?

37 Who was a 'Sex Bomb' with Tom Jones?

38 What was Mel'isa Morgan's saucy request in 1986, a cover of the Prince original?

39 Who would have us believe that Sheffield is the 'Sex City'?

40 Before confessing 'now I need you more than ever', what improper suggestion did Mick Jagger make in 1967?

QUIZ 76

THE REVOLUTION STARTS NOW

Popular music has long been, and hopefully long will remain, a valid voice of protest. Whenever you hear men and women in suits crying foul and calling for a clampdown, you know healthy protest is afoot and the towers of the citadel have been rocked. We need more of it, perhaps following the examples of some of the acts featured in these 30 questions.

Answers: page 525

1   What was the subject matter of the Who's 1967 single 'Pictures of Lily'? On the same subject, which 1980 single turned the Vapors into one-hit wonders?

2   Who received abuse from many right-wing American figures when he released 'John Walker's Blues', a reflection on the war in Afghanistan and Iraq from the perspective of a jihadist? Which all-female country band saw their records effectively banned by some US radio stations after they spoke out against the war?

3   Which D:Ream hit was adopted by the Labour Party for their 1997 general election campaign? Which Lighthouse Family song did the party favour in 2001?

4   Who wrote 'Ohio', a protest song about the deaths of four people that occurred when the National Guard opened fire on unarmed peace protesters? What was the name of the university where the shootings took place?

5   'September '77, Port Elizabeth, weather fine.' So begins 'Biko', one of the most powerful anti-apartheid songs by a western artist. Who was the singer? And what was the number of the police room where Steve Biko was murdered by the South African police, as referenced in the song?

6   What is the anthemic opening track on Patti Smith's 1988 comeback album *Dream of Life*? Who used the track as a call-to-arms on his Vote for Change shows in 2004, in support of Democratic Presidential candidate John Kerry?

7   What is the lengthy experimental track on the fourth and final side of the vinyl release of the Beatles' *White Album*? On the third side of the same album, who, apart from John Lennon, had nothing to hide?

8   John Lennon's first two solo singles, credited to the Plastic Ono Band, were a peace anthem and a drug recovery song. What are their titles?

9   Who wrote the anti-poverty classic 'This Land Is Your Land' in 1940? And to which Irving Berlin song was it a riposte?

10   Why was the Beatles' 'Come Together' denied prime-time airplay on BBC radio? Which Kinks song was banned by the Beeb for very similar reasons?

11 Which 16-year-old schoolgirl killed two teachers and injured many of her classmates at Cleveland Elementary School in San Diego after she had been bought a gun for Christmas in 1978? Which Boomtown Rats hit was inspired by the incident?

12 *Words for the Dying*, a 1989 album by John Cale, was written in 1982 in response to which event? Which fellow Welshman's words did Cale draw on heavily for this semi-orchestral piece?

13 Covered by the Horrors and the White Stripes, 'Jack the Ripper' was originally a Joe Meek-produced recording by which singer in the 1960s? In what guise did he try and affect British politics between 1983 and 1999?

14 Before becoming Australian Minister for the Environment, Heritage & the Arts, Peter Garrett was the singer with which successful rock band? Which vehement anti-nuclear protest took them into the British Top 10 and the American Top 20 in 1987?

15 Which band got into in trouble after appearing at a Lollapalooza gig in Philadelphia in 1993 wearing nothing but gaffa tape over their mouths, a protest against censorship? From which New York building were they ejected while trying to film a video for 'Sleep Now in the Fire'?

BONUS TRACKS

16 Leon Rosselson's political song 'The World Turned Upside Down' was taken into the charts in 1985 by which artist on his *Between the Wars* EP? What was the title of this singer's first album, which introduced his unique brand of folk rock to an unsuspecting world?

17 Which English Catholic suggested that we ought to 'Give Ireland Back to the Irish' in 1972? And who sang about the need for an 'Alternative Ulster' in 1978?

18 Where did police attack a group of travellers known as the Peace Convoy as they tried to set up camp for a free festival in 1985? Which band wrote 'Battle of the Beanfield' about the incident?

19 Who included a track called 'Reggae fi Peach' on his 1980 album *Bass Culture*, a song about about the death of New Zealander Blair Peach at the hands of the police while he was protesting against the National Front in 1979? Who was this artist's regular producer and musical guide on many of his dub poetry recordings?

20 Whose 1978 EP *Rise Free* included the anthem '(Sing If You're) Glad to Be Gay', an originally written for the 1976 Gay Pride march? What's the title of the band's debut album, full of powerful political invective?

21 Which song was released as a single by Buffalo Springfield in response to the police action during the Sunset Strip riots in Los Angeles in 1966? Which famous club, located at 8901 Sunset Boulevard, were Buffalo Springfield in residence at the time?

22 Who is the openly gay lead singer of the Britpop band Ocean Colour Scene? What's the title of the anti-war song he penned with the band and released as the first single off their fourth album *One from the Modern*?

23 Whose debut album featured an anti-corporate song called 'Nat West – Barclays – Midlands – Lloyds'? A cover of which anti-war movie theme gave the band their first British Top 10 hit?

24 Which band changed a crucial lyric to 'duck my sick' in an attempt to get more airplay for 'Big Gay Heart' in 1993? Who is the band's lead singer and songwriter?

25 Which Canadian singer came out in a magazine article in 1992, one of the first high-profile music stars to do so? And which American star followed suit in January 1993, coming out publicly at a ball to celebrate President Clinton's inauguration?

26 Which band's name is a slightly modified version of the Italian for 'political writings'? And which eighties act named themselves after a group of 19th-century political revolutionaries?

27 'Seconds' by the Human League and U2's 'Pride (In the Name of Love)' were both written about assassinations. Who were the respective victims?

28 Which band incited their audience to 'rise above state control' on the opening track of *Damaged*, their 1981 debut? Which vocalist made his debut with the band on the album, after three previous singers had come and gone from the role?

29 Members of which band were arrested and imprisoned by the Russian government in 2012? In which American TV drama did they appear as themselves in 2015, featuring alongside main star Kevin Spacey?

30 Which incoming US President used Bruce Springsteen's 'Born in the USA' as his campaign song, apparently oblivious to its anti-government message? And which politician was sued by Jackson Browne in 2008 for using 'Running on Empty' without permission?

QUIZ 77

NOT SO RIOT GIRLS

When Kate Bush emerged at the end of the seventies, she was greeted as a freak. When she played her comeback shows in 2014, she was feted as a goddess and a national institution. Following a short quiz about Bush's nearly 40-year career, you'll find questions about some of her successors and contemporaries.

Answers: page 526

1   How old was Kate Bush when 'Wuthering Heights' topped the UK singles chart in 1978? What's the title of her debut album, released shortly afterwards? (2)

2   'Wuthering Heights' has been Bush's only British number one so far, but which other five have taken her into the Top Ten? (One song managed it twice, once in the shape of a 2012 remix; and one other song was a duet.) (5)

3   What's the title of the suite of songs that makes up the second half of *Hounds of Love*? (1)

4   What's the name of the suite that occupies disc two of *Aerial*? (1)

5   'Egypt', 'The Wedding List' and 'Army Dreamers' appear on which Bush album? What was the album's first single from the album, the video for which featured the singer writhing around like a foetus in the womb? Which sixties cult folkie provided backing vocals? (3)

6   Which 2005 Bush single was a dreamy take on the Elvis-is-alive theme? And which Marvin Gaye song appeared on its B-side? (2)

7   Released in 2011, *Director's Cut* consists of restructured or re-recorded songs from which two studio albums? (2)

8   Which Bush song was used at the opening ceremony to the 2012 London Olympics, amid rumours (false) that Kate herself would sing at the event? (1)

9   Where did Bush perform her long-awaited live shows in 2014? What was the name of the show? (2)

10 Who appeared in the show as 'the painter' and a number of other roles? (1)

BONUS TRACK I

11 *Come Away with Me* took Norah Jones to number one in the UK and the US. What are the titles of her second and third albums, which both also topped the charts on both sides of the Atlantic?

12 Which 1994 single took Tori Amos into the British Top 10 for the first time? Which other single from *Under the Pink*, her chart-topping second album, followed it into the Top 10 later the same year?

13 Who had UK Top 10 hits with the singles 'Left Outside Alone' and 'Sick and Tired' in 2004? The same singer's debut album reached number two in the UK in 2000 – what's it called?

14 Who had a number one hit in 2013 with a cover of Keane's 'Somewhere Only We Know'? What was her next single, an attack on body image expectations?

15 'Professional Widow' by Tori Amos reached number one after it was remixed by which DJ? Who, allegedly, is the subject of the song's caustic lyrics?

16 What was Lene Lovich's 'Lucky Number', according to her 1979 single? What's the title of her second and highest-charting album, which features the single 'Birdsong' and a cover of 'The Night' by Frankie Valli & the Four Seasons?

17 The widely acclaimed *Give My Love to London* was released in 2014 by which enduring female singer? Which Americana star co-wrote and played guitar on the title track?

18 'Burn' was the first UK number one for which homegrown singer-songwriter? Which movie gave her a second chart-topper with 'Love Me Like You Do'?

19 What was Amy Winehouse wearing on her debut album? And what, rather poignantly, did she ask on the fourth track of the posthumously-released album *Lioness*?

20 Released in 2002, which Beth Orton album is the only one to have reached the British Top 10? 'Concrete Sky', the album's first single, featured vocals from Ryan Adams and was co-written by which indie guitar hero?

BONUS TRACK 2

Match the album to the artist.

21 *Under My Skin.* 22 *Yours Truly, Cellophane Nose.* 23 *Drastic Fantastic.* 24 *Trailer Park.* 25 *Fellow Workers.* 26 *Our Version of Events.* 27 *To Survive.* 28 *Sometimes I Sit and Think, and Sometimes I Just Sit.* 29 *Vespertine.* 30 *Born to Die.*

Artists: Courtney Barnett, Björk, Ani DiFranco, Lana Del Rey, Beth Jeans Houghton, Joan as Policewoman, Avril Lavigne, Beth Orton, Emeli Sandé, KT Tunstall.

QUIZ 78

ROCKERS

If a band is more than a pop group, but not a metal band, what are they? These are the rockers, the bands who are very definitely rock and roll, but aren't extreme enough to be metal or punk or any of those clannish genres. The first section is a straight Q&A, while the second follows a double mix-and-match format. Confused? Read on to find out...

Answers: page 527

1   The 2016 box set *The Last of the Teenage Idols* was a definitive collection of whose recordings? What unfortunate fate befell his younger brother Les, in 1972?

2   In Bon Jovi's monster hit 'Livin' on a Prayer', where does Tommy, one of the protagonists, earn his living? On which platinum-selling album does the song appear?

3   Which band's sound revolved around the twin guitars of Andy Powell, complete with Flying V, and Ted Turner? What's the title of their well-received third album from 1972, a critical and commercial high point for the band?

4   Which Canadian band originally consisted of three brothers, Randy, Robbie and Tim, plus bassist/singer Fred Turner? What was their breakthrough single, which topped the US chart and went to number two in the UK in 1974?

5   If, in the late eighties, you saw Duff McKagan, Izzy Stradlin and Steven Adler on stage, which two other musicians would you probably have been watching alongside them?

6   Bruce Dickinson has always been the most high-profile member of Iron Maiden, but who's the band's bass player, principal songwriter and de facto leader? And who's been Maiden's drummer since 1982?

7   Led Zeppelin were formed to fulfil tour dates booked for Jimmy Page's previous band. Who were they? And what was the name of singer Robert Plant's previous band, which he revived for a 2010 album?

8   Which Scottish rockers only hit it big with their fourth album, *Puzzle*? Which Daft Punk classic did they cover on Dermot O'Leary's *Saturday Sessions* in 2014?

9   Which glam rocker broke six ribs after falling offstage while touring his 1975 album *Welcome to My Nightmare*? What's the title of the 2011 release that served as a kind of sequel to the album?

10 Which 1983 album was the biggest commercial hit for ZZ Top, largely off the back of the lead single 'Gimme All Your Lovin'? Which song by Doc Pomus

and Mort Shuman, originally written for Elvis Presley, gave them their only other UK Top 10 hit?

11 Meat Loaf released *Bat out of Hell* in 1977. What were the subtitles of *Bat out of Hell II* and *III*, released in 1993 and 2006 respectively?

12 What was the lead single from Thin Lizzy's 1976 album *Jailbreak*? What was the band's equally excellent follow-up album, issued only six months later?

13 AC/DC took which damned route to chart success in 1979? Two years earlier, on *Let There Be Rock*, what had they already determined about this same destination?

14 Which album took Lenny Kravitz to number one in the UK, with a Top 10 single of the same name leading the way? What part did Kravitz play in the first two films in the popular *Hunger Games* series?

15 Who replaced Ian Gillan as lead vocalist with Deep Purple in 1973? Which band did he go on to form after leaving in 1976?

BONUS TRACKS

Below, three lists. The first features 15 epic songs. The second contains 15 bands. The third takes in 15 albums. All you have to do is match each song with its artist and the album from which it originally came. If you match all three, score two points. If you get the right artist but the wrong album or vice versa, score one point. But if you match up artist and album but get the wrong song, you get nowt. Because, let's face it, matching The Who to *Who's Next* ain't really that tricky.

Songs:

1 'Won't Get Fooled Again'. 2 'Stargazer'. 3 'Like a Hurricane'. 4 'Tyrants'. 5 'Child in Time'. 6 'War Pigs'. 7 'Keeper of the Seven Keys'. 8 'Ocean In Between the Waves'. 9 'Homecoming'. 10 'In My Time of Dying'. 11 'Free Bird'. 12 'I Would Do Anything for Love (But I Won't Do That)'. 13 'This Corrosion'. 14 'Prophet's Song'. 15 'The Rime of the Ancient Mariner'.

Artists:

Black Mountain, Black Sabbath, Deep Purple, Green Day, Helloween, Iron Maiden, Led Zeppelin, Lynyrd Skynyrd, Meat Loaf, Queen, Ritchie Blackmore's Rainbow, Sisters of Mercy, the War on Drugs, the Who, Neil Young.

Albums:

American Idiot, American Stars n Bars, Bat out of Hell II: Back into Hell, Floodland, In the Future, In Rock, Keeper of the Seven Keys: Part II, Lost in the Dream, A Night at the Opera, Paranoid, Powerslave, Physical Graffiti, (Pronounced 'Lěh-'nérd 'Skin-'nérd), Rainbow Rising, Who's Next.

QUIZ 79

MORE EIGHTIES

We said our piece about this pernicious decade back in Quiz 15. Here's more of the same: dozens of embarrassing coiffures with the occasional decent song hidden among them. After 15 straight questions, three lists – the last one with a twist.

Answers: page 528

1   Which Glaswegian band was, and still is, fronted by singers Ricky Ross and Lorraine McIntosh? What was their first UK Top 10 single, the first to be taken from their album *When the World Knows Your Name*?

2   Which classic 1983 album by New Order saw them develop a poppier sound? Which massive track, originally released only as a 12-inch single, was added to the album for its American release?

3   Who is the other member of Pet Shop Boys alongside vocalist Neil Tennant? Who added guitar and harmonica to their 2009 album *Yes*?

4   From which band did Malcolm McLaren pinch three musicians to back teenage singer Annabella Lwin in Bow Wow Wow? What was Bow Wow Wow's first UK Top 10 hit, released in 1982?

5   What was the first single, a number four hit in the UK, from Peter Gabriel's 1986 album *So*? And who sang with Gabriel on the Top 10 follow-up 'Don't Give Up'?

6   A Volkswagen advert shot which Scottish band to number one in the UK with 'Young at Heart' in 1993, nine years after the same song had reached number eight? Who co-wrote the song and recorded it with her bandmates on their debut album *Deep Sea Skiving* in 1983?

7   Eighties supergroup the Power Station featured John Taylor and Roger Taylor from Duran Duran, drummer Tony Thompson and which singer? With which seventies disco band had Thompson come to prominence?

8   Who was the male singer in the Human League? What was the smash hit he had in 1984 with electro maestro Giorgio Moroder?

9   Which Neil Diamond song gave UB40 their first British number one? And who sang with them on their later number-one hit, 'I Got You Babe'?

10 Who played 'hard to get' and smiled 'from time to time'? The song, the band's only British number one, was released in the UK at the end of 1981 as the B-side to which song from the same album, before reaching the top of the charts in its own right the following year?

11 George Michael had five number one singles in the UK as part of which eighties pop duo? Which solo single took him to the top of the charts while he was still part of the band?

12 In which nightclub did Steve Strange and Rusty Egan showcase new electronic music in the early to mid eighties? In which band did Egan and Strange play together?

13 What did Echo & the Bunnymen 'Bring On' as a specially released single to accompany their first compilation, *Songs to Learn and Sing*? For which John Hughes movie was the song recorded?

14 Who had hits in the late eighties with 'Forgotten Town', 'Ideal World' and 'Hooverville (And They Promised Us the World)'? Where did the band get their name?

15 Cyndi Lauper has had four Top 10 hits in the UK. Two of them have been different versions of 'Girls Just Wanna Have Fun' – what are the other two, one a ballad and the other a song originally written for Roy Orbison?

BONUS TRACK 1

Who had hits with the following singles?

1 'Favourite Shirts (Boy Meets Girl)' (1982). 2 'Ordinary Day' (1987). 3 'Love Is a Stranger' (1983). 4 'Twist in My Sobriety' (1988). 5 'New Song' (1983). 6 'Baby I Don't Care' (1989). 7 'Only When You Leave' (1984). 8 'The Living Years' (1989). 9 'You Give Love a Bad Name' (1986). 10 'Private Investigations' (1982).

BONUS TRACK 2

Who reached number one in the UK singles chart with these hits?

1 'Together We Are Beautiful' (1980). 2 'Frankie' (1985). 3 'You Win Again' (1987 – careful!). 4 'The Reflex' (1984). 5 'The Lion Sleeps Tonight' (1982). 6 'Belfast Child' (1989). 7 '19' (1985). 8 'Swing the Mood', 'That's What I Like' and 'Let's Party' (1989). 9 'Crying' (1980). 10 'Orinoco Flow' (1988).

BONUS TRACK 3

Here are successful albums from the eighties, one from each year – 1980 through 1989. Simply match each album to the year in which it was released.

1 *The Art of Falling Apart* (Soft Cell). 2 *Flesh and Blood* (Roxy Music). 3 *The Gift* (The Jam). 4 *Misplaced Childhood* (Marillion). 5 *The Raw and the Cooked* (Fine Young Cannibals). 6 *The Riddle* (Nik Kershaw). 7 *The Seeds of Love* (Tears for Fears). 8 *Solitude Standing* (Suzanne Vega). 9 *Through the Barricades* (Spandau Ballet). 10 *Wired for Sound* (Cliff Richard).

QUIZ 80

GOOD DAY, BAD DAY

Steve Lamacq is on 6 Music most days and regularly invites his listeners to submit a pair of songs which highlight the difference between a good day and a bad day. Here we have 15 questions on upbeat good day music, followed by 15 questions on miserable bad day tunes.

Answers: page 529

GOOD DAY

1 Captain Sensible had a novelty UK number one in 1982 with a version of the Rodgers & Hammerstein song 'Happy Talk'. From which musical is it taken? What was his similarly wacky follow-up?

2 'Summer Holiday' was a 1963 UK number one taken from a feel-good movie showcasing the talents of which singer? Which song by his backing band, also from the film, bumped 'Summer Holiday' off the top?

3 What was the last track on the first side of the Undertones' debut album, later released in a speeded-up version as a single? Who was the writer of the song, one of two brothers in the band?

4 What was the 1978 debut single by the Undertones, a minor chart hit partly due to incessant plugging by John Peel? What was the 2012 film about the independent record label that launched the band's career?

5 What was the massive 1993 global hit that launched Swedish pop band Ace of Base? Apart from Abba, who are the only other Swedish act to have sold more records than Ace of Base?

6 Which upbeat chunk of funk provided Kool and the Gang with their only US number one single in 1980? Which pop icon recorded it as her last single with Stock Aitken Waterman?

7 'Happy Hour' was a 1986 hit for which Northern jangly guitar pop band? What unlikely football score was the title of their debut album?

8 Which track, first recorded by Elvis on the 1957 film soundtrack *Loving You*, was a hit for Wanda Jackson in 1960? Which 1989 Robin Williams school-based film used it on the soundtrack?

9 Which actor/comedian appeared in the video for Bobby McFerrin's 1988 novelty hit 'Don't Worry, Be Happy'? Which Indian guru did the song quote in its title?

10 'Buddy Holly, Scammell lorries, yellow socks, sitting on the potty, the Marx Brothers and Salvador Dali' were all what, in 1979? What part?

11 Which song from U2's album *All That You Can't Leave Behind* became their fourth UK number one single in 2000? Which TV sports programme adopted the song as its theme?

12 Which upbeat song was Chic's biggest UK hit? It was based on the 1929 song "Happy Days Are Here Again': which US President used this song as his campaign theme in 1932?

13 Which jazz artist had a UK number one with 'What A Wonderful World' in 1967? A Joey Ramone version of the song was used at the end of which 2002 Michael Moore film?

14 Which song, released at the end of 2013, became the biggest selling single of 2014? Which animated movie propelled it to that level of success?

15 *The Roar of the Greasepaint – The Smell of the Crowd* (1964) isn't the most renowned musical, but it spawned a stonewall classic when one of its songs was covered by Nina Simone the following year. What was it and who included a super version on their 2001 album *Origin of Symmetry*?

BAD DAY

16 When Nick Cave released his new album in 1996, its title hinted it would be low on giggles: what was it? Which fellow Aussie duetted with him on 'Where the Wild Roses Grow'?

17 Who bowed to public demand and recorded a duet of the break-up song 'You Don't Bring Me Flowers', after their two solo versions were spliced together by a radio producer?

18 Who had a UK number one in 1960 with 'Tell Laura I Love Her', the dying words of Tommy, who loves Laura but will not make their wedding day. How does Tommy meet his end?

19 Which country star sang 'I Fall to Pieces' in 1961? Who did the backing vocals, taking time off from their day job as Elvis's backing singers?

20 Which 1971 song, about an abused woman snapping and retaliating against her man, was US soul band the Persuaders' biggest hit? Which band gave it a twist with female vocals on their 1984 album *Learning To Crawl*?

21 Where, according to a track on their 1992 album *Bricks Are Heavy*, would you end up if you upset L7? Which musician and producer, fresh from success on Nirvana's *Nevermind*, produced the album?

22 Which 1999 Bloodhound Gang album led off with the entertainingly offensive 'I Hope You Die'? Who was the porn star referenced in the title of another track on this album?

23 What is Eleanor Rigby doing in the first line of Paul McCartney's lyric about 'all the lonely people'? And who is writing a sermon that no-one will hear?

24 What is the junction in question in Squeeze's 'Up the Junction'? In their 'Labelled With Love', what does the protagonist sell off along with her silver and china?

25 Who topped the US chart in 2005 with 'Bad Day'? Which cartoon band covered the song for their eponymous 2007 movie?

26 Which American country pop act recorded 'The Ballad of Lucy Jordan' in 1974? Who included an edgier electronic version of the song on her 1979 album, *Broken English*?

27 What was the characteristically gloomy title of the Smiths' first UK Top 10 single from 1984? What was the subject matter of the single's controversial B-side 'Suffer Little Children'?

28 American couple Brett and Rennie Sparks record under what name? Their song 'Far From Any Road' was used as the theme tune for the first season of which gothic TV crime drama series?

29 Based on news stories that executed American murderer Gary Gilmore had donated his eyes to science, which punk band sang 'Gary Gilmore's Eyes'? Which new wave band's song 'Bring On the Night' was also inspired by Gilmore?

30 What is the 1991 Richard Thompson song about a biker, James, who suffers a fatal accident and bequeaths his beloved bike to his girlfriend? What is her name?

QUIZ 81

OUTTAKES

In recent years, many albums have been repackaged with a host of extras or outtakes tagged on to the end, or perhaps on a second CD. Most of the time, it turns out that these outtakes were left off the original album for good reason, but the odd gem does get unearthed. Here are 30 questions that were all dropped from this book during the edit, most (but not all) because we couldn't find the right section for them. This pick-and-mix selection comes in two sections, each with 15 questions.

Answers: page 530

1   Where was the Killers' only live album recorded in 2009? Which Joy Division song is the sole cover version on it?

2   *The Genius After Hours* and *The Genius Sings the Blues* were released by which artist in 1961? Which Don Gibson song gave him an international number one the following year?

3   'Can You Feel It', 'Don't Stop', 'Jai Ho!', 'Tubthumping', 'Never Forget', 'Hey Jude' and 'One Day Like This'. What's the connection. (We need a detailed answer for both points.)

4   Which two artists collaborated on *Mirror Ball* in 1995?

5   In 1939, whose band recorded 'In the Mood', a tune that became synonymous with their success? In what circumstances did he go missing in 1944?

6   Which artist has made the most appearances to date on the *Now!* series of compilations? And what was the significance of *Now! 62*, released in 2005?

7   Which member of Bruce Springsteen's band appeared in *The Sopranos* as club owner Silvio Dante? Who stood in for him on guitar for Springsteen's 2014 *High Hopes* tour after playing on the album of the same name?

8   The composer George Frideric Handel lived at 25 Brook Street in London's Mayfair. Which more contemporary musician has been honoured with an English Heritage blue plaque at number 23, commemorating the fact that he lived there in the late sixties? And which other artist has a blue plaque at 34 Montagu Square, where he lived for much of 1968?

9   'Sister Morphine' is a track on the Rolling Stones album *Sticky Fingers*. Who had to fight a legal battle to have her part in the song's composition acknowledged? Her own version was eventually released on a reissue of which classic 1979 album?

10 After his music career, Sonny Bono was elected to which august body after spending four years as the Mayor of Palm Springs in California? Who was Sonny's second wife?

11 *Here Lies Love* is a 2010 rock opera and album about the life of which controversial figure? Who co-wrote it with former Talking Heads frontman David Byrne?

12 Who made his jazz masterpiece *Kind of Blue* in just nine studio hours in 1959? Which noted pianist plays on four of the album's five tracks?

13 Who took the bold song *The Killing of Georgie*, about the murder of a gay man in New York, to number two in the UK in 1976? The album from which the song was taken, *A Night on the Town*, reached number one in the UK. In 2013, what became this singer's next British number-one long-player, setting a record for the longest gap between chart-topping albums?

14 Very introspective behaviour? Yes please – actually fundamental, bilingual. Release super electric nightlife. What are we talking about, and what's missing?

15 In 1994, Danish singer Sannie Carlson became the first act to go straight to number in the UK singles chart with her debut single. What's her stage name? And what was the song?

BONUS TRACKS

16 Messrs. Hodges and Peacock achieved notable chart success between 1978 and 1987 with a series of novelty songs. What's their stage name? And what was their first UK Top 10 single, a plea to a chatterbox other 'alf?

17 Jack White had a good 2005 – he headlined Glastonbury and got married. To whom? And which album, their fifth, did the White Stripes release in the same year?

18 'Standing Stone', 'Ecce Cor Meum' and 'Ocean's Kingdom' are all classical pieces composed by which popular musician? What is the meaning of 'Ecce Cor Meum', which the composer adopted as his motto when invited to create a coat of arms on receipt of his knighthood?

19 The Attractions, the First Men, the Imposters, the Roots, the Vaudeville. Which two of these have never been the names of backing bands used by Elvis Costello?

20 Who went to the top of the UK singles chart in April 2016 and was still there in the middle of the summer, an unprecedented run for the modern chart of 16 weeks (and counting)? Which Nigerian artist guests on the song?

21 In the list of the bestselling albums in US chart history, who's the leading country artist? She sits at sixth place on the list, one place ahead of Fleetwood Mac's *Rumours* – with which album?

22 Which Scottish rock musician suffered a brain haemorrhage in 2005? Which four-word phrase did he keep repeating as he began to recover, a phrase that was later used as the title of a 2014 documentary chronicling his illness and recovery?

23 What was Frank Sinatra's last solo UK number one, released in 1966? On which song did he duet with Bono in 1994?

24 Under which name did Ian Kilmister achieve rock and roll fame? His band got their name from a song by his previous group, from which he was sacked: which band?

25 Which saxophonist lent his name to a famous London jazz club? And which other saxophonist founded the club with him and ran it for nearly 50 years?

26 Neil Hannon and Thomas Walsh have combined under which name to release two albums of songs about cricket? Which Pakistani batsman is mentioned by name in the title of a track on their debut?

27 'The Whole of the Moon', the Waterboys' biggest hit, appears on which 1985 album? In which British town was the album recorded?

28 With which classical ensemble did Elvis Costello collaborate on the 1993 project *The Juliet Letters*? Which 70-year-old songwriting legend worked with Costello on the 1998 album *Painted from Memory*?

29 Which two blonde vocalists were the only white female singers to have a solo line on the 1985 USA for Africa single 'We Are the World'?

30 Which jazz clarinettist was the first British artist to top the US pop charts in 1962? What was the track, an instrumental that became the UK's biggest selling single of the year despite never reaching number one over here?

QUIZ 82

RADIOHEAD

How do you categorise a band as unique, adventurous and sometimes even strange as Radiohead? They truly are musical Marmite. There are two parts to this quiz: the first is on the Oxford boys themselves, while the second spotlights a number of other modern acts who've pushed the musical envelope in similar ways.

Answers: page 531

1   *Hail to the Thief* is, so far, the band's most overtly political album. Who was the 'thief' of the title? And which single used an Orwellian conceit of bad arithmetic as a political metaphor? (2)

2   Along with Thom Yorke, who are Radiohead's two guitarists? (2)

3   What was the name of the band formed by Thom Yorke's brother, Andy, who had a minor hit with their debut album *Almost Here* in 1998? (2)

4   What was the name of the supergroup formed by Thom Yorke to play songs from his solo album *The Eraser*? Which Red Hot Chili Pepper took part in the project? (2)

5   Which 2000 Radiohead album set a precedent for their new modus operandi when it was released with no singles and no advance publicity? What's the name of the band's 2016 album, announced only a week before its release? (2)

6   Which jazz musician's band guested on 'Life in a Glasshouse' on *Amnesiac*? (1)

7   Which song did Radiohead release on Christmas Day in 2015? For what was it originally written? (2)

8   Which Talking Heads album features the song 'Radio Head' from which the band took their name? What were Radiohead previously called, an acknowledgment that they couldn't rehearse more than once a week due to their educational commitments? (2)

9   Which Academy Award-winning 2007 film features a much-praised score by Jonny Greenwood? (1)

10 What was the first track released from *A Moon Shaped Pool* on 3 May 2016? Who directed the video to accompany 'Daydreaming', the second release? (2)

11 What's the title of the 1999 documentary that followed Radiohead on tour? Which album were the band promoting on the tour that features in the film? (2)

12 Which single from *In Rainbows* was written around a decade before its release, and had been a staple of the band's live shows for years? (1)

13 Up until 2016, which seven Radiohead singles have reached the British Top 10? (7)

14 Which two Radiohead albums, released in 2000 and 2001, were recorded in the same sessions and represented a major departure from *OK Computer*? (2)

15 What was the name of the war veteran, the last surviving combat soldier from World War I, about whom Radiohead wrote a song to raise funds for the British Legion? (1)

BONUS TRACKS

16 *Narrow Stairs* is the US chart-topping sixth album by which group? From which comic British band of the sixties did they get their name?

17 *Love This Giant* is a 2012 collaboration between which two artists?

18 Which act was asked to remix Jean Michel Jarre's 'Oxygene' and instead came up with a very different piece called 'Toxygene'? What's the title of their 1991 debut, a groundbreaking collection of ambient techno?

19 Which female singer guested on Snow Patrol's 'Set the Fire to the Third Bar', taken from their 2006 album *Eyes Open*? Which single from the same album gave the band their biggest worldwide hit, reaching number six in the UK and number five in the US?

20 As well as releasing albums under the name Panda Bear, Noah Lennox is also a member of which band? Who did Panda Bear meet on his 2015 album?

21 Which Manchester techno act got their name from a Roland drum machine? Which 1989 single gave them their first UK hit?

22 Which band made their debut in 1989 with an EP called *Scar*, issued more than two years before their debut album *Spooky*? Which Britpop hero added guest vocals to the track 'Ciao!' on *Lovelife*, their third album?

23 Which nineties band named a track on their 1993 album *Chrome* after influential guitarist Robert Fripp? Which American rock singer guested with the group two years later on their 'Judy Staring at the Sun'?

24 Which Welsh band introduced a psychedelic edge to Britpop with their albums *Fuzzy Logic* and *Radiator*? They played live only once between 2009 and 2014 at a memorial concert – to whom?

25 Which act's ten albums include *Crumbling the Antiseptic Beauty, Ignite the Seven Cannons* and *Forever Breathes the Lonely Word*? Which cult hero founded the band?

26 Which singer-songwriter reached number three in the UK albums chart in 2012 with *Standing at the Sky's Edge*? The streets and scenery of which English city colour much of his work?

27 Released in 2012 and 2014, *World Music* and *Commune* are the two albums by which post-prog band, which performs in masks and costumes? From which country do they hail?

28 In 2011, which band issued a monthly series of bizarre releases that included a flash drive embedded in a replica foetus and an EP containing a single track that lasts for 24 hours? The latter release came in a limited edition of 13, cost $5,000 and arrived packaged in what ghoulish wrapper?

29 What is the significance of the title of Kasabian's album *48:13*? What graphic stylisation did the band apply to the track listing on the album cover?

30 In 2007, *Neon Bible* represented a commercial leap forward for which Canadian rock band? Who directed the 30-minute film that accompanied their even more successful third album, *The Suburbs*?

QUIZ 83

CLASSIC ALBUMS #5:
21ST CENTURY

This latest classic albums section concentrates on modern times and runs the noughties and the teens together – after all, it can take a while to see which albums are destined to be classics.

We'll say it again: you have three tracks and the year, and need to find the band and the title of the album. Although I suspect this is getting increasingly hard in the era of the single-track download.

Answers: page 532

1   'I Wish I Was a Girl'; 'Teenage Icon'; 'No Hope' (2012)

2   'Wrestlers'; 'Shake a Fist'; 'Ready for the Floor' (2008)

3   'Blame Game'; 'All of the Lights'; 'Runaway' (2010)

4   'Alone in Kyoto'; 'Surfing on a Rocket'; 'Cherry Blossom Girl' (2004)

5   'Waiting for a Sign'; 'Shut Up'; 'Husbands' (2013)

6   'Renegade'; 'Takeover'; 'Girls, Girls, Girls' (2001)

7   'Bitter Branches'; 'On Battleship Hill'; 'The Glorious Land' (2011)

8   'Troublemaker'; 'Lazuli'; 'Myth' (2012)

9   'Dungeness'; 'You Got the Style'; 'El Salvador' (2003)

10 'Extreme Ways'; 'In My Heart'; 'We Are All Made of Stars' (2002)

11 'One and Only': 'Turning Tables'; 'Rolling in the Deep' (2011)

12 'So Here We Are'; 'Pioneers'; 'Helicopter' (2005)

13 'In the Morning of thee Magicians'; 'Ego Tripping at the Gates of Hell'; 'Do You Realize??' (2002)

14 'Paper Gangsta'; 'Beautiful, Dirty, Rich'; 'Poker Face' (2008)

15 'Living for the Weekend'; 'Cash Machine'; 'Hard to Beat' (2005)

BONUS TRACKS

16 'Mary's in India'; 'Sand in My Shoes'; 'White Flag' (2003)

17 'Velvet Snow'; 'Taper Jean Girl'; 'The Bucket' (2004)

18 'Push That Knot Away'; 'Glamour Puss'; '(Still A) Weirdo' (2010)

19 'Shattered and Hollow'; 'Heaven Knows'; 'My Silver Lining' (2014)

20 'Twisted Logic'; 'White Shadows'; 'Speed of Sound' (2005)

21 'Reckless Serenade'; 'Brick By Brick'; 'Don't Sit Down Cause I've Moved Your Chair' (2011)

22 'Stuck in a Rut'; 'Growing On Me'; 'I Believe in a Thing Called Love' (2005)

23 'Time Honoured Tradition'; 'Everyday I Love You Less and Less'; 'I Predict a Riot' (2005)

24 'In the Garden of Edie'; 'Cool Papa Bell'; 'The Werewolf' (2016)

25 'Throw Away Your Television'; 'Dosed'; 'Can't Stop' (2002)

26 'Complicated'; 'Raining Men'; 'Only Girl (In the World)' (2010)

27 'Beat Goes On'; 'Candy Shop'; 'Give It 2 Me' (2008)

28 'Walk the Fleet Road'; 'Et Raw Meat = Blood Drool'; 'Papillon' (2009)

29 'Witch Doctor'; 'Someday (Place in the Sun)'; 'Trampoline' (2013)

30 'Milk & Black Spiders'; 'Inhaler'; 'My Number' (2013)

CLASSIC ALBUMS #6: 21ST CENTURY 2

So here's one more set of classic albums from the last 16 years – after all, nobody can claim 6 Music only ever plays old stuff. One last time: you have three tracks and the year, and need to find the band and the title of the album.

Answers: page 533

1 'The End of the Movie'; 'We are the Battery Human'; 'Zorbing' (2010)

2 'Cassy O'; 'Blame It On Me'; 'Budapest' (2014)

3 'Bubbles'; 'Many of Horror'; 'Mountains' (2009)

4 'Dawn Chorus', 'Something Like Happiness', 'Kamakura' (2015)

5 'Sawdust & Diamonds'; 'Cosmia'; 'Emily' (2006)

6 'Waiting for a Sign'; 'Dead Nature'; 'Shut Up' (2013)

7 'Hunter'; 'It Girl'; 'Marilyn Monroe' (2014)

8 'Crimson Day'; 'This Means War'; 'Shepherd of Fire' (2013)

9 'Desire'; 'Eyes Shut'; 'Shine' (2015)

10 'Architect's Dream'; 'Joanni'; 'Mrs Bartolozzi' (2005)

11 'Satin Chic'; 'Ride a White Horse'; 'Number 1' (2005)

12 'The Cave'; 'Dust Bowl Dance'; 'Little Lion Man' (2009)

13 'Universal Speech'; 'The Wrath of Marcie'; 'Grip Like a Vice' (2007)

14 'Dog Days Are Over'; 'Kiss with a Fist'; 'You've Got the Love' (2009)

15 'Littlest Things'; 'Alfie'; 'Smile' (2006)

BONUS TRACKS

16 'The Good Old Days'; 'Death on the Stairs'; 'Time for Heroes' (2002)

17 'Rumour Mill'; 'Never Let You Go'; 'Bloodstream' (2015)

18 'Don't Mug Yourself'; 'Let's Push Things Forward'; 'Geezers Need Excitement' (2002)

19 'Starlight'; 'Invincible'; 'Knights of Cydonia' (2006)

20 'Atlantis'; 'Explosions'; 'Anything Could Happen' (2012)

21 'Oceans Burning'; 'Changing the Rain'; 'I Can See Through You' (2011)

22 'Moonshine'; 'Fast Car/Slow Traffic'; 'Find the Torch, Burn the Plans' (2010)

23 'Tessellate'; 'Fitzpleasure'; 'Breezeblocks' (2012)

24 'Dollar Days'; 'Lazarus'; 'Tis a Pity She was a Whore' (2016)

25 'Work Song'; 'Foreigner's God'; 'Take Me to Church' (2014)

26 'Apollo 13'; 'Autograph'; 'Refugees' (2005)

27 'Weston Road Flows'; 'Controlla'; 'Hotline Bling' (2016)

28 'Cross Your Fingers'; 'Old Stone'; 'The Captain and the Hourglass' (2007)

29 'Black Plant'; 'The Time Has Come Again'; 'Standing Next To Me'(2008)

30 'Voyeur'; 'I Am Sold'; 'Retrograde' (2013)

QUIZ 85

POP STARS IN THE MOVIES

They all want a go, don't they? Not content with the kudos of being a rock star, they want the added ego boost of having cinemagoers hang on their every word as well. It's a step too far for some, but others surprise us by displaying acting chops that we didn't think would be there.

Two parts to this quiz. The first is a series of questions on pop stars who have appeared in movies: they are mainly straight roles that don't involve music. The second section is very definitely about music-related movies: we have listed 15 roles in music biopics or films that directly take the music industry and its stars as their subject matter, and we have also given you a list of 15 performers. You just have to match the actor to the film.

Answers: page 533

1   When Icelandic band the Sugarcubes disbanded in 1992, their singer pursued a solo career: who is she? Which 2000 film lead role won her a Palme d'Or?

2   Which two singers starred in the 1976 film, *A Star is Born*, about the rise of a star while her older lover's career goes into decline?

3   Who appeared as Max Zorin's sidekick, May Day, in the 1985 Bond movie *View to a Kill*? And who provided the film's theme tune?

4   Who provided the voice of Chef in *South Park*, a number one chart artist in 1998? In which 1981 cult movie directed by John Carpenter did he appear as a gang leader known as the Duke?

5   Which singer-as-actor connects *Down By Law* (Jim Jarmusch, 1986), *Short Cuts* (Robert Altman, 1993), *The Imaginarium of Dr Parnassus* (Terry Gilliam, 2009) and *Seven Psychopaths* (Martin McDonagh, 2012)? What part did he play in Bram Stoker's *Dracula* (Francis Ford Coppola, 1992)?

6   *The Social Network* was a 2010 film about the rise of Mark Zuckerberg and which social media phenomenon? Who played Zuckerberg's business partner, Sean Parker?

7   The *People vs Larry Flynt* was a 1996 film about a court case brought against Larry Flynt, the founder and owner of which adult magazine? Which rock star played Flynt's wife?

8   The 2009 against-the-odds film *Precious* starred which singer as a social worker? Which Chris O'Donnell/Renee Zellweger romantic comedy gave the singer her first film role?

9   Which singer played Meryl Streep's lesbian flatmate in the 1983 political drama *Silkwood*? Which 1987 movie won her an Academy Award?

10 Who earned plaudits for his portrayal of boxer Micky Ward in David O. Russell's *The Fighter* (2010)? What was the name of the actor's band during his pop star years at the start of his career?

11 Which 1983 David Cronenberg film gave Debbie Harry her first major film role? In which 1988 John Waters movie did she play Velma von Tussle, a role that Michelle Pfeiffer would later play?

12 *That'll be the Day* was a 1973 film about growing up in the rock and roll age starring David Essex. Who starred alongside him as a worldly teddy boy, Mike? And who co-starred as his friend and manager in the 1974 sequel, *Stardust*?

13 Who played the misfit Eddie in the cult movie version of the musical *The Rocky Horror Picture Show*? Which Academy Award-winning superstar in the making played winsome Janet Weiss?

14 Who played Great Train Robber Buster Edwards in the 1988 crime comedy *Buster*? Eight years earlier there was a darker drama about the armed robber, John McVicar: who played the title role?

15 Which rapper appeared in *Get Him to the Greek* (2010) as record company owner Sergio Roma? And which rapper co-starred in the film version of Starsky & Hutch as the street snitch, Huggy Bear?

BONUS TRACKS

Which actors played which roles?

1. John Lennon in *Nowhere Boy*. 2. June Carter Cash in *Walk the Line*. 3. Sid Vicious in *Sid & Nancy*. 4. Ray Charles in *Ray*. 5. Ian Dury in *Sex & Drugs & Rock & Roll*. 6. Joan Jett in *The Runaways*. 7. Bob Dylan in *I'm Not There*. 8. Dr Dre in *Straight Outta Compton*. 9. Hank Williams in *I Saw the Light*. 10. Jim Morrison in *The Doors*. 11. Patsy Cline in *Sweet Dreams*. 12. Johnny Cash in *Walk the Line*. 13. Tina Turner in *What's Love Got To Do With It?* 14. Jerry Lee Lewis in *Great Balls of Fire*. 15. Loretta Lynn in *Coal Miner's Daughter*.

Angela Bassett; Cate Blanchett; Jamie Foxx; Corey Hawkins; Tom Hiddleston; Aaron Johnson; Val Kilmer; Jessica Lange; Gary Oldman; Joaquin Phoenix; Dennis Quaid; Andy Serkis; Sissy Spacek; Kristen Stewart; Reese Witherspoon.

QUIZ 86

PEEL SESSIONS

Here is a quiz about bands beloved of the late DJ John Peel. The late night slot that Peel occupied gave him license to pick and choose the music he played without the restrictions of a playlist. Peel would constantly push the boundaries, playing punk when the BBC controllers didn't approve and foisting eclectic and unsigned material on his appreciative audience.

Two sections. The first is a list of tracks from various Peel Sessions. I've put 30 of them in chronological order and then given you a (longer) list of possible answers. The second section is straight questions on Peel himself, in particular his annual Festive Fifty of tracks of the year.

Answers: page 534

Which artisis recorded these sessions for Peel?

1   'Sure 'Nuff 'n Yes I Do', 'Yellow Brick Road', 'Abba Zabba', 'Electricity' (1968)

2   'Canyons of Your Mind', 'I'm the Urban Spaceman', 'Monster Mash' (1968)

3   'Watcher of the Skies', 'Twilight Alehouse', 'Get 'em Out by Friday' (1972)

4   'Keep Yourself Alive', 'Son and Daughter', 'Ogre Battle', 'Great King Rat' (1973)

5   'Slave Driver', 'Rasta Man', 'Concrete Jungle' (1973)

6   'Commune', 'Forever', 'Highway Blues', 'I'll See You Again', 'North Country' (1974)'

7   'Love and Romance', 'Vindictive', 'New Town', 'Shoplifting' (1977)

8   'Rebellious Jukebox', 'Mother Sister', 'Industrial Estate,' 'Futures and Pasts' (1978)

9   'Get Over You', 'Top Twenty', 'She Can Only Say No', 'Male Model' (1978)

10 'Gangsters', 'Too Much Too Young', 'Concrete Jungle' (1979)

11 'Cars', 'Airplane', 'Films', 'Conversation' (1979)

12 'A New England', 'This Guitar Says Sorry', 'Love Gets Dangerous', 'Fear is a Man's Best Friend' (1983)

13 'What Difference Does It Make?', Handsome Devil', 'Reel Around the Fountain' (1983)

14 'Manhenga', 'Writing on the Wall', 'Chemedza Vana', 'Let's Work Together', 'Kuroja Chete' (1986)

15 'Prison Without Walls', 'Deceiver', 'Lucid Fairytale', 'Common Enemy' (1987)

16 'Far Out and Gone', 'Silverblade', 'Here Comes Alice' (1989)

17 'They Spelled My Name Wrong Again', 'Jesse Don't Like It', 'Sunday Time', 'Sometimes I Forget' (1989)

18 'God Knows It's True', 'So Far Gone', 'Alcoholiday', 'Long Hair' (1990)

19 'Circa 1762', 'Kentucky Cocktail', 'Secret Knowledge of Back Roads', 'Here' (1992)

20 'Semi-Detached', 'Attached', Lush (Eurotunnel Disaster 1994)', 'Walk About' (1993)

21 'Tabla Attack', 'Hooba Hooba', 'Non Stop to the Border' (1995)

22 'Wondering Boy Poet', 'Atom Eyes', 'Cut Out Witch', 'Man Called Aerodynamics' (1996)

23 'Bingo England', 'Ultra Paj', 'Safe Cracker', 'Latino' (1996)

24 'Paper Route', 'Wash', 'Sanchez', 'Spokes', 'Drape' (1997)

25 'Autumn Sweater', 'Shadows', 'I Heard You Looking' (1997)

26 'Procedure 4', 'Ex Cowboy', 'Don't Cry', 'New Paths to Helicon (Part II)' (1998)

27 'Raisans', 'Does It Float', 'The Leper', 'Bulbs of Passion' (1988)

28 'Number One Son', 'Sun On His Back', 'Antiwestern', 'Before You Cry' (2001)

29 'Suzi Lee', 'Stop Breaking Down', 'Don't Know', 'Lafayette Blues' (2001)

30 'Last Snowstorm of the Year', 'Canada', 'Li'l Argument with Myself', 'In the Drugs' (2001)

Artists: Arab Strap, Ash, Bhundu Boys, Black Keys, Black Star Liner, Blur, Bong Ra, Bonzo Dog Doo Dah Band, David Bowie, Billy Bragg, Calexico, Camera Obscura, Can, Captain Beefheart and His Magic Band, Cornershop, The Datsuns, Delgados, Dinosaur Jr, The Faces, The Fall, Genesis, Guided By Voices, Roy Harper, P.J. Harvey, Jimi Hendrix, Hole, Jesus and Mary Chain, Low, Mogwai, Bob Marley and the Wailers, My Bloody Valentine, Napalm Death, Gary Numan, Orbital, Pavement, Pop Will Eat Itself, Cat Power, Queen, Scarfo, Scratch Perverts, Slits, The Smiths, Soft Machine, The Specials, Teenage Fanclub, T.Rex, The Undertones, Loudon Wainwright III, White Stripes, Yo La Tengo.

BONUS TRACKS

31 When John Peel played his all-time Festive Fifty for the millennium, which band had four songs in the Top 20? Which very connected band was the only other artist with more than two?

32 Whose debut single, 'Can't Be Sure', topped the Festive Fifty in 1989? What was the album from whence it came, with a title punning on education and also the town where the band formed?

33 'Don't Touch That Dial' was the last Festive Fifty number one before Peel died in 2004: who was the band behind the song? Of which other cult indie band were they a side project?

34 After Peel died, which Radio 1 DJ was chosen to continue his evening slot? Which band was at number one in his first Festive Fifty, in homage to his predecessor?

35 After Radio 1 dropped the Festive Fifty in 2006, which independent online radio station was invited to keep the chart running by Peel's old production team? Which independent release by Cheltenham duo Tall Pony was their first Festive Fifty chart topper?

36 In Peel's millennial Festive Fifty there were two versions of the same song, 'Song to a Siren'. Which two acts – one the co-writer and original singer in 1970, the other an indie collective in 1984 – were they by?

37 Which two Smiths songs, one a 1985 single, the other a track on the 1986 album *The Queenils Dead*, were in the Top 20 of John Peel's millennial Festive Fifty?

38 For which pirate radio station was John Peel working before he joined Radio 1 in 1967? What was the name – one now more readily associated with car enthusiasts – of the show he presented until 1975?

39 What was the name of the producer who worked with Peel from 1969 until his sudden death in 2001? He was best man at Peel's second wedding in 1974 to Sheila Gilhooly: what was Peel's affectionate nickname for her?

40 Of which football team, reflecting his roots, was Peel an avid follower? What song did he have played at his second wedding?

41 Who earned his breakthrough by driving to Radio 1 with a curry for John Peel (along with his demo tape) after the DJ announced he was hungry on air? What was this artist's seven-track less-than-twenty-minutes debut album later that year?

42 The Only Ones were one of the many late-seventies new wave bands championed by Peel. What 1978 single is their most famous song? Who was the guitarist alongside singer and songwriter Peter Perrett?

43 'Teenage dreams, so hard to beat' is a line from 'Teenage Kicks' by which punk/power pop band who owed Peel a huge amount? How will this lyric be forever associated with Peel?

44 What is the name of Peel's DJ son? And what was the title of Peel's posthumous autobiography, completed by his wife?

45 The Festive Fifty wasn't all punk and indie. Which two Beach Boys' songs featured on the millennial list, one from *Pet Sounds* and one from *Smiley Smile*?

QUIZ 87

VIDEO KILLED THE RADIO STAR

Did it? Music videos have almost become a different art form, in some ways separate from the singles they're designed to promote. Videos are simply another way of approaching the music, a different medium through which to hear and experience the tunes. This quiz comes in two parts: the first is a series of straightforward questions about well-known pop videos, while the second is a mix-and-match affair spotlighting famous film directors' forays into the pop video business.

Answers: page 535

1   Which Duran Duran video, directed by Russell Mulcahy (*Highlander*), cost over £1 million to make in 1984? After her work with Hot Gossip, who was hired to come up with the choreography?

2   What was Brandon Flowers' first solo single, a UK Top 10 hit? Which Academy Award-winning actress appeared in the accompanying video?

3   Which Madonna video won director Jonas Akerlund a host of awards in 1998? Who directed the video for her 2001 single 'What It Feels Like for a Girl'?

4   The video for Eminem's debut single featured the singer impersonating Bill Clinton, Marilyn Manson and a member of the Brady Bunch. What was its title? And who appeared in the video as Eminem's doctor?

5   Which funk soul brother sang guest vocals on Fatboy Slim's hit 'Weapon of Choice'? And who danced up a storm on the video, directed by Spike Jonze?

6   Better known as a fashion photographer, Jean-Baptiste Mondino cleaned up most of the big video awards for his work on which 1985 hit for Don Henley? Which major artist has used Mondino on a number of videos, including 'Open Your Heart', 'Justify My Love' and 'Human Nature'?

7   When Billboard magazine ran a poll for the best music video of the 1990s, which 1999 pop song won 40 per cent of the vote? Nigel Dick, its director, also directed which famous 1984 Christmas video?

8   Who directed the soft porn video that accompanied Duran Duran's 'Girls on Film' in 1981? And from which band did this pair split in the late seventies?

9   Which Green Day video won Samuel Bayer a bucketful of awards in 2005? Which actress did Bayer and Justin Timberlake persuade to appear in the video for Timberlake's hit 'What Goes Around... Comes Around'?

10   Francis Lawrence, director of three of the *Hunger Games* movies, also directed which award-winning 2009 Lady Gaga video? Which fashion designer's famous 12-inch heels did Gaga wear in the clip?

11 The popular video to which Queen single saw Freddie Mercury and the rest of the band dress in drag and do a spot of housecleaning? Where did Queen perform two years after the promo was made, a concert that was released on video and became, for a while, the bestselling music video in the UK?

12 Which film director and animator worked with Kate Bush on the concept for the video to 'Cloudbusting'? Which Hollywood star was persuaded (reputedly, by Bush herself) to appear in the narrative film?

13 Which 1994 video caused something of a furore when it showed Prince gyrating, obviously naked, in a bathtub with the New Power Generation writhing around him? Who directed it?

14 Which 21-year-old comedian, about to get a lot more famous, did a Benny Hill-style routine in the video for Blur's 'Country House'? Who directed the video, which also featured the celebrity glamour model Jo Guest?

15 Which 1986 Peter Gabriel video saw director Stephen R Johnson take his work on stop-motion and figurine animation to a new level? Which British animation company wored with him on the video?

BONUS TRACKS

Match each director to the pop video they made and the mainstream movie they directed. If you correctly match a director to both video and movie, score two points. If you match a director to either video or movie, score one. And if you match video and film but put them both with the wrong director, score a big zero.

Directors:

1 Michael Bay. 2 Kathryn Bigelow. 3 Tim Burton. 4 Sofia Coppola. 5 Jonathan Demme. 6 Brian De Palma. 7 David Fincher. 8 Jonathan Glazer. 9 Michel Gondry. 10 Spike Jonze. 11 John Landis. 12 Spike Lee. 13 John Maybury. 14 Michael Moore. 15 Gus van Sant.

Movies:

Being John Malkovich. The Blues Brothers. Bowling for Columbine. Carrie. Do the Right Thing. Drugstore Cowboy. The Edge of Love. Eternal Sunshine of the Spotless Mind. Fight Club. The Hurt Locker. Pearl Harbor. Sexy Beast. The Silence of the Lambs. Sleepy Hollow. The Virgin Suicides.

Videos:

Aerosmith – 'Janie's Got a Gun'. Björk – 'It's Oh So Quiet'. Foo Fighters – 'Everlong'. Michael Jackson – 'Black or White'. The Killers – 'Here with Me'. Meatloaf – 'I'd Do Anything for Love (But I Won't Do That)'. New Order – 'Touched By the Hand of God'. Sinéad O'Connor – 'Nothing Compares 2 U'. Public Enemy – 'Fight the Power'. Radiohead – 'Street Spirit (Fade Out)'. Rage Against the Machine – 'Sleep Now in the Fire'. Red Hot Chili Peppers – 'Under the Bridge'. Bruce Springsteen – 'Dancing in the Dark'. Tom Tom Club – 'Genius of Love'. White Stripes – 'I Just Don't Know What to Do with Myself'.

QUIZ 88

ALL KILLER NO FILLER

How many times have you bought an album based on a couple of cracking tracks you heard on the radio, only to find the rest of the album is pants? This is NOT a quiz about those albums. This is a quiz about those albums where every track is a joy. Those of you who listen to the Liz Kershaw show on Saturday afternoon will know what I mean – we're talking about albums that are All Killer, No Filler.

The first section of the quiz features records that listeners recommended for the slot. The second section of the quiz features 15 albums that this author thinks would merit a place in that slot on Liz's show.

Answers: page 536

1 Whose 1988 second album *It Takes A Nation of Millions To Hold Us Back* is regarded as the record that put hip hop on the map, both artistically and commercially? Which label, founded by Rick Rubin, released it?

2 Kevin Drew and Brendan Canning are the founders of which Canadian musical collective? What was their second, breakthrough album (2002)?

3 Who shares production credits with Mick Ronson on Lou Reed's 1972 album *Transformer*? Which song from the album was a huge selling charity single in 1997?

4 Which Glasgow band won the Mercury Prize with their eponymous debut album in 2004? From whom do they take their name?

5 *Behind the Music* (2002) was the third album for which band, breaking them commercially and earning a Grammy nomination? Where are they from?

6 What was The Cure's brilliant debut album? Under what name was it released in the US and re-released in the UK a year later with a slightly different track listing?

7 Which year was Fleetwood Mac's classic album *Rumours* released? And which song, later used as a sporting intro, opened side two of the record and was the only track credited as written by the entire band?

8 *Daydream Nation* was a 1988 album from which US cult band? What was the uncharacteristically catchy track that opened the album?

9 What was the exciting 1983 debut album from the Chameleons? Who was the band's lead singer and bass player, who still plays the band's material in live shows?

10 Whose *Heaven or Las Vegas* (1990) gave them their first UK Top 10 album? Who was their ethereal, distinctive female singer?

11 What was Goldfrapp's debut album? Who is in the band with singer Alison Goldfrapp?

12 Stuart Staples is the front man and main event in which critically loved indie band? Why was the title of their second album (1995) a tad confusing?

13 The addition of Budgie and John McGeoch to which band changed their sound markedly for their critically acclaimed third album, *Kaleidoscope*? What was the lead single and opening track?

14 Besides 'Tainted Love', which other two singles were taken from Soft Cell's 1981 debut album *Non-Stop Erotic Cabaret*?

15 What was the Clash's second album? 'Guns on the Roof', the opening track on side two of the original vinyl release, unashamedly pinched a riff from which single by the Who?

BONUS TRACKS

Three tracks and a year: name the classic album.

16 'See No Evil'; 'Friction'; 'Prove It' (1977)

17 'As I Sat Sadly by Her Side'; 'Fifteen Feet of Pure White Snow'; 'God is in the House' (2001)

18 'Drink Before the War'; 'Mandinka'; 'Troy' (1987)

19 'Angel from the Coast'; 'Cowboy Song'; 'The Boys are Back in Town' (1976)

20 'Ku Ku Kurama'; 'Love of the Common People'; 'Come Back and Stay' (1983)

21 'Bend in the Road'; 'Man Made Lake'; 'Two Silver Trees' (2008)

22 'A Change is Gonna Come'; 'Satisfaction'; 'Respect' (1965)

23 'Bargain'; 'Baba O'Riley'; 'Won't Get Fooled Again' (1971)

24 'Bombin' the L'; 'King of New York'; 'Scooby Snacks' (1996)

25 '1984'; 'Better Be Good To Me'; 'What's Love Got To Do With It' (1984)

26 'Jack of All Trades'; 'Rocky Ground'; 'We Take Care of Our Own' (2012)

27 'Protect Me', 'Mother', 'Born of Frustration' (1993)

28 'Girl with a Red Balloon'; 'My Father's Father'; 'I've Got This Friend' (2011)

29 'Thick as Thieves'; 'Smithers-Jones', 'The Eton Rifles' (1979)

30 'So Much Things To Say', 'Three Little Birds'; 'Jamming' (1977)

QUIZ 89

THE NUMBERS GAME 3

Same as twice before. Question one requires one answer, question two requires two, right up to question ten, which requires ten (with the usual question 5a to bring the total number of answers to 60, as in the other chapters). If three answers are required, you must give only three: any more that you suggest will be ignored.

Answers: page 537

1   What was the Eurythmics' sole number one single?

2   Which two brothers – one the drummer in a major veteran British band – make up the Magic Brothers?

3   What are the three studio albums released by Two Door Cinema Club?

4   The Pet Shop Boys' four UK number one singles to date all came between 1985 and 1988: what were they?

5   Who are the five members of Andy Warhol's entourage at the Factory referenced in Lou Reed's 'Walk on the Wild Side'?

5a Can you name the five albums released by the Arctic Monkeys up to the end of 2015?

6   What were the six U2 albums released in the eighties?

7   Name the seven studio albums made by Oasis.

8   What were the first eight songs by Adele to make the Top 10 of the UK charts?

9   Metallica released their tenth studio album in 2016: what were the other nine? (No collaborations or covers projects included)

10 What were the ten Top 10 singles released by the Sweet?

QUIZ 90

WRITERS ON MUSIC

This quiz is about writing about music, concentrating on books rather than magazine journalism. The first section is a series of straight questions about books written by musicians or critics. The second section lists the titles of 15 music biographies and asks you to match them with their subjects.

Answers: page 537

1   *Just Kids* was a 2010 autobiography by which punk poet and rock singer? The book chronicles her relationship with which famous New York photographer in the seventies?

2   *King Ink* (1988) and *King Ink II* (1997) were collections of poetry and writing by which musician and songwriter? What was the title of his first novel (1989)?

3   In 2005, which literary music writer released a book studying the recording and impact of one Bob Dylan song? What was the song?

4   Which musician wrote the 2009 book, *Bicycle Diaries*, extolling the virtues of cycling? What was the title of the same writer's 2012 book, a reflection on music, the industry and his own career within it?

5   Who was the author of a *New York Times* bestseller called *The English Roses,* a picture book for children? What was the name of the outsider envied by the other four girls (the Roses referred to in the title)?

6   Which musical movement was the subject of Jon Savage's book, *England's Dreaming*? Whose second volume of autobiography, *Anger is an Energy*, chronicles some of the same events?

7   *Stoned* was the autobiography of which former Rolling Stones manager? Who wrote *The True Adventures of the Rolling Stones*, regarded by many as a definitive biography?

8   *Psychotic Reactions and Carburettor Dung* is a series of essays by which American rock critic, who died in 1982? Who portrayed him in the 2000 film about the music business, *Almost Famous*?

9   Who wrote classic Bob Marley biography *Catch a Fire*? Which band was the subject matter of his 1994 book, *The Nearest Far Away Place*?

10 Whose hand-written *Journals*, released posthumously in book form in 2002, went to the top of the book bestseller lists in both the US and the UK? What was the title of Charles Cross's book on the same subject, a year earlier?

11 Elvis Costello published his autobiography in 2015, with the title *Unfaithful Music and* .... what? Which writer published two novels, *Less Than Zero* and *Imperial Bedrooms*, with the same titles as two of Costello's albums?

12 *Cider with Roadies* (2005) was which rock journalist and DJ's account of his formative years in the North West? And which poet wrote the 2008 memoir *Gig*?

13 *Apathy for the Devil* was the seventies memoir of which legendary rock journalist? What was the collection of his writings published in 1994?

14 *Thank You for the Days* and *Reelin' in the Years* are volumes of anecdotal autobiography by DJ Mark Radcliffe. Which two bands released those songs?

15 From the Velvets to the ???? Complete the title of Clinton Heylin's 2005 account of the roots and records of the American punk scene. Who was the subject of his first book, *Behind the Shades*?

BONUS TRACKS

Which artists are the following books about? Where no author is given, the author is the artist (or, more likely, their ghost writer).

1 Charles Shaar Murray, *Crosstown Traffic*, 1989. 2 *Scar Tissue*, 2004. 3 *A Bit of a Blur*, 2007. 4 Jerry Hopkins, *No One Gets Out of Here Alive*. 1980 5 *Take It Like a Man*, 1995. 6 *Dirty Blonde*, 2007. 7 *I'll Never Write My Memoirs*, 2016. 8 Tony Fletcher, *Dear Boy*, 2010. 9 *Secrets of a Sparrow*, 1993. 10 *Life*, 2010. 11 *Chronicle, Volume 1*, 2003. 12 *The Heroin Diaries*, 2007. 13 Barry Miles, *Many Years from Now*, 1997. 14 *Reckless*, 2015. 15 Philip Norman, *Shout!* 1991.

Possible answers: The Beatles; Boy George; The Doors; Bob Dylan; Jimi Hendrix; Chrissie Hynde; Alex James; Grace Jones; Anthony Kiedis; Courtney Love; Paul McCartney; Keith Moon; Keith Richards; Diana Ross; Nikki Sixx.

QUIZ 91

INDIE ROCK

There was a time when indie music was literally defined by its record label – 'indie' was short for the 'independent' record labels that released it. The term has become abused over time, though, and now suggests any artist with a certain spirit or ethos: acts that perhaps don't stick to a formula, that have control over their own creative output and that don't artificially sweeten their music for the commercial market. Here are 30 questions on a wide variety of artists who, however tightly or loosely, fit that billing.

Answers: page 538

1   Bad Lieutenant was formed by Bernard Sumner and Phil Cunningham during a pause in New Order's touring and recording commitments. Which member of Blur contributed to their album *Never Cry Another Tear*? And from where did the band take their name?

2   Who connects the Raconteurs with the Dead Weather? What's the name of the first album that this artist released under his own name in 2012?

3   Which two acts from the following list have reached the Top 100 of the American albums chart: Manic Street Preachers, Muse, the Stone Roses, Suede, Paul Weller, Robbie Williams?

4   With which band did Shaun Ryder sing while Happy Mondays were on hiatus during the mid/late nineties? And to which track on Gorillaz' *Demon Days* did he contribute vocals?

5   Brian Molko and Stefan Oldsal are the two permanent members of which British glam rock band, who emerged during the Britpop era? What's the illicit title of their third album, released in 2000?

6   Which band comprises the siblings Matthew and Eleanor Friedberger? Eleanor is almost certainly the subject of the song 'Eleanor, Put Your Boots On' by which Scottish indie band?

7   Which two modern rock aristocrats released a single together called 'This Old Town' in 2007?

8   The 2015 album *FFS* is a collaboration between which two power pop bands of different vintages?

9   Which band's studio recordings are largely the work of one man, Kevin Parker? What's the name of their 2012 second album, which helped launch them into the mainstream?

10 Which New York band's fourth album, *Mosquito* (2013), was their most successful to date worldwide? In which country was singer and keyboard player Karen O born?

11 Brothers Alan White and Steve White were both drummers in the British rock scene of the nineties and noughties. With which two artists are they primarily associated?

12 Johanna Bennett co-wrote which Arctic Monkeys hit while she was dating singer Alex Turner? Which rock star did she marry in 2009?

13 What's the name of the stunning debut album by American indie guitar band the Strokes? In which year was it released?

14 Rapper Ninja provides most of the on-stage vocals for which British band? What's the name of their Mercury Music Prize-nominated 2004 debut album, featuring the single 'The Power Is On'?

15 Which song gave the B-52s a surprise hit single in 1989, reaching number three in the US and number two in the UK? Which movie theme song gave them another UK Top 10 hit in 1994?

BONUS TRACKS

16 'When this River Rolls over You' is the 2003 debut single by which highly touted British band? Released the following year, on which album does it appear?

17 Which duo makes up the Stone Roses' songwriting team?

18 Which album by alt-J topped the British charts in 2014? Which soul classic appears as a hidden track at the end of the album?

19 Which band have been 'The Drowners', 'The Wild Ones' and 'Lazy'? With which album did the band return in 2013 after an 11-year break?

20 What was the name of the band formed by the Stone Roses' guitarist after that band broke up? What's the title of their one and only album, which shares its title with the second album by Ian Dury & the Blockheads?

21 Which New York band's most successful single so far has been 'Evil', a song about the wife and abettor of serial killer Fred West? 'Evil' appears on the band's second album, *Antics* – but what was the name of the follow-up album, which reached number two in the UK?

22 Which band consists of the Jarman brothers, Gary, Ross and Ryan? Who joined them on guitar for their 2009 album *Ignore the Ignorant*?

23 Which nineties band were named after a character from Harper Lee's *To Kill a Mockingbird*? Which 1995 single gave them their biggest hit?

24 In 2006, which Sheffield band set the record for the fastest-selling debut album in UK history? Which single, their first on Domino Records and a UK number one in October 2005, set the ball rolling?

25 *Mistaken for Strangers* is a 2013 tour documentary focusing on which American band? From which album, the band's fourth, does the film take its title?

26 What were *Champion Versions*, *The Patty Patty Sound* and *Los Amigos del Beta Bandidos*?

27 Favouring orchestral arrangements rather than jangly guitars, which band was – and, occasionally, still is – fronted by singer and songwriter Jake Shillingford? Drummer Jason Cooper now plays for which enduring post-punk band?

28 In the gospel according to Alex Turner, who 'flicks a red hot revelation off the tip of her tongue'? And what may 'her steady hands have done'?

29 Annie Clark's fourth album won her a Grammy for Best Alternative Album: under what name does she perform? For whom did she substitute at the Rock and Roll Hall of Fame induction ceremony in 2014, singing 'Lithium' with the rest of the band?

30 What's the name of Alex Turner's side project, which he fronts alongside fellow singer/guitarist Miles Kane? Their producer, James Ford, is a member of which electronic duo?

PEOPLE'S PLAYLIST: LOVE

We can't have a music quiz book without acknowledging the L word. Love has infused popular music since the very beginning and is now probably both the most overused and the most inappropriately used word in the musical lexicon. Here are 40 straight questions. Do it with love.

Answers: page 539

1   What would Meat Loaf do for love?

2   And what wouldn't he do?

3   Where did 'Love Grow' for Edison Lighthouse at the beginning of the seventies?

4   What did the Darkness believe in?

5   Who gave us the eighties indie anthem 'Shine On'?

6   *Love Is Hell*, according to which tortured American singer in 2004?

7   Who does Father John Misty love?

8   In 1994, what was the purpose of PJ Harvey's third album?

9   What was Paolo Nutini's kind of love in 2014?

10 In 1973, how long was Donny Osmond prepared to love his girl?

11 What kind of solid love did the Courteeners enjoy in 2014?

12 Who enjoyed 'Big Love' in 1987 (and many other times, according to repeated rumours about their inter-band relationships)?

13 What fact about love did Rose Royce reveal in 1978?

14 Which unanswered question gave Buzzcocks their biggest hit single?

15 What was Amy Winehouse's bleak take on love on *Back to Black*?

16 What did Madonna want you to do with her love in 1991?

17 Which group took 'Chanson d'Amour' to number one in 1977?

18 Who co-wrote 'Will You Love Me Tomorrow?', then recorded it herself in 1971?

19 Who had a 'Love Hangover' in 1976?

20 Who ordered us to 'Stop! In the Name of Love'?

21 Who told us *The Truth about Love* on her 2012 album?

22 Jennifer Rush, Frankie Goes to Hollywood and Sam Bailey all warned us about what?

23 Which Katrina & the Waves song gave the UK a rare Eurovision win in 1997?

24 There are all sorts of love songs – but who complained about silly ones in 1976?

25 What was Killing Joke's 'Love Like'?

26 Whose 2009 concept album warned us about *The Hazards of Love*?

27 Who thought your love was royalty in 1984?

28 What were the dying words of the victim of a motorcycle accident in Ricky Valance's 1960 smash hit?

29 Which kind of love made the British Top 40 in every decade from the 1960s to the 2000s, including a number one for Love Affair in 1968?

30 Who was 'Addicted to Love' in 1986?

31 Which 'Kind of Love' did Phil Collins take to number one in the UK in 1988?

32 Which song did the Beatles premiere in 1967 on *Our World*, the world's first global satellite television production?

33 What was love to the Eurythmics in 1982?

34 And what was it for Pat Benatar in 1983?

35 Who swore that she'd never fall in love again on her British number one single in 1969?

36 What did Yazz cry that we needed to 'Stand Up for' in 1988?

37 What came with the 'Love' on the title of Michael Kiwanuka's 2016 album?

38 Who topped the chart in 1975 by insisting they weren't in love?

39 'Home is a love that I miss very much, but the past has been bottled and...'
What?

40 Who presumably needed to tow their love around in 1986?

QUIZ 93

NAME THE BAND #4

This one is not quite so simple as it seems. Unlike previous Name the Band quizzes, where you had just to name the band, here you have to specify the decade in which the band released their first album. (The answers state the exact year, but for the extra point you just need the decade).

Answers: page 539

QUIZ 93: NAME THE BAND

1 Joseph Mount, Oscar Cash, Anna Prior, Gbenga Adelekan

2 George Cummings, Jay David, Rik Elswit, Billy Francis, Jayce Garfat, Dennis Locorriere, Ray Sawyer

3 Benji Blakeway, Johnny Bond, Bob Hall, Van McCann

4 Steve Boone, Joe Butler, John Sebastian, Zal Yanovsky

5 Jam Master Jay, Darryl McDaniels, Joseph Simmons

6 Ed Lay, Russell Leetch, Tom Smith, Chris Urbanowicz

7 Tom Hamilton, Joey Kramer, Joe Perry, Steven Tyler, Brad Whitford

8 Jimmy Dixon, Tommy Grace, David Maclean, Vincent Neff

9 Bev Bevan, Trevor Burton, Ace Kefford, Carl Wayne, Roy Wood

10 Felix Buxton, Simon Ratcliffe

11 Aaron Escolopio, Benji Madden, Joel Madden, Billy Martin, Paul Thomas

12 Gillian Gilbert, Peter Hook, Stephen Morris, Bernard Sumner

13 Mark Foster, Cubbie Fink, Mark Pontius

14 Ralf Hutter, Florian Schneider

15 Andy Cato, Tom Findlay

BONUS TRACKS

16 Jonathan Horne, Jeff Olson, James Petralli, Steven Terebecki

17 Gary Daly, Eddie Lundon, Dave Reilly

18 Jehnny Beth, Ayse Hasssan, Fay Milton, Gemma Thompson

19 Simon Gallup, Robert Smith, Lol Tolhurst, Porl Thompson

20 Apollo 9, Atom, JC2000, ND, Petey X, Speedo

21 Jamie Reynolds, Jamie Righton, Simon Taylor-Davies

22 Tim Bricheno, Andy Cousin, Mark Price, Julianne Regan

23 Gary Brooker, Matthew Fisher, Dave Knights, Robin Trower, B.J. Wilson

24 Terry Chambers, Dave Gregory, Colin Moulding, Andy Partridge

25 Stanley Demeski, Sean Eden, Justin Harwood, Dean Wareham

26 Johnny Christ, Synyster Gates, The Rev, M.Shadows, Zacky Vengeance

27 Lee Rocker, Brian Setzer, Slim Jim Phantom

28 Doris Coley, Addie Harris, Beverly Lee, Shirley Owens

29 Martin Rev, Alan Vega

30 Martin Blunt, Jon Brookes, Tim Burgess, Mark Collins, Rob Collins, Martin Duffy

QUIZ 94

ELECTRIC LADYLAND

Late on a Friday night (or, to be more accurate, very early on a Saturday morning) Nemone presents her own mix of hip hop, beats and electronic music. The show mixes old and new but focuses largely on the digital-music era, from house and trance through to modern beats and grime. Guests have numbered most of the prestigious mixers and DJs of recent years, as well as electro pioneers such as Jean Michel Jarre.

The second set of questions here is inspired by the Wind Down playlist: the segment of the show where listeners suggest a Saturday night chill-out track. All the artists have been featured in the Wind Down slot – but not necessarily with the track or record you're being asked about.

Answers: page 540

1   Who would you be listening to if the DJ was Alexander Coe from Bangor in Wales? What was his 1999 EP which still makes many lists of the best dance songs of the last couple of decades?

2   Which popular movie theme gave Moby his second UK Top 10 hit in 1997? What was the title of his massive 1999 album that saw him cross over to mainstream success?

3   'Theme from S-Express (by S-Express)' was one of the earliest big chart hits in the UK to be mainly based on a sample. What was the title of their debut album, from which it was taken? Who was the DJ and producer at the core of the band?

4   Saul Milton and Will Kennard are a DJ partnership who release records under which name? Which white British urban star, with his best days ahead of him, provided the vocals for their 2008 single 'Pieces'?

5   Which American producer had a UK number one with 'You Don't Know Me', sung by Duane Harden, in 1999? Who went 'Bonkers' and gave him another chart-topper as producer and co-writer?

6   *Random Album Title, For Lack of a Better Name* and *>album title goes here<* are all albums by Joel Zimmerman. Under what name does he DJ/produce/record, and where is he from?

7   LA electronic duo Ken Jordan and Scott Kirkland perform under what name? In 2005 the duo composed the theme to which hugely successful TV cop show based on the books by forensic expert Kathy Reichs?

8   What was the controversially-titled third single from the Prodigy's *Fat of the Land*? Who is the band leader and songwriter in the band?

9   The Chemical Brothers. They aren't. Who are they?

10 Which German film composer and producer wrote 'He's a Pirate' for the soundtrack of *Pirates of the Caribbean: Curse of the Black Pearl*? Who released a special remix of the track in 2006?

11 Which massive club hit, the second single from Fathless' debut album, Reverence, reached number one in the UK in 1995? What saucy business does the narrator get up to with his girl while 'making mad love on the heath'?

12 Which drum and bass artist won the Mercury Prize in 1997 with *New Forms*? What was the side project with which the main man released an album, *Ultra-Obscene*, in 1999??

13 Which 1976 electronic suite was Jean Michel Jarre's massive commercial breakthrtough? Which collaborative project took him back to the upper reaches of the UK charts in 2015?

14 Who sang on David Guetta's two UK number ones from his 2009 album *One Love*, 'When Love Takes Over' and 'Sexy Bitch'?

15 Here are the Chemical Brothers albums: *Exit Planet Dust*, MISSING, *Surrender*, *Come With Us*, *Push the Button*, MISSING, *Further*, *Born in the Echoes*. What are the two missing albums?

BONUS TRACKS

16 Which country was Future Sound of London's 1991 debut single – since remixed and released many times – named after? Where are they from?

17 Portishead's only UK Top 10 single was the first released from their self-named 1997 second album: what was it? What was the somewhat unimaginative title of their next album, in 2008?

18 What was Gary Numan's 1979 debut solo single and number one? With which band had he already topped the chart that year with 'Are Friends Electric?'

19 French duo Nicola Godin and Jean-Benoit Dunckel perform under what name? Their second album was a soundtrack to which *2000* movie directed by Sofia Coppola?

20 Underworld released the single 'Born Slippy' in 1995 with little success. It reached number two when rereleased the following year with what suffix after the title? What status at school did the band claim in the title of their 1996 album?

21 What style of music do the Gotan Project use as their base? In which European city are this multi-national act based?

22 *The Bath*, *The Yellow* and *The Midnight* were three EPs put together to make the debut album of which lo-fi trip hop band in 2000? Which claiming-to-be-loud single off their third album sampled, 'Horrorshow', a single by cult punk band the Scars?

23 Which band boasted that Daft Punk were playing at their house? What was their third album, which reached the Top 10 in both the US and the UK in 2010?

24 William Orbit's second, third, fourth and fifth albums all shared a title theme: what? Which other album title has he used twice, in 1999 and 2010, for classical works remixed and reworked electronically?

25 Who made a comeback in 2014 with *Syro*, his first studio album for 14 years?? What was his most successful single, a 1999 track with a ten-minute video spoofing gangsta rappers?

26 Easy Star All-Stars are a collective who specialise in reworking classic albums in what style? Which classic 1973 prog rock album was their debut project in 2003?

27 DJ Shadow produced the 1998 debut album *Psyence Fiction* for which band, comprising James Lavelle and Tim Goldsworthy? What was the title of his own debut, released in 1996?

28 Where did the electronic band Ladytron get their name? Where are they based?

29 Which pioneer of electronic music began his career playing keyboards for Roxy Music? With whom did he collaborate on *Evening Star* in 1975, and again on *The Equatorial Stars* in 2004?

30 Singer Skye Edwards and the Godfrey brothers are the core of which downtempo band? What was their platinum-selling 1998 album containing chill-out classics 'Part of the Process' and 'The Sea'?

QUIZ 95

POST-PUNK & THE NEXT GENERATION

Punk had blown itself out and been fully absorbed into the mainstream even by the end of the seventies, but the baton was soon passed on through a new generation of indie bands, even if they had a slightly different energy. Then, in the early nineties, a new wave of disaffected youth seemed ready to throw themselves around at gigs by guitar bands playing at a million miles an hour. Punk had been reborn – except it had never really gone away. This quiz comes in two sections – one about the new wave of punk-style bands and one about the eighties post-punk scene, when established bands started to reinvent their sound and a new wave of noise hit the stores.

Answers: page 541

1 Which Tunbridge Wells duo were nominated for the BBC Sound of 2015 award after a livewire appearance on *Later... with Jools Holland*? What's the title of their official debut album, which was nominated for the Mercury Music Prize?

2 Which East Midlands modern punk band features Jason Williamson shouting aggressively agit vocals over Andrew Fearn's minimalist backing? What's the title of their 2014 album, a critical and commercial breakthrough?

3 Which band did John Lydon form after the break-up of the Sex Pistols? With which punk group did the band's guitarist Keith Levene briefly play before they recorded their first album?

4 *The Unravelling* was the 2001 independent label debut by which Chicago hardcore band? Released five years later, what's the title of their breakthrough album, which made the American Top 10?

5 Which new British band is fronted by Justin Hayward-Young? What's the name of their debut album, which won them a host of new-act awards in 2012?

6 'Council Flat Blues' was the first self-released single by which Leeds punk band? Their second album, released in 2016, showed the band refusing to compromise their hard-edged sound – but what's it called?

7 Who were *Your New Favourite Band* in 2001? And what, on the same record, did they hate?

8 Along with Pete Doherty, who is the other main songwriter in the Libertines? Which punk legend produced their first two albums?

9 Which power pop band's first, third and sixth records are all eponymously titled and are referred to as the Blue, Green and Red albums? What colour did they give to their tenth album, released in 2016 and also eponymous?

10 Which label, whose roster eventually included Arcade Fire, Caribou and Camera Obscura, was started by two members of North Carolina punk band Superchunk to release their own material? What's the title of Superchunk's own 1989 debut single, a cornerstone release in the new wave of slacker punk?

11 Wattie Buchan has been the lead singer of which Scottish punk band since 1979? Responding to the Crass song 'Punk Is Dead', what did they call their first album in 1981?

12 After starting out as a punk outfit, which band softened their sound and achieved commercial success with a stream of pop punk singles, including the 1998 British number one 'Pretty Fly (For a White Guy)'? Released in 1994, which album was their commercial breakthrough, hitting the Top 10 in the US and selling more than 11 million copies around the world?

13 JN, JW, MB, MJ and SS are the five initial (geddit?) members of which post-punk band from West Yorkshire? What's the title of their third album, the first not simply to be named after the band?

14 Which foul-smelling punk revivalist band released their eponymous debut in 1993 and their eighth, ...Honor Is All We Know, in 2014? Who was briefly a member of the band in 1993, co-writing the song 'Radio' and playing a couple of gigs with the group?

15 Who were Generation Terrorists in 1992? What's the title of their collectible debut single, released nearly four years before their debut album came out?

BONUS TRACKS

16 Who found themselves in 'A Forest' for their first single of the eighties? From which album was the single taken, a much longer record than its name suggests?

17 Formed by Ana Da Silva and Gina Birch, which post-punk band released their eponymous debut album in 1979? What's the title of their second album, either a mess or a classic according to taste?

18 The band's last release for the independent Lookout label, Green Day's second album was named after whih children's game? What's the name of the band's drummer, who joined in 1990 and still plays with the group?

19 Released on three 45rpm 12inch records in deluxe packaging, what was Public Image Ltd's second album? Who provided the band's distinctive dub reggae-style basslines?

20 What was Ian Dury & the Blockheads' only British number one? And what was the sad significance of Dury's 1998 album, *Mr Love Pants*?

21 Released in 2016, *Nocturnal Koreans* is the 15th studio album by which post-punk band? With which album did they make their debut in 1977?

22 A UK Top 20 hit three times over, which Joy Division song has come to define the dark sound of post-punk? What was the double A-side of its original release?

23 Who was the Clash's visual chronicler? He later formed Big Audio Dynamite with Mick Jones from the band – which song, apparently inspired by the films of Nicolas Roeg, did they take into the British Top 20 in 1986?

24 Written by Joy Division before Ian Curtis's death, which song was released as New Order's first single in 1981? Closely associated with both bands, which producer worked on the single and also produced New Order's first album?

25 Which Beatles song gave Siouxsie & the Banshees a UK No3 hit in 1983? What's the name of their 1987 covers album?

26 Which band did Billy Idol sing with before starting his solo career? The band's bassist, Tony James, went on to form which notorious eighties act?

27 What was the Clash's fourth album, a triple LP that saw them shift heavily towards dub and reggae? Which single from the album, its title a nod to Motown, featured Mick Jones's then-girlfriend Ellen Foley on vocals?

28 *The Second Annual Report* (1977) was actually the first album by which art punk band? What was the stage name adopted by bassist, violinist and vocalist Neil Megson?

29 Andy Gill and Jon King were the main men in which cult post-punk band, formed at the University of Leeds in the seventies? What's the mildly sarcastic title of the band's 1979 debut album?

30 Whose 1978 debut album *Real Life* was a leading influence on many later post-punk bands? Who was the band's bass player, who later recorded with Visage and the Bad Seeds before embarking on a solo career?

MOTOWN

It is possibly the most famous record label of all. Ask anyone what EMI or RCA Victor or Polydor were famous for and you would be met with a host of different answers. Not so Motown – it was a feel and a beat and a movement, not just a record label.

Here are two different sections, comprising straight questions and the mix-and-matches. The first section is pretty easy – but they get progressively tougher.

Answers: page 541

1 What was the name of the house band that played on most of Motown's hits between 1959 and 1972? What was the title of Paul Justman's 2002 documentary about this band?

2 Who played the scarecrow opposite Diana Ross's Dorothy in *The Wiz*, Motown Productions 1978 musical re-imagining of *The Wizard of Oz*? Who directed the movie?

3 Who were the two backing singers behind Diana Ross in the classic Supremes line-up from 1962 to 1967?

4 Brian, Eddie and Lamont: explain, in a Motown context.

5 In 1972, Motown relocated from Detroit to which city, partly to set up a film and TV company, Motown Productions? Who was the subject of this company's first film release, *Lady Sings the Blues*, starring Diana Ross?

6 Which 1970 hit was the last time the Supremes hit the Top 10 in both the US and the UK? Who sang lead vocals on this song, with Diana Ross having left to start a solo career?

7 Who were Motown's biggest chart act of the nineties, with five US number ones? What was their only number one in the UK?

8 Who was the founder and controlling influence in Motown Records? Who was his brother-in-law from 1963 to 1975 after marrying his sister, Anna?

9 Who sang the lead vocal on The Four Tops' biggest hit, 'Reach Out (I'll Be There)'? What was his contribution to 1986 musical comedy film *The Little Shop of Horrors*?

10 Who recorded Motown's first US number one single, 'Please Mr Postman'? Which brother-and-sister soft rock duo covered it in 1975?

11 Otis Williams, David Ruffin and Eddie Kendricks were prominent singers in which Motown vocal group? What was their first big hit in 1965, reaching number one in the US and number two in the UK?

12 Who duetted with Marvin Gaye on 'It Takes Two'? And which other frequent Gaye collaborator collapsed in the singer's arms at a 1967 concert and later died of a brain tumour?

13 How did Berry Gordy start out in the music industry? And what name did Motown use outside North America?

14 'Do You Love Me' was the only US Top 40 single for the Contours. Which beat group took it to number one in Britain the following year? Which 1987 film revived its popularity, along with 'Unchained Melody'?

15 Who had US Top 30 hits for Motown with 'Every Little Bit Hurts' and 'When I'm Gone'? The followers of which UK dance-club scene revived her popularity in the nineties?

BONUS TRACKS: I

Simply match the artists to the songs.

1 'Papa Was a Rolling Stone'. 2 'Touch Me in the Morning'. 3 'I Can't Help Myself (Sugar Pie Honey Bunch)'. 4 'Truly'. 5 'ABC' 6 'I Heard it Through the Grapevine'. 7 'My Guy'. 8 'Superstition'. 9 'Stop! in the Name of Love'. 10 'On Bended Knee'.

a The Supremes. b Lionel Richie. c The Temptations. d Mary Wells. e Boyz II Men. f The Four Tops. g Stevie Wonder. h The Jackson 5. i Diana Ross. j Marvin Gaye.

BONUS TRACKS: II

1 'Ain't Too Proud to Beg'. 2 'Love Hangover'. 3 '(Love is Like A) Heat Wave'. '4 Shop Around'. 5 'Fingertips (part 1)'. 6 'Can I Get a Witness'. 7 'Somebody's Watching Me'. 8 'Don't Leave Me This Way' 9 'Don't Let Him Shop Around'. 10 'Baby I Need Your Loving'.

a Rockwell. b The Temptations. c Debbie Dean. d The Miracles. e Marvin Gaye. f Thelma Houston. g The Four Tops. h Little Stevie Wonder. i Diana Ross. j Martha and the Vandellas.

BONUS TRACKS: III

1 'It's a Shame'. 2 'Stubborn Kind of Fellow'. 3 'Going to the Hop'. 4 'Solid Sender'. 5 'Heaven Must Have Sent You'. 6 'Please, Mr Postman'. 7 'Devil with the Blue Dress'. 8 'Shotgun'. 9 'He Was Really Sayin' Something'. 10 'Take Me In Your Arms (Rock Me a Little While)'.

a Junior Walker & the All-Stars. b Chico Leverett. c Shorty Long. d Kim Weston. e The Satintones. f The Velvelettes. g Marvin Gaye. h The Marvelettes. i The Elgins. j The (Detroit) Spinners.

QUIZ 97

PEOPLE'S PLAYLIST: CARS, TRAINS, BOATS & PLANES

This last People's Playlist is about getting around. The usual deal: 40 quickfire questions. Remember to keep the theme in mind, and don't hesitate. You have five minutes, so off you go – as fast as an HS2 train, if they ever get built...

Answers: page 542

1 Which out-and-about track closes Red Hot Chili Peppers' *Californication*?

2 How did Johnny Cash build his bespoke car?

3 Where did Frank Sinatra want you to fly him?

4 *Southern Rock Opera* was the breakthrough album for which Athens, Georgia rockers?

5 What was the name of the Beach Boys' sailing vessel in 1966?

6 Who caught the 'Marrakesh Express' in 1969?

7 Which road out of London did Billy Bragg eulogise?

8 In 2013, which band released the *Music for Cars* EP just before their debut album?

9 Who took his 'Roadrunner' into the UK Top 20 in 1976?

10 What kind of transport did Queen use to race on *Jazz*?

11 Who reimagined the M25 as 'The Road to Hell' in 1989?

12 Who were riding *Bicycles and Tricycles* in 2004?

13 What was Status Quo's unsafe-sounding mode of flight, a single from their 1972 album *Piledriver*?

14 The Saw Doctors held a soft spot for which road between Galway and Sligo?

15 Who was *Wanted on Voyage* in 2014?

16 Which singer was 'Leaving on a Jet Plane' in the sixties, then died piloting a much smaller plane in 1997?

17 Which train did Jimmy catch in *Quadrophenia*?

18 'Riding along in my automobile, my baby beside me at the wheel.' Where was Chuck Berry heading?

19 In which seaworthy craft did the Beatles all live?

20 Which legendary session guitarist had a one-off UK hit in 1975 with 'Motor Bikin"?

21 Which flashy motor did Prince drive?

22 Who threatened that 'One Day I'll Fly Away' in 1980?

23 What was the Clash's prize possession on *London Calling*?

24 In which direction was Joe Bonamassa driving in 2012?

25 Who rode a 'Silver Machine' in 1972?

26 Which train did the Monkees catch on their first single?

27 How did the boy in Avril Lavigne's second single, another UK Top 10 hit after 'Complicated', get around?

28 Who were 'Driving in my Car' in the UK Top 10 in 1982?

29 Who was concerned with 'Crosstown Traffic' in 1968?

30 Who were 'Jumping Someone Else's Train' in 1979?

31 In 1988, which British band got 'Behind the Wheel'?

32 Who drove a 'Car 67' in 1978?

33 How did Tom Robinson count in his freeway?

34 Whose second album advised us to *Take Them On, On Your Own*?

35 Which band fell for the singer's 'Best Friend's Girl'?

36 Who probably regretted using the underground, if 'Down in the Tube Station (At Midnight)' is anything to go by?

37 Which band suggested we 'Keep the Car Running' at the start of their 2007 album, but had changed their mind by the time 'No Cars Go' appeared as the record's penultimate track?

38 Who was the air hostess who saved the singer's life in 10cc's UK Top 10 hit from 1976?

39 Who wanted to go to sea by themselves in 1989?

40 Where have Bobby Troup, Chuck Berry and the Rolling Stones all got their kicks?

QUIZ 98

AMERICANA

Americana, alt.country – call it what you will, but we're using it as a catch-all for music with a country-tinged sound or its roots in the country scene. Some of these acts have a full-on Dolly-style attitude, while others are closer to rock and roll with just a hint of pedal steel. It's an exciting scene, certainly not the reactionary hillbilly cartoon music that some British listeners imagine inner-state American music to be. Here are 30 questions about some of the old guard and the new kids on the scene.

Answers: page 542

1   When an album tops the US country chart, it can sometimes stay there for a while. For example: Glen Campbell held the top spot from November 1968 until June 1969 the following year with two successive releases. Named after two of his most famous songs, what were they called?

2   *Car Wheels on a Gravel Road* launched which alt.country artist towards into the mainstream? Released in 2014, which of her albums gave the singer her highest UK chart placing when it reached number 23?

3   What was the name of the psychedelic protest band formed by Joe McDonald and Barry Melton? A performance at which festival remains their finest moment?

4   Who was the original 'King of the Road', topping the UK singles chart in 1965? Which Scottish band took the same number back into the Top 10 in 1990?

5   With which bands did Graham Nash and David Crosby play before forming Crosby, Stills & Nash with Stephen Stills?

6   *Luxury Liner* and *Wrecking Ball* are two of many career highlights for which enduringly successful country singer? With whom has she made two well-received albums in recent years, *Old Yellow Moon* and *The Traveling Kind*?

7   Chicago have given many of their album titles a Roman numeral: *Chicago V*, *Chicago XIV* and so on. What was the title of their 1969 debut LP, which was also at that time the name of the band? And what has been their biggest hit single, reaching number one in the US and the UK in 1976?

8   Released in 2002, what was Shania Twain's fourth album and the follow-up to the massive *Come On Over*? Why shouldn't the singer be hailed as the all-American icon she appears to be?

9   Which classic Gram Parsons album was released posthumously in early 1974, months after his death from a drugs overdose? Which band did he form after leaving the Byrds?

10 Released in 2014, *Out Among the Stars* was a posthumous album by which singer? Who had previously released *The List*, an album based on a list she had found in the singer's house after his death?

11 *Evil Urges* was the 2008 breakthrough album for which alternative American rock band? Who is their charismatic songwriter and singer?

12 Which supergroup includes Scott McCaughey of the Minus 5, Belle & Sebastian's drummer Richard Colburn and REM's guitarist Peter Buck? Who is their singer and frontman?

13 Released in 1987, *Trio* was a collaboration between Dolly Parton and which two other country legends?

14 In 2009, *Raising Sand* garnered almost universal praise from critics. Which two artists, one a rock singer and the other a bluegrass star, collaborated on the project?

15 Whose brand of Latino country gave them a massive hit with 'Dance the Night Away' in 1998? What's the name of the band's singer and guitarist, who has also released six solo albums?

BONUS TRACKS

16 Whose beauty was beyond compare? And what colour were her eyes, to go with her 'flaming locks of auburn hair'?

17 Which country album by Bobbie Gentry, named after the biggest hit single taken from it, replaced *Sgt Pepper's Lonely Hearts Club Band* at the top of the US albums chart? Two years later, in 1969, which Bacharach and David song gave Gentry her only British number one?

18 *The People's Key* is the final studio album by which American band, fronted by Conor Oberst? What's the name of the backing band that Oberst sometimes uses for his solo projects?

19 Which band is led by Jakob Dylan, the son of Bob Dylan and Sara Lownds? What was the title of their most successful album so far, released in 1996 and produced by T-Bone Burnett?

20 Which massive US star had a rare UK chart entry with the album *In Pieces* in 1994? Which country singer became his second wife 11 years later?

21 Kurt Wagner is the main creative influence and only permanent member of which alt.country band? In 2004, the band released two albums. One was called *Aw C'mon* – what was the other?

22 Who wrote and recorded 'Your Cheatin' Heart', one of the most covered country songs? How old was this singer when he died in 1953, months after recording it?

23 *The Dirty South*, *The Big To-Do* and *English Oceans* are albums by which Alabama rock band? The band used to have three singer/guitarist/songwriters: which one left and now records with the 400 Unit?

24 In 1997, who won two Grammy Awards for her song and album 'Blue' at the age of just 14? Which song, the theme tune from the film *Coyote Ugly*, scored the singer her only British number one?

25 What's the title of Ryan Adams' impressive solo debut? And what was the name he used for his backing band on *Cold Roses* and *Jacksonville City Nights*?

26 Who is the only permanent member of longstanding US act Giant Sand? The two principal members of which other American band once served as the group's rhythm section?

27 Which song topped the US charts and went Top 10 in the UK for Kenny Rogers and Dolly Parton? Who wrote it, apparently intending for it to be recorded by Marvin Gaye?

28 What's the name of John Grant's third solo album, released in 2015? With which band did Grant release six studio albums before embarking on a solo career?

29 *Highwayman* is a 1985 album by a supergroup featuring Johnny Cash, Willie Nelson and which two other country legends?

30 Taken from a classic country song written by the answer to question 22, what's the title both of Steve Earle's 2011 album and his first novel? Which country singer became Earle's seventh wife in 2005 (and his seventh ex-wife in 2014)?

BOB DYLAN

It's impossible to have a quiz book of this ilk without a section devoted to rock's great cryptic troubadour. Not just a rock and roll figure, Bob Dylan was (though he might deny it) one of the most significant figures in sixties counter-culture. Here, the first 20 questions are about his work and life. The last ten take the format of the Classic Albums quizzes, whereby you get three tracks and have to deduce which album they were on, and its decade of release.

Answers: page 543

1 When Dylan won a Lifetime Achievement Grammy in 1991, which of his sixties songs did he sing in response to the Gulf War? Which world leader, at a presentation six years later, praised him for having 'disturbed the peace and discomfited the powerful'?

2 What was the title of the 1975 album by Bob Dylan and the Band from recordings made while he was recuperating from a motorcycle accident in 1966? Under what name did the Band act as Dylan's touring band during 1965?

3 Who was Bob Dylan's first wife, and what name did he give her in the film he directed in 1978?

4 Jacques Levy, a trained psychologist and the director of the erotic Broadway stage show *Oh Calcutta!*, was an odd co-writer for Dylan – but on which album did he co-write all but two of the songs? One of them, 'Hurricane', was about the wrongful arrest and prosecution of which boxer?

5 'Come in, she said, I'll give you ....' on Dylan's 1975 classic *Blood on the Tracks*? On the same album is a narrative song called 'Lily, Rosemary and the Jack of Hearts': which mean mine owner do that trio thwart?

6 The seventh volume of the *Bootleg* series of Dylan releases was the soundtrack to a 1995 TV documentary. What was it called and who directed it?

7 Which 1979 album is regarded as the first of Dylan's Christian albums? Which famous studio in Sheffield, Alabama, known for its soul sounds and top drawer horn section, was it made in?

8 'Baby Stop Crying' was one of two only UK Top 20 singles Dylan enjoyed post-1970. The other was a 1973 track from the *Pat Garrett and Billy the Kid* soundtrack: what was the song? Who directed the film?

9 In the mid-nineties Dylan released two albums of traditional folk songs. What marked *Good as I Been to You* (1992) as the first of its kind since *Another Side of Bob Dylan* in 1964? The song 'Blackjack Davey' was a rendering of which Scottish folk ballad?

10 Which Jamaican rhythm section did Dylan hire to work on his 1983 album, *Infidels*? Who played guitar on, and also produced, the album?

11 In which year did Dylan's eponymous debut album hit the stores? What was the oft-covered Blind Lemon Jefferson song, a mordant take on impending death?

12 Which Dylan album, released in April, 2009, was his first UK number one since 1970's *New Morning*? Robert Hunter, Dylan's songwriting partner on the 2009 album, was also a member of, and the lyricist, in which band?

13 The patchy 1986 *Knocked Out Loaded* contains one masterpiece, an 11-minute track that opens side two of the vinyl release. What is the song and which American playwright is credited as co-writer?

14 Which long narrative song took up the entire fourth side of *Blonde on Blonde*? Where and with what did Dylan get stuck on this album?

15 The royalties from Dylan's first Christmas album, *Christmas in the Heart* (2009) were given to charities in which area of work? Which of these Christmas songs does NOT appear on the album: 'Hark the Herald Angels Sing'; 'Little Drummer Boy'; 'Silent Night'; 'Winter Wonderland?'

16 What was the 1965 Festival where Dylan was booed for playing an electric set? Who was his guitarist that day, known also for his work with the Paul Butterfield Blues Band and Electric Flag?

17 Which song from *Freewheelin' Bob Dylan* did the artist re-record as a duet on 'Nashville Skyline', and which country legend sang with him?

18 *Shadows in the Night* (2015) saw Dylan covering popular jazz standards. What was his main criterion for selection? Which song from *South Pacific* appeared on there?

19 Which Dylan song was voted as the greatest rock song of all time in polls published by *Rolling Stone* magazine in both 2004 and 2011? What is the first line of the song?

20 Which legendary critic and enthusiastic chronicler of Bob Dylan began his
    review of *Self Portrait* (1970) in *Rolling Stone* with the words, 'What is this
    shit?' Which Paul Simon song from *Bridge Over Troubled Water* did Dylan
    cover on the album?

BONUS TRACKS

Like we said, identify the album and decade of release from these song titles.

21 'Lenny Bruce'; 'Property of Jesus'; 'Every Grain of Sand'

22 'Standing in the Doorway'; 'Cold Irons Bound'; 'Not Dark Yet'

23 'We Better Talk This Over'; 'Is Your Love In Vain?'; 'Changing of the Guards'

24 'Bob Dylan's Dream'; 'Don't Think Twice, It's Alright'; 'A Hard Rain's a Gonna Fall'

25 'Disease of Conceit'; 'Man in the Long Black Coat'; 'Everything is Broken'

26 'Tin Angel'; 'Duquesne Whistle'; 'Long and Wasted Years'

27 'Wiggle Wiggle'; 'Cat's in the Well'; 'Born in Time'

28 'On a Night Like This'; 'Never Say Goodbye'; 'Forever Young'

29 'The Levee's Gonna Break'; 'Thunder on the Mountain'; 'Rollin' and Tumblin''

30 'Just Like Tom Thumb's Blues'; 'Desolation Row'; 'Like a Rolling Stone'

ANSWERS

QUIZ 16 MUSIC RECOMMENDS

1 Battles; Ian Williams. 2 I Am Kloot; 'Over My Shoulder'. 3 Future Islands; Samuel T Herring. 4 Dan Auerbach; Patrick Carney. 5 'The horror (here) …'; *Total Life Forever*. 6 *Under the Blacklight*; The Elected. 7 'Post Break-Up Sex'; *English Graffiti*. 8 Lykke Li; *Wounded Rhymes*. 9 *Michigan* (he has since added only *Illinois*, saying that his earlier claim was a joke the music press took too seriously); *Carrie & Lowell*. 10 Poliça; Channy Leaneagh. 11 Klara and Johanna. 12 *Lost in the Dream*; An Ocean. 13 The Wave Pictures; Billy Childish. 14 Midlake; *Antiphon*. 15 Dave Grohl; Mark Lanegan.

16 Fat White Family; Mark E. Smith of the Fall (in 'I Am Mark E Smith'). 17 Dry The River; 'in the best way possible'. 18 'Munich'; 'Smokers Outside the Hospital Doors'. 19 St Paul and the Broken Bones; *Half the City*. 20 Django Django; *Born Under Saturn*. 21 Band of Skulls; Diamonds and Pearls. 22 Christine and the Queens; *Chaleur Humaine*; the UK release has some songs re-sung in English and a couple of new English-language numbers. 23 War On Drugs; The Violators. 24 Frightened Rabbit; *Painting of a Panic Attack*. 25 Augustines; *Rise Ye Sunken Ships*. 26 Hozier; Sinéad O'Connor. 27 *Depression Cherry*; the band (all two of them) are from Baltimore, where *The Wire* is set. 28 Alabama Shakes; *Boys & Girls*. 29 Johnny Marr; Isaac Brock. 30 Beirut; trumpet.

QUIZ 2 THE BEATLES

1 *Sgt Pepper's Lonely Hearts Club Band*; Dame Vera Lynn. 2 They are all on the cover of *Sgt Pepper's Lonely Hearts Club Band*, which was designed and composed by the two artists. 3 'Eleanor Rigby'; 'Yellow Submarine'. 4 Cellophane; marshmallow pies. 5 George Harrison wrote and sang them all; 'Within You, Without You' was also George's. 6 Four thousand; it is a line from 'A Day in the Life'. 7 Paul McCartney; The Beach Boys' 'California Girls', whose chorus and lyrics it echoes. 8 Pepperland; the Little Blue Meanies. 9 Sir George Martin; piano and other keyboards. 10 *Let It Be*; on the roof of the Apple building in Savile Row, central London. 11 Richard Lester; *A Hard Day's Night*. 12 'You're Sixteen' (it seemed innocent then, but not in this post-Yewtree age); Johnny Burnette. 13 They are the opening songs on their first eleven studio albums, so 'Two of Us' (from the twelfth, *Let It Be*) completes the set. 14 'It Don't Come Easy'; *The Concert for Bangladesh* organised by George Harrison. 15 'When I'm Sixty-Four'; Vera, Chuck and Dave.

16 'Handle With Care'; Nelson Wilbury. 17 *With the Beatles*; Chuck Berry. 18 *All Things Must Pass*; 'If Not For You'. 19 'You Really Got a Hold on Me'; 'Dizzy Miss Lizzy'. 20 Dark Horse; 'Got My Mind Set on You'. 21 'Penny Lane'; 'The Ballad of John and Yoko'. 22 *Imagine* and *Double Fantasy*. 23 Sitar; Ravi Shankar. 24 'Imagine'; 'Jealous Guy'. 25 *Revolver*; 1966. 26 Gideon's Bible; piggies. 27 John Lennon's claim that the band had become 'bigger than Jesus'. 28 'What's That You're Doing' and 'Ebony and Ivory'. 29 The Quarrymen were a Liverpool band started by John Lennon with school friends and later joined by Paul McCartney and George Harrison; Ringo Starr left Rory Storm and the Hurricanes to replace Pete Best in the Beatles. 30 *Flaming Pie* and *New*.

QUIZ 3 MONEY MONEY MONEY

1 Rich Kids; Midge Ure. 2 Barenaked Ladies; 'One Week'. 3 Thin Lizzy (Phil Lynott) and the Sex Pistols (Paul Cook and Steve Jones). 4 *Innocent Man*; *Wrecking Ball*. 5 *She Works Hard for the Money*; Musical Youth. 6 'Free Money'; Penetration. 7 *Good Kid, m.A.A.d.*; Jay Rock. 8 Bruno Mars; The Queen. 9 Marco Pirroni; 'Made of Money'. 10 At the Sorbonne in Paris; (*Let's Make Lots of Money*). 11 Mötley Crüe; Sex Pistols. 12 *The Dark Side of the Moon*; David Gilmour. 13 'Take the Money and Run'; they robbed a bank in El Paso. 14 A diamond ring; vocal harmonies. 15 Sting; *Brothers in Arms*.

16 'Material Girl'; Marilyn Monroe. 17 Dizzee Rascal; 'Dirtee Cash'. 18 U2; Rolling Stones. 19 'Money Changes Everything'; The Brains: Gray was their singer. 20 'Money (That's What I Want)'; Tamla Motown. 21 U2 and Elton John. 22 Mercedes Benz (the title of the song); a colour TV. 23 'Money Honey'; The Drifters. 24 Alice Cooper (when the name still meant the band, not the singer); 'School's Out'. 25 Cole Porter; Frank Sinatra. 26 Notorious B.I.G.; Puff Daddy. 27 Daryl Hall and John Oates. 28 50 Cent; *Get Rich or Die Tryin'*. 29 'Money's Too Tight (To Mention)'; Frantic Elevators. 30 The rights to the Beatles song catalogue; Michael Jackson, who sold it in 2006 to offset his rising debts.

QUIZ 4 CLASSIC ALBUMS #1: THE SIXTIES

1 The Kinks; *Something Else by the Kinks*. 2 Simon and Garfunkel; *Sounds of Silence*. 3 Johnny Cash; *Live at San Quentin* 4 The Velvet Underground & Nico; *The Velvet Underground & Nico*. 5 The Beach Boys; *Pet Sounds*. 6 Them; *The Angry Young Them*. 7 Creedence Clearwater Revival; *Green River*. 8 Van Morrison; *Astral Weeks*. 9 Led Zeppelin; *I*. 10 Love; *Forever Changes*. 11 Isaac Hayes; *Hot Buttered Soul*. 12 Jefferson Airplane; *Surrealistic Pillow*. 13 Fairport Convention; Liege & Lief. 14 The Zombies; *Odessey and Oracle*. 15 The Bonzo Dog Doo Dah Band; *Gorilla*.

16 The Jimi Hendrix Experience; *Electric Ladyland*. 17 Phil Spector; *A Christmas Gift For You*. 18 The MC5; *Kick Out the Jams*. 19 The Mamas and the Papas; *If You Can Believe Your Eyes and Ears*. 20 The Beatles; *Please Please Me*. 21 Rolling Stones; *Beggars' Banquet*. 22 The Monkees; *More of the Monkees*. 23 The Byrds; *Fifth Dimension*. 24 The Small Faces; *Ogden's Nut Gone Flake*. 25 Aretha Franklin; *Lady Soul*. 26 Cream; *Goodbye*. 27 The Who; *Tommy*. 28 Otis Redding; *Otis Blue: Otis Redding Sings Soul*. 29 Leonard Cohen; *Songs from a Room*. 30 Dusty Springfield; *A Girl Called Dusty*.

QUIZ 5 **ROCK AND ROLL**

1 Bill Haley and his Comets. 2 Lonnie Donegan; Van Morrison. 3 Johnny Kidd and the Pirates; Mick Green. 4 Roy Orbison; 'Claudette'. 5 Hank Marvin; 'Apache'. 6 Bo *Diddley; 'Who Do You Love?'* 7 Del Shannon; The Travelling Wilburys. 8 The Teddy Bears; Phil Spector. 9 'Cathy's Clown'; Phil and Don. 10 'Johnny Remember Me'; 'Telstar'. 11 'Lucille'; B.B. King – the story goes that it helped remind him of a foolish act as a young man, when he ran back into a burning building to retrieve his guitar. 12 'Peggy Sue'; She got married (in Holly's song, 'Peggy Sue Got Married'). 13 Johnny and the Hurricanes; 'Red River Rock'. 14 'Johnnie Ray'; 'Come On Eileen'. 15 'Sweet Little Sixteen'; 'My Ding-a-Ling'.

16 Loads of Elvis-stamped letters were sent to fictitious addresses in the hope that the mail service would stamp them 'return to sender'. 17 'An American Trilogy'; the American Civil War. 18 'Jailhouse Rock'; it was the thousandth UK number one. 19 'All Shook Up'; 'Jailhouse Rock'. 20 RCA Victor; Colonel Tom Parker. 21 'A Little Less Conversation'; *Ocean's Eleven.* 22 *Love Me Tender*; Hawaii – it was screened as *Aloha from Hawaii!* 23 'My Way'; Paul Anka. 24 *G.I. Blues* and *Blue Hawaii.* 25 'Way Down'; 'The Wonder of You'. 26 Dire Straits; *On Every Street.* 27 'Elvis has left the building...' (in Zappa's case 'just left the building'); Tiny Tim released 'I Saw Mr Presley Tiptoeing Through the Tulips'. 28 Marc Cohn; Cher. 29 A chip shop ('There's a Guy Works Down the Chip Shop Swears He's Elvis'; 'A New England'. 30 George Michael; Lennon.

QUIZ 6 PEOPLE'S PLAYLIST: ALL AROUND THE WORLD

1 China Crisis. 2 Teenage Fanclub. 3 Mink Deville. 4 Paris ('Une Nuit a Paris').
5 *Siamese Dream*. 6 'Warszawa' (Warsaw). 7 Mozambique. 8 'One Night in
Bangkok'. 9 Toto. 10 'Cuba'. 11 Alphaville. 12 The Mamas & the Papas. 13 The
band's first hit was 'Native New Yorker'. 14 They were 'Going Back to My Roots'.
15 'Spanish Harlem' (aka East Harlem). 16 San Francisco. 17 'Berlin Got Blurry'.
18 'I'm in Love with a German Film Star'. 19 The album title is *Around the World
in a Day*. 20 'Holiday in Cambodia'. 21 'The Lebanon'. 22 Super Furry Animals.
23 'Vienna' by Ultravox. 24 'All Around the World'. 25 'Massachusetts'. 26 Supergrass.
27 'Budapest'. 28 The Ramones. 29 Swedish House Mafia. 30 David Bowie.
31 *Andorra*. 32 'Australia'. 33 'Bloodbuzz Ohio'. 34 The Stranglers, on 'Goodbye
Toulouse', 'Dagenham Dave', 'Sweden' and 'Dead Loss Angeles'. 35 Boards of Canada.
36 'Norwegian Wood (This Bird Has Flown)'. 37 *To the 5 Boroughs*. 38 'Mambo
Italiano'. 39 *Be Here Now*. 40 'Paris, Munich'.

QUIZ 7 NAME THE BAND #1

1 Kajagoogoo. 2 Silversun Pickups. 3 The Blue Nile. 4 Shalamar. 5 Nine Black Alps.
6 Kasabian. 7 Gerry and the Pacemakers. 8 Alt-J. 9 Everything Everything. 10 The
Mission. 11 Best Coast. 12 The Ting Tings.13 Blue Oyster Cult. 14 Maximo Park.
15 Royal Blood. 16 Scorpions. 17 Stornoway. 18 The Four Tops. 19 The Tourists.
20 Imagine Dragons. 21 War On Drugs. 22 The Dead Kennedys. 23 Weezer. 24 The
Lighthouse Family. 25 Steel Pulse. 26 My Bloody Valentine. 27 A Certain Ratio.
28 Supertramp. 29 Powderfinger. 30 Fat White Family,

31 Odyssey. 32 Stereo MCs. 33 The Cramps. 34 Manfred Mann (not Manfred Mann's
Earthband, which came later and had a different line-up). 35 The Saw Doctors.
36 The Crickets (Buddy Holly's band). 37 Freddie and the Dreamers. 38 Stone Temple
Pilots. 39 Temples. 40 Colin Blunstone (formerly of the Zombies). 41 Hurricane #1.
42 Calexico. 43 The Levellers. 44 Westlife. 45 Reef. 46 Aztec Camera. 47 Saint Etienne.
48 Glasvegas. 49 The Lumineers. 50 Kitchens of Distinction. 51 Drive-By Truckers.
52 Doves. 53 Go West. 54 London Grammar. 55 Wild Beasts. 56 The Cars. 57 The
Temper Trap. 58 The Au Pairs. 59 Spear of Destiny. 60 The Leisure Society,

QUIZ 8 DJS & RADIO

1 Simon Bates; Classic FM. 2 Fun Lovin' Criminals; Huey Morgan. 3 Radio Luxembourg; 208 MW. 4 'The Riverboat Song'; *Don't Forget Your Toothbrush*. 5 Zoë Ball; she presents *It Takes Two*, having previously competed on *Strictly Come Dancing*. 6 Alan Freeman; *Pick of the Pops*. 7 Xfm; Johnny Vaughan. 8 Kenny Everett; Captain Kremmen. 9 Manchester; Damon Albarn. 10 *The Old Grey Whistle Test*; country and Americana music. 11 Terry Wogan; Lynn Bowles. 12 *Multi-Coloured Swap Shop* (*Swap Shop* is an acceptable answer); he resigned after Michael Lush died while rehearsing a stunt for the show. 13 Sara Cox; Comedy Dave (Dave Vitty). 14 Matt Everitt; Menswear. 15 Nick Grimshaw; *The One Show*.

16 Capital Gold; Jonathan Pearce, who presented *Capital Gold Sportstime*. 17 Tony Blackburn; *I'm a Celebrity... Get Me Out of Here!*. 18 Charlie Gillett; *The Sound of the City*. 19 Annie Nightingale; *The Old Grey Whistle Test*. 20 Gilles Peterson, Worldwide. 21 Heart FM; Emma Bunton. 22 *MV Fredericia* became *MC Caroline*, the host ship of Radio Caroline; it was named after Caroline Kennedy, John F Kennedy's daughter. 23 Steve Wright, who has hosted shows called *Steve Wright in the Afternoon* on BBC Radios 1 and 2; Mr Angry was purportedly from Purley. 24 Marc Riley; The Fall. 25 Mark Lamarr; *Never Mind the Buzzcocks*. 26 John Peel; Bob Harris. 27 Jo Whiley; Simon Mayo. 28 Harry Enfield and Paul Whitehouse, for *Harry Enfield's Television Programme*. 29 Scott Mills; Mark Chapman ('Chappers'). 30 Paul Gambaccini; *America's Greatest Hits*.

QUIZ 9 LOU REED

1 Edgar Allan Poe; Julian Schnabel. 2 Max's Kansas City, a New York nightclub; 'I'm Waiting for the Man'. 3 Tom Tom Club; a cover of the Velvet Underground song 'Femme Fatale'. 4 Jesse Jackson and Pope John Paul II (identified simply as 'Pontiff'). 5 The 9/11 attacks; 'Laurie' is Laurie Anderson, Reed's wife. 6 Delmore Schwartz; Andy Warhol, who died in 1987. 7 A version of the song featuring numerous guest singers was used on a video designed to showcase the diversity of the BBC's music coverage; *Trainspotting*. 8 'Sweet Jane'; Mott the Hoople. 9 *Metal Machine Music*; *The Creation of the Universe*. 10 'Sister Ray', sometimes referred to as the source of the 'shoegaze' scene; *White Light/White Heat*. 11 *NYC Man*; 'Satellite of Love'. 12 Maureen 'Mo' Tucker; it was the first time since the break-up of the Velvet Underground that Tucker, Lou Reed, John Cale and Sterling Morrison had appeared on record together. 13 *Ecstasy*; Fernando Saunders. 14 *Street Hassle*; Bruce Springsteen. 15 'Heroin' appears on the first Velvet Underground album, while 'Sex with Your Parents' features on *Set the Twilight Reeling*.

16 'Like a bird on the wire; 'Bird on the Wire' features on *Songs from a Room*. 17 *Kicking Against the Pricks*; 'All Tomorrow's Parties'. 18 Mick Harvey; Barry Adamson. 19 *Harvest*; a moon – in 1992, Young released *Harvest Moon*, a follow-up of sorts to *Harvest*. 20 'Heart of Gold'; '... And I'm getting old'. 21 'Famous Blue Raincoat'; 'Joan of Arc'. 22 *Americana*; 'God Save the Queen'. 23 *Abattoir Blues* and *The Lyre of Orpheus*. 24 'Hallelujah'; *Various Positions*. 25 *The Proposition*; *20,000 Days on Earth*. 26 *Natural Born Killers*; the Berlin Wall. 27 *Living with War*; 'Let's Impeach the President'. 28 *Old Ideas*; *Popular Problems*. 29 The Boys Next Door; Grinderman. 30 They're all Neil Young live albums; *Arc*.

QUIZ 10 **NOW PLAYING @6**

1 *Breaking Glass*; 'Will You?'. 2 'Is Vic There?' *Department S* was a sixties TV spy show. 3 Creedence Clearwater Revival; John Fogerty. 4 *Who the Fuck Are Arctic Monkeys?* 'The View from the Afternoon'. 5 'Life On Mars?' and 'Where Are We Now?'. 6 'The Boy With the Arab Strap'; Isobel Campbell. 7 Oasis, *(What's the Story) Morning Glory?*; Alanis Morissette, *Jagged Little Pill*. 8 Paul Young; David Bowie. 9 The Moody Blues; Justin Hayward. 10 'Do You Know the Way to San Jose?'; Dionne Warwick. 11 *Who's Next* and *Who Are You*. 12 'Who Am I? (What's My Name?)'. 13 Edward Tudor-Pole; Nobody — it was Bambi's mum who was killed by a hunter. 14 Jimmy Ruffin; 1966. 15 Elvis Costello and the Attractions; Brinsley Schwarz.

Bonus tracks

1 'What Do I Get?' Therapy?. 2 Frankie Lymon (and the Teenagers); 'Why do birds sing so gay?' 3 Eurythmics; Madonna. 4 'How Soon is Now?' *Charmed*. 5 'Is There Something I Should Know'; 'The Reflex'. 6 The Bees; Isle of Wight. 7 'Will You Love Me Tomorrow?'; *Tapestry*. 8 *I Am A Bird Now*; Rufus Wainwright. 9 'Where Did Our Love Go?'; David Ball. 10 'What Have I Done to Deserve This?'; Dusty Springfield. 11 'What's a Girl To Do?'; Natasha Khan. 12 Drake; Robyn Rihanna Fenty. 13 'Blowin' in the Wind'; *The Freewheelin' Bob Dylan*. 14 Connie Francis; *A Night in Casablanca*. 15 'Does Chewing Gum Lose Its Flavour (On the Bedpost Overnight)?' 'My Old Man's a Dustman'.

QUIZ 11 THIS IS REGGAE MUSIC

1 Dillinger; the CB200 was his Honda motorcycle. 2 The I Threes; Bob Marley's backing singers: Rita was his wife. 3 'Don't worry 'bout a thing, cause every little thing gonna be alright'. 4 'Don't Turn Around'; Aswad is Arabic for black. 5 Bunny Wailer; Bob Marley. 6 Carlton and Aston 'Family Man' Barrett; The Upsetters. 7 Burning Spear; a pre-war Jamaican politician and writer seen as a prophet by many Rastafarians. 8 'Young, Gifted and Black' and 'Pied Piper'. 9 Peter Tosh; Mick Jagger. 10 The Lyceum; *Babylon By Bus*. 11 UB40 (Ali and Robin Campbell); Eddy Grant. 12 Bob Marley's *Legend*; *The Dark Side of the Moon*. 13 Buju Banton; he is serving ten years for cocaine trafficking. 14 Peter Tosh and Bunny Wailer. 15 The Folkes Brothers; 'Boombastic'.

16 Coventry; 2 Tone. 17 *Dutty Rock*; Sasha. 18 *Burnin'*; John Brown. 19 Chaka Demus & Pliers with 'Twist & Shout'; 'Tease Me'. 20 'Police and Thieves'; Junior Murvin. 21 Gregory Isaacs; The Cool Ruler. 22 Trenchtown; England. 23 'You Don't Love Me (No, No, No)'; Rihanna. Penn originally released the song in the sixties in a much more basic, rocksteady style. 24 Prince Buster; All Stars. 25 Horace Andy; Massive Attack. 26 *Uprising*; *Confrontation*. 27 Finley Quaye; Edinburgh. 28 Trojan Records; skinheads. 29 The Paragons; John Holt. 30 Sun Is Shining; *Soul Revolution*.

QUIZ 12 GIRLS & BOYS

1 'Maria'; Rage Against the Machine. 2 Bruce Springsteen & the E Street Band; Thin Lizzy. 3 'Henrietta'; 'Mistress Mabel'. 4 'Valerie'; Mark Ronson. 5 'Rhiannon'; 'Sara'. 6 'Mary of the 4th Form'; '(I Never Loved) Eva Braun'. 7 'Jenny Was a Friend of Mine'; 'Smile Like You Mean It'. 8 'Judy in Disguise (With Glasses)'; 'Judy is a Punk'. 9 'Delilah'; the Sensational Alex Harvey Band. 10 'Suzanne' and Marianne (on 'So Long, Marianne'). 11 'Charlotte Sometimes'; 'Charlotte the Harlot'. 12 'Geraldine'; 'Euphoria, Take My Hand'. 13 Barry Manilow; Westlife. 14 Paolo Nutini and Robbie Williams. 15 Hot Chocolate; 'Grace Kelly'.

16 'Gloria' and 'Iris (Hold Me Close)'. 17 Caroline, in 'Sweet Caroline' by Neil Diamond and 'Caroline' by Status Quo; 'Cracklin' Rosie'. 18 'Mustang Sally'; 'Lay Down, Sally'. 19 Terrorvision; Smokie. 20 'Lucille'; 'four hungry children and a crop in the field'. 21 Sham 69, 'Hurry Up Harry'; the Stranglers, '(Don't Bring) Harry'. 22 Charlie Brown; *Mylo Xyloto*. 23 Elton John; Bat for Lashes. 24 Jack and Diane; John Mellencamp. 25 Chuck Berry; Palma Violets. 26 'A Boy Named Sue'; it was recorded live at San Quentin State Prison. 27 Abba and the Brotherhood of Man. 28 The Undertones; Green Day on *American Idiot*. 29 'Jackie'; 'Jackie Wilson Said (I'm in Heaven When You Smile)'. 30 Robert Palmer; Bryan Ferry.

QUIZ 13 STADIUM ROCK

1 Peter Green; Bob Welch. 2 Paul Rodgers; *The Cosmos Rocks*. 3 'Exogenesis'; 'Uprising'. 4 The Valley, home of Charlton Athletic FC; the 1976 show entered *The Guinness Book of World Records* as the loudest concert in history. 5 'Helter Skelter'; 'Desire'. 6 Willie Dixon; 'Bring it on Home'. 7 'I Can't Explain'; 'I'm a Boy'. 8 'Supermassive Black Hole'; 'Knights of Cydonia'. 9 George Michael and Lisa Stansfield. 10 *The Joshua Tree*; Anton Corbijn. 11 'Kashmir'; 'Achilles Last Stand'. 12 'Bohemian Rhapsody'; it was re-released as a tribute to Freddie Mercury following his death. 13 *The Dance*; *Say You Will*. 14 *War*; 'Sunday Bloody Sunday'. 15 The album is officially untitled, but is commonly known as *Led Zeppelin IV*; the album cover doesn't contain the band's name or writing of any sort, apparently Jimmy Page's response to the ordinary reviews received by the band's previous album.

16 'Love, Reign o'er Me', subtitled 'Pete's Theme', and 'Bell Boy (Keith's Theme)'. 17 *Flash Gordon*; *Highlander*. 18 Stevie Nicks and Lindsey Buckingham. 19 'Stockholm Syndrome'; 'Thoughts of a Dying Atheist'. 20 'Vertigo' and 'Sometimes You Can't Make It on Your Own'. 21 'The Song Remains the Same'; *Physical Graffiti*. 22 Mick Fleetwood, the drummer, and John McVie, the bass player. 23 Palestrina; 'Feeling Good'. 24 *Made in Heaven*; Lake Geneva. 25 'Won't Get Fooled Again' (*CSI: Miami*) and 'Baba O'Riley' (*CSI: NY*). 26 Passengers; 'Miss Sarajevo'. 27 *In Through the Out Door*; *Coda*. 28 Size: the hits were 'Big Love' and 'Little Lies'. 29 *Showbiz*; Mushroom Records. 30 Kenney Jones of the Faces; Zak Starkey, Ringo Starr's son.

QUIZ 14 DAVID BOWIE

1 A founder member of Kraftwerk; *"Heroes"*. 2 Labyrinth; Pontius Pilate. 3 Lulu; Bowie himself. 4 He wanted something more glamorous and was fed up of confusion with Davy Jones, singer of the Monkees; from Jim Bowie, the American hero and pioneer of the knife that bears his name. 5 He'd 'shrug and ask to stay'; 'she'd sigh like Twig the Wonder Kid'. 6 New York; Los Angeles. 7 John Lennon; Luther Vandross (the album was *Young Americans*). 8 His middle name, Zowie; *Moon*. 9 Doppelganger and Skeleton Men. 10 Annie Lennox; Imam. 11 'China Girl'; *Let's Dance*. 12 *The Buddha of Suburbia*; Hanif Kureishi. 13 *Blackstar*; *Best of Bowie*, a 2002 compilation. 14 'Starman' (1972); 'Blue Jean' (1984). 15 *Low* and *"Heroes"*.

16 Bing Crosby; 'Little Drummer Boy/Peace on Earth' 17 Carlos Alomar; Robert Fripp. 18 *Life On Mars*; The Jean Genie. 19 Nile Rodgers; Stevie Ray Vaughan. 20 The Thin White Duke; 'Wild is the Wind'. 21 Tin Machine; 'Working Class Hero'. 22 'Space Oddity' as Major Tom reappears; a Pierrot. 23 'Anyway, Anyhow, Anywhere' and 'See Emily Play'. 24 'God Only Knows'; Tina Turner. 25 *Black Tie, White Noise*; 'Where Are We Now?'. 26 Serious Moonlight; Glass Spider. 27 *The Man Who Fell to Earth*; Nicolas Roeg; 28 *Hours*; it was called 'Thursday's Child' (Thursday's Child has far to go, according to the old children's rhyme); 29 *Absolute Beginners*; Patsy Kensit. 30 Dave Grohl; 'Slow Burn'.

QUIZ 15 ACCEPTABLE IN THE 80S

1 Altered Images; Texas. 2 Gary Jules; Tears for Fears. 3 Five Star; *Silk and Steel*.
4 'Stool Pigeon'; 'Annie, I'm Not Your Daddy'. 5 'Fairytale of New York'; Kirsty
MacColl. 6 'Super Trouper'; 'The Visitors'. 7 'I Want to Know What Love Is'; Spooky
Tooth. 8 Heaven 17; *The Luxury Gap*. 9 Prefab Sprout; *From Langley Park to
Memphis*. 10 'Under Pressure'; *Hot Space*. 11 *Ghost in the Machine*; 'Invisible Sun'. 12
Orchestral Manoeuvres in the Dark. 13 Dee C Lee; Wham!. 14 'Personal Jesus'; Johnny
Cash. 15 'Stand and Deliver' and the title track, 'Prince Charming'.

Bonus track 1

1 T'Pau. 2 Ultravox. 3 Terence Trent D'Arby. 4 Nik Kershaw. 5 Paul Young. 6 The
Thompson Twins. 7 Aztec Camera. 8 The Bangles. 9 Soft Cell. 10 Bronski Beat.

Bonus track 2

1 Aneka. 2 Feargal Sharkey. 3 Bros. 4 Shakin' Stevens. 5 Falco. 6 Irene Cara. 7 Jim
Diamond. 8 Phyllis Nelson. 9 Kylie Minogue. 10 Men at Work.

Bonus track 3

1 Belouis Some. 2 Robyn Hitchcock. 3 The Go-Betweens. 4 Sonic Youth. 5 XTC. 6 Nine
Inch Nails. 7 JoBoxers. 8 The Cramps. 9 Bauhaus. 10 Johnny Hates Jazz.

QUIZ 16 PEOPLE'S PLAYLIST: WEATHER WITH YOU

1 A song by Crowded House. 2 Travis. 3 Donna Summer. 4 Cheryl Cole. 5 'Mr Blue Sky'. 6 'Did You Hear the Rain?'. 7 'Beautiful Day'. 8 5 Seconds of Summer. 9 'The Boys of Summer'. 10 The Kinks. 11 'It's Raining Men'. 12 Geri Halliwell. 13 'Holidays in the Sun'. 14 Thunderclap Newman. 15 'Raining in My Heart'. 16 'In the Summertime'. 17 Eurythmics. 18 'The Sun Always Shines on TV'. 19 The Doors. 20 Vanilla Ice. 21 Weather Report. 22 Kate Bush. 23 T-Bone Walker. 24 Madonna. 25 Frankie Valli & the Four Seasons. 26 'The Sun Ain't Gonna Shine Anymore'. 27 Rainbow. 28 Nine Below Zero. 29 Status Quo. 30 'Walking on Sunshine'. 31 The Orb. 32 The Dead Weather. 33 'A Hard Rain's Gonna Fall'. 34 'Summer in the City'. 35 Graham Parker & the Rumour. 36 The Undertones. 37 Nick Cave & the Bad Seeds. 38 'Informer'. 39 'April Skies'. 40 Nick Cave & the Bad Seeds.

QUIZ 17 GUITAR GIRLS

1 Polly Jean; Dorset (Bridport). 2 John Parish; *A Woman a Man Walked By*; Automatic Dlamini. 3 Nick Cave & the Bad Seeds and Tricky. 4 *Stories from the City, Stories from the Sea* and *Let England Shake*. 5 A version of Bob Dylan's 'Highway 61 Revisited'. 6 He's the drummer. 7 Thom Yorke; Mick Harvey. 8 'The Life and Death of Mr Badmouth'; 'Cat on the Wall'; 'The Darker Days of Me and Him'. 9 Flood; Linton Kwesi Johnson. 10 'What if I take my problem to the United Nations?'; 'Summertime Blues' by Eddie Cochran.

11 'Brass in Pocket'; 'Stop Your Sobbing'. 12 Blue Öyster Cult; 'Hey Joe'. 13 *Wave*; First Aid Kit. 14 Billy Bremner; Robbie McIntosh. 15 Arthur Rimbaud, a big influence on her work; CBGB. 16 'I'll Stand by You'; Girls Aloud. 17 *The Isle of View*; they served as the string accompaniment. 18 Tom Verlaine; *Horses*. 19 *Stockholm*; John McEnroe. 20 'The Boy in the Bubble'; 'Everybody Hurts'.

21 Ladytron. 22 Tilly & the Wall. 23 Wolf Alice. 24 Warpaint. 25 Evanescence. 26 Hole. 27 Bikini Kill. 28 Sleater-Kinney. 29 Babes in Toyland. 30 Veruca Salt.

QUIZ 18 **THE SMITHS**

1 *The Smiths, Meat is Murder, The Queen is Dead* and *Strangeways, Here We Come*.
2 *Hatful of Hollow*. 3 Mike Joyce, the drummer, and Andy Rourke, the bass player.
4 *The Messenger* and *Playland*. 5 He didn't 'have a stitch to wear'. 6 Sheila, in 'Sheila
Take a Bow'. 7 'That Joke Isn't Funny Anymore'; 'Some Girls are Bigger than Others'.
8 Steven Patrick. 9 Cicely Courtneidge; 10 Derek Jarman. 11 'There Is a Light that
Never Goes Out'; *Trainspotting*. 12 *Vauxhall and I*; *Ringleader of the Tormentors*.
13 '...I'd like to smash every tooth in your head'; 'Bigmouth Strikes Again'. 14 'Hand
in Glove'; Sandie Shaw. 15 'The Last of the Famous International Playboys'; 'November
Spawned a Monster'; 'You're the One for Me, Fatty'; 'The More You Ignore Me, the
Closer I Get'.

16 The Blue Aeroplanes; he's the group's dancer. 17 Orange Juice; Edwyn Collins.
18 Grimes; *Visions*. 19 The Independent Music Chart; Spizzenergi's 'Where's Captain
Kirk?' was the first song to top the new chart. 20 Echobelly; *Everyone's Got One*.
21 Bobby Gillespie; Primal Scream. 22 *High Land, Hard Rain*; 'Somewhere in My
Heart'. 23 Everything but the Girl; 'Missing'. 24 BEF (British Electric Foundation);
Heaven 17. 25 Julian Cope; The Teardrop Explodes. 26 Albert Camus (*L'Etranger*);
Disintegration. 27 Echo & the Bunnymen; Ian McCulloch. 28 The Virgin Prunes; Gavin
Friday. 29 'I Wanna Be Adored' and 'She Bangs the Drums'. 30 The Auteurs; 'Lenny
Valentino'.

QUIZ 19 CRAIG CHARLES FUNK & SOUL

1 Quincy Jones; Michael Jackson (*Off the Wall*, *Thriller* and *Bad*). 2 George Benson; *Breezin'*. 3 Mary J Blige; George Michael. 4 *Songs in the Key of Life*; Duke Ellington. 5 Martin Luther King; 'Abraham, Martin and John'. 6 'Sexual Healing'; Lionel Richie. 7 'Can't Slow Down'; the Commodores. 8 'Nightshift'; Van Morrison. 9 Dexy's Midnight Runners; Geno (about Geno Washington). 10 Blue-eyed soul; Simply Red. 11 'If You Don't Know Me By Now'; Teddy Pendergrass. 12 Sam Cooke; 'Wonderful World'. 13 'Louie Louie'; Otis Redding. 14 '(Sittin' on) the Dock of the Bay'; Booker T & the M.G.'s. 15 Ain't No Sunshine; Michael Jackson – and so back to question 1.

16 Sam & Dave and Wilson Pickett. 17 Cody Chesnutt; The Roots. 18 Chairmen of the Board; General Johnson – it was, apparently, his given name. 19 Freda Payne; it was a Vietnam War protest. 20 K.C. of K.C. & the Sunshine Band; 'Give It Up'. 21 They were all in Sly & The Family Stone; 'Everyday People'. 22 The Isley Brothers. Family: the three older Isleys were acknowledging the influence of their younger siblings on the band. 23 Aretha Franklin; 'Respect'. 24 Kool and the Gang; Atomic Kitten. 25 Billy Paul; Nike. Paul won. 26 Al Green, 'Let's Stay Together'. 27 Leon Bridges; Apple iPhone 6. 28 Jocelyn Brown; Right Said Fred. 29 'Boogie Nights'; Paul Thomas Anderson. 30 'War'. Absolutely nothing.

QUIZ 20 **PROG ROCK**

1 *The Lamb Lies Down on Broadway*; Rael. 2 Hawkwind; Michaeal Moorcock. 3 The Doors; Ian Astbury from the Cult. 4 Emerson, Lake & Palmer: Keith Emerson was in the Nice, Greg Lake in King Crimson and Carl Palmer in Atomic Rooster. 5 Barclay James Harvest; 'Mockingbird'. 6 Richard Wright; Roger Waters. 7 Donald Fagen and Walter Becker. 8 *Tales of Topographic Oceans*; Jon Anderson. 9 Jeff Wayne; Richard Burton. 10 *Uriah Heep*; David Copperfield. 11 Peter Gabriel and Steve Hackett. 12 Vangelis (Papathanassiou) was the maestro; Demis Roussos.13 Brian Eno; he had produced three Talking Heads albums. 14 Fish; Marillion, 15 Jethro Tull; *Thick as a Brick*.

1. Emerson, Lake & Palmer; 20:40 (allow 20-23m). 2. Genesis; 23:01 (allow 22-25). 3. Marillion; 8.13 (allow 8-9). 4. The Doors; 11:41 (allow 10-12). 5. Iron Butterfly; 17:05 (allow 16-19). 6. Wishbone Ash; 9:42 (allow 9-11). 7. Spock's Beard; 27:02 (allow 25-30). 8. Yes; 21:55 (allow 20-23). 9. King Crimson; 12:13 (allow 11-13). 10. Pink Floyd; 13:32 (allow 12-14). 11. Rush; 19:57 (allow 18-21). 12. Caravan; 22:43 (allow 20-24). 13. Savoy Brown; 9:15 (allow 8-10). 14. The Flower Kings; 31:01 (allow anything over 30m). 15. Jethro Tull; 8:58 (allow 8-10).

QUIZ 21 **WORLD MUSIC**

1 *Songlines*; Australian Aborigines. 2 Peter Gabriel; Real World. 3 Amadou & Mariam; Both are blind. 4 Staff Benda Bilili; Mbongwana Star. 5 Tango; Gotan Project. 6 Shakira is from Colombia, Wyclef Jean is from Haiti. 7 Tinariwen; Turaeg, i.e. Saharan desert nomads. 9 *Buena Vista Social Club*; Wim Wenders. 10 Gipsy Kings; they are gypsies from the south of France who sing in Andalusian Spanish. 11 Manu Chao; Paris. 12 Peter Gabriel; Youssou N'Dour. 13 *Abraxas*; he was the percussionist who supplied the distinctive congas and timbales. 14 Songhoy Blues; Mali. 15 Ladysmith Black Mambazo; Paul Simon.

16. Fela Kuti. 17. Gogol Bordello. 18. Yothu Yindi. 19. Sepultura. 20. Mariza. 21. Bhundu Boys. 22. Salif Keita. 23. Rodrigo y Gabriela. 24. Ernest Ranglin. 25. Cheikh Lo. 26. Shajarian. 27. Billy Ocean. 28. Raghu Dixit. 29. Nixlopi. 30. Heather Nova.

QUIZ 22 MICHAEL JACKSON

1 Seven; 50. 2 Jackie; Jermaine. 3 Rod Temperton; Lincolnshire. 4 *Music & Me* (1973); *Forever, Michael* (1975). 5 Princess Stéphanie of Monaco; 'Irresistible'. 6 *HIStory: Past, Present and Future, Book 1*: 'Come Together'. 7 'You're So Vain' by Carly Simon – the full title was 'Son of a Gun (I Betcha Think This Song Is About You)'; Carly Simon. 8 'Girlfriend'; 'The Girl is Mine'. 9 Martin Scorsese; *West Side Story*. 10 The Notorious B.I.G.; 'They Don't Care About Us'. 11 (Tamla) Motown; Diana Ross. 12 'Tonight's the Night'; 'Big Yellow Taxi'. 13 24; five years. 14 Annie; 'Dirty Diana'. 15 *Blood on the Dance Floor (HIStory in the Mix)*; Nile Rodgers.

16 'One Day in Your Life'; *Forever Michael*. 17 Damita Jo; James DeBarge. 18 'I Want You Back'; The Corporation. 19 'Smooth Criminal'; Alien Ant Farm. 20 2009; Conrad Murray was convicted of involuntary manslaughter. 21 John Landis; Vincent Price. 22 Marlon; La Toya. 23 'Show You the Way to Go'; Epic. 24 *Bad*; Katy Perry. 25 Elvis Presley; Debbie Rowe. 26 His sister Janet; R Kelly. 27 'Let's Get Serious'; Iman. 28 *Got to Be There*; 'Rockin' Robin'. 29 'Black or White'; Macaulay Culkin. 30 *Invincible*; *Xscape*.

QUIZ 23 THE NUMBERS GAME #1

1 'Can't Help Falling In Love'. 2 'Too Much Too Young'; 'Ghost Town'. 3 Pink Floyd, *The Dark Side of the Moon*; Meat Loaf, *Bat Out of Hell*; Fleetwood Mac, *Rumours*. 4 *Purple Rain*; *Under the Cherry Moon*; *Sign o' the Times*; *Graffiti Bridge*. 5 *Rated R*; *Songs for the Deaf*; *Lullabies to Paralyze*; *Era Vulgaris*; *...Like Clockwork*. 5a 'You Wear It Well'; 'Sailing'; 'I Don't Want To Talk About It' (actually a double-A side with 'The First Cut is the Deepest', so accept either); 'Do Ya Think I'm Sexy?'; 'Baby Jane'. 6 Elvis Presley (21); The Beatles (17); Cliff Richard, Westlife (14); Madonna (13); Take That (12). 7 Spice Girls; All Saints; Eternal; Pussycat Dolls; Girls Aloud; Bananarama; Destiny's Child. 8 'Love Action (I Believe in Love)'; 'Open Your Heart'; 'Don't You Want Me'; 'Being Boiled' (it was originally released in 1978 and failed to chart but hit number six when re-released after 'Don't You Want Me'); 'Mirror Man'; '(Keep Feeling) Fascination'; 'Human'; 'Tell Me When'. 9 'Michelle'; 'Eleanor (Rigby)'; 'Lucy (in the Sky with Diamonds)'; '(Lovely) Rita'; 'Julia'; '(Sexy) Sadie'; 'Martha (my Dear)'; '(Polythene) Pam'; '(The Ballad of John and) Yoko'. 10 *Movement*; *Power, Corruption & Lies*; *Low-Life*; *Brotherhood*; *Technique*; *Republic*; *Get Ready*; *Waiting for the Sirens' Call*; *Lost Sirens*; *Music Complete*.

QUIZ 24 **FESTIVALS**

1 Knebworth; Jason Bonham. 2 Latitude; Snow Patrol. 3 Creamfields; Cheshire. 4 T in the Park; Strathallan Castle. 5 Cornbury Music Festival; Cornbury Park is now the venue for the Wilderness Festival. 6 The state of New York; Ang Lee. 7 Woodstock – they covered the Joni Mitchell song of the same name; Fairport Convention. 8 Roskilde; a naked run, which is now so oversubscribed that there are qualifying runs beforehand. 9 Derek & the Dominoes and Arthur Lee & Love. 10 Altamont; the Rolling Stones. 11 Rock Werchter; TW Classic. 12 Jay Z; Kanye West. 13 The Big Feastival; Jamie Oliver. 14 Exit Festival; Sea Dance Festival. 15 135,000 (one point if within 5,000); Pilton. 16 Beyoncé in 2011 and Adele in 2016. Kylie Minogue was booked in 2005 but had to pull out. 17 Randalls Island, New York (just 'New York' is fine); it rained so hard that the venue was deemed unsafe and the event was cancelled. 18 The Glastonbury Festival; David Bowie. 19 End of the Road; Bella Union. 20 Lollapalooza; Santiago in Chile – the concept has since expanded to include Rio de Janeiro, Buenos Aires and Bogotá.

Bonus track 1

1 Camp Bestival. 2 Truck. 3 WOMAD. 4 Lovebox. 5 Download. 6 Beautiful Days. 7 Bestival. 8 Meltdown. 9 Green Man. 10 The Great Escape.

Bonus track 2

1 Barcelona. 2 Byron Bay. 3 Iceland. 4 California. 5 Manchester. 6 Rajasthan. 7 Switzerland. 8 Austin. 9 Mexico. 10 The Nevada desert.

QUIZ 25 **EARWORMS**

1 'Wannabe'; 1996. 2 'Eye of the Tiger'; 'Burning Heart'. 3 'Gimme! Gimme! Gimme! (A Man After Midnight)'; 'Voulez-Vous'. 4 They are the girls name-checked in the chorus of Lou Bega's Mambo #5; Jessica. 5 *The Fame Monster*; 'Bad Romance'. 6 'Only the Lonely (Know the Way I Feel)'; 'Thunder Road'. 7 'Beat It'; Eddie Van Halen. 8 Susan Ann Sulley; as a waitress in a cocktail bar. 9 A monster; The Automatic. 10 A cowboy and a construction worker. 11 *Sunshine on Leith*; Hibernian FC. 12 'Karma Chameleon'; red, gold and green. 13 'All About the Bass'; *Title*. 14 Crazy Frog; 'Axel F'. 15 'Smoke on the Water'; Montreux.

16 'Can't Get you Out of My Head'; Mud. 17 Baha Men; *Rugrats in Paris*. 18 'Call Me Maybe'; Canada. 19 Black Eyed Peas ('My Humps'); 'Pump It'. 20 Toni Basil; 'Kitty'. 21 Boney M; 'Brown Girl in the Ring'. 22 Kelly Clarkson; anything that doesn't kill you – 'Stronger (What Doesn't Kill You)' was the song. 23 'The Final Countdown'; Joey Tempest. 24 'Doctor Jones' and 'Turn Back Time'. 25 Chumbawamba; 'Tubthumping'. 26 Blondie's 'One Way or Another' and the Undertones' 'Teenage Kicks'. 27 Bucks Fizz; the two boys in the group pulled off the two girls' skirts, to reveal more skirts. 28 'Seven Nation Army'; Jack White's guitar played through an effects pedal. 29 'I Will Survive'; Gloria Gaynor. 30 Cheerleader; Simon Cowell

QUIZ 26 CLASSIC ALBUMS #2: THE SEVENTIES

1 Public Image Ltd; *Metal Box*. 2 Elvis Costello and the Attractions; *Armed Forces*.
3 Joni Mitchell; *Blue*. 4 Madness; *One Step Beyond*. 5 Stevie Wonder; *Songs in the Key of Life*. 6 Steely Dan; *Pretzel Logic*. 7 Tom Petty and the Heartbreakers; *Damn the Torpedoes*. 8 Joy Division; *Unknown Pleasures*. 9 Curtis Mayfield; *Superfly*. 10 Bob Marley and the Wailers; *Catch a Fire*. 11 Paul Simon; *Still Crazy After All These Years*. 12 The Ruts; *The Crack*. 13 XTC; *Drums and Wires*. 14 Patti Smith; *Easter*. 15 The Stranglers; *No More Heroes*.

16 Neil Young; *Harvest*. 17 Talking Heads; *Fear of Music*. 18 Supertramp; *Breakfast in America*. 19 The Sensational Alex Harvey Band; *Framed*. 20 Paul McCartney and Wings; *Band on the Run*. 21 Blondie; *Parallel Lines*. 22 Led Zeppelin; *Physical Graffiti*. 23 The Cure; *Three Imaginary Boys*. 24 John Martyn; *Solid Air*. 25 Boomtown Rats; *A Tonic for the Troops*. 26 David Bowie; *Station to Station*. 27 Bruce Springsteen; *Darkness on the Edge of Town*. Roxy Music; *For Your Pleasure*. 29 Lou Reed; *Berlin*. 30 Electric Light Orchestra; *Out of the Blue*.

QUIZ 27 **PAUL WELLER**

1 *Studio 150*; Gil Scott-Heron. 2 'In the Midnight Hour'; 'Heat Wave'. 3 They were all written by bassist Bruce Foxton. 4 Playing 'Little Boy Soldiers'; 'The Eton Rifles'; 'Smithers-Jones'. 5 Wormwood Scrubs; 'Down in the Tube Station at Midnight'.
6 Entertainment: they're among the things listed in 'That's Entertainment'. 7 'Going Underground' (twinned with 'Dreams of Children'), 'Start!', 'Town Called Malice' (twinned with 'Precious') and 'Beat Surrender'. 8 'News of the World'; 'Funeral Pyre'.
9 *Fire and Skill*; they're the words inscribed on Weller's guitar amp. 10 *Stanley Road*; it's the street where he was brought up in Woking, Surrey; 'You Do Something to Me'.
11 *Our Favourite Shop*; Lenny Henry. 12 *Absolute Beginners*. 13 *Heavy Soul*. 14 *22 Dreams*. 15 *Heliocentric*. 16 *Wild Wood*. 17 *Sonik Kicks*.

18 Alison Mosshart and Jack White. 19 Cerys Matthews; 'Baby, It's Cold Outside'.
20 They're three of the cartoon characters that make up the band Gorillaz; the missing member is Noodle. 21 Neil Hannon; the Divine Comedy. 22 The Charlatans; Rob Collins, their keyboard player, was killed in a car crash. 23 Quentin Tarantino; 'Swashbucklin' in Brooklyn'. 24 Athlete; 'Wires'. 25 *I'm with Stupid*; *Magnolia*.
26 Ocean Colour Scene; Paul Weller. 27 Speech Debelle and Young Fathers. 28 Texas; Sharleen Spiteri. 29 'Weak Become Heroes'; *A Grand Don't Come for Free*. 30 'A Little Time'; Paul Heaton. 31 The Housemartins and Beats International. 32 Richard Ashcroft; the Verve.

QUIZ 28 PEOPLE'S PLAYLIST: DRINK & DRUGS

1 One Scotch and one Beer. 2 'Itchycoo Park'. 3 Bowling for Soup. 4 James Taylor.
5 Oasis. 6 Wiz Khalifa. 7 *The Who by Numbers*. 8 JJ Cale. 9 Mary Coughlan.
10 Queens of the Stone Age. 11 Milk. 12 They 'don't do anything at all', according
to Jefferson Airplane's 'White Rabbit'. 13 Vodka and cider. 14 'Ebeneezer Goode'.
15 'Brass Monkey'. 16 'Eight Miles High'. 17 'Gin and Juice'. 18 Cypress Hill. 19 Kris
Kristofferson. 20 The Notorious BIG. 21 'The Bartender and the Thief'. 22 Acid – they
were Gaye Bykers on Acid. 23 Motörhead. 24 'Love Is the Drug'. 25 *Whiskey for the
Holy Ghost*. 26 Plan B. 27 Status Quo. 28 Amy Winehouse. 29 'Lilac Wine'. 30 Canned
Heat. 31 Sailor. 32 The Darkness. 33 'Mistletoe and Wine'. 34 Pulp. 35 Bruno Mars.
36 Plan B. 37 'Drinking from the Bottle'. 38 Black Sabbath. 39 Caro Emerald.
40 Placebo.

QUIZ 29 THE SEVENTIES

1 'Low Rider'; Cheech & Chong. 2 'Radar Love'; the Netherlands – they were Dutch.
3 Peter Frampton; 'Show Me the Way'. 4 'Sylvia's Mother'; they wanted to be on 'The
Cover of *Rolling Stone*'. 5 They were named in the titles of the five tracks that comprise
Pink Floyd's *Animals*; Battersea Power Station. 6 Joe Walsh; 'Life's Been Good'.
7 'Baker Street'; Stealers Wheel. 8 Boston; er, Boston. 9 *News of the World*; 'Sheer Heart
Attack', which had previously served as the name of their third album, released in 1974.
10 Midge Ure; Thin Lizzy. 11 Curved Air; 'Back Street Luv'. 12 'Dance Away' and
'Angel Eyes'. 13 Lindisfarne; Paul Gascoigne – it was credited to 'Gazza & Lindisfarne'.
14 'Hocus Pocus'; 'Sylvia'. 15 They were the Spiders from Mars, David Bowie's backing
band; Uriah Heep.

16 Clive Dunn; 'Ride a White Swan'. 17 *Band on the Run* by Wings; 'Jet'.
18 Showaddywaddy; 'Under the Moon of Love'. 19 'Ma Baker'; 'Rasputin'. 20 'What's
Going On'; Marvin Gaye, the first time he'd produced his own material. 21 *Rock
Follies*; Andy Mackay. 22 'No More Mr Nice Guy'; 'Elected'. 23 'The Chain'; 'Silver
Springs'. 24 *Saturday Night Fever*; *The Sound of Music*. 25 Electric Light Orchestra;
Wizzard. 26 'Coz I Luv You'; 'Merry Xmas Everybody'. 27 'I'm Still Waiting'; Tony
Blackburn. 28 'Down Down'; 'Rockin' All Over the World'. 29 'Honaloochie Boogie';
'All the Way from Memphis'. 30 Ron and Russell Mael; *Kimono My House*.

QUIZ 30 **GIRL POWER**

1 Lily Allen; *It's Not Me, It's You*. 2 Cher; 'The Shoop Shoop Song (It's in His Kiss)' – her previous chart-topper had been 'I Got You Babe', a duet with then-husband Sonny Bono. 3 The Runaways; Dakota Fanning. 4 The Smiths, although they spelt it 'Shakespeares Sister'; Marcella Detroit. 5 Alison Moyet; 'That Ole Devil Called Love'. 6 The Go-Go's; 'Our Lips Are Sealed'. 7 Kate Bush, with *Never for Ever*. 8 Lulu; Take That. 9 *Crazysexycool*; 'Creep'. 10 Bat for Lashes; Sexwitch. 11 Annie Lennox – her 1995 album was called *Medusa*, while her 2002 release was *Bare*; 'Love Song for a Vampire'. 12 Louise Wener, the singer of Sleeper, whose second album was called *The It Girl*; she is now a novelist. 13 'Wannabe'; 'Stop' was the only one of the ten not to top the UK singles chart. 14 Catatonia; the album was called *Scissors, Paper, Stone*. 15 Salt-N-Pepa; DJ Spinderella. 16 Billie (later Billie Piper); Chris Evans. 17 Haim; *Days Are Gone*. 18 Bernard Butler; *Endlessly*. 19 All Saints; 'Never Ever'. 20 Suzi Quatro; 'Devil Gate Drive'.

Bonus track 1

1 The Saturdays. 2 Sugababes. 3 Pussycat Dolls. 4 B*Witched. 5 Hepburn. 6 All Saints. 7 tATu. 8 Girls Aloud. 9 Spice Girls. 10 Atomic Kitten.

Bonus track 2

1 Janis Joplin. 2 Mary Timony. 3 Kim Deal. 4 Belinda Carlisle. 5 Carol Dekker. 6 Annie Lennox. 7 Lzzy Hale. 8 Ari Up. 9 Erika Wennerstrom. 10 Margo Timmins.

QUIZ 31 **PUNK I**

1 Richard Hell; Television. 2 Eddie & the Hot Rods; Graeme Douglas. 3 The Flamin' Groovies; Dave Edmunds. 4 The Dictators; 'California Sun'. 5 The eponymous debut album by the New York Dolls; David Johansen. 6 Joe Strummer and Ian Dury. 7 'The Passenger'; Siouxsie & the Banshees. 8 Kim Fowley; 'Cherry Bomb'. 9 The Heartbreakers; Richard Hell. 10 Graham Parker (with the Rumour); *Stick to Me*. 11 Dr Feelgood; Lee Brilleaux. 12 The MC5; *Kick Out the Jams*. 13 'Judy is a Punk' and 'Suzy is a Headbanger' – they're all tracks by the Ramones. 14 Dr Feelgood; 'Johnny B Goode'. 15 The Stooges; 'Search and Destroy'.

Bonus tracks

16 'Janie Jones' on *The Clash*. 17 'Gary Gilmore's Eyes' by the Adverts. 18 Squeeze are being 'Tempted'. 19 According to the Clash, 'White Riot'. 20 'There's gonna be a borstal breakout', from Sham 69's 'Borstal Breakout'. 21 'Rockaway Beach' (the Ramones). 22 'No More Heroes' by the Stranglers. 23 'Alternative Ulster' (Stiff Little Fingers). 24 'Pretty Vacant' (the Sex Pistols). 25 The Dead Kennedys, on 'California Über Alles'. 26 'What Do I Get?' (Buzzcocks). 27 'Mary of the 4th Form' (the Boomtown Rats). 28 'New Rose' by the Damned). 29 Blondie's 'Rip Her to Shreds'. 30 'My Perfect Cousin' by the Undertones.

QUIZ 32 TEATIME THEME

1 Echo: McCulloch is the singer in Echo and the Bunnymen, Martha and the Muffins had a hit with 'Echo Beach' and the Floyd compilation was called *Echoes*. 2 Heaven: Bob Dylan's 'Knockin' On Heaven's Door', Bruno Mars' 'Locked Out of Heaven' and Led Zeppelin's 'Stairway To Heaven'. 3 Pictures: The Who's 'Pictures of Lily' Status Quo's 'Pictures of Matchstick Men'and Emerson, Lake & Palmer's 'Pictures At An Exhibition'. 4 Mountain: *In The Future* is by Black Mountain, *Heretic Pride* is by the Mountain Goats, and Fleet Foxes released their self-named debut album, which contained the tracks 'Blue Ridge Mountains' and 'Tiger Mountain Peasant Song'.
5 Slow Down: the Beatles and the Jam covered the Williams song, Foreigner's album was *Can't Slow Down,* and Oasis released a download-only single called 'Lord Don't Slow Me Down'. 6 'Spaceman', 'Mr Spaceman' and 'I Thought I Was A Spaceman' respectively. 7 Set fire: 'We Didn't Start the Fire', 'Set Fire to the Rain' and ' Set the Fire to the Third Bar' respectively. 8 House: Blur's 'Country House', Madness's 'House of Fun' and Ed Sheeran's 'Lego House'. 9 Party: Beastie Boy's '(You Gotta) Fight for Your Right (To Party)', Pink's 'Get the Party Started, and Courtney Barnett's 'Nobody Really Cares if You Don't Go to the Party'.10 Garden: Lynn Anderson's '(I Never Promised You A) Rose Garden', the Beatles' 'Octopus's Garden' and Siouxsie and the Banshees' 'Hong Kong Garden'. 11 Breathe: Laura Marling did it on her 2013 album *Once I Was an Eagle*. 12 Electric: 'Feel Electric, 'Electric Body', 'Electric Lady; and Duran Duran had a single called 'Electric Barbarella'. 13 Moonlight: *Moonlight Sonata*, 'Moonlight Serenade, and Toploader and Thin Lizzy both sang songs called.'Dancing in the Moonlight'. 14 Blood: Bastille's 'Bad Blood', Kanye's 'Blood on the Leaves' and Norah's 'Young Blood'; Kerr and Thatcher are the two members of Royal Blood. 15 Jump: Van Halens's 'Jump', House of Pain's 'Jump Around' and Metallica's 'Jump in the Fire'; Flo Rida.

16 Ginger Baker; Blind Faith. 17 Bruce Foxton and Rick Buckler. 18 'Biscuits'; *Same Trailer, Different Park.* 19 Half Man Half Biscuit; *Achtung Bono.* 20 King Biscuit Time; *Meet the Humans.* 21 Sodomy ('Cake and Sodomy'); Brian Warner. 22 Hot Chocolate; 'So You Win Again'. 23 Pennyroyal; abortion – pennyroyal tea is said to induce miscarriage if consumed in vast quantities. 24 'Honey Pie'; Moby. 25 'Black Coffee'; in bed ('Black Coffee in Bed'). 26 'Peaches N Cream'; Charlie Wilson. 27 Sugar; Spice ('Sugar and Spice'). 28 *Sgt Pepper's Lonely Heart Club Band*; as bubblegum ('Strawberry Bubblegum'). 29 Garbage; Benny Hill. 30 Bread; 'Make It With You'.

QUIZ 33 IN THE YEAR 2525

1 1982. 2 1975. 3 1991. 4 1966. 5 1986. 6 1963. 7 1958. 8 2001. 9 1964. 10 1990. 11 1969. 12 2003. 13 1978. 14 1997. 15 1960.

16 2005. 17 1979. 18 1988. 19 2012. 20 1961. 21 1977. 22 1956. 23 1995. 24 2010. 25 2000. 26 1965. 27 1984. 28 2002. 29 1970. 30 1992.

QUIZ 34 COVER ME

1 Robbie Williams and Nicole Kidman. 2 Tori Amos; the Stranglers. 3 Elvis's 'Suspicious Minds' and the Beatles''The Long and Winding Road'. 4 'I Will Always Love You'; Dolly Parton. 5 U2; the Skids. 6 *An Innocent Man*; Westlife. 7 'Don't Let Me Be Misunderstood'; *Notting Hill*. 8 The Marmalade; 'Ob-la-di Ob-la-da'. 9 'Sound and Vision'; Girls Aloud. 10 Robbie Williams; Michael Bublé. 11 Lulu; Dan Hartman. 12 'Santa Claus Is Coming To Town'; Björn Again. 13 Talking Heads; Big Mouth Billy Bass, a singing fish head. 14 David Bowie and Amii Stewart. 15 Take That and Boyzone respectively.

16 The Isley Brothers; The Christians. 17 Tom Waits; 'Heigh-Ho' from *Snow White and the Seven Dwarfs*. 18 Joe Cocker; Wet Wet Wet. 19 Kate Bush; 'Candle in the Wind'. 20 Thin Lizzy; Metallica. 21 'Heroes'; Brian Eno, who co-wrote 'Heroes' with Bowie, did a version of Gabriel's song 'Mothers of Violence'. 22 Dave Edmunds and Robert Wyatt respectively. 23 'Victoria' and 'There's a Ghost In My House'. 24 'Whole Lotta Love'; 'Asteroid' (but a point for saying 'the Pearl & Dean song'). 25 Village People; David Bowie. 26 'Only Love Can Break Your Heart'; it was sung not by Sarah Cracknell but by session singer Moira Lambert. 27 Flaming Lips; *Sgt Pepper's Lonely Hearts Club Band* (the album was entitled With a Little Help from My Fwends). 28 Dave Edmunds and the Ramones respectively. 29 To celebrate the 50th anniversary of Amnesty International; Bryan Ferry. 30 'Make You Feel My Love' and 'Lovesong'.

QUIZ 35 TABLOID TALES

1 L7 (drummer Dee Plakas was apparently quite relaxed about the incident); *The Word*. 2 Boy George; Kirk Brandon. 3 'Go Ape Crazy!'; the album's cover, a pastiche of Manet's *Le Déjeuner sur l'herbe*, showed singer Annabella Lwin naked – she was 14 at the time. 4 Chuck Berry; tax evasion. 5 Madonna; Live Aid. 6 Eminem; 'Cleaning out My Closet'. 7 'Golden Brown'; Hugh Cornwell. 8 A lawn mower – he was stopped by police about ten miles away; Tammy Wynette. 9 Jim Morrison; he died while the sentence was on appeal. 10 Burglary – while the rest of the Libertines were on tour, Doherty broke into bandmate Carl Barât's flat and stole property. 11 Larry Hagman; Oliver Reed. 12 Nicole was married to Liam Gallagher from 2008 to 2014, while Natalie's second husband is Liam Howlett of the Prodigy. 13 He was never done for fraud or manslaughter. 14 Queens of the Stone Age; Josh Homme. 15 Elton John; flowers.

16 Ian Brown of the Stone Roses; Diana Ross. 17 Mötley Crüe; Pamela Anderson. 18 Eddie Van Halen; Harry Connick Jr. 19 Elvis Presley; his future wife, Priscilla. 20 *Penthouse*; *The Daily Sport*. 21 Wendy O Williams; the Plasmatics. 22 Lee 'Scratch' Perry; bananas. 23 The Bling Ring; she was sent to prison for the theft of a necklace. 24 Mandy Smith; Mandy Smith's mum. 25 *Today*, hosted by Bill Grundy; 'The Filth and the Fury'. 26 Debbie Reynolds and Elizabeth Taylor. 27 P Diddy; Farnsworth was his butler. 28 Phil Spector; *Fast Times at Ridgemont High*. 29 Sid Vicious; Rikers Island. 30 Lil' Kim; tax evasion.

QUIZ 36 ALTERNATIVE JUKEBOX

1 Horace Andy; Neneh Cherry. 2 Sonic Youth; *Dirty*. 3 The Michael Faraday Memorial, near Elephant & Castle; 'Given to the Wild'. 4 Brighton; Brakes. 5 Rufus Wainwright; Florence Welch. 6 *Sea Change*; *Modern Guilt*. 7 1983; three. 8 *Power, Corruption and Lies*; 808 State. 9 The Streets; 'Dry Your Eyes'. 10 Jamie xx; *In Colour*. 11 Chubby Checker; The Fat Boys. 12 Shortened it from Tyrannosaurus Rex to T. Rex; 'Hot Love'. 13 Joanna Newsom; harp. 14 *Trainspotting*; David Bowie. 15 Desmond Dekker; 'You Can Get It If You Really Want'.

16 Bill Callahan; *Dream River*. 17 Death In Vegas; Iggy Pop. 18 Little Richard; 'Tutti-Frutti'. 19 Daughter; *Not To Disappear*. 20 *Is This It*; Julian Casablancas. 21 Kraftwerk; *Autobahn*. 22 The delta sign Δ; *An Awesome Wave*. 23 The Wedding Present; Elvis Presley. 24 A: *We Are Devo*. Mothersbaugh. 25 Gossip; 'Standing in the Way of Control'. 26 John Lee Hooker; 'One Bourbon, One Scotch and One Beer'. 27 'Mr Tambourine Man'; 'All I Really Want to Do'. 28 Goldie; *The World is Not Enough*. 29 Throwing Muses and the Breeders. 30 'You Walk Like a Peasant'; 'Want to Dance'.

QUIZ 37 **AT THE MOVIES**

1 'Falling Slowly'; *The Commitments*. 2 Brian Slade; David Bowie. 3 *Ghost*;
25. 4 Mogwai; he was the furry hero of *Gremlins*. 5 Los Lobos; *La Bamba*. 6 Chesney
Hawkes; Nik Kershaw. 7 *Footloose*; 'Holding Out for a Hero'. 8 *Butch Cassidy and
the Sundance Kid*; Burt Bacharach and Hal David. 9 *The Woman in Red*; 'I Just
Called to Say I Love You'. 10 *The Three Musketeers*; Rod Stewart. 11 Propellerheads;
Decksanddrumsandrockandroll. 12 *24 Hour Party People*; *Control*. 13 *Mamma Mia*;
Madonna – the album was *The Power of Madonna*. 14 Radio Caroline'; Richard
Curtis. 15 John Carpenter and Kurt Russell.

16 *Robin Hood: Prince of Thieves*; 16 weeks. 17 *Four Weddings and a Funeral*; the
Troggs. 18 Denzel Washington; Branford Marsalis Quartet. 19 'Stuck in the Middle
with You'; Steppenwolf. 20 Anvil; Tokyo. 21 Beyoncé Knowles; Jennifer Hudson.
22 Ken Russell; Elton John. 23 *Crazy Heart*; Colin Farrell. 24 Kim Basinger; 'Lose
Yourself'. 25 *Leningrad Cowboys Go America*; *Total Balalaika Show*. 26 *High Fidelity*;
Jack Black. 27 *Pulp Fiction*; Neil Diamond. 28 Ice Cube (O'Shea Jackson); his son,
O'Shea Jackson Jr. 29 Chess Records; Mos Def. 30 *Smell the Glove*; Rob Reiner, the
film's director.

QUIZ 38 **METAL**

1 Dream Theater; *Black Clouds and Silver Linings*. 2 'Ace of Spades'; Hammersmith – the album was called *No Sleep 'Til Hammersmith*. (A later live album was called *No Sleep at All*.) 3 Venom; *Black Metal*. 4 Brain Donor; Julian Cope. 5 Deep Purple; Ian Gillan. 6 Avenged Sevenfold; Mike Portnoy. 7 Metallica; 'Symphony' – it was recorded with the San Francisco Symphony. 8 Rage Against the Machine; 'Killing in the Name'. 9 Iowa; a clown mask. 10 System of a Down; *Mezmerize/Hypnotize*. 11 Megadeth; Kirk Hammett. 12 Saxon; 'And the Bands Played on'. 13 Slayer; *Reign in Blood*. 14 Helloween; *Keeper of the Seven Keys*. 15 Anthrax; Joey Belladonna.

16 Girlschool; *Hit and Run*. 17 *Follow the Leader*; Fred Durst. 18 Iron Maiden; 'Bring Your Daughter… to the Slaughter'. 19 Judas Priest; he came out as gay. 20 Rammstein; 'Stripped'. 21 Ronnie James Dio; Rainbow. 22 Linkin Park; *Hybrid Theory*. 23 *Load*; *St Anger*. 24 Limp Bizkit; DJ Lethal. 25 Mutt Lange; *Pyromania*. 26 The Scorpions (Rudolf) and UFO (Michael, also briefly a member of the Scorpions). 27 They're the character make-up masks worn by the members of Kiss; *The Elder* was a concept album by the group, released in 1981. 28 Tony Iommi and Geezer Butler. 29 Pantera; Abbott was killed by a fan at a concert in Ohio. 30 'Enter Sandman'; *Live Shit: Binge & Purge*.

QUIZ 39 **BLUR VS OASIS**

1 Graham Coxon, Alex James and Dave Rowntree. 2 Food Records; Seymour. 3 'She's So High'. 4 *Live at the De De De Der*; the Royal Albert Hall in London. 5 'This Is a Low'; Dogger Bank. 6 Phil Daniels. 7 *Everyday Robots*; Brian Eno. 8 'Country House'; 'Beetlebum'. 9 William Orbit. 10 *Monkey: Journey to the West* (Albarn reworked the music for the CD release, which was just called *Journey to the West*); *Dr Dee*. 11 It was the first single on which Graham Coxon sang lead vocals; a milk carton (called Milky). 12 *Tank Girl*. 13 Neneh Cherry, De La Soul and Dennis Hopper. 14 *No Distance Left to Run*; 'Fool's Day'. 15 Snoop Dogg. 16 Fela Kuti; the Clash; the Verve.

17 Beady Eye. 18 Harmonica. 19 *Definitely Maybe*. 20 Paul Arthurs, Paul McGuigan and Tony McCarroll; Alan White replaced McCarroll in 1995 and Andy Bell replaced McGuigan in 1999. 21 Johnny Depp. 22 Paul Stacey (his brother Jeremy is also a High Flying Bird). 23 Chasing Yesterday. 24 Rodney Marsh; *The Good, the Bad and the Ugly*. 25 Seven. 26 'Some Might Say', 'Don't Look Back in Anger', 'D'You Know What I Mean?', 'All Around the World', 'Go Let It Out', 'The Hindu Times', 'Lyla' and 'The Importance of Being Idle'. 27 *Familiar to Millions*; *Time Flies… 1994–2009* (*Time Flies* is fine). 28 Knebworth House. 29 Jay Z. 30 Meg Matthews and Sara MacDonald; Russell Brand.

QUIZ 40 **AKA**

1 Adamski; Seal. 2 Lady Gaga; 2008. 3 Pink and Little Boots. 4 Maxi Jazz and Sister Bliss. 5 Elvis Costello and Wreckless Eric. 6 D'Angelo; The Vanguard. 7 Skin; Skunk Anansie. 8 Alice Cooper; golf. 9 The shows were by comedian Bill Bailey, whose real name is Mark Bailey; Bill Bailey is Guns N' Roses singer Axl Rose's real name. 10 The Fratellis; Mince Fratelli. 11 Chuck D and Flavor Flav. 12 Badly Drawn Boy; *About a Boy*. 13 Chris De Burgh; 'The Lady in Red'. 14 Gabrielle; *Rise*. 15 Example; Professor Green.

Bonus tracks

Boys: 1-b; 2-e;3-f;4-g; 5-i; 6-c; 7-d; 8-a; 9-j; 10-h

Girls: 1-j; 2-d; 3-h; 4-c; 5-g; 6-e; 7-I; 8-f; 9-a;10-b

Rappers: 1-g; 2-d; 3-j; 4-i; 5-a;6-f; 7-b; 8-h; 9-c;10-e.

QUIZ 41 WORDS, WORDS, WORDS

1 'Puppet on a String' by Sandie Shaw. 2 'Kiss with a Fist' by Florence + the Machine. 3 'Don't Bomb When You're the Bomb' by Blur. 4 'Subterranean Homesick Blues' by Bob Dylan. 5 'Parachutes' by Coldplay. 6 'It's the End of the World as We Know It (And I Feel Fine)' by REM. 7 'Changed the Way You Kiss Me' by Example. 8 'He Ain't Heavy, He's My Brother' by the Hollies. 9 'We Hate It When Our Friends Become Successful' by Morrissey. 10 'The Importance of Being Idle' by Oasis. 11 'English Riviera' by Metronomy. 12 'I Still Haven't Found What I'm Looking For' by U2. 13 'Make Me Smile (Come Up and See Me)' by Steve Harley & Cockney Rebel. 14 'She Wolf (Falling to Pieces)' by David Guetta featuring Sia. 15 'Where Do You Go To (My Lovely)' by Peter Sarstedt. 16 'A Momentary Lapse of Reason' by Pink Floyd. 17 'Shoplifters of the World Unite' by the Smiths. 18 'Grand Prix' by Teenage Fanclub. 19 'Wherever I Lay My Hat (That's My Home)' by Paul Young, after Marvin Gaye. 20 'The Yeah Yeah Yeah Song' by the Flaming Lips.

21 'Russian Roulette' by Rihanna. 22 'With a Little Help from My Friends' by the Beatles (and, later, Joe Cocker). 23 'Monkey Wrench' by Foo Fighters. 24 'I Wish I Was a Punk Rocker (With Flowers in My Hair)' by Sandi Thom. 25 'Paranoid Android' by Radiohead. 26 'Life Begins at the Hop' by XTC. 27 'You Can Get It If You Really Want' by Desmond Dekker. 28 'Fit But You Know It' by the Streets. 29 'You Don't Have to Say You Love Me' by Dusty Springfield, born Mary O'Brien. 30 'This Is Not a Love Song' by Public Image Ltd. 31 'Without You I'm Nothing' by Placebo. 32 'I Need a Forest Fire' by James Blake featuring Bon Iver. 33 'Is She Really Going Out With Him?' by Joe Jackson. 34 'I Wanna Be Your Dog' by Iggy & the Stooges – Iggy Pop's real name is James Osterberg. 35 'Written in the Stars' by Tinie Tempah featuring Eric Turner. 36 'Sisters Are Doin' It for Themselves' by the Eurythmics with Aretha Franklin. 37 'Have You Seen Your Mother, Baby, Standing in the Shadow?' by the Rolling Stones. 38 'These Boots Are Made for Walkin'' by Nancy Sinatra. 39 'If You Tolerate This Your Children Will Be Next' by Manic Street Preachers. 40 'Talking with the Taxman about Poetry' by Billy Bragg.

QUIZ 42 PEOPLE'S PLAYLIST: LIVING THINGS

1 *Heavy Horses*. 2 'Digital Lion'. 3 *The Dream of the Blue Turtles*. 4 'Rattlesnakes'.
5 Toots & the Maytals. 6 The Specials. 7 'Rock Lobster'. 8 Paul Weller. 9 The
Boomtown Rats. 10 Band of Horses. 11 He managed to 'Fly Like an Eagle'. 12 America.
13 The opening lines from 'Black Dog' by Led Zeppelin. 14 *Mink, Rat or Rabbit*.
15 'Chestnut Mare'. 16 'The bird', on the song 'Surfin' Bird'. 17 *The Lion and the
Cobra*. 18 The Walrus. 19 A Flock of Seagulls. 20 The Jam. 21 Doves. 22 Antony (now
Anohni) & the Johnson. 23 'The Love Cats'. 24 *Horses*, her first album. 25 Foals. 26
'When Doves Cry'. 27 'The Size of a Cow'. 28 Tame Impala. 29 The Frog Chorus, who
joined McCartney to record 'We All Stand Together'. 30 Snoop Doggy Dogg, or Snoop
Dogg as he's now known. 31 Wolf Alice. 32 Squeeze. 33 'Black Horse and the Cherry
Tree'. 34 The Jayhawks. 35 'Crocodile Rock'. 36 'Bird Dog'. 37 *Seven and the Ragged
Tiger*. 38 *The Raven*. 39 'Hound Dog'. 40 'Snake Eyes'.

QUIZ 43 SONGWRITERS

1 *Hopelessness*; Hudson Mohawke. 2 Gruff Rhys, the singer in Super Furry Animals; *American Interior*. 3 Benny Andersson and Björn Ulvaeus. 4 Jimmy Webb; 'Up, Up and Away'. 5 They're the words used to distinguish between the first four albums by Peter Gabriel, which are all officially called *Peter Gabriel* – the words are inspired by images on each album's cover. 6 *Smile*; Van Dyke Parks. 7 Doc Pomus and Mort Shuman; the Beat. 8 Dave Matthews Band; they're the only band to go straight to the top of the US albums chart with six different albums. 9 George Gershwin; 'You've Got a Friend in Me'. 10 Bruce Springsteen and Patti Smith. 11 Alanis Morissette; Tori Amos. 12 Jackson Browne; 'Stay'. 13 Andrew Lloyd Webber and Tim Rice; Elaine Paige. 14 Leonard Cohen; Rufus Wainwright – the film itself featured John Cale's version of the song. 15 'River of Dreams'; 'Piano Man'.

16 Burt Bacharach and Hal David; ABC. 17 Jerry Leiber and Mike Stoller; the Coasters. 18 *White Ladder*; 'Say Hello, Wave Goodbye'. 19 Joe Jackson; *Night and Day*. 20 'Morning Dew'; the Grateful Dead. 21 'Sacrifice'; Bernie Taupin. 22 'Locomotion'; Gerry Goffin and Carole King. 23 Cat Stevens; 'Matthew and Son'. 24 *Sleep Through the Static* and *To the Sea*. 25 Lisa Hannigan; 9. 26 *Release the Stars*; Richard Thompson, father of Wainwright's longtime friend Teddy Thompson. 27 Judy Collins; Joni Mitchell. 28 Ben Howard; *I Forget Where We Were*. 29 February; James Dean. 30 'Watching the Detectives'; 'filing her nails'.

QUIZ 44 NAME THE BAND #2

1 Beyoncé Knowles; Destiny's Child. 2 Natalie Merchant; 10;000 Maniacs. 3 Dan Smith; Bastille. 4 Nina Persson; the Cardigans. 5 Michael Stipe; R.E.M. 6 Alex Kapranos; Franz Fredinand. 7 Johnny Thunders; New York Dolls. 8 Gavin Rossdale; Bush. 9 Stuart Staples; Tindersticks. 10 Chris Martin; Coldplay. 11 Julian Casablancas; the Strokes. 12 Alex Harvey; Sensational Alex Harvey Band. 13 E (aka Mark Everett); Eels. 14 Nick Cave; The Birthday Party. 15 Michael Hutchence; INXS.

16 Ian Hunter; Mott the Hoople. 17 Bob Geldof; Boomtown Rats. 18 Heather Small; M People. 19 Pauline Black; Selecter. 20 Billy Corgan; Smashing Pumpkins. 21 Fred Durst; Limp Bizkit. 22 Nancy Wilson; Heart. 23 Lauren Laverne; Kenickie. 24 Mick Hucknall; Simply Red. 25 Marcus Mumford; Mumford and Sons. 26 Liela Moss; Duke Spirit. 27 Ranking Roger; The Beat. 28 Cerys Matthews; Catatonia. 29 Tom Petty; Tom Petty and the Heartbreakers. 30 Brandon Flowers; the Killers.

QUIZ 45 **EVERYBODY DANCE**

1 Haçienda; New Order. 2 'I Can't Explain'; *Better Living Through Chemistry*. 3 'Don't Leave Me This Way'; 'Yes Sir, I Can Boogie'. 4 Madison Avenue; Australia. 5 Paul Oakenfold; Heaven. 6 Elton John; *Ta-Dah*. 7 *Saturday Night Fever*; 'If I Can't Have You'. 8 Brandon Flowers; Elly Jackson. 9 'Firestarter' and 'Breathe'. 10 'Don't Stop (Wiggle Wiggle)' and 'Boom Boom Boom'. 11 *Disco 1, 2, 3* and *4*; *Disco 4* was remixes of other people's songs, not their own. 12 'Levels'; Dead or Alive. 13 Ottawan; 'Funkytown'. 14 Jamiroquai; *Emergency on Planet Earth*. 15 'Titanium' and 'She Wolf (Falling To Pieces)'.

16 Jackie Wilson; Jocky Wilson. 17 'Pompeii'; *Twin Peaks*. 18 'The Power' and 'Rhythm is a Dancer'. 19 Calvin Harris (*I Created Disco*); the eighties. 20 Moloko; *Hairless Toys*. 21 Tiesto; William Orbit. 22 DJ Fresh; Rita Ora. 23 The Pointer Sisters; excitement – 'I'm So Excited'. 24 Dido; she is the sister of the band's leader, Rollo Armstrong. 25 Gotye; 'Somebody That I Used to Know'. 26 The Moonwalk, later adopted by Michael Jackson; 'I Can Make You Feel Good'. 27 Electric Six; 'Radio Ga Ga'. 28 Orbital; Hartnoll. 29 Rose Royce; 'Car Wash'. 30 Nile Rodgers and Bernard Edwards (or Chic); 'Upside Down'.

QUIZ 46 ALL MY COLOURS

1 'Whiter Shade of Pale'; *The Commitments*. 2 Psychedelic Furs; Molly Ringwald.
3 'Purple Haze'; Monterey Pop Festival. 4 'Brown Eyed Handsome Man'; Van
Morrison, 'Brown Eyed Girl'. 5 *Little Red*; Katy B. 6 *The Beatles*; *Yellow Submarine*.
7 *Otis Blue: Otis Redding Sings Soul*; Sam Cooke. 8 AC/DC; Amy Winehouse. 9 Pink;
You+Me. 10 Professor Green; Emeli Sandé. 11 'Misty Blue'; Eddy Arnold. 12 Visage;
Midge Ure. 13 White Lies; *Ritual*. 14 David Soul and David Essex. 15 '(There'll be
Bluebirds Over) The White Cliffs of Dover'; Robson and Jerome.

16 Electric Light Orchestra, *Out of the Blue*. 17 The Corrs, *In Blue*. 18 David Gray, *White
Ladder*. 19 Flaming Lips, *Yoshimi Battles the Pink Robots*. 20 Culture Club, *Colour By
Numbers*. 21 Elton John, *Goodbye Yellow Brick Road*. 22 Tori Amos, *Under the Pink*.
23 Radiohead, *In Rainbows*. 24 The National, *High Violet*. 25 Florence + the Machine,
How Big, How Blue, How Beautiful. 26 The Stranglers, *Black and White*. 27 John Grant,
Pale Green Ghosts. 28 Taylor Swift, *Red*. 29 Kate Bush, *The Red Shoes*. 30 R.E.M., *Green*.

QUIZ 47 SUNDAY SERVICE WITH JARVIS

1 They are both Mormons; Gladys Knight. 2 Joan Osborne; *Relish*. 3 Like a Prayer;
Pepsi. 4 Gloria; Van Morrison. Smith changed many of the lyrics, and the spoken part
at the beginning is taken from her own poem, 'Oath'. 5 Chocolate and Personal. 6 'Let
It Be'; words of wisdom. 7 'A Place on Earth'; Three steps. 8 Morrissey; 'Jesus was
an Only Son'. 9 Hindu Love Gods; 'Raspberry Beret'. 10 George Harrison; his death.
11 *Nirvana: MTV Unplugged in New York*; the Vaselines: it was a spoof of an old
Christian ditty. 12 The Mountain Goats; *Neon Bible*.13 The Cure in 1981 and George
Michael in 1987. 14 Aretha Franklin; Duran Duran. 15 *My Fair Lady*; 'Modern Love'.

16 Marianne Faithfull; 'Somewhere (A Place for Us)'. 17 Meltdown; Guy Garvey.
18 Iggy Pop; Sunday at 4pm. 19 Stuart Maconie; *Separations*. 20 Russell Senior; he
was president of the band's fan club (and occasional tour manager). 21 Weird Sisters;
Radiohead. 22 Sculpture; a supermarket. 23 *This is Hardcore*; 'Help the Aged'.
24 'Mis-Shapes'; *Daily Mirror*. 25 'Do You Remember the First Time?'; Jo Whiley.
26 'Bad Cover Version'; Nick Cave. 27 Beth Ditto; they are both from Sheffield.
28 Nancy Sinatra; Richard Hawley. 29 Island; Rough Trade. 30 Deep; 'Caucasian Blues'.

QUIZ 48 CLASSIC ALBUMS #3: THE EIGHTIES

1 U2; *War.* 2 Echo and the Bunnymen; *Ocean Rain.* .3 Happy Mondays; *Bummed.*
4 Pixies; *Doolittle.* 5 Talking Heads; *Little Creatures.* 6 The Cure; *Pornography.* 7 John
Lennon and Yoko Ono; *Double Fantasy.* 8 Pet Shop Boys; *Actually.* 9 Madonna; *True
Blue.* 10 David Bowie; *Scary Monsters (and Super Creeps).* 11 New Order; *Technique.*
12 Guns N' Roses; *Appetite for Destruction.* 13 The Police; *Synchronicity.* 14 De La
Soul; *3 Feet High and Rising.* 15 AC/DC; *Back in Black.*

16 REM; *Life's Rich Pageant.* 17 Heaven 17; *Penthouse and Pavement.* 18 Depeche
Mode; *Music for the Masses.* 19 Iron Maiden; *The Number of the Beast.* 20 Def
Leppard; *Hysteria.* 21 Yazoo; *Upstair's at Eric's.* 22 Edie Brickell and the New
Bohemians; *Shooting Rubberbands at the Stars.* 23 Soul II Soul; *Club Classics Vol
I.* 24 The Associates; *Sulk.* 25 The Pogues; *Rum; Sodomy & the Lash.* 26 Talk
Talk; *The Colour of Spring.* 27 The Cramps; *A Date with Elvis.* 28 Tom Waits;
Swordfishtrombones. 29 George Michael; *Faith.* 30 Sisters of Mercy; *Floodland.*

QUIZ 49 **MADONNA**

1 Don McLean; *The Next Best Thing*. 2 Sean Penn; Guy Ritchie. 3 Britney Spears; Cristina Aguilera. 4 Mirwais; 'What it Feels Like for a Girl'. 5 Maverick; Alanis Morissette's *Jagged Little Pill*. 6 *Desperately Seeking Susan*; Rosanna Arquette. 7 John 'Jellybean' Benitez; 'Holiday'. 8 'Like a Virgin'; 'Into the Groove'. 9 A cowboy hat; the Drowned World tour. 10 The love affair between King Edward VIII and Wallis Simpson; 'Masterpiece'. 11 *I'm Breathless*; Warren Beatty. 12 'Frozen'; William Orbit. 13 Justin Timberlake and Timbaland. 14 *Erotica*; *Body of Evidence*. 15 *Austin Powers: the Spy who Shagged Me*; *Evita* ('Don't Cry for Me, Argentina' and 'Another Suitcase in Another Hall').

16 Britney Spears; Rihanna. 17 No Doubt; *This is What the Truth Feels Like*. 18 *Back to Basics*; 'Moves Like Jagger'. 19 *Funhouse*; 'So What'. 20 'True Colors'; 'What's Going On'. 21 Kerry Katona; *Snog Marry Avoid?* 22 Melanie Blatt and Shaznay Lewis. 23 Little Boots; *Dead Disco*. 24 Pixie Lott; 'Mama Do (Uh Oh Uh Oh)'. 25 Ladyhawke; Michelle Pfeiffer. 26 Beyoncé; Britney Spears. 27 2014; 52nd Street. 28 A dress made of meat; a murderer. 29 Tony Bennett; 'The Lady is a Tramp'. 30 *American Horror Story* (the fifth series was called *Hotel*); The Born This Way Foundation to help young people overcome issues with bullying and low self-esteem.

QUIZ 50 **PUNK II**

1 *Spiral Scratch*; Howard Devoto. 2 The Slits; Palmolive. 3 'Don't Dictate'; the Invisible Girls, who were actually formed as a backing band for John Cooper Clarke. 4 The Rezillos; 'Ballroom Blitz'. 5 'Too Drunk to Fuck' and 'Nazi Punks Fuck Off'. 6 The Lurkers; 'Then I Kicked Her', a take on 'Then I Kissed Her'. 7 Paul Cook; Glen Matlock. 8 The Saints; 'This Perfect Day'. 9 Crass; *Penis Envy*. 10 X-Ray Spex; 'Germfree Adolescents'. 11 The Ruts; 'Staring at the Rude Boys'. 12 'Oh Bondage Up Yours!'; Poly Styrene, the singer with X-Ray Spex. 13 Angelic Upstarts; Liddle Towers, on 'The Murder of Liddle Towers'. 14 *Rocket to Russia*; 'Needles and Pins'. 15 'Smash It Up'; 'Eloise'.

16 The Boomtown Rats; 'Rat Trap'. 17 'Anarchy in the UK'; *Never Mind the Bollocks, Here's the Sex Pistols*. 18 *Damned Damned Damned*; 'Neat Neat Neat'. 19 'God Save the Queen' by the Sex Pistols; Rod Stewart, with a double-A side of 'I Don't Want to Talk about It' and 'The First Cut is the Deepest'. 20 Sham 69; 'If the Kids Are United'. 21 The Dickies; 'Silent Night'. 22 Iggy & the Stooges; *Coming Up for Air*. 23 'I'm So Bored with the USA'; 'Lost in the Supermarket'. 24 Ronnie Biggs; 'Somethin' Else'. 25 Stiff Little Fingers; *Inflammable Material*. 26 Captain Sensible (Raymond Burns); a red beret. 27 The Rezillos; 'I Can't Stand My Baby'. 28 Black Flag; 'Louie Louie'. 29 The Adverts; 'Bored Teenagers'. 30 *Another Music in a Different Kitchen*; *Love Bites*.

QUIZ 51 **RAP & HIP HOP**

1 MC Hammer; Hammer pants. 2 Will Smith; 'Boom! Shake The Room'. 3 The Dogg Pound; *Dogg Food*. 4 Dido; *No Angel*. 5 D12; Proof. 6 Kanye West – *The College Dropout* was his debut album; *Graduation*, the title of his third album. 7 Beastie Boys; Madonna. 8 50 Cent; *The Massacre*. 9 A Tribe Called Quest; *Beats, Rhymes and Life*. 10 Snoop Dogg; Snoop Lion. 11 The Outhere Brothers; *The Fucking Hits*. 12 The Bomb Squad; Terminator X. 13 Kim Kardashian; Paul McCartney. 14 Royce da 5'9"; *Hell: the Sequel*. 15 Nelly; Kelly Rowland.

16 Roots Manuva; 'Witness (1 Hope)'. 17 *Me Against the World*; 'California Love'. 18 Coolio; *Celebrity Big Brother*. 19 *Straight Outta Compton* by NWA. 20 *American Gangster*; *Bonnie and Clyde*. 21 Slim Shady; *The Marshall Mathers LP* and *The Marshall Mathers LP 2*. 22 Drake – they're the titles of his first two albums; *Views*, the title of his 2016 album. 23 Cypress Hill; they were a Latino collective rather than an African American group. 24 Tupac Shakur; the Notorious BIG (aka Biggie Smalls). 25 Puff Daddy; the Police's 'Every Breath You Take'. 26 Ice Cube; *Predator*. 27 'Run this Town' and 'Empire State of Mind'. 28 *Encore* followed *The Eminem Show*; after *Relapse* came *Recovery*. 29 Rihanna; 'What's My Name?'. 30 Soul II Soul; *IV* was a best-of compilation.

QUIZ 52 **PEOPLE'S PLAYLIST: DATE STAMP**

1 'Blue Monday' by New Order. 2 Judas Priest. 3 'Days are Forgotten'. 4 August – their debut album was *August and Everything After*. 5 Sheryl Crow. 6 '1959'. 7 Bryan Adams. 8 'Two More Years'. 9 Blancmange. 10 The 1975. 11 The Cure. 12 The Sundays. 13 'Sunday Girl'. 14 Richard Thompson. 15 'When the Sun Goes Down'. 16 The Bangles. 17 'Hymn for the Weekend'. 18 The Strokes. 19 'Eighth Day'. 20 Enter Shikari. 21 The Gaslight Anthem. 22 Buddy Holly. 23 Saturday. 24 'Another Day'. 25 Ian Brown. 26 *October*. 27 *In this Light and on this Evening*. 28 'Friday on My Mind'. 29 *Come Around Sundown*. 30 Melanie. 31 Culture Club. 32 'The Year of the Cat'. 33 '1999'. 34 *Sunday at Devil Dirt*, their second album. 35 'Wednesday Week'. 36 'Watch the Sun Come Up'. 37 Shed Seven. 38 Pet Shop Boys. 39 Altered Images. 40 He sang 'Millennium'.

QUIZ 53 KEEP IT IN THE FAMILY

1 Gary and Martin Kemp. 2 The Breeders; *Last Splash*. 3 Anorexia; she was the drummer. 4 Jay Z and Beyoncé. 5 The Jesus & Mary Chain (Jim and William Reid) and the Proclaimers (Charlie and Craig Reid). 6 Win and Will Butler; Régine Chassagne is married to Win. 7 The Magic Numbers; 'Forever Lost'. 8 Ray Davies of the Kinks and Jim Kerr of Simple Minds. 9 Kate McGarrigle; Judy Garland. 10 Norma Waterson; *Bottle*. 11 Carrie Fisher and Edie Brickell. 12 Carl and Dennis Wilson; cousin. 13 The Corrs; *Talk on Corners*. 14 The Followill family are better known as Kings of Leon; Nashville, Tennessee. 15 Lourdes and Rocco.

16 The Bellamy Brothers. 17 The Scissor Sisters. 18 Damien Rice. 19 Aretha Franklin. 20 Paul Simon. 21 Loretta Lynn. 22 Shakespears Sister. 23 Uncle Tupelo. 24 Sisters of Mercy. 25 Simone Felice. 26 The Black Keys. 27 *Hunky Dory*. 28 *Desire*. 29 Mystery Jets. 30 Dutch Uncles. 31 Father John Misty. 32 The Indigo Girls. 33 'My Brother Jake'. 34 Natalie Merchant. 35 The Punch Brothers. 36 The Righteous Brothers. 37 'Mother's Little Helper'. 38 *Brothers in Arms*. 39 Vampire Weekend. 40 *Graduation*. 41 Sons and Daughters. 42 Young Fathers. 43 James. 44 *If You Leave*. 45 Chris Robinson.

QUIZ 54 **BRITPOP**

1 Bernard Sumner (New Order) and Johnny Marr (the Smiths). 2 Longpigs; Richard Hawley. 3 The La's; Cast. 4 Gene; *Olympian*. 5 *Urban Hymns* (the Verve); 'Bitter Sweet Symphony'. 6 'In My Place'; Darius. 7 The La's; 'There She Goes'. 8 'Weekender'; Maher. 9 Shed Seven; 'Going for Gold'. 10 Their breakthrough single was 'Mulder and Scully', named after the show's two lead characters; *International Velvet*. 11 Supergrass; *I Should Coco*. 12 Ash released the album *1977* in 1995; 1977 was also the year *Star Wars* was released, and there are references to the film on the album. 13 Alex James; Keith Allen. 14 Kula Shaker; Crispian Mills, the son of Hayley Mills, the grandson of Sir John Mills and the nephew of Jonathan Mills. 15 Brett Anderson; the Tears.

16 The band was called Marion, and Marion Morrison was John Wayne's real name; New Order. 17 Gary 'Mani' Mounfield; they're all ardent Manchester City supporters. 18 'Viva la Vida' and 'Paradise'. 19 Pulp; *It*. 20 Sleeper; the press called them 'Sleeperblokes', and the musicians responded by using the term as a badge of honour. 21 'Step On' and 'Kinky Afro'. 22 'Yes'; David McAlmont. 23 *Second Coming*; 'Love Spreads'. 24 Inspiral Carpets; Noel Gallagher. 25 Elastica; Blur's Damon Albarn. 26 Stereophonics; Kelly Jones. 27 Mansun; *Attack of the Grey Lantern*. 28 *Plastic Beach*; Bobby Womack. 29 'Common People' was kept off the top spot by 'Unchained Melody', and 'Wonderwall' was blocked by 'I Believe'. 30 Ian Brown; Sinéad O'Connor.

QUIZ 55 **SOUL DIVAS**

1 *Unbreakable*; Jimmy Jam. 2 Jessie J; 'Do It Like a Dude'. 3 Pointer Sisters; 'Fire'.
4 Mary J Blige; *Share My World*. 5 Lisa Stansfield; 'All Around the World'. 6 Neneh
Cherry; *Raw Like Sushi*. 7 'Crazy' by Gnarls Barkley, 'Umbrella' by Rihanna and
'One Dance' by Drake. 8 'Love the Way You Lie' and 'Monster'. 9 'Dreams'; East 17.
10 Destiny's Child; Beyoncé. 11 Mariah Carey; Boyz II Men. 12 Laura Mvula; a new
version with a full orchestra. 13 Macy Gray; *The Id*. 14 Leona Lewis; *Spirit*. 15 Erykah
Badu; *New Amerykah Part One* and *Part Two*.

16 Mary J Blige; 'One'. 17 'Crazy in Love' and 'Déjà Vu'. 18 En Vogue; *Funky Divas*.
19 'Midnight Train to Georgia'; *Licence to Kill*. 20 Oleta Adams; Tears for Fears.
21 Mica Paris; *What Not to Wear*. 22 'Chain Reaction'; Barry, Robin and Maurice
Gibb. 23 Toni Braxton; 'Un-Break My Heart'. 24 'Ring My Bell' and 'Jump to the Beat'
respectively. 25 Deniece Williams; Johnny Mathis. 26 Jennifer Lopez; *Selena*. 27 Randy
Crawford; *Jackie Brown*. 28 *janet*. – with a lower-case 'j' and a full stop. 29 *Sade*;
Diamond Life. 30 TLC; Lisa Left-Eye Lopes.

QUIZ 56 **THE NUMBERS GAME #2**

1 'Hotel California'. 2 'Setting Sun'; 'Block Rockin' Beats'. 3 'Do Wah Diddy Diddy',
Pretty Flamingo' and Dylan's 'Mighty Quinn'. 4 'Hot Love'; 'Get It On'; 'Telegram
Sam'; Metal 'Guru'. 5 *Performance and Cocktails*; *Just Enough Education to Perform*;
You Gotta Go There to Come Back; *Language. Sex. Violence. Other?*; *Pull the Pin*.
5a Gary Barlow, Howard Donald, Jason Orange, Mark Owen and Robbie Williams.
6 'Public Image'; 'Death Disco'; 'Flowers of Romance'; 'This is Not a Love Song'; 'Rise';
'Don't Ask Me'. 7 'Space Oddity'; 'Ashes to Ashes'; 'Under Pressure' (with Queen); 'Let's
Dance'; 'Dancing in the Street' (with Mick Jagger). 8 *39/Smooth*; *Kerplunk*; *Dookie*;
Insomniac; *Nimrod*; *Warning*; *American Idiot*; *21st Century Breakdown*. 9 Paul: Linda
Eastman, Heather Mills, Nancy Shevell. John: Cynthia Powell, Yoko Ono. George:
Patti Boyd, Olivia Trinidad Arias. Ringo: Maureen Cox, Barbara Bach. 10 Elvis Presley;
Elton John; Diana Ross; Paul McCartney and Wings; Rod Stewart; Marc Bolan and T.
Rex; David Bowie; Cliff Richard; Hot Chocolate; Abba.

QUIZ 57 MAKING MUSIC

1 Pete Best; Nirvana. 2 Clem Cattini; James Corden. 3 Vivienne Westwood; Bow Wow Wow. 4 A mixtape is a collection of songs, beats and samples, often but not always released as a precursor to an 'official' album, and often free. 5 Record Store Day; Metallica. 6 They were all used in a series of Levi's ads that changed the game as regards the use of popular music in TV advertising. 7 Fender Stratocaster; a wah-wah pedal. 8 *Aerial* by Kate Bush. 9 Bruce Dickinson; Ronnie James Dio. 10 Hipgnosis; UFO. 11 Ritchie Blackmore and Jack White. 12 David Bowie; 'The Laughing Gnome'. 13 They're all synthesizers; the Minimoog. 14 They're all the nicknames of guitars played by Eric Clapton; George Harrison. 15 A hi-hat; Ringo Starr.

16 Mick Fleetwood and Samantha Fox. 17 Dido and Adele. 18 The KLF; Extreme Noise Terror. 19 The Eurovision Song Contest; Terry Wogan. 20 John Prescott; Vic Reeves. 21 Jarvis Cocker; 'Earth Song'. 22 The Union Jack dress; David Bowie. 23 Sting (he's won six); David Bowie. 24 The Rock and Roll Hall of Fame; Ohio, in the city of Cleveland. 25 Liam Gallagher; Villain of the Year. 26 2008; Elbow. 27 2003; Dizzee Rascal. 28 1998; Gomez. 29 2010; The xx. 30 1995; Portishead.

QUIZ 58 PEOPLE'S PLAYLIST: OUT OF TOWN

1 'This River is Wild'. 2 'Thunder in the Mountains'. 3 The Stone Roses. 4 Ike & Tina Turner. 5 Kacey Musgraves. 6 The Rolling Stones. 7 The Outlaws. 8 The Waterboys. 9 Aztec Camera. 10 The Kinks. 11 'The Sensual World'. 12 The Move, on 'I Can Hear the Grass Grow'. 13 Manic Street Preachers. 14 alt-J. 15 Villagers. 16 Panic! At the Disco. 17 *The Waterfall*. 18 John Denver. 19 Olivia Newton-John. 20 REM. 21 'A Waterfall'. 22 Roxy Music. 23 Led Zeppelin. 24 The Deep Dark Woods. 25 Echo & the Bunnymen. 26 *The Endless River*. 27 The Jayhawks. 28 'Mountains'. 29 Idlewild. 30 'Into the Valley'. 31 Joe Walsh. 32 'River Lea'. 33 Creedence Clearwater Revival. 34 *Our Version of Events* by Emeli Sandé. 35 Black Mountain. 36 'One Tree Hill'. 37 'Cotton Fields', written by Leadbelly and covered by the Beach Boys (as 'Cottonfields'). 38 'Rivers of Babylon'. 39 The Shires. 40 Iron Maiden.

QUIZ 59 **NIRVANA**

1 Krist Novoselic; Fecal Matter. 2 Sub Pop; $600 ($200 either way is acceptable). 3 He was the drummer; Them Crooked Vultures. 4 'Love Buzz'; 'Sliver'. 5 'About a Girl'; the Meat Puppets. 6 'In Bloom' and 'Come as You Are'. 7 1992; Frances Bean. 8 *In Utero*; Steve Albini. 9 *From the Muddy Banks of the Wishkah*; the Wishkah is the river that runs through Aberdeen in Washington state, where Kurt Cobain was brought up. 10 Foo Fighters; 'This Is a Call'. 11 He's the drummer; Shirley Manson. 12 *Romeo + Juliet*; *The World Is Not Enough*. 13 'You Know You're Right'; 'The Man Who Sold the World'. 14 Hole; they were formed and are fronted by Courtney Love, Kurt Cobain's widow. 15 Gus van Sant; *Journals*.

16 *Surfer Rosa* by Pixies. 17 *Version 2.0* by Garbage. 18 *Bricks are Heavy* by L7. 19 *University* by Throwing Muses. 20 *Vitalogy* by Pearl Jam. 21 *Superunknown* by Soundgarden. 22 *Clairvoyance* by Screaming Trees. 23 *In Utero* by Nirvana. 24 *Rust Never Sleeps* by Neil Young. 25 *Every Good Boy Deserves Fudge* by Mudhoney. 26 *Rehab Doll* by Green River. 27 *Without a Sound* by Dinosaur Jr. 28 *Wasting Light* by Foo Fighters. 29 *Mellon Collie and the Infinite Sadness* by Smashing Pumpkins. 30 *Copper Blue* by Sugar.

QUIZ 60 A SONG FOR GUY

1 'Way Down in the Hole'; Steve Earle. 2 Rilo Kiley; Jonathan Rice. 3 Amen Corner;
Augusta National. 4 Iron & Wine; Jesca Hoop. 5 'Crocodile Rock'; Bernie Taupin.
6 Zero 7; Sia. 7 '10538 Overture'; 'Xanadu'. 8 Captain Beefheart; the Magic Band.
9 Beck; *Odelay*. 10 'Lola'; 'Apeman'. 11 The Walkmen; 'The Rat'. 12 The Byrds; Roger
McGuinn.13 Ty Segall; Fuzz. 14 Elvis Costello; 'A Good Year for the Roses'. 15 Arcade
Fire; Merge Records – and they have stayed with them ever since.

16 Nick Lowe; Rockpile. 17 Billy Swan; 'Don't Be Cruel'. 18 Men At Work; *Business
as Usual*. 19 Mark Kozelek; Sun Kil Moon. 20 The National; Matt Berenger. 21 Turin
Brakes; 'Pain Killer (Summer Rain)'. 22 Cat Power; *The Greatest*. 23 The Delgados;
Scotland. 24 Split Enz; Crowded House. 25 Feist; Broken Social Scene. 26 Bury.
27 Ivor Novello; the closing ceremony of the London Olympics. 28 Potter; drummer.
29 'Grounds for Divorce'; 'Forget Myself'. 30 *Asleep in the Back*; *Dead in the Boot*.

QUIZ 61 **NEW WAVE**

1 Ian Dury & the Blockheads; a top-shelf magazine. 2 'Psycho Killer'; 'Once in a Lifetime'. 3 Squeeze; Jools Holland. 4 The Only Ones; *Baby's Got a Gun*. 5 Jerry Harrison; Jonathan Richman. 6 'Little Johnny Jewel'; 'Prove It'. 7 Hugh Cornwell; Baz Warne. 8 '(I Love the Sound of) Breaking Glass' and 'Cruel to Be Kind'. 9 'Take Me to the River', originally by Al Green; *Little Creatures*. 10 Chris Difford and Glenn Tilbrook. 11 The Jam; *In the City*. 12 John McGeoch; 'Shot by Both Sides'. 13 'Mongoloid'; '(I Can't Get No) Satisfaction'. 14 'Should I Stay or Should I Go'; *London Calling*. 15 *New Boots and Panties*; *Lord Upminster*.

16 'So Good to Be Back Home Again'; Eurythmics. 17 '(I Don't Want to Go to) Chelsea'; '(The Angels Wanna Wear My) Red Shoes'. 18 'Denis'; 'Heart of Glass'. 19 'Statue of Liberty'; 'Senses Working Overtime'. 20 Ultravox; Midge Ure. 21 'Down in the Sewer'; '(Get a) Grip (on Yourself)'. 22 Steve Nieve; guitar. 23 Joe Jackson; a pair of very cool white shoes, laced at the sides. 24 *Get Happy!!*; 'I Can't Stand Up for Falling Down'. 25 'Hanging on the Telephone'; 'I'm Gonna Love You Too'. 26 Siouxsie & the Banshees; *The Scream*. 27 The Members; Nicky Tesco. 28 Feargal Sharkey; 'More Songs About Chocolate and Girls'. 29 Tommy, Marky and Richie; Clem Burke. 30 Bad Religion; Greg Graffin.

QUIZ 62 CLASSIC ALBUMS #4: THE NINETIES

1 Travis; *The Man Who*. 2 REM; *Up*. 3 Ride; *Nowhere*. 4 Faithless; *Sunday 8pm*. 5 The Jesus and Mary Chain; *Stoned and Dethroned*. 6 Public Enemy; *Fear of a Black Planet*. 7 Tori Amos; *Boys for Pele*. 8 Jane's Addiction; *Ritual de lo Habitual*. 9 Stone Temple Pilots; *Purple*. 10 Massive Attack; *Blue Lines*. 11 Lou Reed; *Magic and Loss*. 12 M People; *Bizarre Fruit*. 13 The Wedding Present; *Seamonsters*. 14 Gin Blossoms; *New Miserable Experience*. 15 Stereo MCs; *Connected*.

16 New Order; *Republic*. 17 My Chemical Romance; *Black Parade*. 18 Edwyn Collins; *Gorgeous George*. 19 Jamiroquai; *The Return of the Space Cowboy*. 20 Cast; *Mother Nature Calls*. 21 Tindersticks; *Curtains*. 22 Cypress Hill; *Black Sunday*. 23 Gomez; *Bring It On*. 24 The Cardigans; *Gran Turismo*. 25 The Cranberries; *Everybody Else is Doing It So Why Can't We?* 26 Lauryn Hill; *The Miseducation of Lauryn Hill*. 27 Spiritualized; *Ladies and Gentlemen We Are Floating in Space*. 28 U2; *Achtung Baby*. 29 Mercury Rev; *Deserter's Songs*. 30 The Divine Comedy; *Fin de Siècle*.

QUIZ 63 LIVE AND DANGEROUS

1 *The Song Remains the Same*; 'Moby Dick'. 2 Talking Heads; Jonathan Demme.
3 *Concrete*; Robbie Williams. 4 *The Tube*; Squeeze. 5 'Summertime Blues'; The Who.
6 Pink; by the recently fallen Berlin Wall. 7 Status Quo; 'Rockin' All Over the World'.
8 Blond Ambition; Sticky and Sweet. 9 Paul McCartney; *No Quarter: Jimmy Page and
Robert Plant Unledded*. 10 The Specials; Fox News. 11 The Eagles; *Long Road Out
of Eden*. 12 Harlem, New York (accept New York). 'Say It Loud – I'm Black and I'm
Proud'. 13 Eagles of Death Metal; Bataclan. 14 Rollercoaster; Blur. 15 'Got to Give It
Up'; Florence Lyles.

16 Leeds University; Hull. 17 Philadelphia; Midge Ure. 18 The Rolling Thunder Revue;
Joan Baez. 19 Joe Strummer; Rock Against the Rich. 20 The opening ceremony to
the 1994 World Cup in the US. Ross had to kick a ball into an open goal, but missed;
Oprah Winfrey stumbled and nearly fell off the stage as she introduced her. 21 The
Stranglers; 'Nice 'N' Sleazy'. 22 Live8; U2. 23 Misty in Roots; it was the band's first
album – debut albums are rarely live. 24 Neil Young and Crazy Horse; 'Hey Hey, My
My'. 25 John Peel; 'Reason to Believe'. 26 The Band; Martin Scorsese. 27 When Jack
White toured his first solo album, *Blunderbuss*, he alternated an all-male backing band,
the Buzzards, and an all-female one, the Peacocks. 28 New York and San Francisco.
29 The Budokan in Tokyo; The Grateful Dead. 30 Simon & Garfunkel; 'Mrs Robinson'.

QUIZ 64 **FOLK MUSIC**

1 Fairport Convention; Dave Swarbrick, who died in 2016. 2 Joe Strummer;
Spider Stacy. 3 Ralph McTell; the Anti-Nowhere League. 4 Woody Guthrie; Wilco.
5 Cambridge; Cropredy, near Banbury. 6 Noah & the Whale; Marcus Mumford. 7 Karl
Wallinger; the Waterboys. 8 Josh Tillman; Fleet Foxes. 9 Joan Baez; Bob Dylan – the
two were lovers for a spell in the sixties. 10 The Saw Doctors; he 'made an ostentatious
contribution'. 11 The Civil Wars; Smashing Pumpkins. 12 Seasick Steve; *I Started
Out with Nothin' and I Still Got Most of It Left*. 13 Joni Mitchell; 'Big Yellow Taxi'.
14 Mike Scott; WB Yeats – the album was called *An Appointment with Mr Yeats*.
15 Be Good Tanyas; Frazey Ford.

16 'Fast Car'; the Nelson Mandela 70th Birthday Tribute Concert. 17 Stornoway;
Beachcomber's Windowsill. 18 'Theme from *Harry's Game*'; *Robin of Sherwood*.
19 Richard & Linda Thompson; *Shoot Out the Lights*. 20 'Scarborough Fair'; Simon
& Garfunkel. 21 They were both titled *Live at the Point*; 'Ride On'. 22 Fairground
Attraction; Eddi Reader. 23 *Still*; Jeff Tweedy. 24 Nick Drake; *Bryter Later*. 25 The
Decemberists; *The King Is Dead*. 26 Steeleye Span; 'All Around My Hat'. 27 She is
Kami Thompson, daughter of Richard and Linda Thompson; Eliza Carthy. 28 Ewan
MacColl; Kirsty MacColl. 29 Thea Gilmore; Sandy Denny. 30 Hothouse Flowers;
'Don't Go'.

QUIZ 65 **FREAK ZONE**

1 *The Madcap Laughs*; Mick Rock. 2 The Fall; a modern ballet by Michael Clark & Company. 3 *In the Land of Grey and Pink*; Pye Hastings. 4 Gong; Daevid Allen. 5 Boards of Canada; *Tomorrow's Harvest*. 6 Dadaism; birdsong. 7 Pere Ubu; Dirty Carrots. 8 David Sylvian; Japan. 9 King Crimson; Greg Lake. 10 The Residents; who knows? They are as anonymous as Banksy. 11 'Car parts, bottles and cutlery'; 'It's Oh So Quiet'. 12 They (and a few guests, including Wolfgang's daughter) recorded music using the drone of 40,000 bees in a hive as a soundscape. The result was the album *One*, under the band name Be. 13 Sigur Rós; Icelandic (in which they also sing). 14 William Shatner; *Seeking Major Tom*. 15 Double bass; Tom Waits.

16 Laurie Anderson; Jules Massenet: the full title was 'O Superman (for Massenet)'. 17 The Velvet Underground; John Cale. 18 The Mothers of Invention; weasels. 19 Stereolab; Australia. 20 Public Service Broadcasting; Wrigglesworth. 21 Gorky's Zygotic Mynci; Euros Childs. 22 The Creatures; Budgie. 23 Mr Bungle; *The Place Beyond the Pines*. 24 Joe Jackson; Steve Vai. 25 Efterklang; Denmark. 26 Laibach; Ljubljana in Slovenia. 27 10cc; video – the pair directed their own videos as well as for artists including the Police, INXS, Peter Gabriel and Lou Reed. 28 Brigitte Bardot; Jane Birkin. 29 Tortoise; Jehovah's Witnesses. 30 *The Fall of the House of Usher*; Van der Graaf Generator.

QUIZ 66 THOSE WHO DIED YOUNG

1 Jim Morrison; Paris. 2 Def Leppard; Steve Clark. 3 Marvin Gaye; 'Sexual Healing'. 4 Elvis Presley and Kurt Cobain. 5 Lynyrd Skynyrd; *Street Survivors*. 6 Average White Band; 'Pick Up the Pieces'. 7 Marc Bolan; '20th Century Boy'. 8 John Lennon; Mark Chapman. 9 Pretenders; 'Back on the Chain Gang'. 10 Chicago; he shot himself in the head while playing with a gun that he didn't think was loaded. 11 Nick Drake; *Pink Moon*. 12 Eddie Cochran; Gene Vincent. 13 The Strawbs and Fairport Convention. 14 Patti Smith; MC5. 15 Kirsty MacColl; Steve Lillywhite.

16 Thin Lizzy; he was the bass player. 17 Mel and Kim (Appleby); 'Respectable'. 18 Michael Hutchence; Paula Yates. 19 Jimi Hendrix and Janis Joplin. 20 Richie Valens and the Big Bopper. 21 Lowell George; *Dixie Chicken*. 22 Bob Marley; Peter Tosh. 23 Paul Kossoff; Back Street Crawler. 24 'Me and Bobby McGee'; Kris Kristofferson. 25 Keith Moon; Uncle Ernie. 26 Jeff Buckley; he drowned while swimming in the Mississippi. 27 Brian Jones; Mick Taylor. 28 Eva Cassidy; Christine McVie of Fleetwood Mac. 29 Aaliyah; R Kelly. 30 Sid Vicious; *Sid Sings*.

QUIZ 67 **THE ROLLING STONES**

1 *Let It Bleed*; *Bridges to Babylon*. 2 *Sticky Fingers*; a hammer and sickle. 3 *Emotional Rescue* and *Voodoo Lounge*. 4 Keyboards; Lisa Fischer. 5 *She's the Boss* was by Mick Jagger and *Talk Is Cheap* was Keith Richards' debut. 6 'Come On'; it was the only song on the record written by Jagger and Richards. 7 'Start Me Up'; *GRRR!*. 8 'It's All Over Now'; 'Honky Tonk Women'. 9 *Some Girls*; 'Just My Imagination (Running Away with Me)'. 10 *Get Yer Ya-Ya's Out*; Madison Square Garden – 'Love in Vain', the exception, was recorded in Baltimore.

11 *American Idiot*; 'Jesus of Suburbia'. 12 'The One I Love'; *Out of Time*. 13 *X&Y*; Adele, with *25*. 14 William Shakespeare; 72 weeks (score one point for ten weeks either side). 15 *Everything Must Go*; Nicky Wire. 16 *Mylo Xyloto*; Gwyneth Paltrow. 17 Singer Michael Stipe and guitarist Peter Buck. 18 'The Love of Richard Nixon'; 'Your Love Alone Is Not Enough'. 19 'Geek Stink Breath'; 'Good Riddance (Time of Your Life)'. 20 *Collapse into Now*; *Part Lies, Part Heart, Part Truth, Part Garbage 1982-2011* (you don't need the years to get the points).

21 *Automatic for the People*; 'Crush with Eyeliner' is on *Monster*. 22 *...And Justice for All*; 'Enter Sandman' is on *Metallica*. 23 *A Rush of Blood to the Head*; 'Yellow' is on *Parachutes*. 24 *Powerage*; 'Touch Too Much' is on *Highway to Hell*. 25 *Babel*; 'Dust Bowl Dance' is on *Sigh No More*. 26 *Exile on Main Street*; 'Angie' is on *Goat's Head Soup*. 27 Stadium *Arcadium*; 'Dosed' is on *By the Way*. 28 *Empire*; 'Goodbye Kiss' is on *Velociraptor!*. 29 *Dookie*; 'Nice Guys Finish Last' is on *Nimrod*. 30 *The Holy Bible*; 'Motorcycle Emptiness' is on *Generation Terrorists*.

QUIZ 68 **PRODUCERS & LABELS**

1 4AD; This Mortal Coil. 2 Stax (Atlantic); green – 'Green Onions' was the band's big hit. 3 Phil Spector; 'Happy Xmas (War Is Over)'. 4 Sub Pop; Seattle. 5 Jim Steinman; Todd Rundgren. 6 Nude; One Little Indian. 7 They were all produced by Phil Spector; 'The Long and Winding Road'. 8 Lee 'Scratch' Perry; *Arkology*. 9 Island Records; *The Joshua Tree*. 10 Paul Epworth; Florence + the Machine. 11 Paul Oakenfold; Perfecto. 12 Josh Homme; James Ford. 13 Alan McGee; Poptones. 14 Trevor Horn; ZTT. 15 Rough Trade; Beggars Group.

16 Stephen Street; *Parklife* by Blur. 17 Stargate; Rihanna. 18 Brian Epstein; Parlophone. 19 Factory Records; Tony Wilson. 20 Kevin Campbell; Mark Morrison. 21 Daniel Lanois and Brian Eno. 22 Tony Visconti; Badfinger. 23 EMI; Virgin Records – who were eventually bought by EMI. 24 Domino; Sheffield. 25 Tuff Gong; Island. 26 Death Row Records; Suge Knight. 27 Island Records; Polygram – both are now subsidiaries of Universal. 28 Bella Union; Cocteau Twins. 29 1983 – two points if you got it spot on, or one point if you said anywhere from 1981 to 1985. 30 Nick Lowe; *Armed Forces*.

QUIZ 69 SWEET SOUL MUSIC

1 Sharon Jones and the Dap-Kings; Amy Winehouse (Mark Ronson used the New York studio for much of the work on *Back to Black*). 2 Bruno Mars; Prince. 3 The New Power Generation; O2 Arena. 4 Saxophone; James Brown. 5 The JB's; Bootsy Collins. 6 'One Nation Under a Groove'; 'TEAR the ROOF off the SUCKER'. 7 'Tell Me Something Good'; Chaka Khan. 8 Melle Mel; Grandmaster Flash and the Furious Five. 9 He played harmonica; Philip Bailey. 10 'September'; 'The Best of My Love'. 11 The Staple Singers; Curtis Mayfield. 12 *Super Fly*; The Impressions. 13 The Isley Brothers; Rod Stewart; 14 Jimi Hendrix; Otis Redding. 15 Charles Bradley; Daptone (and we've gone full circle).

16 Dexy's Midnight Runners; Kevin Rowland. 17 Wigan Casino; Northern Soul. 18 Luther Vandross and Mariah Carey. 19 Twelve; 'Superstition'. 20 Erykah Badu; André 3000 of Outkast. 21 Sam Cooke; 'Summertime'. 22 D'Angelo; *Voodoo*. 23 'Across 110th Street'; Sam Cooke. 24 'Teardrops', The xx. 25 'When a Man Loves a Woman and 'Stand By Me'. 26 Ben E. King; 'Kissing in the Back Row of the Movies'. 27 'Freeway of Love'; *The Blues Brothers*. 28 Smokey Robinson; 'Tears of a Clown'. 29 'Tracks of My Tears'; 'Love Machine'. 30 Joss Stone; SuperHeavy.

QUIZ 70 NAME THE BAND #3

1 ZZ Top. 2 Grandaddy. 3 Magazine. 4 Clannad. 5 Augustines. 6 The Stooges. 7 Eddie and the Hot Rods. 8 The Pigeon Detectives. 9 Fugees. 10 The Sweet. 11 The Feeling. 12 Teenage Fanclub. 13 The E Street Band. 14 McFly. 15 Interpol. 16 Crazy Horse. 17 Blink 182. 18 Fleet Foxes. 19 The Spinners. 20 My Chemical Romance. 21 Buffalo Springfield. 22 Three Degrees. 23 Underworld. 24 De La Soul. 25 Love. 26 Mercury Rev. 27 Jane's Addiction. 28 The Hollies. 29 Elastica. 30 The Band.

31 Traffic. 32 Ride. 33 Bad Company. 34 Booker T and the MGs. 35 The Primitives. 36 Thee Oh Sees. 37 Lush. 38 Third Eye Blind. 39 Wilco. 40 The Horrors. 41 The Go-Gos. 42 Fall Out Boy. 43 Chvrches. 44 Kid Creole and the Coconuts. 45 The Hold Steady. 46 Dsiclosure. 47 Psychedelic Furs. 48 Crystal Castles. 49 Local Natives. 50 Aswad. 51 The Bravery. 52 Girls Aloud. 53 Simple Minds. 54 The Jam; 55 The The. 56 Thompson Twins. 57 Black Angels. 58 Barclay James Harvest. 59 The Dream Syndicate. 60 Biffy Clyro.

QUIZ 71 THE SWINGING SIXTIES

1 Jimi Hendrix Experience; The Animals. 2 The Spencer Davis Group; Steve and Muff Winwood (Winwood will do it). 3 The Easybeats; Australia. 4 The Crystals; Darlene Love. 5 The Cavern; Focus. 6 False – Dave was the drummer; 'Glad All Over'. 7 The Animals; Frijid Pink. 8 Grace Slick; she formed a new band called Jefferson Starship. 9 Paul Jones; Cream. 10 'Good Vibrations'; 'Do It Again'. 11 *My People Were Fair and Had Sky in Their Hair... But Now They're Content to Wear Stars on Their Brows*. 12 Tom Jones; 'Green, Green Grass of Home'. 13 The Pretty Things; the Rolling Stones. 14 Them; Van Morrison. 15 'Silence Is Golden'; Brian Poole.

16 Syd Barrett; David Gilmour. 17 Georgie Fame; the Blue Flames. 18 The Seekers; Judith Durham. 19 Arthur Lee; 1967. 20 'You Really Got Me'; Ray Davies. 21 A total of 24, from *Kinks* in 1964 to *Phobia* in 1993. 22 PJ Proby; 'Hold Me'. 23 'I Can Hear the Grass Grow'; 'Flowers in the Rain'. 24 The Hollies; 'He Ain't Heavy, He's My Brother'. 25 The Small Faces; 'Lazy Sunday'. 26 The Monkees; Bob Rafelson. 27 The Searchers; 'Needles and Pins'. 28 Christine Perfect; 'I'd Rather Go Blind'. 29 The Doors; *Strange Days*. 30 The Yardbirds; John Mayall's Bluesbreakers.

QUIZ 72 **THE CHAIN**

1 Mark Knopfler. 2 *Private Dancer* (Knopfler wrote the title track). 3 'I Might Have Been Queen'. 4 *A Night at the Opera*. 5 'Bohemian Rhapsody'. 6 'Bohemian Like You'. 7 The Velvet Underground and Nico. 8 Lou Reed. 9 Metallica. 10 'One'. 11 Johnny Cash. 12 Rick Rubin. 13 Red Hot Chili Peppers. 14 Danger Mouse. 15 'Crazy'. 16 Patsy Cline. 17 'Sweet Dreams'. 18 Eurythmics. 19 Clem Burke. 20 Atomic Kitten. 21 It is the name of the bomber that dropped the atomic bomb on Hiroshima. 22 The Stranglers. 23 Dionne Warwick. 24 The Gibb brothers (accept the Bee Gees). 25 It wasn't used in the film. 26 Barry Gibb (don't accept the Bee Gees). 27 Frankie Valli; 28 'I Want To Hold Your Hand' (the link is that 'December 1963 (Oh What A Night)' was a hit for Frankie Valli and the Four Seasons). 29 Dave Clark Five. 30 'Bits and Pieces'.

31 'I Love Rock 'n' Roll'. 32 Britney Spears. 33 Matthew Sweet. 34 The Bangles. 35 'Walk Like an Egyptian'. 36 'Egyptian Reggae'. 37 *The Great Rock 'n 'Roll Swindle*. 38 Dr Feelgood. 39 Wilko Johnson. 40 Pete Townshend (accept the Who). 41 Phil Daniels (the film was *Quadrophenia*). 42 Sting. 43 'Message in a Bottle' – the band was the Police. 44 UB40. 45 'I Can't Help Falling In Love With You'. 46 *Moody Blue*. 47 The Moody Blues. 48 *Jeff Wayne's War of the Worlds*. 49 Phil Lynott. 50 Gary Moore. 51 Peter Green of Fleetwood Mac. 52 'Albatross'. 53 Stevie Nicks. 54 Tom Petty. 55 Bob Dylan. 56 The Travelling Wilburys. 57 *Pretty Woman* used the song 'Oh, Pretty Woman' by Roy Orbison and borrowed its name for the film title. 58 Julia Roberts was also in *Notting Hill*. 59 The Notting Hillbillies, a side project of Mark Knopfler. 60 Dire Straits – and so the circle is closed.

QUIZ 73 **CULT BANDS**

1 The Mountain Goats; Mexican professional wrestling. 2 BEF (British Electric Foundation); *Dark*. 3 Big Star; the Box Tops. 4 Talk Talk; Mark Hollis. 5 Tom Waits; *Mule Variations*. 6 Was (Not Was); 'Papa Was a Rollin' Stone'. 7 Guided by Voices; *Suitcases*. 8 Baader Meinhof; Black Box Recorder. 9 Sparklehorse; *Dark Night of the Soul*. 10 Luna; Tom Verlaine. 11 Jason Pierce; Spacemen 3. 12 Violent Femmes; 'Blister in the Sun'. 13 The Avalanches; *Wildflower*. 14 My Bloody Valentine; Creation Records. 15 The Tubes; 'White Punks on Dope'.

16 Young Marble Giants; *Colossal Youth*. 17 'While turning you blue'; Billy MacKenzie. 18 'Wordy Rappinghood'; the Drifters. 19 The B52s; Fred Schneider. 20 Black Francis, aka Frank Black; Pixies. 21 Cud; *Rich and Strange*. 22 Grizzly Bear; *Veckatimest*. 23 60 Ft Dolls; 'Happy Shopper'. 24 Bristol; Beth Gibbons. 25 'Voodoo Ray'; Peter Cook and Dudley Moore. 26 The Durutti Column; Morrissey. 27 Jaz Coleman; Killing Joke. 28 *The Sopranos*; 'Woke Up this Morning'. 29 Deerhoof; 'La Isla Bonita'. 30 The Wedding Present; the Ukrainians.

QUIZ 74 **THE BOSS**

1 *Nebraska*; 'Born in the USA' – Springsteen released the demo to clear up any supposed ambiguities about the song's lyrics after it was hijacked as a jingoistic anthem. 2 Julianne Phillips; *Tunnel of Love*. 3 'Streets of Philadelphia' from the movie *Philadelphia*; *The Ghost of Tom Joad*. 4 '57 Channels (and Nothin' On)'; *Lucky Town*. 5 'American Skin (41 Shots)'; *High Hopes*. 6 Pete Seeger – the album is called *We Shall Overcome: The Seeger Sessions*; Dublin – the live release was called *Bruce Springsteen with the Sessions Band: Live in Dublin*. 7 *Working on a Dream*; 'Outlaw Pete'. 8 *Lilyhammer*, which starred and was co-written and co-produced by E Street band member Steven van Zandt; 'Hunter of Invisible Game'. 9 Paul McCartney; Clarence Clemons, founder member and the band's saxophonist, who was saluted during a rendition of 'Tenth Avenue Freeze Out' on the rest of the tour. 10 Patti Scialfa; equestrianism.

11 '... On a last chance power drive'. 12 '... Fix your hair up pretty'. 13 '... Down along the strand'. 14 '... No flowers, no wedding dress'. 15 '... Kill the yellow man'. 16 '... Hotter than hell'. 17 '... An eye for an eye'. 18 '... Trouble in the heartland'. 19 '... Freight train running through the middle of my head'. 20 '... Please don't stop me'.

Bonus track 2

21 *Darkness on the Edge of Town*; 'State Trooper' is on *Nebraska*. 22 *Wrecking Ball*; 'Hunter of Invisible Game' is on *High Hopes*. 23 *Born in the USA*; 'Hungry Heart' is on *The River*. 24 *Magic*; 'Maria's Bed' is on *Devils and Dust*. 25 *The Wild, the Innocent and the E Street Shuffle*; 'Mary Queen of Arkansas' is on *Greetings from Asbury Park, NJ*. 26 *Tunnel of Love*; 'If I Should Fall Behind' is on *Lucky Town*. 27 *The Promise*; 'Adam Raised a Cain' was on *Darkness on the Edge of Town* – *The Promise* is the album of outtakes from these sessions. 28 *Nebraska*; 'Youngstown' is on *The Ghost of Tom Joad*. 29 *Born to Run*; 'New York City Serenade' is on *The Wild, the Innocent and the E Street Shuffle*. 30 *The Rising*; 'My Best Was Never Good Enough' is on *The Ghost of Tom Joad*.

QUIZ 75 PEOPLE'S PLAYLIST: YOU SEXY THING

1 Captain & Tennille. 2 Donna Summer. 3 Barry White. 4 'Lady Marmalade'. 5 Air.
6 Steely Dan. 7 The Pretenders. 8 Britt Ekland. 9 James Brown. 10 *1984*. 11 'Foxy
Lady'. 12 Madonna. 13 'Hustle'. 14 Prince. 15 'Night Nurse'. 16 Robbie Williams.
17 'Roxanne'. 18 Arctic Monkeys. 19 'Across [his] big brass bed'. 20 'Love Machine',
by the Miracles. 21 The Felice Brothers. 22 George Michael. 23 'Come Baby Come'.
24 Hot Chocolate. 25 James, on 'Laid'. 26 Marvin Gaye. 27 'Sex on the Beach'.
28 Justin Timberlake. 29 'Lick My Love Pump'. 30 Blondie. 31 'Please Be Naked'.
32 Gang of Four. 33 Kings of Leon. 34 Salt-n-Pepa. 35 'Adolescent Sex'. 36 Prince.
37 Mousse T. 38 'Do Me, Baby'. 39 Pulp. 40 'Let's Spend the Night Together'.

QUIZ 76 THE REVOLUTION STARTS NOW

1 Masturbation; 'Turning Japanese'. 2 Steve Earle; the Dixie Chicks. 3 'Things Can Only Get Better'; 'Lifted'. 4 Neil Young; Kent State. 5 Peter Gabriel; 619. 6 'People Have the Power'; Bruce Springsteen. 7 Revolution 9 (just 'Revolution' is not enough, as the album also contains the very different 'Revolution 1'; 'Everybody's Got Something to Hide Except Me and My Monkey'. 8 'Give Peace a Chance' and 'Cold Turkey'. 9 Woody Guthrie; 'God Bless America'. 10 Thanks to the line 'He got monkey finger/ He shoot Coca-Cola', thereby contravening the BBC's ban on advertising in songs; 'Lola', though the band changed the offending lyric to 'cherry cola' to get round the ban. 11 Brenda Spencer; 'I Don't Like Mondays' – it was Spencer's reply to a journalist's question about why she had committed the murders. 12 The Falklands War; Dylan Thomas. 13 Screaming Lord Sutch, the self-styled 3rd Earl of Harrow; he formed and became leader of the Official Monster Raving Loony Party, standing in and losing more than 40 different elections. 14 Midnight Oil; 'Beds Are Burning'. 15 Rage Against the Machine; the New York Stock Exchange.

16 Billy Bragg; *Life's a Riot with Spy vs Spy*. 17 Paul McCartney (the record was credited to Paul McCartney & Wings); Stiff Little Fingers. 18 Stonehenge, Wiltshire; the Levellers. 19 Linton Kwesi Johnson; Dennis Bovell. 20 Tom Robinson Band; *Power in the Darkness*. 21 'For What It's Worth'; the Whisky a Go Go, often referred to as simply the Whisky. 22 Simon Fowler; 'Profit in Peace'. 23 Manic Street Preachers; 'Theme from M*A*S*H (Suicide is Painless)'. 24 Lemonheads; Evan Dando. 25 kd lang; Melissa Etheridge. 26 Scritti Politti – the actual Italian translation of 'political writings' is '*scritti politici*'; the Communards. 27 The Human League were singing about John F Kennedy, while U2 were paying tribute to Martin Luther King. 28 Black Flag; Henry Rollins, erstwhile BBC 6 Music presenter. 29 Pussy Riot; *House of Cards*. 30 Ronald Reagan in 1984; John McCain, the Republican nominee.

QUIZ 77 **NOT SO RIOT GIRLS**

1 She was 19; *The Kick Inside*. 2 'The Man with the Child in His Eyes', 'Babooshka', 'Running up that Hill' (twice), 'King of the Mountain' and 'Don't Give Up', a duet with Peter Gabriel. 3 *The Ninth Wave*. 4 *A Sky of Honey*. 5 *Never for Ever*; 'Breathing'; Roy Harper. 6 'King of the Mountain'; 'Sexual Healing'. 7 *The Sensual World* and *The Red Shoes*. 8 'Running Up That Hill' 9 Hammersmith Apollo; *Before the Dawn*. 10 Albert McIntosh – aka Bertie, Kate Bush's son.

11 *Feels Like Home* and *Not Too Late*. 12 'Cornflake Girl'; 'Pretty Good Year'. 13 Anastacia; *Not That Kind*. 14 Lily Allen; 'Hard Out Here'. 15 Armand van Helden; Courtney Love. 16 Two; *Flex*. 17 Marianne Faithfull; Steve Earle. 18 Ellie Goulding; *Fifty Shades of Grey*. 19 'Fuck Me Pumps'; 'Will You Still Love Me Tomorrow?'. 20 *Daybreaker*; Johnny Marr.

21 Avril Lavigne. 22 Beth Jeans Houghton. 23 KT Tunstall. 24 Beth Orton. 25 Ani DiFranco. 26 Emeli Sandé. 27 Joan as Policewoman. 28 Courtney Barnett. 29 Björk. 30 Lana Del Rey.

QUIZ 78 **ROCKERS**

1 Alex Harvey; he was electrocuted while playing an outdoor gig on a wet stage. 2 'On the docks'; *Slippery When Wet*. 3 Wishbone Ash; *Argus*. 4 Bachman-Turner Overdrive; *You Ain't Seen Nothing Yet*. 5 Axl Rose and Slash – the three were the other original members of Guns 'n Roses. 6 Steve Harris; Nicko McBrain. 7 The Yardbirds (get a bonus point if you also said the New Yardbirds); Band of Joy. 8 Biffy Clyro; 'Get Lucky'. 9 Alice Cooper; *Welcome 2 My Nightmare*. 10 *Eliminator*; 'Viva Las Vegas'. 11 *Part II: Back into Hell* and *Part III: The Monster Is Loose*. 12 'The Boys Are Back in Town'; 'Johnny the Fox'. 13 'Highway to Hell'; 'Hell Ain't a Bad Place to Be'. 14 *Are You Gonna Go My Way*; Cinna, though you also get a point if you knew he played Katniss Everdeen's stylist but couldn't remember the character's name. 15 David Coverdale; Whitesnake.

1 The Who, *Who's Next*. 2 Rainbow, *Rainbow Rising*. 3 Neil Young, *American Stars n Bars*. 4 Black Mountain, *In the Future*. 5 Deep Purple, *In Rock*. 6 Black Sabbath, *Paranoid*. 7 Helloween, *Keeper of the Seven Keys: Part II*. 8 The War on Drugs, *Lost in the Dream*. 9 Green Day, *American Idiot*. 10 Led Zeppelin, *Physical Graffiti*. 11 Lynyrd Skynyrd, *(Pronounced 'Lĕh-'nérd 'Skin-'nérd)*. 12 Meat Loaf, *Bat out of Hell II: Back into Hell*. 13 Sisters of Mercy, *Floodland*. 14 Queen, *A Night at the Opera*. 15 Iron Maiden, *Powerslave*.

QUIZ 79 MORE EIGHTIES

1 Deacon Blue; 'Real Gone Kid'. 2 *Power, Corruption and Lies*; 'Blue Monday'. 3 Chris Lowe; Johnny Marr. 4 Adam & the Ants; 'Go Wild in the Country'. 5 'Sledgehammer'; Kate Bush. 6 The Bluebells; Siobhan Fahey of Bananarama. 7 Robert Palmer; Chic. 8 Philip Oakey; 'Together in Electric Dreams'. 9 'Red, Red Wine'; Chrissie Hynde. 10 'The Model' by Kraftwerk; 'Computer Love', which reached 36 – the single was then re-released with 'The Model' as the A-side when radio plays revealed it to be the more popular song. 11 Wham!; 'Careless Whisper'. 12 Camden Palace; Visage. 13 'Bring on the Dancing Horses'; *Pretty in Pink*. 14 The Christians; it was the surname of the three brothers who formed the band with ex-Yachts guitarist Henry Priestman. 15 'Time After Time' and 'I Drove All Night'.

1 Haircut One Hundred. 2 Curiosity Killed the Cat. 3 Eurythmics. 4 Tanita Tikaram. 5 Howard Jones. 6 Transvision Vamp. 7 Spandau Ballet. 8 Mike + the Mechanics. 9 Bon Jovi. 10 Dire Straits.

1 Fern Kinney. 2 Sister Sledge. 3 The Bee Gees – Hot Chocolate's hit with a similar title was 'So You Win Again' and came out ten years earlier. 4 Duran Duran. 5 Tight Fit. 6 Simple Minds. 7 Paul Hardcastle. 8 Jive Bunny & the Mastermixers. 9 Don McLean. 10 Enya.

1980 – *Flesh and Blood*. 1981 – *Wired for Sound*. 1982 – *The Gift*. 1983 – *The Art of Falling Apart*. 1984 – *The Riddle*. 1985 – *Misplaced Childhood*. 1986 – *Through the Barricades*. 1987 – *Solitude Standing*. 1988 – *The Raw and the Cooked*. 1989 – *The Seeds of Love*.

QUIZ 80 **GOOD DAY, BAD DAY**

1 *South Pacific*; 'Wot'. 2 Cliff Richard; 'Foot Tapper' by the Shadows. 3 'Here Comes the Summer'; John O'Neill. 4 'Teenage Kicks'; *Good Vibrations* – also the name of the Belfast label. 5 'All That She Wants'; Roxette. 6 'Celebration'; Kylie Minogue. 7 The Housemartins; *London 0 Hull 4*. 8 'Let's Have a Party'; *Dead Poets Society*. 9 Robin Williams; Meher Baba. 10 'Reasons to be Cheerful';' Part III' – Ian Dury and the Blockheads song. 11 'Beautiful Day'; *The Premiership* on ITV1. 12 'Good Times'; Franklin D Roosevelt. 13 Louis Armstrong; *Bowling for Columbine*. 14 'Happy' by Pharrell Williams; *Despicable Me 2*. 15 'Feeling Good'; Muse.

16 *Murder Ballads*; Kylie Minogue. 17 Neil Diamond and Barbra Streisand. The producer allegedly put the mix together as a parting shot at his wife, whom he was divorcing. 18 Ricky Valance; he enters a stock-car race and is killed when his car overturns. 19 Patsy Cline; The Jordanaires. 20 'Thin Line Between Love and Hate'; The Pretenders; 21 On their 'Shitlist'; Butch Vig. 22 *Hooray for Boobies*; Chasey Lain: 'The Ballad of Chasey Lain'. 23 'Picking up rice in the church'; Father McKenzie. 24 Clapham; her poodles. 25 Daniel Powter; Alvin and the Chipmunks. 26 Dr Hook and the Medicine Show; Marianne Faithfull. 27 'Heaven Knows I'm Miserable Now'; The Moors Murders. 28 The Handsome Family; *True Detective*. 29 The Adverts; The Police. 30 '1952 Vincent Black Lightning'; Red Molly.

QUIZ 81 **OUTTAKES**

1 The Royal Albert Hall in London; 'Shadowplay'. 2 Ray Charles; 'I Can't Stop Loving You'. 3 They're the songs in the medley that made up the 2009 *Children in Need* song, orchestrated by comedian Peter Kay and credited to Peter Kay's Animated All Star Band. 4 Neil Young and Pearl Jam. 5 Glenn Miller; the plane in which he was travelling to entertain troops went missing over the English Channel. 6 Robbie Williams (29); it was the first *Now!* album to be released digitally as well as in physical form. 7 Steven Van Zandt; Tom Morello of Rage Against the Machine. 8 Jimi Hendrix; John Lennon – they're the only two artists from the world of post-war popular music to be deemed worthy of an English Heritage blue plaque. 9 Marianne Faithfull; *Broken English*. 10 The US House of Representatives; Cher. 11 Imelda Marcos; Fatboy Slim. 12 Miles Davis; Bill Evans. 13 Rod Stewart; *Time*. 14 This gobbledegook contains 12 of the Pet Shop Boys' 13 single-word album titles; the missing word/title is *Elysium*. 15 Whigfield; 'Saturday Night'.

16 Chas & Dave; 'Rabbit'. 17 Karen Elson; *Get Behind Me Satan*. 18 Paul McCartney; 'behold my heart'. 19 The First Men and the Vaudeville. 20 Drake, with 'One Dance'; Wizkid. 21 Shania Twain; *Come on Over*. 22 Edwyn Collins; 'The Possibilities Are Endless'. 23 'Strangers in the Night'; 'I've Got You Under My Skin'. 24 Lemmy; Motörhead got their name from a Hawkwind song. 25 Ronnie Scott; Pete King. 26 The Duckworth Lewis Method, the complicated statistical method by which the results of rain-affected one-day cricket matches are calculated; 'Meeting Mr Miandad', a reference to former Pakistani batsman Javed Miandad. 27 *This Is the Sea*; Hastings. 28 The Brodsky Quartet; Burt Bacharach. 29 Kim Carnes and Cyndi Lauper. 30 Acker Bilk; 'Stranger on the Shore'.

QUIZ 82 **RADIOHEAD**

1 George W. Bush; '2 + 2 = 5'. 2 Jonny Greenwood and Ed O'Brien. 3 The Unbelievable Truth. 4 Atoms for Peace; Flea. 5 *Kid A*; *A Moon Shaped Pool*. 6 Humphrey Lyttelton. 7 'Spectre'; it was written as the theme for a James Bond movie, but was rejected. 8 *True Stories*; On a Friday. 9 *There Will Be Blood*. 10 'Burn the Witch'; Paul Thomas Anderson – Jonny Greenwood has previously written film scores for the director. 11 *Meeting People Is Easy*; *OK Computer*. 12 'Nude'. 13 'Creep', 'Street Spirit (Fade Out)', 'Paranoid Android', 'Karma Police', 'No Surprises', 'Pyramid Song' and 'There There'. 14 *Kid A* and *Amnesiac*. 15 'Harry Patch (In Memory of)'.

16 Death Cab for Cutie; the name came from a song by the Bonzo Dog Doo Dah Band. 17 David Byrne and St Vincent. 18 The Orb; *The Orb's Adventures Beyond the Ultraworld*. 19 Martha Wainwright; 'Chasing Cars'. 20 Animal Collective; *Panda Bear Meets the Grim Reaper*. 21 808 State; 'Pacific State'. 22 Lush; Jarvis Cocker. 23 The Catherine Wheel; Tanya Donelly. 24 Super Furry Animals; Gary Speed, former manager of the Wales football team. 25 Felt; Lawrence. 26 Richard Hawley; Sheffield. 27 Goat; Sweden. 28 Flaming Lips; each flash drive was contained in a real human skull. 29 It's the running time of the album; everything is in lower case. 30 Arcade Fire; Spike Jonze.

QUIZ 83 CLASSIC ALBUMS #5: 21ST CENTURY

1 The Vaccines; *Come of Age*. 2 Hot Chip; *Made in the Dark*. 3 Kanye West; *My Beautiful Dark Twisted Fantasy*. 4 Air; *Talkie Walkie*. 5 Savages; *Silence Yourself*. 6 Jay-Z; *The Blueprint*. 7 PJ Harvey; *Let England Shake*. 8 Beach House; *Bloom*. 9 Athlete; *Vehicles & Animals*. 10 Moby; *18*. 11 Adele; *21*. 12 Bloc Party; *Silent Alarm*. 13 Flaming Lips; *Yoshimi Battles the Pink Robots*. 14 Lady Gaga; *The Fame*. 15 Hard-Fi; *Stars of CCTV*.

16 Dido; *Life for Rent*. 17 Kings of Leon; *Aha Shake Heartbreak*. 18 KT Tunstall; *Tiger Suit*. 19 First Aid Kit; *Stay Gold*. 20 Coldplay; *X&Y*. 21 Arctic Monkeys; *Suck It and See*. 22 The Darkness: *Permission to Land*. 23 Kaiser Chiefs; *Employment*. 24 Paul Simon; *Stranger to Stranger*. 25 Red Hot Chili Peppers; *By the Way*. 26 Rihanna; *Loud*. 27 Madonna; *Hard Candy*. 28 Editors; *In This Light and On This Evening*. 29 Tinie Tempah; *Demonstration*. 30 Foals: *Hold Fire*.

QUIZ 84 CLASSIC ALBUMS #6: 21ST CENTURY 2

1 Stornoway; *Beachcomber's Windowsill*. 2 George Ezra; *Wanted On Voyage*. 3 Biffy Clyro; *Only Revolutions*. 4 Maccabees; *Marks to Prove It*. 5 Joanna Newsom; *Ys*. 6 Savages; *Silence Yourself*. 7 Pharrell Williams; *G I R L*. 8 Avenged Sevenfold; *Hail to the King*. 9 Years & Years; *Communion*. 10 Kate Bush; *Aerial*. 11 Goldfrapp; *Supernature*. 12 Mumford & Sons; *Sigh No More*. 13 The Go! Team; *Proof of Youth*.14 Florence + the Machine; *Lungs*. 15 Lily Allen; *Alright, Still*.

16 The Libertines; *Up the Bracket*. 17 Rudimental; *We the Generation*. 18 The Streets; *Original Pirate Material*. 19 Muse; *Black Holes and Revelations*. 20 Ellie Goulding; *Halcyon*. 21 The Horrors; *Skying*. 22 Paul Weller; *Wake up the Nation*. 23 alt-J; *An Awesome Wave*. 24 David Bowie; *Blackstar*. 25 Hozier; *Hozier*. 26 The Tears; *Here Come the Tears*. 27 Drake; *Views*. 28 Laura Marling; *Alas, I Cannot Swim*. 29 The Last Shadow Puppets; *The Age of the Understatement*. 30 James Blake; *Overgrown*.

QUIZ 85 POP STARS IN THE MOVIES

1 Björk; *Dancer in the Dark*. 2 Barbra Streisand and Kris Kristofferson. 3 Grace Jones; Duran Duran. 4 Isaac Hayes; *Escape from New York*. 5 Tom Waits; Renfield, the fly-obsessed madman in the asylum. 6 Facebook; Justin Timberlake. 7 *Hustler*; Courtney Love. 8 Mariah Carey; *The Bachelor*. 9 Cher; *Moonstruck*. 10 Mark Wahlberg; Marky Mark and the Funky Bunch. 11 *Videodrome*; *Hairspray*. 12 Ringo Starr; Adam Faith. 13 Meat Loaf; Susan Sarandon. 14 Phil Collins; Roger Daltrey. 15 P Diddy (as Sean Combs); Snoop Dogg.

1 Aaron Johnson. 2 Reese Witherspoon. 3 Gary Oldman. 4 Jamie Foxx. 5 Andy Serkis. 6 Kristen Stewart. 7 Cate Blanchett. 8 Corey Hawkins. 9 Tom Hiddleston. 10 Val Kilmer. 11 Jessica Lange. 12 Joaquin Phoenix. 13 Angela Bassett. 14 Dennis Quaid, 15 Sissy Spacek.

QUIZ 86 **PEEL SESSIONS**

1 Captain Beefheart and his Magic Band. 2 Bonzo Dog Doo Dah Band. 3 Genesis.
4 Queen. 5 Bob Marley and the Wailers. 6 Roy Harper. 7 Slits. 8 The Fall. 9 The
Undertones. 10 The Specials. 11 Gary Numan. 12 Billy Bragg. 13 The Smiths.
14 Bhundu Boys. 15 Napalm Death. 16 The Jesus and Mary Chain. 17 Loudon
Wainwright III. 18 Teenage Fanclub. 19 Pavement. 20 Orbital. 21 Black Star
Liner. 22 Guided By Voices. 23 Scarfo. 24 Calexico. 25 Yo La Tengo. 26 Mogwai.
27 Dinosaur Jr. 28 Camera Obscura. 29 White Stripes. 30 Low.

31 Joy Division; New Order. 32 The Sundays; *Reading, Writing and Arithmetic*.
33 Cinerama; The Wedding Present. 34 Rob Da Bank; The Fall ('Theme from Sparta
FC Part 2'). 35 Dandelion Radio; 'I'm Your Boyfriend Now'. 36 Tim Buckley and
This Mortal Coil. 37 'How Soon Is Now?' and 'There is a Light that Never Goes Out'.
38 'Radio London'; *Top Gear*. 39 John Walters; the pig. 40 Liverpool; 'You'll Never
Walk Alone'. 41 Billy Bragg; *Life's a Riot with Spy vs Spy*. 42 'Another Girl, Another
Planet'; John Perry. 43 The Undertones; It is on his gravestone. 44 6 Music's own Tom
Ravenscroft (Peel's real surname was Ravenscroft); *Margrave of the Marshes*. 45 'God
Only Knows' and 'Good Vibrations'.

QUIZ 87 VIDEO KILLED THE RADIO STAR

1 'The Wild Boys'; Arlene Phillips. 2 'Crossfire'; Charlize Theron. 3 'Ray of Light'; Guy Ritchie. 4 'My Name Is'; Dr Dre. 5 Bootsy Collins; Christopher Walken. 6 'The Boys of Summer'; Madonna. 7 Britney Spears' '... Baby One More Time'; Band Aid's 'Do They Know It's Christmas?'. 8 Godley & Creme; 10cc. 9 'Boulevard of Broken Dreams'; Scarlett Johansson. 10 'Bad Romance'; Alexander McQueen. 11 'I Want to Break Free'; Wembley Stadium. 12 Terry Gilliam; Donald Sutherland. 13 'When Doves Cry'; Prince himself directed it. 14 Matt Lucas; Damien Hirst. 15 'Sledgehammer'; Aardman Animations, now most famous for Nick Park's creations Wallace and Gromit.

1 Michael Bay – *Pearl Harbor* and Meatloaf. 2 Kathryn Bigelow – *The Hurt Locker* and New Order. 3 Tim Burton – *Sleepy Hollow* and the Killers. 4 Sofia Coppola – *The Virgin Suicides* and White Stripes. 5 Jonathan Demme – *The Silence of the Lambs* and Tom Tom Club. 6 Brian de Palma – *Carrie* and Bruce Springsteen. 7 David Fincher – *Fight Club* and Aerosmith. 8 Jonathan Glazer – *Sexy Beast* and Radiohead. 9 Michel Gondry – *Eternal Sunshine of the Spotless Mind* and Foo Fighters. 10 Spike Jonze – *Being John Malkovich* and Björk. 11 Jon Landis – *The Blues Brothers* and Michael Jackson. 12 Spike Lee – *Do the Right Thing* and Public Enemy. 13 John Maybury – *Edge of Love* and Sinéad O'Connor. 14 Michael Moore – *Bowling for Columbine* and Rage Against the Machine. 15 Gus van Sant – *Drugstore Cowboy* and Red Hot Chili Peppers.

QUIZ 88 **ALL KILLER NO FILLER**

1 Public Enemy; Def Jam. 2 Broken Social Scene; *You Forgot It In People*. 3 David Bowie; 'Perfect Day'. 4 Franz Ferdinand; the Austrian Archduke whose assassination by Gavrilo Princip led to the outbreak of the First World War. 5 The Soundtrack of Our Lives; Gothenburg, Sweden. 6 *Three Imaginary Boys*; *Boys Don't Cry*. 7 1977; 'The Chain', now the theme tune to TV coverage of Formula 1.8 Sonic Youth; 'Teen Age Riot'. 9 *Script of the Bridge*; Mark Burgess; 10 Cocteau Twins; Elizabeth Fraser. 11 *Felt Mountain*; Will Gregory. 12 Tindersticks; it was simply called *Tindersticks*, the same as its predecessor. 13 Siouxsie and the Banshees; 'Happy House'. 14 'Bedsitter' and 'Say Hello, Wave Goodbye'. 15 *Give 'em Enough Rope*; 'I Can't Explain'.

16 Television; *Marquee Moon*. 17 Nick Cave and the Bad Seeds: *No More Shall We Part*. 18 Sinéad O'Connor; *The Lion and the Cobra*. 19 Thin Lizzy; *Jailbreak*. 20 Paul Young; *No Parlez*. 21 Calexico, *Carried to Dust*. 22 Otis Redding; *Otis Blue*. 23 The Who; *Who's Next*. 24 Fun Lovin' Criminals; *Come Find Yourself*. 25 Tina Turner; *Private Dancer*. 26 Bruce Springsteen; *Wrecking Ball*. 27 James; *Laid*. 28 The Civil Wars; *Barton Hollow*. 29 The Jam; *Setting Sons*.30 Bob Marley and the Wailers; *Exodus*.

QUIZ 89 THE NUMBERS GAME 3

1 'There Must Be an Angel (Playing with My Heart)'. 2 Nick and Woody Woodgate: Woody is the drummer in Madness. 3 *Tourist History* (2010); *Beacon* (2012); *Gameshow* (2016). 4 'West End Girls'; 'It's a Sin'; 'Always on My Mind'; 'Heart'. 5 Holly (Woodlawn); Candy (Darling); Little Joe (Dallesandro); Sugar Plum Fairy (Joe Campbell); Jackie (Curtis). 5 *Whatever People Say I Am, That's What I'm Not*; *Favourite Worst Nightmare*; *Humbug*; *Suck It and See*; *A.M.* 6 *Boy*; *October*; *War*; *The Unforgettable Fire*; *The Joshua Tree*; *Rattle and Hum.* 7 *Definitely Maybe*; *(What's the Story) Morning Glory?*; *Be Here Now*; *Standing on the Shoulder of Giants*; *Heathen Chemistry*; *Don't Believe the Truth*; *Dig Out Your Soul.* 8 'Chasing Pavements'; 'Make You Feel My Love'; 'Rolling in the Deep'; 'Someone Like You'; 'Skyfall'; 'Hello'; 'When We Were Young'; 'Send My Love (To Your New Lover). 9 *Kill 'em All*; *Ride the Lightning*; *Master of Puppets*; *...And Justice for All*; *Metallica*; *Load*; *Reload*; *St Anger*; *Death Magnetic.* 10 'Co-co'; 'Little Willy'; 'Wig-Wam Bam'; 'Block Buster'; Hell Raiser'; 'The Ballroom Blitz'; Teenage Rampage; The Six Teens'; 'Fox on the Run'; 'Love is Like Oxygen'.

QUIZ 90 WRITERS ON MUSIC

1 Patti Smith; Robert Mapplethorpe. 2 Nick Cave; *And the Ass Saw the Angel.* 3 Greil Marcus; 'Like a Rolling Stone'. 4 David Byrne; *How Music Works.* 5 Madonna; Binah. 6 Punk rock; John Lydon. 7 Andrew Loog Oldham; Stanley Booth. 8 Lester Bangs; Philip Seymour Hoffman. 9 Timothy White; The Beach Boys. 10 Kurt Cobain; *Heavier Than Heaven.* 11 *...Disappearing Ink*; Brett Easton Ellis. 12 Stuart Maconie; Simon Armitage. 13 Nick Kent; *The Dark Stuff.* 14 The Kinks and Steely Dan. 15 Voidoids; Bob Dylan

1 Jimi Hendrix. 2 Anthony Kiedis. 3 Alex James. 4 The Doors. 5 Boy George. 6 Courtney Love. 7 Grace Jones. 8 Keith Moon. 9 Diana Ross. 10 Keith Richards. 11 Bob Dylan 12 Nikki Sixx. 13 Paul McCartney. 14 Chrissie Hynde. 15 The Beatles.

QUIZ 91 **INDIE ROCK**

1 Alex James; a cult 1992 movie directed by Abel Ferrara and starring Harvey Keitel.
2 Jack White; *Blunderbuss*. 3 Muse, who topped the Billboard chart with *Drones* and
have had three other top ten albums in the US, and the Stone Roses. 4 Black Grape;
'Dare'. 5 Placebo; *Black Market Music*. 6 The Fiery Furnaces; Franz Ferdinand –
Eleanor Friedberger used to be in a relationship with Alex Kapranos, the band's singer.
7 Paul Weller and Blur's Graham Coxon. 8 Franz Ferdinand and Sparks. 9 Tame
Impala; *Lonerism*. 10 Yeah Yeah Yeahs; South Korea. 11 Oasis (Alan) and Paul Weller
(Steve); it's believed that Weller recommended Alan to Noel Gallagher when Oasis
found themselves without a drummer in 1995. 12 'Fluorescent Adolescent'; Matthew
Followill of Kings of Leon. 13 *Is This It*; 2001. 14 The Go! Team; *Thunder, Lightning,
Strike*. 15 'Love Shack'; '(Meet) The Flintstones', credited to the BC-52s.

16 The Stands; *All Years Leaving*. 17 Ian Brown and John Squire. 18 *This Is All
Yours*; Bill Withers' 'Lovely Day'. 19 Suede; *Bloodsports*. 20 The Seahorses; *Do
It Yourself*. 21 Interpol; *Our Love to Admire*. 22 The Cribs; Johnny Marr. 23 The
Boo Radleys; 'Wake Up Boo!'. 24 Arctic Monkeys, with *Whatever People Say I Am,
That's What I'm Not*; 'I Bet You Look Good on the Dancefloor'. 25 The National;
Boxer. 26 They were the trio of EPs that the Beta Band later compiled into their first
album. 27 My Life Story; the Cure. 28 'The Hellcat Spangled Shalalala'; 'the Devil's
pedicure'. 29 St Vincent; Kurt Cobain of Nirvana. 30 The Last Shadow Puppets;
Simian Mobile Disco.

QUIZ 92 PEOPLE'S PLAYLIST: LOVE

1 'I Would Do Anything for Love'. 2 '(But I Won't Do That)'. 3 'Love Grows (Where My Rosemary Goes)'. 4 'I Believe in a Thing Called Love'. 5 The House of Love. 6 Ryan Adams. 7 *I Love You, Honeybear*. 8 'To Bring You My Love'. 9 *Caustic Love*. 10 Until 'The Twelfth of Never'. 11 *Concrete Love*. 12 Fleetwood Mac. 13 'Love Don't Live Here Anymore'. 14 'Ever Fallen in Love (With Someone You Shouldn't've)'. 15 'Love is a Losing Game'. 16 'Justify My Love'. 17 Manhattan Transfer. 18 Carole King. 19 Diana Ross. 20 The Supremes. 21 Pink. 22 'The Power of Love'. 23 'Love Shine a Light'. 24 Wings. 25 'Love Like Blood'. 26 The Decemberists. 27 Sade, on 'Your Love Is King'. 28 'Tell Laura I Love Her'. 29 'Everlasting Love'. 30 Robert Palmer. 31 'A Groovy Kind of Love'. 32 'All You Need Is Love'. 33 'Love Is a Stranger'. 34 'Love Is a Battlefield'. 35 Bobbie Gentry. 36 'Stand Up for Your Love Rights'. 37 *Love and Hate*. 38 10cc, with 'I'm Not in Love'. 39 'Labelled with Love' by Squeeze. 40 The Housemartins, with their cover of 'Caravan of Love'.

QUIZ 93 NAME THE BAND #4

1 Metronomy (2006). 2 Dr Hook & the Medicine Show (1971). 3 Catfish and the Bottlemen (2014). 4 The Lovin' Spoonful (1965). 5 Run D.M.C. (1984). 6 Editors (2005). 7 Aerosmith (1973). 8 Django Django (2012). 9 The Move (1968). 10 Basement Jaxx (1999). 11 Good Charlotte (2000). 12 New Order (1981). 13 Foster the People (2012). 14 Kraftwerk (1970). 15 Groove Armada (1998).

16 White Denim (2008). 17 China Crisis (1982). 18 Savages (2013). 19 The Cure (1979). 20 Rocket from the Crypt (1991). 21 Klaxons (2007). 22 All About Eve (1988). 23 Procol Harum (1967). 24 XTC (1978). 25 Luna (1992). 26 Avenged Sevenfold (2001). 27 The Stray Cats (1981). 28 The Shirelles (1961). 29 Suicide (1977). 30 The Charlatans (1990).

QUIZ 94 ELECTRIC LADYLAND

1 Sasha; *Xpander*. 2 'James Bond Theme (Moby's Re-Version)'; *Play*. 3 *Original Soundtrack*; Mark Moore. 4 Chase & Status; Plan B. 5 Armand van Helden; Dizzee Rascal. 6 deadmau5; Ontario, Canada. 7 The Crystal Method; *Bones*. 8 'Smack My Bitch Up'; Liam Howlett. 9 Tom Rowlands and Ed Simons; 10 Klaus Badelt; Tiesto. 11 'Insomnia'; '...tearing off tights with my teeth'. 12 Roni Size Reprazent; Breakbeat Era. 13 *Oxygene*; *Electronica 1 – The Time Machine*. 14 Kelly Rowland and Akon. 15 *Dig Your Own Hole* and *We Are the Night*.

16 Papua New Guinea; Manchester. 17 'All Mine'; *Third*. 18 'Cars'; Tubeway Army. 19 Air; *The Virgin Suicides*. 20 'NUXX'; *Second Toughest in the Infants*. 21 Tango (hence the anagram); Paris. 22 Lemon Jelly (the album was *lemonjelly.KY*); 'The Shouty Track'. 23 LCD Soundsystem; *This Is Happening*. 24 *Strange Cargo*; *Pieces in a Modern Style*. 25 The Aphex Twin; 'Windowlickers'. 26 Dub reggae (accept reggae); Pink Floyd's *The Dark Side of the Moon*, retitled *The Dub Side of the Moon*. 27 Unkle; *Endtroducing...* 28 A track on the first Roxy Music album; Liverpool. 29 Brian Eno; Robert Fripp. 30 Morcheeba; *Big Calm*.

QUIZ 95 POST-PUNK & THE NEXT GENERATION

1 Slaves; *Are You Satisfied?*. 2 Sleaford Mods; *Divide and Exit*. 3 Public Image Ltd (PiL); the Clash. 4 Rise Against; *The Sufferer and the Witness*. 5 The Vaccines; *What Did You Expect from the Vaccines?*. 6 Eagulls; *Ullages*. 7 The Hives; their big single was 'Hate to Say I Told You So'. 8 Carl Barât; Mick Jones of the Clash. 9 Weezer; white. 10 Merge Records; 'Slack Motherfucker'. 11 The Exploited; 'Punks Not Dead'. 12 The Offspring; *Smash*. 13 Hookworms; *Pearl Mystic*. 14 Rancid; Billie Joe Armstrong from Green Day. 15 Manic Street Preachers; 'Suicide Alley'.

16 The Cure; *Seventeen Seconds*. 17 The Raincoats; *Odyshape*. 18 *Kerplunk*; Tré Cool. 19 *Metal Box*; Jah Wobble. 20 'Hit Me with Your Rhythm Stick'; it was his last album before his death in 2000. 21 Wire; *Pink Flag*. 22 'Love Will Tear Us Apart'; 'These Days'. 23 Don Letts; 'E=MC²'. 24 'Ceremony'; Martin Hannett. 25 'Dear Prudence'; *Through the Looking Glass*. 26 Generation X; Sigue Sigue Sputnik. 27 *Sandinista!*; 'Hitsville UK'. 28 Throbbing Gristle; Genesis P-Orridge. 29 Gang of Four; *Entertainment!* 30 Magazine; Barry Adamson.

QUIZ 96 MOTOWN

1 The Funk Brothers; *Standing in the Shadows of Motown*. 2 Michael Jackson; Sydney Lumet. 3 Mary Wilson and Florence Ballard. 4 They were iconic and peerless songwriting team Holland-Dozier-Holland. 5 Los Angeles; Billie Holiday. 6 'Stoned Love'; Jean Terrell. 7 Boyz II Men; 'End of The Road'. 8 Berry Gordy; Marvin Gaye. 9 Levi Stubbs; he provided the voice of Audrey II, the killer plant. 10 The Marvelettes; The Carpenters. 11 The Temptations; 'My Girl'. 12 Kim Weston; Tammi Terrell. 13 He was a songwriter; Tamla Motown. 14 Brian Poole and the Tremeloes; *Dirty Dancing*. 15 Brenda Holloway; she became a cult act in the Northern Soul clubs.

1-c. 2-i.. 3-f. 4-b. 5-h. 6-j. 7-d. 8-g. 9-a. 10-e.

1-b. 2-i.. 3-j. 4-d. 5-h. 6-e. 7-a. 8-f. 9-c. 10-g.

1-j. 2-g. 3-e. 4-b. 5-i.. 6-h. 7-c. 8-a. 9-f. 10-d.

QUIZ 97 PEOPLE'S PLAYLIST: CARS, TRAINS, BOATS & PLANES

1 'Road Trippin''. 2 'One Piece at a Time'. 3 The Moon. 4 Drive-By Truckers. 5 'Sloop John B'. 6 Crosby, Stills & Nash. 7 The A13, on 'A13, Trunk Road to the Sea'. 8 The 1975. 9 Jonathan Richman, credited to the Modern Lovers – either answer is fine. 10 'Bicycle Race'. 11 Chris Rea. 12 The Orb. 13 'Paper Plane'. 14 N17. 15 George Ezra. 16 John Denver. 17 The '5:15'. 18 Nowhere – he had 'No Particular Place to Go'. 19 In a 'Yellow Submarine'. 20 Chris Spedding. 21 'Little Red Corvette'. 22 Randy Crawford. 23 'Brand New Cadillac'. 24 'Driving Towards the Daylight'. 25 Hawkwind. 26 'Last Train to Clarksville'. 27 On a skateboard – he was her 'Sk8er Boi'. 28 Madness. 29 Jimi Hendrix. 30 The Cure . 31 Depeche Mode. 32 Driver 67. 33 '2-4-6-8 Motorway'. 34 Black Rebel Motorcycle Club. 35 The Cars. 36 The Jam. 37 Arcade Fire, on *Neon Bible*. 38 'I'm Mandy, Fly Me'. 39 The Beautiful South, on 'I'll Sail This Ship Alone'. 40 'Route 66'.

QUIZ 98 AMERICANA

1 *Wichita Lineman* and *Galveston*. 2 Lucinda Williams; *Down Where the Spirit Meets the Bone*. 3 Country Joe & the Fish; Woodstock. 4 Roger Miller; the Proclaimers. 5 Nash was a guitarist and songwriter with the Hollies, while Crosby was a member of the Byrds. 6 Emmylou Harris; Rodney Crowell. 7 Chicago Transit Authority; 'If You Leave Me Now'. 8 *Up!*; because she's Canadian. 9 *Grievous Angel*; the Flying Burrito Brothers. 10 Johnny Cash; his daughter, Rosanne Cash. 11 My Morning Jacket; Jim James. 12 Tired Pony; Snow Patrol's Gary Lightbody. 13 Linda Ronstadt and Emmylou Harris. 14 Robert Plant and Alison Krauss. 15 The Mavericks; Raúl Malo.

16 'Jolene', the Dolly Parton song; emerald green. 17 *Ode to Billie Joe*; 'I'll Never Fall in Love Again'. 18 Bright Eyes; the Mystic Valley Band. 19 The Wallflowers; *Bringing Down the Horse*. 20 Garth Brooks; Trisha Yearwood. 21 Lambchop; *No You C'mon*. 22 Hank Williams; 30 years old. 23 Drive-By Truckers; Jason Isbell. 24 LeAnn Rimes; 'Can't Fight the Moonlight'. 25 *Heartbreaker*; the Cardinals. 26 Howe Gelb; Calexico. 27 'Islands in the Stream'; the Bee Gees. 28 *Grey Tickles, Black Pressure*; the Czars. 29 Waylon Jennings and Kris Kristofferson. 30 *I'll Never Get out of This World Alive*; Allison Moorer.

QUIZ 99 **BOB DYLAN**

1 'Masters of War'; President Bill Clinton. 2 *The Basement Tapes*; The Hawks. 3 Sara Lownds; Clara (the film was *Renaldo and Clara*, and starred Dylan, Sara and former girlfriend, Joan Baez). 4 *Desire*; Rubin Carter. 5 'Shelter from the Storm'; Big Jim. 6 *No Direction Home*; Martin Scorsese. 7 *Slow Train Coming*; Muscle Shoals. 8 Knockin' On Heaven's Door; Sam Peckinpah. 9 It was his first solo acoustic album since 1964; 'Raggle Taggle Gypsy'. 10 Sly and Robbie; Mark Knopfler. 11 1962; 'See That My Grave is Kept Clean'. 12 *Together Through Life*; The Grateful Dead. 13 'Brownsville Girl'; Sam Shepard. 14 'Sad Eyed Lady of the Lowlands'; 'Stuck Inside of Mobile with the Memphis Blues Again'. 15 Feeding the poor; 'Silent Night'. 16 Newport; Mike Bloomfield. 17 'Girl from the North Country'; Johnny Cash. 18 They had all been sung by Frank Sinatra; 'Some Enchanted Evening'. 19 'Like a Rolling Stone'; 'Once upon a time you dressed so fine..'. 20 Greil Marcus; 'The Boxer'.

21 *Shot of Love* (1982). 22 *Time Out of Mind* (1997). 23 *Street Legal* (1978). 24 *The Freewheelin' Bob Dylan* (1963). 25 *Oh Mercy* (1989). 26 *Tempest* (2012). 27 *Under a Red Sky* (1990). 28 *Planet Waves* (1974). 29 *Modern Times* (2006). 30 *Highway 61 Revisited* (1965).